Information Privacy Engineering and Privacy by Design

Information Privacy Engineering and Privacy by Design

Understanding Privacy Threats, Technology, and Regulations Based on Standards and Best Practices

Dr. William Stallings

✦Addison-Wesley

For information about buying this title in bulk quantities, or for special sales opportunities (which may include electronic versions; custom cover designs; and content particular to your business, training goals, marketing focus, or branding interests), please contact our corporate sales department at corpsales@pearsoned.com or (800) 382-3419.

For government sales inquiries, please contact governmentsales@pearsoned.com.

For questions about sales outside the U.S., please contact intlcs@pearson.com.

Visit us on the Web: informit.com/aw

Library of Congress Control Number: 2019952003

ISBN-13: 978-0-13-530215-6

ISBN-10: 0-13-530215-3

194 2024

Editor-in-Chief
Mark Taub

Product Line Manager
Brett Bartow

Development Editor
Christopher A. Cleveland

Managing Editor
Sandra Schroeder

Senior Project Editor
Lori Lyons

Copy Editor
Catherine D. Wilson

Production Manager
Gayathri Umashankaran/
codeMantra

Indexer
Tim Wright

Proofreader
Karen Davis

Technical Reviewers
Bruce DeBruhl

Stefan Schiffner

Editorial Assistant
Cindy Teeters

Cover Designer
Chuti Prasertsith

Compositor
codeMantra

To my loving and loyal wife, Tricia

Contents at a Glance

Table of Contents

Chapter 4: Information Privacy Threats and Vulnerabilities 94

Part III   Technical Security Controls for Privacy 117

Chapter 5: System Access 118

Preface

Information privacy is the right of individuals to control or influence what information related to them may be collected, processed, and stored and by whom and to whom that information may be disclosed. In the context of information, the term *privacy* usually refers to ensuring that ostensibly private information about an individual is unavailable to parties that should not have that information.

Information privacy has become a high priority in all private and public organizations. Our society is being exposed to greater privacy threats and developing skills around Internet privacy, and safety is crucial to protecting our organizations and ourselves. The implementation of information privacy is the responsibility of IT organizations, specifically IT management, IT security management, and IT engineers. In addition, most organizations now have a senior privacy official or group to oversee compliance with privacy requirements. Typically, a chief privacy officer, data protection officer, or privacy leader fills this role.

Effective information privacy is very difficult. Increasingly, organizations have adopted an approach based on two concepts:

- **Privacy by design:** Encompasses management and technical means for including privacy considerations throughout the system development life cycle. The goal is to embed privacy in the design and architecture of IT systems and business practices.

- **Privacy engineering:** Encompasses the implementation, deployment, and ongoing operation and management of privacy features and controls in systems. Privacy engineering involves both technical capabilities and management processes.

Both standards documents, such as those issued by the International Organization for Standardization (ISO), and regulations, such as the European Union's General Data Protection Regulation (GDPR), mandate the use of privacy by design and privacy engineering.

The goal of this book is to present a comprehensive treatment of privacy by design and privacy engineering that will enable privacy executives and privacy engineers to manage and implement the privacy requirements dictated by standards, regulations, contractual commitments, and organizational policy.

Organization of the Book

The book consists of six parts:

- **Part I—Overview:** A necessary but insufficient aspect of information privacy is information security and the related field of cryptography; **Chapter 1** provides an overview of these concepts. Then, **Chapter 2** presents a survey of basic information privacy concepts, including privacy by design and privacy engineering.

- **Part II—Privacy Requirements and Threats: Chapter 3** discusses the requirements for information privacy that an organization must address. This discussion includes a definition of the types of personal data for which privacy is of concern, the concept of fair information practice principles, and the privacy regulations, standards, and best practices that drive the development of privacy solutions. Then, **Chapter 4** covers information privacy threats and the privacy vulnerabilities of information systems. Together, an understanding of requirements, threats, and vulnerabilities structure and guide privacy by design and privacy engineering solutions.

- **Part III—Technical Security Controls for Privacy:** There is considerable overlap between the requirements for information security and information privacy. Accordingly, privacy designers and engineers can select appropriate security controls to partially satisfy privacy requirements. Part Three examines in detail these security controls. **Chapter 5** looks at security controls for system access, which encompass the areas of authorization, user authentication, and access control. **Chapter 6** examines countermeasures to malicious software and to intruders.

- **Part IV—Privacy Enhancing Technologies:** Part Four examines technologies and practices that go beyond the traditional security controls in order to satisfy privacy requirements and counter privacy threats. **Chapter 7** discusses the complex issue of privacy in databases. Among the topics covered in this chapter are anonymization, de-identification, and privacy in queryable databases. **Chapter 8** provides a survey of threats, requirements, and approaches to online privacy. **Chapter 9** discusses the concept of data loss prevention and examines privacy issues related to cloud computing and the Internet of Things.

- **Part V—Information Privacy Management:** Part Five examines management and organizational privacy controls and procedures. **Chapter 10** discusses how information privacy governance enables the direction and oversight of information privacy–related activities across an enterprise, as an integrated part of corporate governance. The chapter also focuses on management issues related to information privacy. **Chapter 11** provides a detailed examination of one of the central tasks of information privacy management: privacy impact assessment. **Chapter 12** deals with the essential organizational task of developing a privacy culture based on organization-wide privacy awareness and the training and education of staff who have privacy-related duties. **Chapter 13** discusses techniques for auditing and monitoring the performance of privacy controls, with a view to spotting gaps in the system and devising improvements. The chapter also deals with planning for and reacting to threats through incident management.

- **Part VI—Legal and Regulatory Requirements: Chapter 14** provides a detailed examination of the EU's General Data Protection Regulation, which is the most important privacy regulation that most organizations must deal with. **Chapter 15** surveys the key U.S. federal laws that relate to privacy and the California Consumer Privacy Act.

Supporting Websites

The author maintains a companion website at WilliamStallings.com/ Privacy that includes a list of relevant links organized by chapter and an errata sheet for the book.

WilliamStallings.com/Privacy
Companion Website

The author also maintains the Computer Science Student Resource Site, at ComputerScienceStudent.com. The purpose of this site is to provide documents, information, and links for computer science students and professionals. Links and documents are organized into seven categories:

computersciencestudent.com

- **Math:** Includes a basic math refresher, a queuing analysis primer, a number system primer, and links to numerous math sites.

- **How-to:** Advice and guidance for solving homework problems, writing technical reports, and preparing technical presentations.

- **Research resources:** Links to important collections of papers, technical reports, and bibliographies.

- **Other useful:** A variety of other useful documents and links.

- **Computer science careers:** Useful links and documents for those considering a career in computer science.

- **Writing help:** Help in becoming a clearer, more effective writer.

- **Miscellaneous topics and humor:** You have to take your mind off your work once in a while.

Companion Book on Cybersecurity

I am also the author of *Effective Cybersecurity: A Guide to Using Best Practices and Standards* (Pearson, 2019). This book is addressed to people in both IT and security management, people tasked with maintaining IT security, and a wide range of others interested in cybersecurity and information security. The book enables privacy executives and engineers to gain a better grasp of the technical and management security practices that are essential elements in an information privacy program.

WilliamStallings.com/
Cybersecurity
Companion Website

Register Your Book

Register your copy of *Information Privacy Engineering and Privacy by Design* on the InformIT site for convenient access to updates and/or corrections as they become available. To start the registration process, go to informit.com/register and log in or create an account. Enter the product ISBN (9780135302156) and click Submit. Look on the Registered Products tab for an Access Bonus Content link next to this product and follow that link to access any available bonus materials. If you would like to be notified of exclusive offers on new editions and updates, please check the box to receive email from us.

Acknowledgments

This book has benefited from review by a number of people, who gave generously of their time and expertise. I especially thank Bruce DeBruhl and Stefan Schiffner, who each devoted an enormous amount of time to a detailed review of the entire manuscript. I also thank the people who provided thoughtful reviews of the initial book proposal: Steven M. Bellovin, Kelley Dempsey, Charles A. Russell, Susan Sand, and Omar Santos.

Thanks also to the many people who provided detailed technical reviews of one or more chapters: Kavitha Ammayappan, Waleed Baig, Charlie Blanchard, Rodrigo Ristow Branco, Tom Cornelius, Shawn Davis, Tony Fleming, Musa Husseini, Pedro Inacio, Thomas Johnson, Mohammed B. M. Kamel, Rob Knox, Jolanda Modic, Omar Olivos, Paul E. Paray, Menaka Pushpa, Andrea Razzini, Antonius Ruslan, Ali Samouti, Neetesh Saxena, Javier H. Scodelaro, Massimiliano Sembiante, Abhijeet Singh, and Bill Woolsey.

Finally, I would like to thank the many people at Pearson responsible for the publication of the book. This includes the staff at Pearson, particularly Brett Bartow (director of IT Professional Product Management), Chris Cleveland (development editor), Lori Lyons (senior project editor), Gayathri Umashankaran (production manager), and Kitty Wilson (copyeditor). Thanks also to the marketing and sales staffs at Pearson, without whose efforts this book would not be in front of you.

About the Author

Dr. William Stallings has made a unique contribution to understanding the broad sweep of technical developments in computer security, computer networking, and computer architecture. He has authored 18 textbooks, and, counting revised editions, a total of 70 books on various aspects of these subjects. His writings have appeared in numerous ACM and IEEE publications, including the *Proceedings of the IEEE* and *ACM Computing Reviews*. He has 13 times received the award for the best computer science textbook of the year from the Text and Academic Authors Association.

With more than 30 years in the field, he has been a technical contributor, a technical manager, and an executive with several high-technology firms. He has designed and implemented both TCP/IP-based and OSI-based protocol suites on a variety of computers and operating systems, ranging from micro-computers to mainframes. Currently he is an independent consultant whose clients have included computer and networking manufacturers and customers, software development firms, and leading-edge government research institutions.

He created and maintains the Computer Science Student Resource Site, at computersciencestudent. com. This site provides documents and links on a variety of subjects of general interest to computer science students and professionals.

He is a member of the editorial board of *Cryptologia*, a scholarly journal devoted to all aspects of cryptology.

Dr. Stallings holds a PhD from M.I.T. in Computer Science and a B.S. from Notre Dame in electrical engineering.

Figure Credits

Figure	Attribution/Credit Line
Cover	art_of_sun/Shutterstock; dboystudio/ Shutterstock
FIG01-09a	Iconic Bestiary/Shutterstock
FIG04-01a	cheskyw/123RF
FIG04-05a.1	Sashkin/Shutterstock
FIG04-05a.2	Sashkin/Shutterstock
FIG04-05a.3	Sashkin/Shutterstock
FIG04-05b.1	Jojje/Shutterstock
FIG04-05b.2	Jojje/Shutterstock
FIG04-05b.3	Jojje/Shutterstock
FIG04-05b.4	Jojje/Shutterstock
FIG05-01a	Ganna Rassadnikova/123RF
FIG05-01b	ostapenko/123RF
FIG05-01c	arturaliev/123RF
FIG05-01d	Jojje/Shutterstock
FIG05-01e	Sashkin/Shutterstock
FIG05-02a	Dmitry Rukhlenko/Shutterstock
FIG05-02b	Dmitry Rukhlenko/Shutterstock
FIG05-06a	arturaliev/123RF
FIG05-06b	Lightwave Stock Media/123RF
FIG05-07a	ostapenko/123RF
FIG05-08a	ostapenko/123RF
FIG05-08b.1	Sashkin/Shutterstock
FIG05-08b.2	Sashkin/Shutterstock
FIG06-01a	Arvind Singh Negi/Red Reef Design Studio/Pearson India Education Services Pvt. Ltd
FIG06-01b	DR Travel Photo and Video/Shutterstock
FIG06-01c	Oleksandr_Delyk/Shutterstock
FIG06-01d	Sashkin/Shutterstock
FIG06-01e	yukipon/123RF

FIG08-02a.3	Oleksandr_Delyk/Shutterstock
FIG08-02b.1	DR Travel Photo and Video/Shutterstock
FIG08-02b.2	DR Travel Photo and Video/Shutterstock
FIG08-02c.1	dny3d/Shutterstock
FIG08-02c.2	dny3d/Shutterstock
FIG08-02c.3	dny3d/Shutterstock
FIG08-02d	Sashkin/Shutterstock
FIG08-02e	Alex Mit/Shutterstock
FIG08-03a	yukipon/123RF
FIG08-03b	mipan/Shutterstock
FIG08-03c.1	Jojje/Shutterstock
FIG08-03c.2	Jojje/Shutterstock
FIG08-03c.3	Jojje/Shutterstock
FIG08-03c.4	Jojje/Shutterstock
FIG08-03c.5	Jojje/Shutterstock
FIG08-03c.6	Jojje/Shutterstock
FIG08-03c.7	Jojje/Shutterstock
FIG08-03c.8	Jojje/Shutterstock
FIG08-03d	dny3d/Shutterstock
FIG08-04a	Scott Betts/123RF
FIG09-06a.1	Milos Luzanin/Shutterstock
FIG09-06a.2	Milos Luzanin/Shutterstock
FIG09-10a	Iconic Bestiary/Shutterstock
FIG10-01a	maxuser/Shutterstock
FIG10-01b	David Franklin/123RF
FIG10-01c	Pavel L Photo and Video/Shutterstock
Table 10-6	Copyright © OASIS Open 2016. All Rights Reserved.
FIG13-01a	Sebastian Kaulitzki/Shutterstock

PART I

Overview

Chapter 1

Security and Cryptography Concepts

Learning Objectives

After studying this chapter, you should be able to:

- Describe the five main security objectives
- Explain the main uses of cryptography
- Describe four types of cryptographic algorithms
- Understand the concept of public-key infrastructure

Essential to understanding the concept of information privacy is an understanding of information security. As described in Chapter 2, "Information Privacy Concepts," there are areas of overlap as well as areas of nonoverlap between these two fields. This book provides numerous examples of privacy management, design, and technology concepts that require the use of the corresponding security concepts. This chapter provides a brief overview of information security concepts in Sections 1.1 through 1.4. Then, Sections 1.5 through 1.10 survey important aspects and implications of cryptography, which is the fundamental technology underlying much of information security. Then, Section 1.11 introduces the important topic of public-key infrastructure. Finally, Section 1.12 provides an introduction to network security.

1.1 Cybersecurity, Information Security, and Network Security

It is useful to start this chapter with a definition of the terms *cybersecurity*, *information security*, and *network security*. A reasonably comprehensive definition of **cybersecurity** based on one in NISTIR (*Small Business Information Security: The Fundamentals*, 2016) follows:

Cybersecurity is the prevention of damage to, unauthorized use of, exploitation of, and—if needed—the restoration of electronic information and communications systems, electronic communications services, wire communication, and electronic communication, including information contained therein, to ensure its availability, integrity, authentication, confidentiality, and nonrepudiation.

As subsets of cybersecurity, we can define the following:

- **Information security:** Preservation of confidentiality, integrity, and availability of information. In addition, other properties, such as authenticity, accountability, nonrepudiation, and reliability, can also be involved.

- **Network security:** Protection of networks and their services from unauthorized modification, destruction, or disclosure and provision of assurance that the networks perform their critical functions correctly, without harmful side effects.

Cybersecurity encompasses information security, with respect to electronic information, and network security. Information security also is concerned with physical (e.g., paper-based) information. However, in practice, the terms *cybersecurity* and *information security* are often used interchangeably.

Security Objectives

The cybersecurity definition just given introduces three key objectives that are at the heart of information and network security:

- **Confidentiality:** Also known as *data confidentiality*, the property that information is not made available or disclosed to unauthorized individuals, entities, or processes. A loss of confidentiality is the unauthorized disclosure of information.

- **Integrity:** This term covers two related concepts:
    - **Data integrity:** Ensures that data (both stored and in transmitted packets) and programs are changed only in a specified and authorized manner. A loss of data integrity is the unauthorized modification or destruction of information.
        - **System integrity:** Ensures that a system performs its intended function in an unimpaired manner, free from deliberate or inadvertent unauthorized manipulation of the system.

- **Availability:** Ensures that systems work promptly and that service is not denied to authorized users. A loss of availability is the disruption of access to or use of information or an information system.

> **Note**
>
> We can define *information* as communication or representation of knowledge such as facts, data, or opinions in any medium or form, including textual, numerical, graphic, cartographic, narrative, or audiovisual; and *data* as information with a specific representation that can be produced, processed, or stored by a computer. Security literature typically does not make much of a distinction between the two, nor does this book.

These three concepts form what is often referred to as the *CIA triad*. These three concepts embody the fundamental security objectives for both data and information and computing services. For example, the NIST (National Institute of Standards and Technology) standard FIPS 199 (*Standards for Security Categorization of Federal Information and Information Systems*) lists confidentiality, integrity, and availability as the three security objectives for information and for information systems.

Although the use of the CIA triad to define security objectives is well established, many in the security field feel that additional concepts are needed to present a complete picture, as illustrated in Figure 1.1. The list that follows describes two of the most commonly mentioned additional security concepts:

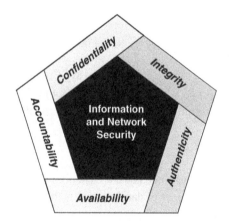

FIGURE 1.1   Essential Information and Network Security Objectives

- **Authenticity:** The property of being genuine and being able to be verified and trusted; confidence in the validity of a transmission, a message, or a message originator. This means verifying that users are who they say they are and that each input arriving at the system came from a trusted source.

- **Accountability:** The security goal that generates the requirement for actions of an entity to be traced uniquely to that entity. This supports nonrepudiation, deterrence, fault isolation, intrusion detection and prevention, and after-action recovery and legal action. Because truly secure systems are not yet an achievable goal, it must be possible to trace a security breach to a responsible party. Systems must keep records of their activities to permit later forensic analysis to trace security breaches or to aid in transaction disputes.

The Challenges of Information Security

Information and network security are both fascinating and complex. Some of the reasons follow:

1. Security is not as simple as it might first appear to the novice. The requirements seem to be straightforward; indeed, most of the major requirements for security services can be given self-explanatory, one-word labels: confidentiality, authentication, nonrepudiation, integrity. But the mechanisms used to meet those requirements can be quite complex, and understanding them may involve rather subtle reasoning.

2. In developing a particular security mechanism or algorithm, designers must always consider potential attacks on those security features. In many cases, successful attacks are designed by looking at the problem in a completely different way and exploiting an unexpected weakness in the mechanism.

3. Because of point 2, the procedures used to provide particular services are often counterintuitive. Typically, a security mechanism is complex, and it is not obvious from the statement of a particular requirement that such elaborate measures are needed. It is only when the various aspects of the threat are considered that elaborate security mechanisms make sense.

4. Having designed various security mechanisms, it is necessary to decide where to use them. This is true both in terms of physical placement (e.g., at what points in a network are certain security mechanisms needed?) and in a logical sense (e.g., should containers or virtual machines be used to isolate personal information, or should an integrated access control mechanism be used to protect all types of data, with access determined by user roles and privileges?).

5. Security mechanisms typically involve more than a particular algorithm or protocol. They also require that participants be in possession of some secret information (e.g., an encryption key), which raises questions about the creation, distribution, and protection of that secret information. There also may be a reliance on communications protocols, whose behavior may complicate the task of developing the security mechanism. For example, if the proper functioning of a security mechanism requires setting time limits on the transit time of a message from sender to receiver, then any protocol or network that introduces variable, unpredictable delays might render such time limits meaningless. It is worth mentioning here that security mechanisms are generally not secret, and indeed they may be open source, but secrecy is provided by maintaining the security of encryption keys, as discussed subsequently.

6. Information and network security are essentially a battle of wits between a perpetrator who tries to find holes and a designer or an administrator who tries to close them. The great advantage that the attacker has is that he or she need find only a single weakness, while the designer must find and eliminate all weaknesses to achieve perfect security.

7. There is a natural tendency on the part of users and system managers to perceive little benefit from security investment until a security failure occurs.

8. Security requires regular, even constant, monitoring, and this is difficult in today's short-term, overloaded environment.

9. Security is still too often an afterthought to be incorporated into a system after the design is complete rather than being an integral part of the design process.

10. Many users and even security administrators view strong security as an impediment to efficient and user-friendly operation of an information system or use of information.

These difficulties apply equally as well to information privacy. The difficulties just enumerated will be encountered in numerous ways as we examine the various privacy threats and mechanisms throughout this book.

1.2 Security Attacks

ITU-T Recommendation X.800 (*Security Architecture for Open Systems Interconnection [OSI]*) defines a general security architecture that is useful to managers as a way of organizing the task of providing security. The OSI security architecture focuses on security attacks, mechanisms, and services. These can be defined briefly as follows:

- **Security attack:** Any action that compromises the security of information owned by an organization.

- **Security mechanism:** A process (or a device incorporating such a process) that is designed to detect, prevent, or recover from a security attack.

- **Security service:** A processing or communication service that enhances the security of the data processing systems and the information transfers of an organization. Security services are intended to counter security attacks, and they make use of one or more security mechanisms to provide the services.

In the literature, the terms *threat* and *attack* are commonly used, with the following meanings:

- **Threat:** Any circumstance or event that has the potential to adversely impact organizational operations (including mission, functions, image, or reputation), organizational assets, individuals, other organizations, or the nation through an information system via unauthorized access, destruction, disclosure, modification of information, and/or denial of service.

■ **Attack:** Any kind of malicious activity that attempts to collect, disrupt, deny, degrade, or destroy information system resources or the information itself.

Sections 1.2 through 1.4 provide an overview of the concepts of attacks, services, and mechanisms. The key concepts that are covered in these sections are summarized in Figure 1.2.

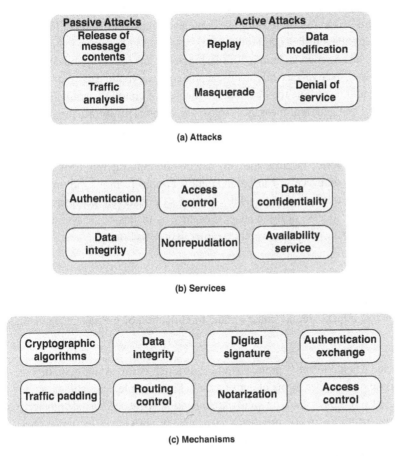

FIGURE 1.2 Key Concepts in Security

X.800 classifies security attacks as either *passive attacks* or *active attacks*. A passive attack attempts to learn or make use of information from the system but does not affect system resources. An active attack attempts to alter system resources or affect their operation.

Passive Attacks

Passive attacks are in the nature of eavesdropping on, or monitoring of, transmissions. The goal of the attacker is to obtain information that is being transmitted. Two types of passive attacks are the release of message contents and traffic analysis:

- **Release of message contents:** The act of an adversary in successfully eavesdropping on a communication, such as a telephone conversation, an electronic mail message, or a transferred file.

- **Traffic analysis:** A form of attack in which the contents of transmitted data blocks are not examined. Assume that there was a way of masking the contents of messages or other information traffic so that adversaries, even if they captured the message, could not extract the information from the message. The common technique for masking contents is encryption. With encryption protection in place, an adversary might still be able to observe the pattern of these messages. The adversary could determine the location and identity of communicating hosts and could observe the frequency and length of messages being exchanged. This information might be useful in guessing the nature of the communication that was taking place.

Passive attacks are very difficult to detect because they do not involve any alteration of the data. Typically, the message traffic is sent and received in an apparently normal fashion, and neither the sender nor the receiver is aware that a third party has read the messages or observed the traffic pattern. However, it is possible to prevent the success of these attacks, usually by means of encryption. Thus, the emphasis in dealing with passive attacks is on prevention rather than detection.

Active Attacks

Active attacks involve some modification of stored or transmitted data or the creation of false data. There are four categories of active attacks: replay, masquerade, modification of messages, and denial of service.

- A *masquerade* takes place when one entity pretends to be a different entity. A masquerade attack usually includes one of the other forms of active attack. For example, authentication sequences can be captured and replayed after a valid authentication sequence has taken place, thus enabling an authorized entity with few privileges to obtain extra privileges by impersonating an entity that has those privileges.

- *Replay* involves the passive capture of a data unit and its subsequent retransmission to produce an unauthorized effect.

- *Data modification* simply means that some portion of a legitimate message is altered or that messages are delayed or reordered to produce an unauthorized effect. For example, a message stating "Allow John Smith to read confidential file Accounts" might be modified to say "Allow Fred Brown to read confidential file Accounts."

- A ***denial-of-service attack*** prevents or inhibits the normal use or management of communication facilities. Such an attack may have a specific target; for example, an entity may suppress all messages directed to a particular destination (e.g., the security audit service). Another form of service denial is the disruption of an entire network, either by disabling the network or by overloading it with messages so as to degrade performance.

Active attacks present the opposite characteristics of passive attacks. Whereas passive attacks are difficult to detect, measures are available to prevent their success. On the other hand, it is quite difficult to prevent active attacks absolutely because to do so would require physical protection of all IT systems, communication facilities, and paths at all times. Instead, the goal is to detect them and to recover from any disruption or delays caused by them. Because detection has a deterrent effect, it may also contribute to prevention.

Figure 1.3 illustrates the types of attacks in the context of a client/server interaction. A passive attack (part b of Figure 1.3) does not disturb the information flow between the client and server but is able to observe that flow.

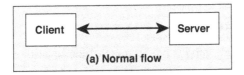

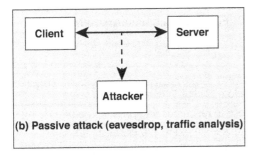

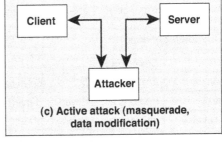

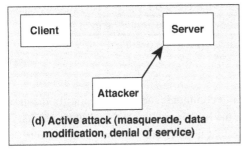

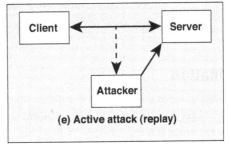

FIGURE 1.3 Security Attacks

A masquerade can take the form of a man-in-the-middle attack (see part c of Figure 1.3). In this type of attack, the attacker intercepts masquerades as the client to the server and as the server to the client. Another form of masquerade is illustrated in part d of Figure 1.3. Here, an attacker is able to access server resources by masquerading as an authorized user.

Data modification may involve a man-in-the middle attack, in which the attacker selectively modifies communicated data between a client and server (see part c of Figure 1.3). Another form of data modification attack is the modification of data residing on a server or another system after an attacker gains unauthorized access (see part d of Figure 1.3).

Part e of Figure 1.3 illustrates the replay attack. As in a passive attack, the attacker does not disturb the information flow between client and server but does capture client messages. The attacker can then subsequently replay any client message to the server.

Part d of Figure 1.3 also illustrates denial of service in the context of a client/server environment. The denial of service can take two forms: (1) flooding the server with an overwhelming amount of data and (2) triggering some action on the server that consumes substantial computing resources.

1.3 Security Services

A security service is a capability that supports one or more of the security requirements (confidentiality, integrity, availability, authenticity, accountability). Security services implement security policies and are implemented by security mechanisms.

The most important security services are shown in part b of Figure 1.2 and summarized in Table 1.1.

TABLE 1.1   Security Services

Service	Description
Authentication	A person's identity is determined before access is granted.
Access Control	Persons are allowed or denied access to resources for specific purposes.
Data Confidentiality	Information is only available to persons intended to use or see it.
Data Integrity	Information is modified only in appropriate ways by persons authorized to change it.
Nonrepudiation	A person cannot perform an action and then later deny performing the action.
Availability	Apps, services, and hardware are ready when needed and perform acceptably.

Authentication

The authentication service is concerned with ensuring that a communication is authentic. In the case of a single message, such as a warning or an alarm signal, the function of the authentication service is to ensure the recipient that the message is from the source that it claims to be from. In the case of an ongoing interaction, such as the connection of a client to a server, two aspects are involved. First, at the time of connection initiation, the service ensures that the two entities are authentic—that is, that each is the entity that it claims to be. Second, the service must ensure that the connection is not interfered with in such a way that a third party can masquerade as one of the two legitimate parties for the purpose of unauthorized transmission or reception.

X.800 defines two specific authentication services:

- **Peer entity authentication:** Provides for the corroboration of the identity of a peer entity in an association. Two entities are considered peers if they implement the same protocol in different systems. Peer entity authentication is provided for use at the establishment of, or at times during the data transfer phase of, a connection. It attempts to provide confidence that an entity is not performing either a masquerade or an unauthorized replay of a previous connection.
- **Data origin authentication:** Provides for the corroboration of the source of a data unit. It does not provide protection against the duplication or modification of data units. This type of service supports applications like electronic mail, where there are no ongoing interactions between the communicating entities.

Access Control

Access control is the ability to limit and control the access to host systems and applications via communications links. To achieve this, each entity trying to gain access must first be identified, or authenticated, so that access rights can be tailored to the individual.

Data Confidentiality

Confidentiality is the protection of transmitted data from passive attacks. With respect to the content of a data transmission, several levels of protection can be identified. The broadest service protects all user data transmitted between two users over a period of time. For example, when a logical network connection is set up between two systems, this broad protection prevents the release of any user data transmitted over the connection.

The other aspect of confidentiality is the protection of traffic flow from analysis. This requires that an attacker not be able to observe the source and destination, frequency, length, or other characteristics of the traffic on a communications facility.

Data Integrity

A connection-oriented integrity service—one that deals with a stream of messages—ensures that messages are received as sent, with no duplication, insertion, modification, reordering, or replays. The destruction of data is also covered under this service. Thus, the connection-oriented integrity service addresses both message stream modification and denial of service. On the other hand, a connectionless integrity service—one that deals with individual messages without regard to any larger context—generally provides protection against message modification only.

We can make a distinction between service with and without recovery. Because the integrity service relates to active attacks, we are concerned with detection rather than prevention. If a violation of integrity is detected, then the service may simply report this violation, and some other portion of software or human intervention is required to recover from the violation. Alternatively, there are mechanisms available to recover from the loss of integrity of data, as we will review subsequently. The incorporation of automated recovery mechanisms is, in general, the more attractive alternative.

Nonrepudiation

Nonrepudiation prevents either a sender or a receiver from denying a transmitted message. Thus, when a message is sent, the receiver can prove that the alleged sender in fact sent the message. Similarly, when a message is received, the sender can prove that the alleged receiver in fact received the message.

Availability Service

Availability means that a system or a system resource is accessible and usable upon demand by an authorized system entity, according to performance specifications for the system; that is, a system is available if it provides services according to the system design whenever users request them. A variety of attacks can result in loss of or reduction in availability. Some of these attacks are amenable to automated countermeasures, such as authentication and encryption, whereas others require some sort of physical action to prevent or recover from loss of availability of elements of a distributed system.

X.800 treats availability as a property to be associated with various security services. However, it makes sense to call out specifically an availability service—that is, a service that protects a system to ensure its availability. This service addresses the security concerns raised by denial-of-service attacks. It depends on proper management and control of system resources and thus depends on access control service and other security services.

1.4 Security Mechanisms

Part b of Figure 1.2 lists the most important security mechanisms, which include:

- **Cryptographic algorithms:** Sections 1.5 through 1.9 cover this topic.

- **Data integrity:** This category covers a variety of mechanisms used to ensure the integrity of a data unit or stream of data units.

- **Digital signature:** Data appended to, or a cryptographic transformation of, a data unit that allows a recipient of the data unit to prove the source and integrity of the data unit and protect against forgery.

- **Authentication exchange:** A mechanism intended to ensure the identity of an entity by means of information exchange.

- **Traffic padding:** The insertion of bits into gaps in a data stream to frustrate traffic analysis attempts.

- **Routing control:** A control that enables selection of particular physically or logically secure routes for certain data and allows routing changes, especially when a breach of security is suspected.

- **Notarization:** The use of a trusted third party to ensure certain properties of a data exchange.

- **Access control:** A variety of mechanisms that enforce access rights to resources.

1.5 Cryptographic Algorithms

The NIST Computer Security Glossary (https://csrc.nist.gov/glossary) provides the following definitions:

> **Cryptography:** 1. The discipline that embodies the principles, means, and methods for the transformation of data in order to hide their semantic content, prevent their unauthorized use, or prevent their undetected modification. 2. The discipline that embodies the principles, means, and methods for the providing information security, including confidentiality, data integrity, non-repudiation, and authenticity.

> **Cryptographic algorithm:** A well-defined computational procedure, pertaining to cryptography, that takes variable inputs, often including a cryptographic key, and produces an output.

Cryptography is an essential component in the secure storage and transmission of data and in the secure interaction between parties. Sections 1.5 through 1.10 provide brief technical introductions to important aspects of the use of cryptography and cryptographic algorithms. For a more detailed treatment, see *Cryptography and Network Security: Principles and Practice* [STAL20].

Cryptographic algorithms can be divided into three categories, as illustrated in Figure 1.4 and described in the list that follows:

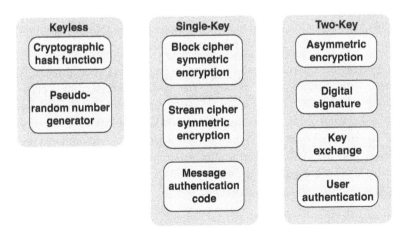

FIGURE 1.4 Cryptographic Algorithms

- **Keyless:** An algorithm that does not use any keys during cryptographic transformations.

- **Single-key:** An algorithm in which the result of a transformation is a function of the input data and a single key, known as a secret key.

- **Two-key:** An algorithm in which, at various stages of the calculation, two different but related keys are used, referred to as the private key and the public key.

Keyless Algorithms

Keyless algorithms are deterministic functions that have certain properties that are useful for cryptography.

One important type of keyless algorithm is the cryptographic hash function. A hash function turns a variable amount of text into a small, fixed-length value called a *hash value*, *hash code*, or *digest*. A *cryptographic hash function* has additional properties that make it useful as part of another cryptographic algorithm, such as a message authentication code or a digital signature.

A *pseudorandom number generator* produces a deterministic sequence of numbers or bits that has the appearance of being a truly random sequence. Although the sequence appears to lack any definite pattern, it will repeat after a certain sequence length. Nevertheless, for some cryptographic purposes, this apparently random sequence is sufficient.

Single-Key Algorithms

Single-key cryptographic algorithms depend on the use of a secret key. This key may be known to a single user; for example, this is the case when protecting stored data that is only going to be accessed by the data creator. Commonly, two parties share the secret key so that communication between the two parties is protected. For certain applications, more than two users may share the same secret key. In this case, the algorithm protects data from those outside the group who share the key.

Encryption algorithms that use a single key are referred to as *symmetric encryption algorithms*. With symmetric encryption, an encryption algorithm takes as input some data to be protected and a secret key and produces an unintelligible transformation on that data. A corresponding decryption algorithm uses the transformed data and the same secret key to recover the original data.

Another form of single-key cryptographic algorithm is the message authentication code (MAC). A MAC is a data element associated with a data block or message. The MAC is generated by a cryptographic transformation involving a secret key and, typically, a cryptographic hash function of the message. The MAC is designed so that someone in possession of the secret key can verify the integrity of the message. Thus, the MAC algorithm takes as input a message and a secret key and produces the MAC. The recipient of the message plus the MAC can perform the same calculation on the message; if the calculated MAC matches the MAC accompanying the message, this provides assurance that the message has not been altered.

Two-Key Algorithms

Two-key algorithms involve the use of two related keys. A private key is known only to a single user or entity, whereas the corresponding public key is made available to a number of users. Encryption algorithms that use two related keys are referred to as ***asymmetric encryption algorithms***. Asymmetric encryption can work in two ways:

- An encryption algorithm takes as input some data to be protected and the private key and produces an unintelligible transformation on that data. A corresponding decryption algorithm uses the transformed data and the corresponding public key to recover the original data. In this case, only the possessor of the private key can have performed the encryption, and any possessor of the public key can perform the decryption.

- An encryption algorithm takes as input some data to be protected and a public key and produces an unintelligible transformation on that data. A corresponding decryption algorithm uses the transformed data and the corresponding private key to recover the original data. In this case, any possessor of the public key can have performed the encryption, and only the possessor of the private key can perform the decryption.

Asymmetric encryption has a variety of applications. One of the most important is the ***digital signature algorithm***. A digital signature is a value computed with a cryptographic algorithm and associated with a data object in such a way that any recipient of the data can use the signature to verify the data's origin and integrity. Typically, the signer of a data object uses the signer's private key to generate the signature, and anyone in possession of the corresponding public key can verify the validity of that signature.

Asymmetric algorithms can also be used in two other important applications. ***Key exchange*** is the process of securely distributing a symmetric key to two or more parties. ***User authentication*** is the process of authenticating that a user attempting to access an application or a service is genuine and, similarly, that the application or service is genuine.

1.6 Symmetric Encryption

Symmetric encryption, also referred to as secret-key encryption, is a cryptographic scheme in which encryption and decryption are performed using the same key. A symmetric encryption scheme has five ingredients, as illustrated in Figure 1.5:

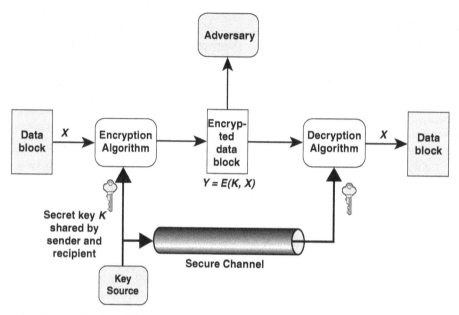

FIGURE 1.5   Model of Symmetric Cryptosystem

- **Plaintext:** The original message or data block that is fed into the algorithm as input.

- **Encryption algorithm:** The algorithm that performs various substitutions and transformations on the plaintext.

- **Secret key:** An input to the encryption algorithm. The exact substitutions and transformations performed by the algorithm depend on the key.

- **Ciphertext:** The scrambled message produced as output. It depends on the plaintext and the secret key. For a given data block, two different keys will produce two different ciphertexts.

- **Decryption algorithm:** The inverse of the encryption algorithm. It uses the ciphertext and the secret key to produce the original plaintext.

There are two requirements for secure use of symmetric encryption:

- A strong encryption algorithm is required. At a minimum, the algorithm should be such that an opponent who knows the algorithm and has access to one or more ciphertexts would be unable to decipher the ciphertext or figure out the key. This requirement is usually stated in a stronger form: The opponent should be unable to decrypt ciphertext or discover the key even if he or she is in possession of a number of ciphertexts together with the plaintext that produced each ciphertext.

- The sender and receiver must have obtained copies of the secret key in a secure fashion and must keep the key secure. If someone can discover the key and knows the algorithm, all communication using this key is readable.

The generation and distribution of secret keys are essential elements of a symmetric cryptography scheme. Typically, a key generation algorithm generates a random number and derives a secret key from that number. For two parties to communicate, there are a number of possibilities for key distribution, including:

- One party generates the key and securely transfers it to the other party.

- The two parties engage in a secure key exchange protocol that enables them to jointly generate a key known only to the two parties.

- A third party generates the key and securely transfers it to the two communicating parties.

Figure 1.5 illustrates the first alternative. One way to establish a secure channel of communication is if the two parties already share an older secret key, and the party that generates the key can encrypt the new key with the older key. Another alternative is the use of public-key cryptography to encrypt the key. Public-key cryptography is discussed subsequently.

Figure 1.5 also indicates the existence of a potential adversary that seeks to obtain the plaintext. It is assumed that the adversary can eavesdrop on the encrypted data and knows the encryption and decryption algorithms that were used.

There are two general approaches an adversary can use to attack a symmetric encryption scheme. One approach is *cryptanalysis*. Cryptanalytic attacks rely on the nature of the algorithm plus perhaps some knowledge of the general characteristics of the plaintext or even some sample plaintext/ciphertext pairs. This type of attack exploits the characteristics of the algorithm to attempt to deduce a specific plaintext or to deduce the key being used. If an attack succeeds in deducing the key, the effect is catastrophic: All future and past messages encrypted with that key are compromised. The second method, known as the *brute-force attack*, involves trying every possible key on a piece of ciphertext until an intelligible translation into plaintext is obtained. On average, half of all possible keys must be tried to achieve success. Thus, a secure symmetric encryption scheme requires an algorithm that is secure against cryptanalysis and a key of sufficient length to defeat a brute-force attack.

1.7 Asymmetric Encryption

Public-key cryptography, also called *asymmetric cryptography*, involves the use of two separate keys, in contrast to symmetric encryption, which uses only one key. The use of two keys has profound consequences in the areas of confidentiality, key distribution, and authentication. A public-key encryption scheme has six ingredients (see part a of Figure 1.6; compare with Figure 1.5):

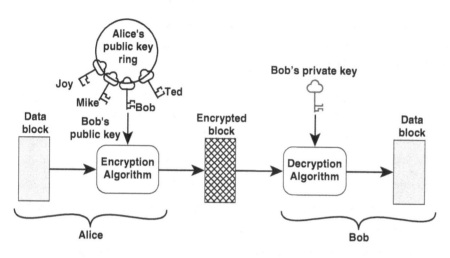

(a) Public-key encryption/decryption (Alice encrypts block for Bob only)

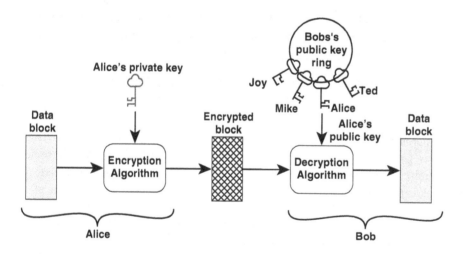

(b) Public-key encryption/decryption (Alice authenticates block for any recipient)

FIGURE 1.6   Model of Asymmetric Cryptosystem

- **Plaintext:** This is the readable message or data block that is fed into the algorithm as input.

- **Encryption algorithm:** The encryption algorithm performs various transformations on the plaintext.

- **Public key and private key:** This is a pair of keys that have been selected so that if one is used for encryption, the other is used for decryption. The exact transformations performed by the encryption algorithm depend on the public or private key that is provided as input.

- **Ciphertext:** This is the scrambled block produced as output. It depends on the plaintext and the key. For a given message, two different keys will produce two different ciphertexts.

- **Decryption algorithm:** This algorithm accepts the ciphertext and the matching key and produces the original plaintext.

The essential steps shown in part a of Figure 1.6 are as follows:

1. Each user generates a pair of keys to be used for the encryption and decryption of messages.

2. Each user places one of the two keys in a public register or another accessible file. This is the public key. The companion key is kept private. As part a of Figure 1.6 suggests, each user maintains a collection of public keys obtained from others.

3. If Alice wishes to send a confidential message to Bob, Alice encrypts the message using Bob's public key.

4. When Bob receives the message, he decrypts it using his private key. No other recipient can decrypt the message because only Bob knows Bob's private key.

The process works (produces the correct plaintext on output) regardless of the order in which the pair of keys is used. With this approach, all participants have access to public keys, and private keys are generated locally by each participant and therefore need never be distributed. As long as a user's private key remains protected and secret, incoming communication is secure. At any time, a system can change its private key and publish the companion public key to replace its old public key. Table 1.2 summarizes some of the important aspects of symmetric and asymmetric encryption.

TABLE 1.2 Symmetric and Asymmetric Encryption

Symmetric Encryption	Asymmetric Encryption
Needed to Work:	*Needed to Work:*
The same algorithm with the same secret key is used for encryption and decryption.	One algorithm is used for encryption and a related algorithm for decryption, with a pair of keys, known as the public key and the private key. The two keys can be used in either order, one for encryption and one for decryption.
The sender and receiver must share the algorithm and the secret key.	The sender and receiver must each have a unique public/private key pair.
Needed for Security:	*Needed for Security:*
The key must be kept secret.	The private key must be kept secret.
It must be impossible or at least impractical to decipher a message if the key is kept secret.	It must be impossible or at least impractical to decipher a message if the private key is kept secret.
Knowledge of the algorithm plus samples of ciphertext must be insufficient to determine the key.	Knowledge of the algorithm plus the public key plus samples of ciphertext must be insufficient to determine the private key.

As with symmetric encryption, asymmetric key generation involves the use of a random number. In this case, the key generation algorithm computes a private key from a random number and then computes a public key as a function of the private key. Without knowledge of the private key, it is infeasible to calculate the public key. On the other hand, knowledge of the public key does not enable calculation of the private key.

Public-key encryption can be used in another way, as illustrated in part b of Figure 1.6. Suppose that Alice wants to send a message to Bob and, although it isn't important that the message be kept secret, she wants Bob to be certain that the message is indeed from her. In this case, Alice uses her private key to encrypt the message. When Bob receives the ciphertext, he finds that he can decrypt it with Alice's public key, thus proving that the message must have been encrypted by Alice: No one else has Alice's private key, and therefore no one else could have created a ciphertext that could be decrypted with Alice's public key.

As with symmetric encryption algorithms, the security of public-key encryption is a function of the strength of the algorithm and the length of the private key. Public-key cryptographic algorithms are considerably slower than symmetric algorithms for a given data block length. Accordingly, public-key cryptography is almost always limited to use with small blocks of data, such as a secret key or, as discussed subsequently, a hash value.

1.8 Cryptographic Hash Functions

A hash function takes an input of arbitrary length and maps it to a fixed-length data block that is typically shorter than the input data block. This is therefore a many-to-one function; that is, multiple input blocks produce the same output. The output is known as the hash value or hash digest. A cryptographic hash function, also known as a secure hash function, is a hash function with specific properties that are useful for various cryptographic algorithms, as explained subsequently. Secure hash functions are an essential element of many security protocols and applications. To be useful for security applications, a hash function called H must have the properties indicated in Table 1.3.

TABLE 1.3 Requirements for Cryptographic Hash Function H

Requirement	Description
Variable input size	H can be applied to a block of data of any size.
Fixed output size	H produces a fixed-length output.
Efficiency	$H(x)$ is relatively easy to compute for any given x, making both hardware and software implementations practical.
Preimage resistant (one-way property)	For any given hash value h, it is computationally infeasible to find y such that $H(y) = h$.
Second preimage resistant (weak collision resistant)	For any given block x, it is computationally infeasible to find $y \neq x$ with $H(y) = H(x)$.
Collision resistant (strong collision resistant)	It is computationally infeasible to find any pair (x, y) such that $H(x) = H(y)$.
Pseudorandomness	Output of H meets standard tests for pseudorandomness; that is, the output appears to be a random sequence of bits.

Figure 1.7 indicates two common ways in which hash functions are used. Part a of Figure 1.7 illustrates the use of a hash function to ensure the data integrity of a block of data, generally referred to as message authentication. The two important aspects of message authentication are to verify that the contents of the message have not been altered and that the source is authentic. The hash function can also verify a message's timeliness (to see if it has been artificially delayed and replayed) and sequence relative to other messages flowing between two parties by including timestamps and sequence numbers in the message.

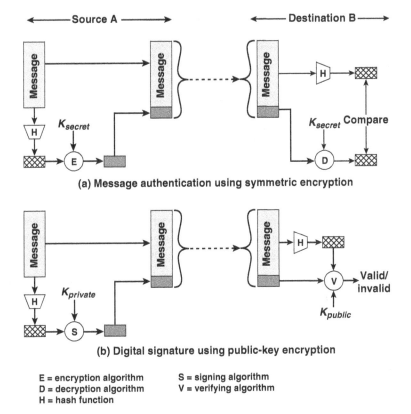

(a) Message authentication using symmetric encryption

(b) Digital signature using public-key encryption

E = encryption algorithm   S = signing algorithm
D = decryption algorithm   V = verifying algorithm
H = hash function

FIGURE 1.7   Uses for a Secure Hash Function

Message authentication using a hash value proceeds as follows. First, generate a hash value for the source message. Next, encrypt the hash value using a secret key shared by a cooperating partner. Then, transmit the message plus encrypted hash value to the destination. The recipient decrypts the incoming encrypted hash value, generates a new hash value from the incoming message, and compares the two hash values. If only the receiver and the sender know the identity of the secret key, and if the received code matches the calculated code, then:

- The receiver is assured that the message has not been altered. If an attacker alters the message but does not alter the code, then the receiver's calculation of the code will differ from the received code. For a secure hash function, it is infeasible for an attacker to alter the message in such a way that the hash value is not altered.

■ The receiver is assured that the message is from the alleged sender. Because no one else knows the secret key, no one else could prepare a message with a proper code.

■ If the message includes a sequence number (as is used with TCP), then the receiver can be assured of the proper sequence because an attacker cannot successfully alter the sequence number.

A second important use for hash functions is in the digital signature process, explained next.

1.9 Digital Signatures

NIST FIPS 186-4 (*Digital Signature Standard*) defines a digital signature as follows:

> The result of a cryptographic transformation of data that, when properly implemented, provides a mechanism for verifying origin authentication, data integrity, and signatory non-repudiation.

Thus, a digital signature is a data-dependent bit pattern, generated by an agent as a function of a file, message, or other form of data block. Another agent can access the data block and its associated signature and verify that (1) the data block has been signed by the alleged signer, and (2) the data block has not been altered since the signing. Further, the signer cannot repudiate the signature.

Part b of Figure 1.7 provides a simplified illustration of the digital signature process. Suppose that Bob wants to sign a document or message. Although it is not important that the message be kept secret, he wants others to be certain that the message is indeed from him. For this purpose, Bob uses a secure hash function to generate a hash value for the message. Together, that hash value and Bob's private key serve as input to a digital signature generation algorithm that produces a short block that functions as a digital signature. Bob sends the message with the signature attached. Any other user can calculate a hash value for the message. The user then inputs that hash value, the attached signature, and Bob's public key to a digital signature verification algorithm. If the algorithm returns the result that the signature is valid, the user is assured that the message must have been signed by Bob. No one else has Bob's private key; therefore, no one else could have created a signature that could be verified for this message with Bob's public key. In addition, it is impossible to alter the message without access to Bob's private key, so the message is authenticated both in terms of source and in terms of data integrity. The message also has the feature of nonrepudiation. Bob cannot deny having signed the message because no one else could have done so.

Digital signatures are widely used for a number of purposes, including:

■ Digitally signing email messages to authenticate the sender

■ Digitally signing software programs to authenticate the source of the program and to counter the threat of software tampering

■ Verifying the authorship or origin of digital data

■ Ensuring the integrity of digital data against tampering

■ Authenticating online entities

1.10 Practical Considerations

This section examines two practical aspects of the use of cryptographic algorithms: the selection of specific algorithms and the accompanying key lengths and implementation considerations.

Selection of Cryptographic Algorithms and Key Lengths

As processor speeds and capacity have increased, and as cryptographic algorithms are subjected to increased scrutiny, algorithms that were once considered secure have been abandoned. Similarly, key lengths and hash value lengths that were once considered secure are now too weak for secure use. Accordingly, security managers should take care to choose algorithms and lengths to achieve a desired level of security. A useful source of guidance for algorithm selection is FIPS 140-2A (*Approved Security Functions for FIPS PUB 140-2*) and for key and hash length is SP 800-131A (*Transitioning the Use of Cryptographic Algorithms and Key Lengths*). Similar recommendations are in the ENISA report *Algorithms, Key Size and Protocol Report* [ECRY18].

For symmetric encryption, NIST recommends the use of the Advanced Encryption Standard (AES), with a key length of 128, 192, or 256 bits. AES is widely accepted worldwide and has become the standard symmetric encryption algorithm.

For the hash function, NIST recommends one of two NIST standard hash functions: SHA-2 or SHA-3. The approved hash lengths for both functions range from 224 to 512 bits. The structure and functions used for SHA-3 are substantially different from those of SHA-2. Thus, if weaknesses are discovered in either SHA-2 or SHA-3, users have the option to switch to the other standard. SHA-2 has held up well, and NIST considers it secure for general use. So for now SHA-3 is a complement to SHA-2 rather than a replacement for it. The relatively compact nature of SHA-3 may make it useful for "embedded" or smart devices that connect to electronic networks but are not themselves full-fledged computers. Examples include sensors in a building-wide security system and home appliances that can be controlled remotely.

For digital signatures, NIST recommends three alternative digital signature algorithms:

■ Digital Signature Algorithm (DSA) with length of 2048 bits

■ RSA algorithm with 2048 bits

■ Elliptic-Curve Digital Signature Algorithm with length of 224 bits

SP 800-131A also includes recommendations for random bit generation algorithms, message authentication codes, key agreement algorithms, and key encryption algorithms.

Implementation Considerations

SP 800-12 (*An Introduction to Information Security*) lists the following as important management considerations for implementing cryptography within an organization:

- **Selecting design and implementation standards:** It is almost always advisable not to rely on a proprietary cryptographic algorithm, especially if the algorithm itself is secret. Standardized algorithms, such as AES, SHA, and DSS, have been subject to intense scrutiny by the professional community, and managers can have a high degree of confidence that the algorithms themselves, used with the recommended lengths, are secure. NIST and other organizations have developed numerous standards for designing, implementing, and using cryptography and for integrating it into automated systems. Managers and users of systems should choose the appropriate cryptographic standard based on cost-effectiveness analysis, trends in the standard's acceptance, and interoperability requirements.

- **Deciding between hardware, software, and firmware implementations:** The trade-offs among security, cost, simplicity, efficiency, and ease of implementation need to be studied by managers acquiring various security products meeting a standard.

- **Managing keys:** Key management is the process of administering or managing cryptographic keys for a cryptographic system or application. It involves the generation, creation, protection, storage, exchange, replacement, and use of keys and enables selective restriction for certain keys. In addition to access restriction, key management also involves the monitoring and recording of each key's access, use, and context. A key management system also includes key servers, user procedures, and protocols, including cryptographic protocol design. This complex topic is beyond the scope of this book; see *Effective Cybersecurity: A Guide to Using Best Practices and Standards* [STAL19] for a discussion.

- **Security of cryptographic modules:** A cryptographic module contains the cryptographic algorithm(s), certain control parameters, and temporary storage facilities for the key(s) being used by the algorithm(s). The proper functioning of cryptography requires the secure design, implementation, and use of the cryptographic module. This includes protecting the module against tampering. A useful tool is the NIST Cryptographic Module Validation Program (CMVP), which validates vendor offerings using independent accredited laboratories. The validation is against the security requirements in FIPS 140-2 (*Security Requirements for Cryptographic Modules*). FIPS 104-2 provides a detailed set of requirements at four security levels, against which vendor hardware, firmware, and software offerings can be evaluated.

Lightweight Cryptographic Algorithms

Two recent areas of strong interest in the field of cryptography are lightweight cryptography and post-quantum cryptography. It is likely that, in the coming years, a number of new algorithms in both areas will be widely deployed. In essence, lightweight cryptography is focused on developing algorithms that, while secure, minimize execution time, memory usage, and power consumption. Such algorithms are suitable for small embedded systems such as those in wide use in the Internet of Things. Work on lightweight cryptography is almost exclusively devoted to symmetric (secret key) algorithms and cryptographic hash functions.

In 2018, NIST announced a project to solicit designs for lightweight cryptographic algorithms. NIST is planning to develop and maintain a portfolio of lightweight algorithms and modes that are approved for limited use. Each algorithm in the portfolio will be tied to one or more profiles, which consist of algorithm goals and acceptable ranges for metrics. NISTIR 8114 (*Report on Lightweight Cryptography*) indicates that the initial focus is the development of symmetric encryption and secure hash functions. NIST has issued a preliminary set of two profiles for these algorithms: one for implementations in both hardware and software and one for hardware-only implementations.

Post-Quantum Cryptographic Algorithms

Post-quantum cryptography is an area of study that arises from the concern that quantum computers would be able to break currently used asymmetric cryptographic algorithms. Recent research demonstrates feasible ways to break the commonly used asymmetric algorithms. Thus, work on post-quantum cryptography is devoted to developing new asymmetric cryptographic algorithms.

There is no single widely accepted alternative to the existing algorithms currently in use, and researchers are exploring a number of mathematical approaches. An indication of the interest shown in these approaches is found in the submissions to the NIST effort at post-quantum standardization. As reported in NISTIR 8105 (*Report on Post-Quantum Cryptography*), NIST hopes to standardize a number of algorithms that can be used to replace or complement existing asymmetric schemes. See [STAL20] for a study of lightweight and post-quantum cryptographic algorithms.

1.11 Public-Key Infrastructure

A public-key infrastructure (PKI) supports the distribution and identification of public encryption keys, enabling users and computers to both securely exchange data over networks such as the Internet and verify the identity of the other party. A PKI is used to bind public keys to entities, enable other entities to verify public key bindings, revoke such bindings, and provide other services that are critical to managing public keys.

Before providing an overview of PKI, this section introduces the concept of public-key certificates.

Public-Key Certificates

A public-key certificate is a set of data that uniquely identifies an entity. The certificate contains the entity's public key and other data and is digitally signed by a trusted party, called a *certification authority*, thereby binding the public key to the entity.

Public-key certificates are designed to provide a solution to the problem of public-key distribution. Typically, in a public-key scheme, multiple users need to have access to the public key of a given entity A, whether to encrypt data to send to A or to verify a digital signature signed by A. Each holder of a public/private key pair could simply broadcast its public key for anyone to read. The problem with this approach is that it would be easy for some attacker X to impersonate A and to broadcast X's public key improperly labeled as A's public key. To counter this, it would be possible to set up some trusted central authority that would interact with each user to authenticate and then maintain a copy of A's public key. Any other user could then consult the trusted central authority over a secure, authenticated communication channel to obtain a copy of the key. It should be clear that this solution would not scale efficiently.

An alternative approach is to rely on public-key certificates that can be used by participants to exchange keys without contacting a public-key authority, in a way that is as reliable as if the keys were obtained directly from a public-key authority. In essence, a certificate consists of a public key plus an identifier of the key owner, and the whole block is signed by a trusted third party. Typically, the third party is a *certification authority* (CA), such as a government agency or a financial institution, that is trusted by the user community. A user can present his or her public key to the authority in a secure manner and obtain a certificate. The user can then publish the certificate. Anyone needing this user's public key can obtain the certificate and verify that it is valid by way of the attached trusted signature. A participant can also convey its key information to another by transmitting its certificate. Other participants can verify that the certificate was created by the authority.

Figure 1.8 illustrates the overall scheme for generation of a public-key certificate. The certificate for Bob's public key includes unique identifying information for Bob, Bob's public key, identifying information about the CA, and certificate information, such as expiration date. This information is then signed by computing a hash value of the information and generating a digital signature using the hash value and the CA's private key. Bob can then either broadcast this certificate to other users or attach the certificate to any document or data block he signs. Anyone who needs to use Bob's public key can be assured that the public key contained in Bob's certificate is valid because the certificate is signed by the trusted CA.

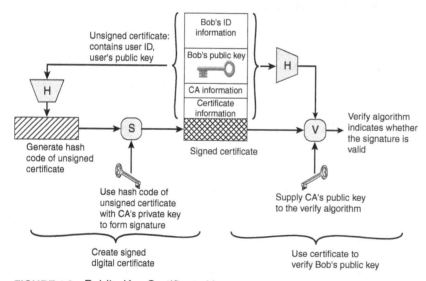

FIGURE 1.8 Public-Key Certificate Use

The standard ITU-T X.509 (*The Directory: Public-Key and Attribute Certificate Frameworks*) has become universally accepted for formatting public-key certificates.

PKI Architecture

A PKI architecture defines the organization and interrelationships among CAs and PKI users. PKI architectures satisfy the following requirements:

- Any participant can read a certificate to determine the name and public key of the certificate's owner.
- Any participant can verify that the certificate originated from the certification authority and is not counterfeit.
- Only the certification authority can create and update certificates.
- Any participant can verify that the certificate is currently valid.

Figure 1.9 provides a typical architecture for a PKI, the essential components of which are defined in the list that follows:

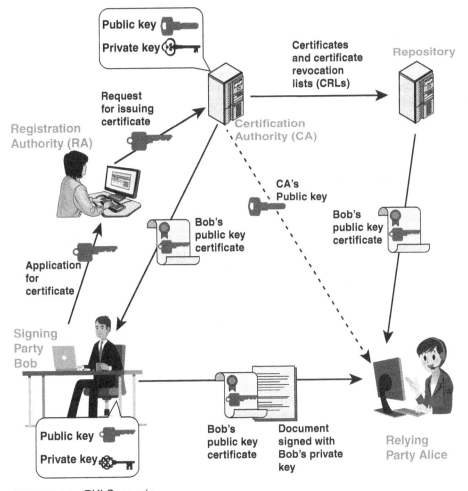

FIGURE 1.9   PKI Scenario

- **End entity:** An end user, a device (such as a router or server), a process, or any item that can be identified in the subject name of a public-key certificate. End entities can also be consumers of PKI-related services and, in some cases, providers of PKI-related services. For example, a registration authority is considered to be an end entity from the point of view of the certification authority.

- **Certification authority (CA):** An authority trusted by one or more users to create and assign public-key certificates. Optionally the certification authority may create the subjects' keys. A CA digitally signs a public-key certificate, which effectively binds the subject name to the public key. CAs are also responsible for issuing certificate revocation lists (CRLs). A CRL identifies certificates previously issued by the CA that are revoked before their expiration date. A certificate could be revoked because the user's private key is assumed to be compromised, the user is no longer certified by this CA, or the certificate is assumed to be compromised.

- **Registration authority (RA):** An optional component that can be used to offload many of the administrative functions that a CA ordinarily assumes. The RA is normally associated with the end entity registration process. This includes the verification of the identity of the end entity attempting to register with the PKI and obtain a certificate for its public key.

- **Repository:** Any method for storing and retrieving PKI-related information, such as public-key certificates and CRLs. A repository can be an X.500-based directory with client access via Lightweight Directory Access Protocol (LDAP). It also can be something simple, such as a means for retrieval of a flat file on a remote server via File Transfer Protocol (FTP) or Hypertext Transfer Protocol (HTTP).

- **Relying party:** Any user or agent that relies on the data in a certificate in making decisions.

Figure 1.9 illustrates the interaction of the various components. Consider a relying party Alice that needs to use Bob's public key. Alice must first obtain in a reliable, secure fashion a copy of the public key of the CA. This can be done in a number of ways, depending on the particular PKI architecture and enterprise policy. If Alice wishes to send encrypted data to Bob, Alice checks with the repository to determine whether Bob's certificate has been revoked, and if not, she obtains a copy of Bob's certificate. Alice can then use Bob's public key to encrypt data sent to Bob. Bob can also send to Alice a document signed with Bob's private key. Bob may include his certificate with the document or assume that Alice already has or can obtain the certificate. In either case, Alice first uses the CA's public key to verify that the certificate is valid and then uses Bob's public key (obtained from the certificate) to validate Bob's signature.

Rather than using a single CA, an enterprise may need to rely on multiple CAs and multiple repositories. CAs can be organized in a hierarchical fashion, with a root CA that is widely trusted signing the public-key certificates of subordinate CAs. Many root certificates are embedded in web browsers, so they have built-in trust of those CAs. Web servers, email clients, smartphones, and many other types of hardware and software also support PKI and contain trusted root certificates from the major CAs.

1.12 Network Security

Network security is a broad term that encompasses security of the communications pathways of a network and the security of network devices and devices attached to the network.

Communications Security

In the context of network security, communications security deals with the protection of communications through the network, including measures to protect against both passive and active attacks (see Figure 1.10).

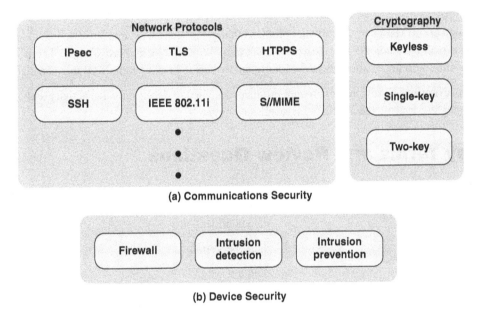

(a) Communications Security

(b) Device Security

FIGURE 1.10   Key Elements of Network Security

Communications security is implemented primarily using network protocols. A network protocol consists of the format and procedures that govern the transmission and receipt of data between points in a network. A protocol defines the structure of the individual data units (e.g., packets) and the control commands that manage the data transfer.

With respect to network security, a security protocol may be an enhancement that is part of an existing protocol or a standalone protocol. Examples of the former are IPsec, which is part of Internet Protocol (IP), and IEEE 802.11i, which is part of the IEEE 802.11 Wi-Fi standard. Examples of the latter are Transport Layer Security (TLS) and Secure Shell (SSH).

One common characteristic of all of these protocols is that they use a number of cryptographic algorithms as part of the mechanism to provide security.

Device Security

In addition to communications security, the other aspect of network security is the protection of network devices, such as routers and switches, and end systems connected to the network, such as client systems and servers. The primary security concerns are intruders gaining access to the system to perform unauthorized actions, insert malicious software (malware), or overwhelm system resources to diminish availability. Three types of device security are noteworthy:

- **Firewall:** A hardware and/or software capability that limits access between a network and a device attached to the network, in accordance with a specific security policy. The firewall acts as a filter that permits or denies data traffic, both incoming and outgoing, based on a set of rules based on traffic content and/or traffic pattern.

- **Intrusion detection:** Hardware or software products that gather and analyze information from various areas within a computer or a network for the purpose of finding and providing real-time or near-real-time warning of attempts to access system resources in an unauthorized manner.

- **Intrusion prevention:** Hardware or software products designed to detect intrusive activity and attempt to stop the activity, ideally before it reaches its target.

1.13   Key Terms and Review Questions

Key Terms

accountability	data confidentiality
asymmetric cryptography	data encryption
availability	data integrity
authenticity	decryption algorithm
brute-force attack	digital signature
certification authority (CA)	encryption algorithm
ciphertext	end entity
confidentiality	information security
cryptanalysis	integrity
cryptographic algorithm	network security
cryptography	nonrepudiation
cybersecurity	PKI architecture
data authenticity	plaintext

privacy	relying party
private key	repository
public key	secret key
public-key certificate	secure hash function
public-key encryption	symmetric encryption
public-key infrastructure (PKI)	system integrity
registration authority (RA)	user authentication

Review Questions

1. List and define the principal security objectives.

2. Describe the uses of data encryption.

3. What are the essential ingredients of a symmetric cipher?

4. What are the two basic functions used in encryption algorithms?

5. How many keys are required for two people to communicate via a symmetric cipher?

6. Describe the two general approaches to attacking a cipher.

7. What are the principal ingredients of a public-key cryptosystem?

8. List and briefly define three uses of a public-key cryptosystem.

9. What is the difference between a private key and a secret key?

10. What is a message authentication code?

11. What is a digital signature?

12. Describe the use of public-key certificates and certificate authorities.

13. Describe the functions of the various components in Figure 1.8.

1.14 References

ECRY18: European Union ECRYPT Project. *Algorithms, Key Size and Protocols Report.* February 2018. https://www.ecrypt.eu.org/csa/publications.html

STAL19: Stallings, W. *Effective Cybersecurity: A Guide to Using Best Practices and Standards.* Upper Saddle River, NJ: Pearson Addison Wesley, 2019.

STAL20: Stallings, W. *Cryptography and Network Security: Principles and Practice,* 8th ed. Upper Saddle River, NJ: Pearson, 2020.

Chapter | **2**

Information Privacy Concepts

Learning Objectives

After studying this chapter, you should be able to:

- Explain the difference between privacy by design and privacy engineering
- Understand how privacy-related activities fit into the system development life cycle
- Define *privacy control*
- Discuss the areas of overlap between security and privacy and the areas that are distinct to either security or privacy
- Explain the trade-off between privacy and utility
- Explain the distinction between privacy and usability

This chapter provides a roadmap for the remainder of the book, introducing the key information privacy concepts and indicating how they relate to one another. The chapter begins by defining key terms in the field of information privacy. Then, Sections 2.2 and 2.3 introduce the concepts of privacy by design and privacy engineering. Sections 2.4 through 2.6 deal with the relationship between privacy and security, the trade-off between privacy and utility, and the concept of usable privacy.

2.1 Key Privacy Terminology

The term *privacy* is used frequently in ordinary language as well as in philosophical, political, and legal discussions. However, there is no single definition or analysis or meaning of the term; a good survey of this topic is the privacy entry in the *Stanford Encyclopedia of Philosophy* [DECE18]. Two general characteristics of privacy are the right to be left alone—that is, free from being observed or disturbed—and the ability to control the information released about oneself.

This book is concerned with a concept of privacy referred to as ***information privacy***. ITU-T Recommendation X.800 (*Security Architecture for Open Systems Interconnection*) defines *privacy* as the right of individuals to control or influence what information related to them may be collected and stored and by whom and to whom that information may be disclosed. A U.S. National Research Council report (*At the Nexus of Cybersecurity and Public Policy: Some Basic Concepts and Issues*) [CLAR14] indicates that in the context of information, the term *privacy* usually refers to making ostensibly private information about an individual unavailable to parties that should not have that information. Privacy interests attach to the gathering, control, protection, and use of information about individuals.

Information privacy generally pertains to what is known as ***personally identifiable information*** (PII), as opposed to, say, video surveillance. PII is information that can be used to distinguish or trace an individual's identity. NIST SP 80-122 (*Guide to Protecting the Confidentiality of Personally Identifiable Information*) gives the following examples of information that might be considered PII:

- Name, such as full name, maiden name, mother's maiden name, or alias
- Personal identification number, such as Social Security number (SSN), passport number, driver's license number, taxpayer identification number, patient identification number, and financial account or credit card number
- Address information, such as street address or email address
- Asset information, such as Internet Protocol (IP) or media access control (MAC) address or other host-specific persistent static identifier that consistently links to a particular person or to a small, well-defined group of people
- Telephone numbers, including mobile, business, and personal numbers
- Personal characteristics, including photographic images (especially of the face or other distinguishing characteristic), x-rays, fingerprints, or other biometric image or template data (e.g., retinal scan, voice signature, facial geometry)
- Information identifying personally owned property, such as vehicle registration number or title number and related information
- Information about an individual that is linked or linkable to one of the above (e.g., date of birth, place of birth, race, religion, weight, activities, geographic indicators, employment information, medical information, education information, financial information)

In dealing with the privacy of PII, two new concepts have emerged: privacy by design (PbD) and privacy engineering. The goal of ***privacy by design*** is to take privacy requirements into account throughout the system development process, from the conception of a new IT system through detailed system design, implementation, and operation. ISO 29100 (*Information Technology—Security Techniques—Privacy Framework*) views PbD as the practice of considering privacy safeguarding measures at the time of the design of the system; that is, designers should consider privacy compliance during the design phase for systems processing PII rather than address compliance only at a subsequent stage.

Privacy engineering involves taking account of privacy during the entire life cycle of ICT (information and communications technology) systems, such that privacy is and remains an integral part of their function. NISTIR 8062 (*An Introduction to Privacy Engineering and Risk Management in Federal Systems*) defines privacy engineering as a specialty discipline of systems engineering focused on achieving freedom from conditions that can create problems for individuals with unacceptable consequences that arise from the system as it processes PII. Privacy engineering focuses on implementing techniques that decrease privacy risks and enables organizations to make purposeful decisions about resource allocation and effective implementation of controls in information systems. Such techniques decrease risks related to privacy harms and enable purposeful decisions about resource allocation and effective implementation of controls.

The European Data Protection Supervisor (EDPS), an independent institution of the European Union, relates the two concepts by indicating that the principles of privacy by design must be translated into privacy engineering methodologies [EDPS18].

Figure 2.1 provides an overview of the major activities and tasks involved in integrating information privacy protection into any information system developed by an organization. The upper part of the figure encompasses design activities that deal with determining what is needed and how to satisfy requirements. The lower part of the figure deals with implementation and operation of privacy features as part of the overall system.

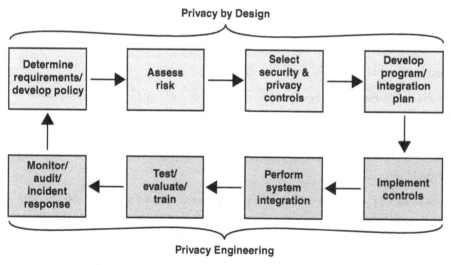

FIGURE 2.1   Information Privacy Development Life Cycle

Section 2.2 provides an overview of PbD, and Section 2.3 looks at privacy engineering.

2.2 Privacy by Design

PbD, as defined earlier, is concerned with ensuring that privacy features are designed into a system before implementation begins. PbD is a holistic concept that applies to information technology, business practices, processes, physical design, and networked infrastructure.

Privacy by Design Principles

A useful guide to the development of a PbD approach is the set of foundational principles for PbD first proposed by Ann Cavoukian, the information and privacy commissioner of Ontario [CAVO09]. These principles were later widely adopted as a resolution by other prominent policymakers at the 32nd Annual International Conference of Data Protection and Privacy Commissioners meeting [ICDP10]. Figure 2.2 illustrates the foundational principles of PbD, which are further described in the list that follows:

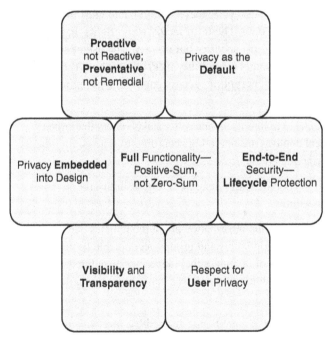

FIGURE 2.2   Foundational Principles of Privacy by Design

- **Proactive not reactive; preventive not remedial:** PbD is an approach that anticipates privacy issues and seeks to prevent problems before they arise. In this approach, designers must assess the potential vulnerabilities in a system and the types of threats that may occur and then select technical and managerial controls to protect the system.

- **Privacy as the default:** This principle requires an organization to ensure that it only processes the data that is necessary to achieve its specific purpose and that PII is protected during collection, storage, use, and transmission. In addition, individuals need not take affirmative action to protect their PII.

- **Privacy embedded into design:** Privacy protections should be core, organic functions, not added on after a design is complete. Privacy should be integral both to the design and architecture of IT systems and to business practices.

- **Full functionality: positive-sum, not zero-sum:** An essential goal of PbD is that it not degrade either the system functionality that is required or the security measures that are part of the system. Designers should seek solutions that avoid requiring a trade-off between privacy and system functionality or between privacy and security.

- **End-to-end security—life cycle protection:** This principle encompasses two concepts. The terms *end-to-end* and *life cycle* refer to the protection of PII from the time of collection through retention and destruction. During this life cycle, there should be no gaps in the protection of the data or in accountability for the data. The term *security* highlights that security processes and controls are used to provide not just security but privacy. The use of security measures ensures the confidentiality, integrity, and availability of PII throughout the life cycle. Examples of security measures include encryption, access controls, logging methods, and secure destruction.

- **Visibility and transparency:** PbD seeks to assure users and other stakeholders that privacy-related business practices and technical controls are operating according to state commitments and objectives. Key aspects of this principle are the following:

  - **Accountability:** The organization should clearly document responsibility for all privacy-related policies and procedures.

  - **Openness:** The organization should provide information about the policies and practices related to managing PII, as well as the individuals and groups accountable for protecting PII within the organization. The concept of openness includes a clearly defined organizational privacy policy for internal distribution as well as a privacy notice available to outsiders, such as web users.

  - **Compliance:** The organization should have compliance and redress mechanisms.

- **Respect for user privacy:** The organization must view privacy as primarily being characterized by personal control and free choice. Key aspects of this principle are the following:

  - **Consent:** Except where otherwise mandated by law, each individual should be empowered with consent for the collection, use, or disclosure of PII.

- **Accuracy:** The organization is responsible for ensuring that any PII that it maintains is accurate and up-to-date.

- **Access:** Individuals should be able to access any PII maintained by an organization, be informed of its uses and disclosures, and be able to challenge its correctness.

- **Compliance:** The organization should have compliance and redress mechanisms.

These principles are fundamental tenets that guide a privacy program, which an organization must translate into specific practices. The remainder of this section looks at the major activities involved in planning and designing information privacy protection for an information system. In essence, the PbD principles are requirements for the way in which systems are designed and implemented. The descriptions throughout this book of the various aspects of information privacy reflect these requirements.

Requirements and Policy Development

Refer to Figure 2.1 and notice that the first stage of privacy by design deals with privacy planning and policy. An essential element of planning for information privacy is the definition of the privacy requirements. The specific requirements for privacy features and protections drive the planning, design, and implementation of these features and protections. Key sources of requirements include regulations, standards, and the organization's contractual commitments. Chapter 3, "Information Privacy Requirements and Guidelines," examines this topic in detail.

A key actor at this stage is the *system owner*, which is the person or organization having responsibility for the development, procurement, integration, modification, operation, maintenance, and final disposition of an information system. The system owner needs to identify the standards and regulations that apply and develop an overall plan for privacy milestones during system development. It is also important to ensure that all key stakeholders have a common understanding, including privacy implications, considerations, and requirements. This planning activity enables developers to design privacy features into the project.

An expected output of this activity is a set of supporting documents that provide a record of the agreed planning decisions, including how these decisions conform to overall corporate privacy policy. Another key output is an initial set of privacy activities and decisions related to the overall development of the information system.

This stage is explored in more detail in Part V, "Information Privacy Management."

Privacy Risk Assessment

The ultimate objective of a privacy risk assessment is to enable organization executives to determine an appropriate budget for privacy and, within that budget, implement the privacy controls that optimize the level of protection. This objective is met by providing an estimate of the potential cost to the organization of privacy violations, coupled with an estimation of the likelihood of such breaches. Four elements are involved in the assessment:

- **Privacy-related asset:** Anything that has value to the organization and that therefore requires protection. With respect to privacy, the primary asset is PII of employees, customers, patients, business partners, and so on. This category also includes intangible assets such as reputation and goodwill.

- **Privacy threat:** A potential for violation of privacy, which exists when there is a circumstance, a capability, an action, or an event that could violate privacy and cause harm to an individual. That is, a threat is a possible danger that might exploit vulnerability. A related term is ***threat action***, which is a realization of a threat—that is, an occurrence in which a vulnerability is exploited as a result of either an accidental event or an intentional act.

- **Privacy vulnerability:** A flaw or weakness in a system's design, implementation, or operation and management that could be exploited by a threat action to violate the system's privacy policy and compromise PII.

- **Privacy controls:** The management, operational, and technical controls (i.e., countermeasures) prescribed for an information system to protect PII and ensure that the organization's privacy policy is enforced.

Using these four elements, a privacy risk assessment consists of these three steps:

1. Determine the harm, or impact, to individuals and the organization of a privacy violation. For each privacy-related asset, determine the possible threats to that asset. Then determine the impact to individuals if their privacy rights are violated and the impact to the organization, in terms of cost or lost value, if a threat action occurs.

2. Determine the likelihood of a privacy incident, where a ***privacy incident*** is defined as an occurrence that actually or potentially violates the privacy of PII or that constitutes a violation or an imminent threat of violation of privacy policies, privacy procedures, or acceptable use policies. For each asset, three factors determine the likelihood: the relevant threats to the asset, the vulnerability of the asset to each threat, and the privacy controls currently in place that reduce the likelihood that each threat will cause harm.

3. Determine the level of risk as the combination of the cost if the privacy incident occurs and the likelihood that that incident occurs.

An organization should use the level of risk to determine a budget allocation for security controls. The combination of privacy risk assessment and privacy control selection is referred to as a *privacy impact assessment* (PIA). Chapter 11, "Risk Management and Privacy Impact Assessment," discusses PIAs in detail.

Privacy and Security Control Selection

The privacy protection of PII involves the use of both controls that are specific to privacy and the use of controls developed for information security requirements. This section discusses both.

Privacy Controls

Privacy controls are the technical, physical, and administrative (or management) measures employed within an organization to satisfy privacy requirements. Privacy controls might result in:

- Removing the threat source
- Changing the likelihood that the threat can exploit a vulnerability by reducing or eliminating the vulnerability or by changing the amount of PII collected or the way it is processed
- Changing the consequences of a privacy event

Two especially valuable sources of information on privacy controls can be used as guidance in control selection. NIST SP 800-53 (*Security and Privacy Controls for Information Systems and Organizations*) is an invaluable and extraordinarily detailed discussion of controls and should be consulted in the development of any risk treatment plan. This 500-page document provides plenty of guidance on the overall development of a treatment plan and includes an extensive catalog of security controls and privacy controls. ISO 29151 (*Code of Practice for Personally Identifiable Information Protection*) offers guidance on a broad range of privacy controls that are commonly applied in many different organizations that deal with protection of PII.

Part IV, "Privacy Enhancing Technologies," provides a detailed examination of technical privacy controls that can be implemented as part of an IT system or subsystem. Part V includes a discussion of administrative and managerial controls.

Security Controls

Security controls are safeguards or countermeasures prescribed for an information system or an organization that are designed to protect the confidentiality, integrity, and availability of its information and to meet a set of defined security requirements. As discussed in Section 2.4, there is an overlap in the areas of concern of information security and information privacy. Security controls, when selected and implemented for information systems that create, collect, use, process, store, maintain, disseminate, disclose, or dispose of PII, address both security and privacy concerns. For example, access control mechanisms can be used to limit the access to PII stored in a database.

Nonetheless, individual privacy cannot be achieved solely through securing personally identifiable information. Hence, both security and privacy controls are needed.

As discussed previously, SP 800-53 is an excellent source of security controls. ISO 27002 (*Code of Practice for Information Security Controls*) is another good source. Part III, "Technical Security Controls for Privacy" covers this topic.

The Selection Process

Selecting and documenting security and privacy controls should be synchronized with the risk assessment activity. Typically, a baseline set of controls is selected and then adjusted, with additional controls based on a refinement of the risk assessment. The refinement considers any possible secondary risks that result from the baseline controls and how they affect the risk assessment.

Privacy Program and Integration Plan

The principal objective of PbD is to ensure that information privacy considerations are considered at every stage of system development and that privacy protection measures are designed into the system during the system design and development process rather than retrofitted. An essential element in achieving this objective is a documented and approved privacy program. Elements of such a program should include:

- Identifying key privacy roles that will be active throughout the system design and implementation

- Identifying standards and regulations that apply

- Developing an overall plan for privacy milestones during system development

- Ensuring that all key stakeholders have a common understanding, including privacy implications, considerations, and requirements

- Describing the requirements for integrating privacy controls within the system and the process for coordinating privacy engineering activities with overall system development

Part of the privacy program document, or provided as a separate document, is a privacy plan that deals with the implementation of privacy features and their integration with the rest of the system. This is a formal document that provides an overview of the privacy requirements for the information system and describes the privacy controls that are in place or planned for meeting those requirements. Key components of the plan are a privacy categorization, which gives the acceptable level of risk for each distinct element of the system, and a description of each privacy control and its implementation plan.

This stage should also produce a detailed architecture that incorporates privacy features and controls into the system design. Expected outputs include:

- A schematic of privacy integration that provides details on where, within the system, privacy is implemented and, if applicable, where privacy mechanisms are shared by multiple services or applications

- A list of shared services and resulting shared risk

- Identification of common controls used by the system

Chapter 10, "Information Privacy Governance and Management," discusses privacy programs and plans.

2.3 Privacy Engineering

Figure 2.1 indicates that privacy engineering encompasses the implementation, deployment, and ongoing operation and management of privacy features and controls in systems. Privacy engineering involves both technical capabilities and management processes. The primary goals of privacy engineering are to:

- Incorporate functionality and management practices to satisfy privacy requirements

- Prevent compromise of PII

- Mitigate the impact of breach of personal data

Although Figure 2.1 shows privacy engineering as being distinct from, and following on, PbD, the term *privacy engineering* is often used to encompass privacy-related activities throughout the system development life cycle. An example of this is shown in Figure 2.3, adapted from NISTIR 8062.

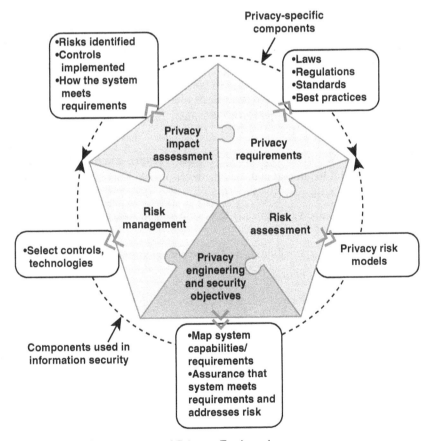

FIGURE 2.3   Components of Privacy Engineering

As illustrated in Figure 2.3, the NIST document lists five components of privacy engineering—two that are specific to the privacy engineering process and three that are components typically used in information security management. The components are:

- **Security risk assessment:** A security risk is an expectation of loss expressed as the probability that a particular threat will exploit a particular vulnerability with a particular harmful result. Security risk assessment is a process that systematically (a) identifies valuable system resources and threats to those resources, (b) quantifies loss exposures (i.e., loss potential) based on estimated frequencies and costs of occurrence. Thus, risk assessment follows two parallel paths. First, for each threat to a resource, the value of the resource is assessed and the potential impact, or cost, if the threat to that resource becomes a successful threat action. Second, based on the strength of a threat, the probability of the threat becoming an actual threat action, and the vulnerability of the resource, a likelihood of a successful threat action is determined. Finally, the potential impact of the threat and the likelihood of its success are factors in determining the risk.

- **Risk management:** NIST SP 800-37 (*Risk Management Framework for Information Systems and Organizations*) states that risk management includes a disciplined, structured, and flexible process for organizational asset valuation; security and privacy control selection, implementation, and assessment; system and control authorizations; and continuous monitoring. It also includes enterprise-level activities to help better prepare organizations to execute the RMF at the system level. Risk management is an iterative process, as illustrated in Figure 2.4, based on one in ITU-T X.1055 (*Risk management and risk profile guidelines for telecommunication organizations*), consisting of four steps:

  1. Assess risk based on assets, threats, vulnerabilities, and existing controls. From these inputs determine impact and likelihood and then the level of risk. This is the risk assessment component described in the preceding bullet.

  2. Identify potential security controls to reduce risk, prioritize their use, and select controls for implementation.

  3. Allocate resources, roles, and responsibilities and implement controls.

  4. Monitor and evaluate risk treatment effectiveness.

In the context of privacy engineering, the emphasis is on privacy risk and the implementation of privacy controls. Chapter 11 discusses risk management.

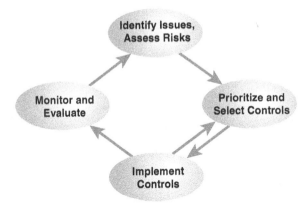

FIGURE 2.4   Risk Management Cycle

■ **Privacy requirements:** These are system requirements that have privacy relevance. System privacy requirements define the protection capabilities provided by the system, the performance and behavioral characteristics exhibited by the system, and the evidence used to determine that the system privacy requirements have been satisfied. Privacy requirements are derived from a variety of sources including laws, regulations, standards, and stakeholder expectations. Chapter 3 examines privacy requirements.

■ **Privacy impact assessment:** The NIST Computer Security Glossary (https://csrc.nist.gov/glossary) defines a PIA as an analysis of how information is handled: (i) to ensure handling conforms to applicable legal, regulatory, and policy requirements regarding privacy; (ii) to determine the risks and effects of collecting, maintaining, and disseminating information in identifiable form in an electronic information system; and (iii) to examine and evaluate protections and alternative processes for handling information to mitigate potential privacy risks. In essence, PIA consists of privacy risk assessment followed by a selection of privacy and security controls to reduce the risk. Chapter 11 examines the PIA.

■ **Privacy engineering and security objectives:** Information security risk assessment focuses on meeting the common security objectives, including confidentiality, integrity, and availability (Figure 1.1). Similarly, privacy engineering objectives focus on the types of capabilities the system needs in order to demonstrate implementation of an organization's privacy policies and system privacy requirements. NISTIR 8062 proposes three privacy objectives, illustrated in Figure 2.5. Chapter 3 expands on this topic.

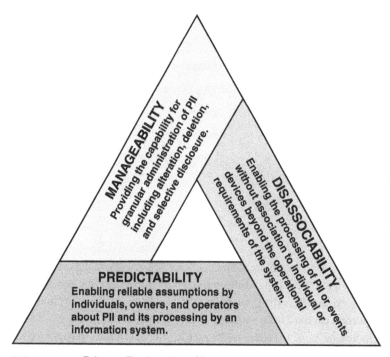

FIGURE 2.5   Privacy Engineering Objectives

The remainder of this section provides an overview of the major stages of privacy engineering (refer to Figure 2.1). Chapter 10 addresses the management and operational aspects of these stages.

Privacy Implementation

During the privacy implementation stage, developers configure and enable system privacy features. Implementation includes alignment and integration of privacy controls with system functional features. As part of implementation, an organization should perform developmental testing of the technical and privacy features/functions to ensure that they perform as intended prior to launching the integration phase.

System Integration

System integration activity occurs at the point of deployment of the system for operation. Privacy control settings are enabled, and other privacy features need to be integrated at this point. The output of this activity is a verified list of operational privacy controls integrated into the completed system documentation.

Privacy Testing and Evaluation

Privacy testing includes the following types of testing:

■ **Functional testing:** Advertised privacy mechanisms of an information system are tested under operational conditions to determine whether a given function works according to its requirements.

■ **Penetration testing:** Evaluators mimic real-world attacks in an attempt to identify ways to circumvent the privacy features of an application, a system, or a network.

■ **User testing:** The software or system is tested in the "real world" by the intended audience. Also called *end user testing*.

This stage should result in formal management certification and accreditation of the system with its privacy features. *Certification* involves a comprehensive assessment of the management, operational, and technical privacy controls in an information system to determine the extent to which the controls are implemented correctly, operating as intended, and producing the desired outcome with respect to meeting the security requirements for the system. *Accreditation* is the official management decision given by a senior agency official to authorize operation of an information system and to explicitly accept the risk to agency operations (including mission, functions, image, or reputation), agency assets, or individuals, based on the implementation of an agreed-upon set of privacy controls.

Privacy Auditing and Incident Response

In the privacy auditing and incident response stage, systems and products are in place and operating, enhancements and/or modifications to the system are developed and tested, and hardware and/or software is added or replaced. During this stage, the organization should continuously monitor performance of the system to ensure that it is consistent with pre-established privacy requirements and that needed system modifications are incorporated.

Two key activities during this stage are as follows:

■ **Auditing:** Auditing involves independent examination of records and activities to ensure compliance with established controls, policy, and operational procedures and to recommend any indicated changes in controls, policies, or procedures.

■ **Incident response:** An IT security incident is an adverse event in a computer system or network caused by the failure of a security mechanism or an attempted or threatened breach of such mechanisms. Incident response involves the mitigation of violations of security policies and recommended practices.

Chapter 13, "Event Monitoring, Auditing, and Incident Response," discusses auditing and incident response.

2.4 Privacy and Security

The two concepts of privacy and information security are closely related. On the one hand, the scale and interconnectedness of personal information collected and stored in information systems has increased dramatically, motivated by law enforcement, national security, and economic incentives. Economic incentives perhaps have been the main driving force. In a global information economy, it is likely that the most economically valuable electronic asset is aggregations of information on individuals [JUDY14]. On the other hand, individuals have become increasingly aware of the extent to which government agencies, businesses, and even Internet users have access to their personal information and private details about their lives and activities.

Areas of Overlap Between Security and Privacy

Although security and privacy are related, they are not equivalent. Figure 2.6, from NISTIR 8062, shows a non-proportional representation of the relationship between the privacy and security domains. While some privacy concerns arise from unauthorized activity, privacy concerns also can arise from authorized processing of information about individuals. Recognizing the boundaries and overlap between privacy and security is key to determining when existing security risk models and security-focused guidance may be applied to address privacy concerns—and where there are gaps that need to be filled in order to achieve an engineering approach to privacy. For instance, existing information security guidance does not address the consequences of a poor consent mechanism for use of PII, the purpose of transparency, what PII is being collected, correction of PII, or which changes in use of PII are permitted if authorized personnel are conducting the activity. Given these material distinctions in the disciplines, it should be clear that agencies will not be able to effectively manage privacy solely on the basis of managing security.

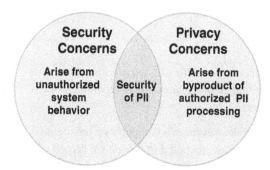

FIGURE 2.6   Overlap Between Information Security and Privacy

Figure 2.7, from the technical paper *Privacy Fundamentals: What an Information Security Officer Needs to Know* [BAKI05], further illustrates the overlap and distinctions between security and privacy by listing key objectives. Some objectives—such as availability, system and data protection from threats, and physical protection—are primarily information security objectives. Objectives dealing specifically with the management and use of PII are primarily or exclusively privacy objectives. The technical paper just mentioned identifies five objectives that are relevant to both privacy and security [BAKI05]. Table 2.1 indicates the difference in emphasis for each objective for privacy and security.

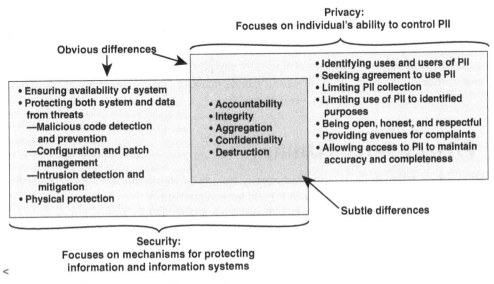

FIGURE 2.7 Privacy and Security Objectives

TABLE 2.1 Overlapping Security and Privacy Objectives

	Security	Privacy
Accountability	Focuses on tracking an individual's actions and manipulation of information	Focuses on tracking the trail of PII disclosure
Integrity	Protects against the corruption of data by authorized or unauthorized individuals	Seeks to ensure that inaccurate PII is not used to make an inappropriate decision about a person
Aggregation	Focuses on determining the sensitivity of derived and aggregated data so that appropriate access guidance can be defined	Dictates that aggregation or derivation of new PII should not be allowed if the new information is neither authorized by law nor necessary to fulfill a stated purpose
Confidentiality	Focuses on processes and mechanisms (e.g., authenticators) that prevent unauthorized access	Focuses on ensuring that PII is only disclosed for a purpose consistent with the reason it was collected
Destruction	Focuses on ensuring that the information cannot be recovered once deleted	Addresses the need for the complete elimination of collected information once it has served its purpose

Trade-Offs Between Security and Privacy

To some extent, information security measures can protect privacy. For example, an intruder seeking ostensibly private information (e.g., personal emails or photographs, financial or medical records, phone calling records) may be stymied by good cybersecurity measures. In addition, security measures can protect the integrity of PII and support the availability of PII. But the National Research Council paper *At the Nexus of Cybersecurity and Public Policy: Some Basic Concepts and Issues* points out that certain measures taken to enhance cybersecurity can also violate privacy [CLAR14]. For example, some firewalls use technical measures to block Internet traffic containing malware before it reaches its destination. To identify malware-containing traffic, the content of all in-bound network traffic must be inspected. But some regard inspection of traffic by any party other than its intended recipient as a violation of privacy because most traffic will in fact be malware free. Under many circumstances, inspection of traffic in this manner is also a violation of law.

2.5   Privacy Versus Utility

An important consideration in the provision of privacy features in an information system or database is the potential conflict between the privacy of PII and the potential utility of collections of PII to third parties. In this context, the term *utility* can be defined as a quantifiable benefit to multiple legitimate information consumers [SANK11]. How specifically to quantify the utility of information depends on the nature of the information and the application context.

Utility and privacy are often competing requirements. Any access of data that contains or is derived from PII has the potential to leak information that the source of the PII wishes to keep private. On the other hand, increasing the privacy restrictions on information increases the restrictions on the flow of potentially useful information. For example, databases of individual data records can facilitate beneficial research in areas such as public health, medicine, criminal justice, and economics. Several strategies can be used to protect privacy, such as making available only aggregations of data or removing key identifiers and/or altering values of sensitive attributes before releasing the data. It should be clear that the more aggressive the measures to protect privacy, the less utility the information will have for researchers.

Figure 2.8 illustrates the trade-off between utility and privacy. With no special measures taken, there is a clear loss of privacy with increased utility and vice versa. One of the objectives of privacy by design and privacy engineering is to provide technical and managerial safeguards to privacy while enabling a high degree of utility. The upper line in the figure indicates this.

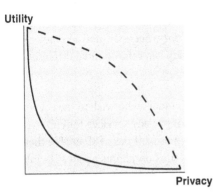

Solid line: little or no use of PbD and privacy engineering techniques
Dashed line: cost-effective use of PbD and privacy engineering techniques

FIGURE 2.8   Utility–Privacy Trade-Off

2.6   Usable Privacy

Like utility, usability is an important constraint in PbD and privacy engineering. ISO 9241-11 (*Ergonomic Requirements for Office Work with Visual Display Terminals (VDTs)—Part 11: Guidance on Usability*) defines **usability** as "the extent to which a product can be used by specified users to achieve specified goals with effectiveness, efficiency and satisfaction in a specified context of use." The key terms in this definition are:

- **Effectiveness:** Accuracy and completeness with which users achieve specified goals. This is typically based on error rates.

- **Efficiency:** Resources expended in relation to the accuracy and completeness with which users achieve goals. This is typically based on the time required to complete a task or subtask, taking into account accuracy goals.

- **Satisfaction:** Freedom from discomfort and positive attitudes toward the use of the product. This is a subjective parameter and can be judged using questionnaires.

- **Context of use:** Users, tasks, equipment (hardware, software, and materials), and the physical and social environments in which a product is used.

- **User:** A person who interacts with the product.

- **Goal:** The intended outcome.

- **Task:** An activity (physical or cognitive) required to achieve a goal.

- **Product:** Part of the equipment (hardware, software, and materials) for which usability is to be specified or evaluated.

Users of Privacy Services and Functions

The National Research Council publication *Toward Better Usability, Security, and Privacy of Information Technology* points out that usability in the context of privacy can refer to three different classes of users [NRC10]:

- **End users of IT systems:** End users of IT systems are individuals who wish to have as much control as possible over the privacy of their PII. Examples of privacy services for end users are those that allow individuals to opt in or opt out of certain uses of their PII, enable them to determine the accuracy of their PII stored in databases, and file complaints about PII violations. Frequently, end users find these services difficult to understand and use.

- **Administrators of IT systems:** Administrators need to configure IT systems to enable or disable specific privacy features for individuals or groups of individuals whose PII is stored in the system. Administrators often contend with systems that are difficult to understand and configure.

- **System developers:** Developers need usable tools that make it easy to avoid or detect design and coding errors that affect privacy.

Usability and Utility

Usability and utility are distinct concepts. *Usability* refers to the ease of use of privacy features. *Utility* refers to the functionality available for databases containing PII with privacy protection in place. Both concepts need to be considered through the design, implementation, and operation of IT systems containing PII.

2.7 Key Terms and Review Questions

Key Terms

accreditation	personally identifiable information (PII)
auditing	privacy
certification	privacy by design (PbD)
end user testing	privacy control
functional testing	privacy engineering
incident response	privacy impact assessment (PIA)
information privacy	privacy-related asset
penetration testing	privacy requirements

privacy threat	system owner
privacy vulnerability	threat action
risk assessment	usability
risk management	user testing
security	utility
stakeholder	V model
system development life cycle (SDLC)	

Review Questions

1. Explain the term *information privacy*.
2. What is personally identifiable information?
3. Explain the manner in which privacy by design and privacy engineering operate together.
4. What are the commonly accepted foundational principles for privacy by design?
5. What elements are involved in privacy risk assessment?
6. Describe the various types of privacy controls.
7. What issues should be considered in selecting privacy controls?
8. Explain the difference between privacy risk assessment and privacy impact assessment.
9. What are the types of privacy testing?
10. What are the overlapping and non-overlapping areas of concern with respect to information security and information privacy?
11. Explain the trade-off between privacy and utility.
12. What is the difference between usability and utility?

2.8 References

BAKI05: Bakis, B. *Privacy Fundamentals: What an Information Security Officer Needs to Know.* Mitre Technical Paper, October 18, 2005. https://www.mitre.org/publications/technical-papers

CAVO09: Cavoukian, A. *Privacy by Design: The 7 Foundational Principles.* Information and Privacy Commissioner of Ontario, Canada, 2009.

CLAR14: Clark, D., Berson, T., and Lin, H. (eds.). *At the Nexus of Cybersecurity and Public Policy: Some Basic Concepts and Issues.* National Research Council, 2014.

DECE18: DeCew, J. "Privacy." *The Stanford Encyclopedia of Philosophy*, Spring 2018, Edward N. Zalta (ed.), https://plato.stanford.edu/archives/spr2018/entries/privacy

EDPS18: European Data Protection Supervisor. *Preliminary Opinion on Privacy by Design.* May 31, 2018. https://edps.europa.eu/sites/edp/files/publication/18-05-31_preliminary_opinion_on_privacy_by_design_en_0.pdf

ICDP10: International Conference of Data Protection and Privacy Commissioners. *Resolution on Privacy by Design.* October 2010. https://icdppc.org/document-archive/adopted-resolutions/

JUDY14: Judy, H., et al. "Privacy in Cyberspace." In Bosworth, S., Kabay, M., and Whyne, E. (eds.). *Computer Security Handbook.* New York: Wiley, 2014.

NRC10: National Research Council. *Toward Better Usability, Security, and Privacy of Information Technology.* The National Academies Press, 2010.

SANK11: Sankar, L., and Poor, H. "Utility–Privacy Tradeoffs in Databases: An Information-Theoretic Approach." *IEEE Transactions on Information Forensics and Security.* February 2011.

PART II

Privacy Requirements and Threats

Chapter | **3**

Information Privacy Requirements and Guidelines

Learning Objectives

After studying this chapter, you should be able to:

- Explain the concept of PII sensitivity
- Discuss the different types of personal information
- Understand the OECD fair information practice principles
- Present an overview of the EU General Data Protection Regulation
- Summarize important U.S. privacy laws
- Present an overview of privacy-related standards from ISO
- Present an overview of privacy-related standards and documents from NIST

Three main categories of specifications drive the set of requirements used by organizations in the design and implementation of information privacy protection features:

- **Regulations:** National and regional regulations and laws mandate the types of protection of personally identifiable information (PII) that organizations must provide. In some cases, the regulations and laws mandate specific features and procedures that organizations must implement to protect PII.

- **Standards:** National and international information privacy standards are guidelines that specify features and procedures of protecting PII.

- **Best Practices:** Best practices documents developed by relevant industry organizations recommend policies, procedures, and controls that have been found to be effective in protecting PII.

Standards and best practices documents provide guidance to designers and implementers. Frequently, organizations treat these documents as sources of specific requirements in policies, procedures, design, and implementation, for the following reasons:

- Government agencies and private sector customers may require contractually that a providing organization conform to certain standards as a condition of providing service.

- If an organization can demonstrate that it has faithfully implemented the guidance in standards and best practices documents, this may limit its liability in the event of a privacy breach.

- These documents represent the collective experience and wisdom of a broad range of concerned government and industry groups and hence provide authoritative guidance as to the best ways to achieve protection of PII.

Before looking at these sources of requirements for the protection of PII, this chapter begins, in Sections 3.1 and 3.2, by discussing the characteristics of PII and other forms of personal information. Section 3.3 covers one of the earliest sets of requirements used for the development of privacy regulations—and one that is still in use today—known as fair information practice principles. Section 3.4 provides an overview of information privacy regulations. Sections 3.5 and 3.6 cover standards and best practices, respectively.

3.1 Personally Identifiable Information and Personal Data

In the context of information systems, privacy deals with the protection of information about individuals that can be stored and transmitted. Standards, regulations, and laws in the United States make this concept more specific by using the term *personally identifiable information* (PII). NIST SP 800-122 (*Guide to Protecting the Confidentiality of Personally Identifiable Information*) defines PII as:

> Any information about an individual maintained by an agency, including (1) any information that can be used to distinguish or trace an individual's identity, such as name, social security number, date and place of birth, mother's maiden name, or biometric records; and (2) any other information that is linked or linkable to an individual, such as medical, educational, financial, and employment information.

SP 800-122 clarifies the terms that are important in this definition as follows:

- **Distinguish an individual:** Information that can be used to identify a specific individual, such as name, passport number, or biometric data. In contrast, a list of items containing only credit scores without any additional information concerning individuals would not be sufficient to distinguish an individual.

- **Trace an individual:** To process sufficient information to determine a specific aspect of an individual's activities or status. For example, an audit log containing records of user actions could make it possible to trace an individual's activities.

- **Linked information:** Information about or related to an individual that is logically associated with other information about the individual.

- **Linkable information:** Information related to an individual for which there is a possibility of logical association with other information about the individual. For example, if two databases contain different PII elements, then someone with access to both databases might be able to link the information from the two databases and identify individuals, as well as access additional information about or relating to the individuals. If the secondary information source is present on the same system or a closely related system and does not have security controls that effectively segregate the information sources, then the data are considered linked. If the secondary information source is maintained more remotely, such as in an unrelated system within the organization, available in public records, or otherwise readily obtainable (e.g., Internet search engine), then the data are considered linkable.

The definition of PII just given is wide, and many other countries use similar definitions to delimit the items that need to be protected. An even broader term, *personal data*, is used in the General Data Protection Regulation (GDPR), which was issued by the European Union (EU) and came into force in May 2018. The GDPR defines *personal data* as:

> Any information relating to an identified or identifiable natural person ("data subject"); an identifiable natural person is one who can be identified, directly or indirectly, in particular by reference to an identifier such as a name, an identification number, location data, an online identifier or to one or more factors specific to the physical, physiological, genetic, mental, economic, cultural or social identity of that natural person.

There are four key elements to the GDPR definition:

- **Any information:** In essence, the GDPR considers any data that can be used to identify an individual as personal data. It includes, for the first time, things such as genetic, mental, cultural, economic, and social information. There may be a wide variety in the nature and content of the information, as well as its technical format.

- **Relating to:** This phrase implies that the regulation applies to information that relates to an individual on the basis of its content, purpose, or result. This phrase also covers information that may have an impact on the way in which and individual is treated or evaluated.

- **Identified or identifiable:** To determine whether a person is identifiable, account should be taken of all the means likely reasonably to be used to identify the person and that the principles of protection shall not apply to data rendered anonymous in such a way that the data subject is no longer identifiable.

- **Natural person:** A natural person is a real human being, as distinguished from a corporation, which is often treated at law as a fictitious person.

In the United States as well as many other countries, a somewhat restrictive view is taken of PII, which frequently focuses on whether the data are actually linked to an *identified* person. In contrast, EU privacy laws and regulations, culminating in GDPR, are more expansive and broadly define PII to encompass all data that can be used to make a person *identifiable*. As pointed out in the *California Law Review* article "Reconciling Personal Information in the United States and European Union," in the EU interpretation, "even if the data alone cannot be linked to a specific individual, if it is reasonably possible to use the data in combination with other information to identify a person, then the information is PII" [SCHW14].

An even broader interpretation of PII is used in the recent California Consumer Privacy Act (CCPA), which uses the term "personal information," defined as "any information that identifies, relates to, describes, is capable of being associated with, or could reasonably be linked, directly or indirectly, with a particular consumer or household."

This book covers how to protect data that have privacy implications, not with the policy and regulatory decisions related to what data to protect. Accordingly, the book uses the term *PII* throughout, with an understanding that the PbD and privacy engineering techniques described in this book apply regardless of the precise definition of personal data in use.

Sources of PII

Individuals share PII with a variety of organizations for a variety of purposes. Chapter 2, "Information Privacy Concepts," lists some examples of PII. The following are some examples of categories of PII:

- **Government-issued identification:** For example, driver's license, passport, birth certificate, and pension and medical benefits identifiers (e.g., in the United States, Social Security number and Medicare number)

- **Contact information:** For example, email address, physical address, and telephone numbers

- **Online information:** For example, Facebook and other social media identifiers, passwords, and PINs (personal identification numbers)

- **Geolocation data:** From smartphones, GPS devices, and cameras

- **Device address:** Such as an IP address of a device connected to the Internet or the media access control (MAC) address of a device connected to a local area network

- **Verification data:** For example, mother's maiden name, pets' and children's names, and high school

- **Medical records information:** Such as prescriptions, medical records, exams, and medical images

- **Biometric and genetic information:** Such as fingerprints, retinal scans, and DNA

- **Account numbers:** Such as bank, insurance, investment, and debit/credit cards

Organizations also collect and store PII based on the role of the individual in relation to the data collected by the organization. Examples include:

- Parent
- Citizen
- Employee
- Consumer
- Investor
- Patient
- Internet user
- Hobbyist
- Volunteer

Sensitivity of PII

Although organizations have a duty to protect all PII, both as a matter of policy and regulatory requirement, they frequently make a distinction between sensitive PII and non-sensitive PII. The implication of the designation of some PII as sensitive is that the release of such information would have greater impact of some sort than would the release of non-sensitive PII and that therefore an organization should have stronger privacy controls for sensitive PII. There is no widely accepted definition of sensitive PII. The International Association of Privacy Professionals (IAPP) proposes the following somewhat general definition: "Data which is more significantly related to the notion of a reasonable expectation of privacy, such as medical or financial information. However, data may be considered more or less sensitive depending on context or jurisdiction" (https://iapp.org/resources/glossary).

On the other hand, *The OECD Privacy Framework* document [OECD13] states that *"it is probably not possible to identify a set of data which are universally regarded as being sensitive."*

On organization can make the distinction between sensitive and non-sensitive PII by enumerating specific items. As an example, the U.S. Commerce Department defines *sensitive PII* as "PII which if lost, compromised, or disclosed without authorization, could result in harm, embarrassment, inconvenience, or unfairness to an individual" [DOC17]. The document lists the following types of PII as sensitive when associated with an individual:

- Social Security number (including in truncated form)
- Place of birth

- Date of birth

- Mother's maiden name

- Biometric information

- Medical information (excluding brief references to absences from work)

- Personal financial information

- Credit card/purchase card account numbers

- Passport numbers

- Potentially sensitive employment information (e.g., performance ratings, disciplinary actions, results of background investigations)

- Criminal history

- Information that may stigmatize or adversely affect an individual

Examples of non-sensitive PII include an individual's name, work email address, work address, and work phone number.

The context is important in determining the sensitivity of PII. PII that might not include elements normally identified as sensitive may still be sensitive and require special handling if its compromise could cause substantial harm, inconvenience, embarrassment, or unfairness to an individual. For example, the U.S. Homeland Security Department provides the following examples in the *Handbook for Safeguarding Sensitive PII* [DHS17]:

> A collection of names is not SPII if it is a list, file, query result of:
>
> - Attendees at a public meeting or
> - Stakeholders who subscribe to a DHS email distribution list
>
> It is SPII if it is a list, file, query result of:
>
> - Law enforcement personnel, such as investigators, agents, or support personnel, or
> - Employee performance ratings, or
> - Employees with overdue mandatory training course completions

3.2 Personal Information That Is Not PII

Figure 3.1, based on a figure in the article "Experimentation with Personal Identifiable Information" [ALFE12], illustrates the position of PII within the totality of information maintained in an information system.

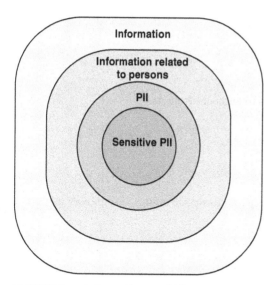

FIGURE 3.1   Information and PII

As already mentioned, some portion of PII is sensitive PII, depending on the specific listing or definition of sensitive PII categories; however, PII is only a subset of all of the information related to persons that may exist in an information system.

It is useful to define four categories of information that relates to persons:

- **Personally identifiable information:** Simply put, information that leads to the identification of a unique individual.

- **De-identified personal information:** Information that has had enough PII removed or obscured that the remaining information does not identify an individual, and there is no reasonable basis to believe that the information can be used to identify an individual.

- **Anonymous personal information:** Information not related to an identified or an identifiable person and that cannot be combined with other information to re-identify individuals. It has been rendered unidentifiable.

- **Aggregated (group) information:** Information elements abstracted from a number of individuals, typically used for the purposes of making comparisons, analyzing trends, or identifying patterns.

De-identification of data refers to the process of removing or obscuring any personally identifiable information from individual records in a way that minimizes the risk of unintended disclosure of the identity of individuals and information about them. Anonymization of data refers to the process of data de-identification that produces data where individual records cannot be linked back to an original, as they do not include the required translation variables to do so.

In many cases, organizations can perform useful work on personal information without having PII, as for example, for some forms of research, resource planning, and examination of correlations and trends. Frequently, the de-identification process is done in such a way that the organization can re-identify the data. ***Re-identification*** is a process that reestablishes the relationship between personally identifiable data and de-identified data. The organization can achieve this by using a code, an algorithm, or a pseudonym that is assigned to individual records, with the enabling information protected by encryption or other means. Another approach is to encrypt identifying elements within data records.

There is, however, a risk that an adversary can re-identify data records by making use of publicly available information to deduce the identity associated with an individual data record.

Anonymization of data is a process of de-identification for which a code or other means of association for re-identification does not exist. Anonymization is commonly used by government agencies to release datasets to the public for research purposes. It is also useful for system testing. Robust testing involves simulating real conditions as closely as possible, so it should involve testing real-world data. However, because of the processing and operational burdens involved in protecting PII, it is more efficient to work with an anonymized dataset.

Aggregation of group information should remove all PII. An example from SP 800-122 is the aggregation and use of multiple sets of de-identified data for evaluating several types of education loan programs. The data describes characteristics of loan holders, such as age, gender, region, and outstanding loan balances. With this dataset, an analyst could draw statistics showing that 18,000 women in the 30–35 age group have outstanding loan balances greater than $10,000. Although the original dataset contained distinguishable identities for each person, the de-identified and aggregated dataset would not contain linked or readily identifiable data for any individual.

Aggregation in the sense used here involves abstracting or summarizing properties about groups of persons. This is the sense used, for example, in the GDPR, which states:

> Where personal data are processed for statistical purposes, this Regulation should apply to that processing. Statistical purposes mean any operation of collection and the processing of personal data necessary for statistical surveys or for the production of statistical results. Those statistical results may further be used for different purposes, including a scientific research purpose. The statistical purpose implies that the result of processing for statistical purposes is not personal data, but aggregate data, and that this result or the personal data are not used in support of measures or decisions regarding any particular natural person.

ENISA also uses this sense of the term *aggregate* in defining a design pattern for privacy [ENIS14]:

> The fourth design pattern, AGGREGATE, states that Personal data should be processed at the highest level of aggregation and with the least possible detail in which it is (still) useful. Aggregation of information over groups of attributes or groups of individuals,

restricts the amount of detail in the personal data that remains. This data therefore becomes less sensitive if the information is sufficiently coarse grained, and the size of the group over which it is aggregated is sufficiently large. Here coarse-grained data means that the data items are general enough that the information stored is valid for many individuals hence little information can be attributed to a single person, thus protecting its privacy.

Even aggregated data can pose a privacy risk. NIST SP 188 (*De-Identifying Government Datasets*) gives the example of a school that uses aggregation to report the number of students performing below, at, or above grade level, within a range of time. For example, if there are 29 students performing above grade level, the entry is 20–29. Part a of Table 3.1 shows the totals for a given period of time. Part b of Table 3.1 shows the results when the table is republished after a new student enrolls. By comparing the two tables, one can readily infer that the student who joined the school is performing above grade level.

TABLE 3.1   Example of Privacy Risk Using Aggregation Techniques

(a) Totals before new student enrolls		(b) Totals after new student enrolls	
Performance	**Students**	**Performance**	**Students**
Below grade level	30–39	Below grade level	30–39
At grade level	50–59	At grade level	50–59
Above grade level	20–29	Above grade level	30–39

Unfortunately, the term *aggregation* is used in the privacy literature in two senses: the one provided above and to refer to the consolidation or combination of multiple datasets on the same or overlapping sets of individuals. For example, the paper *A Taxonomy of Privacy* [SOLO06] provides the following definition:

Aggregation is the gathering together of information about a person. A piece of information here or there is not very telling. But when combined together, bits and pieces of data begin to form a portrait of a person. The whole becomes greater than the parts. This occurs because combining information creates synergies. When analyzed, aggregated information can reveal new facts about a person that she did not expect would be known about her when the original, isolated data were collected.

Usually, the reader can discern the sense of the term from the context.

Figure 3.2 illustrates the degree of privacy risk associated with various categories of personal information. Chapter 7, "Privacy in Databases," examines these concepts in greater detail.

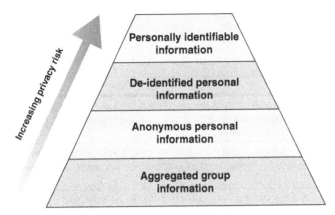

FIGURE 3.2   Degrees of Privacy Risk

3.3   Fair Information Practice Principles

A set of fair information practice principles (FIPPs) for the protection of personal information were first enunciated in a 1973 report of the U.S. Department of Health, Education, and Welfare (HEW) titled *Records, Computers, and the Rights of Citizens*. The HEW report listed five principles. It is useful to review what the HEW report cited as the essence of the privacy objective [HEW73]:

> Personal privacy, as it relates to personal-data record keeping must be understood in terms of a concept of mutuality. Accordingly, we offer the following formulation: An individual's personal privacy is directly affected by the kind of disclosure and use made of identifiable information about him in a record. A record containing information about an individual in identifiable form must, therefore, be governed by procedures that afford the individual a right to participate in deciding what the content of the record will be, and what disclosure and use will be made of the identifiable information in it. Any recording, disclosure, and use of identifiable personal information not governed by such procedures must be proscribed as an unfair information practice unless such recording, disclosure or use is specifically authorized by law.

In 1980, the Organisation for Economic Co-operation and Development (OECD) expanded this to a list of eight principles [OECD80]. These eight principles are widely considered as minimum standards for the protection of individual privacy. The OECD principles function as a high-level set of privacy requirements, suitable for an organization's privacy policy document, and as guidelines for the design and implementation of information privacy mechanisms.

Table 3.2 lists the OECD FIPPs. These principles are still relevant, and many standards, regulations, and organizational policy statements employ some version of these principles. These principles enumerate standards of practice intended to ensure that entities that collect and use personal information provide adequate privacy protection for that information.

TABLE 3.2   OECD Fair Information Practice Principles

Principle	Description
Collection limitation	There should be limits to the collection of personal data, and any such data should be obtained by lawful and fair means and, where appropriate, with the knowledge or consent of the data subject.
Data quality	Personal data should be relevant to the purposes for which they are to be used, and, to the extent necessary for those purposes, should be accurate, complete, and kept up-to-date.
Purpose specification	The purposes for which personal data are collected should be specified not later than at the time of data collection, and the subsequent use should be limited to the fulfilment of those purposes or such others as are not incompatible with those purposes and as are specified on each occasion of change of purpose.
Use limitation	Personal data should not be disclosed, made available, or otherwise used for purposes other than those specified in accordance with the Purpose Specification except with the consent of the data subject or by the authority of law.
Security safeguards	Personal data should be protected by reasonable security safeguards against such risks as loss or unauthorized access, destruction, use, modification, or disclosure of data.
Openness	There should be a general policy of openness about developments, practices, and policies with respect to personal data. Means should be readily available of establishing the existence and nature of personal data and the main purposes of their use, as well as the identity and usual residence of the data controller.
Individual participation	An individual should have the right: (a) to obtain from a data controller or otherwise confirmation of whether or not the data controller has data relating to him; (b) to have communicated to him data relating to him within a reasonable time; at a charge, if any, that is not excessive; in a reasonable manner; and in a form that is readily intelligible to him; (c) to be given reasons if a request made under subparagraphs (a) and (b) is denied, and to be able to challenge such denial; and (d) to challenge data relating to him and, if the challenge is successful to have the data erased, rectified, completed or amended.
Accountability	A data controller should be accountable for complying with measures which give effect to the principles stated above.

The OECD document uses the same definition of personal data as is subsequently used in the GDPR—namely, any information relating to an identified or identifiable natural person. The OECD document defines the term ***data controller*** as a party who is competent to decide about the contents and use of personal data, regardless of whether such data are collected, stored, processed, or disseminated by that party or by an agent on its behalf.

It is useful to elaborate somewhat on the implications and meaning of the eight OECD principles, as follows:

- **Collection limitation:** Companies should only collect the personal data they need to accomplish a specific business purpose. Similarly, government organizations should limit collection of personal data to what is needed for a given mission. Organizations should obtain consent from an individual before collecting or processing that individual's personal data, where possible. There are exceptions, such as for data needed for law enforcement or national security purposes.

- **Data quality:** This principle highlights two concepts: relevancy and accuracy. With respect to relevancy, an organization should only collect information that is not only relevant to a specific purpose but also limited to the amount and type of data that is actually needed. With respect to accuracy, an organization should ensure not only that the data are accurate when collected but that data integrity is maintained so long as the data are held and processed. In addition, where possible, an organization should provide means for a subject to review and correct personal information.

- **Purpose specification:** Organizations should provide notice of the specific purpose for which personal data are collected and should only use, process, store, maintain, disseminate, or disclose personal data for a purpose that is explained in the notice and is compatible with the purpose for which the personal data were collected or that is otherwise legally authorized.

- **Use limitation:** This principle reinforces the limits for data processing as well as the expectations of data subjects. It also places a burden on organizations to ensure that if personal data is transmitted or made available to another party, the use limitations remain in force.

- **Security safeguards:** Organizations should enforce the same security mechanisms and procedures for PII as are used for other sensitive data. These safeguards include confidentiality, integrity, availability, and authenticity. The security measures include physical measures (e.g., locked doors, identification cards), organizational measures (e.g., authority levels with regard to access to data), and technical measures (e.g., access control mechanisms, firewalls). Technical measures, also called *technical controls*, safeguard or provide countermeasures for an information system that are primarily implemented and executed by the information system through mechanisms contained in the hardware, software, or firmware components of the system.

- **Openness:** Organizations should make their privacy policy documents readily and publicly available. The OECD lists the following as examples of additional measures: regular information from data controllers on a voluntary basis, publication in official registers of descriptions of activities concerned with the processing of personal data, and registration with public bodies [OECD80]. The phrase *means which are readily available* implies that individuals should be able to obtain information without unreasonable effort as to time, advance knowledge, traveling, and so forth, and without unreasonable cost.

- **Individual participation:** As with the principle of openness, this principle implies that there is a user-friendly process for individual participation. Participation includes the rights to obtain confirmation of whether the data controller has one's personal data; have one's personal data communicated to him or her; and challenge data relating to him or her and have data modified or erased, if appropriate.

- **Accountability:** This principle dictates that the individual (data controller) who is in charge of determining how personal data are going to be processed and used will be held responsible for ensuring that the data are processed in an authorized, fair, and legitimate manner. Of course, breaches of privacy will raise issues of accountability not only for the data controller but for the organization as a whole. Accountability refers to accountability supported by legal sanctions, as well as to accountability established by codes of conduct and contractual obligations.

3.4   Privacy Regulations

A number of national governments have introduced laws and regulations intended to protect individual privacy in information processing. There is a great deal of overlap and similarity across different nations. This section provides two regional examples that are by far the most influential and that encompass virtually all of the requirements imposed in other nations. Part VI, "Legal and Regulatory Requirements," examines these two examples in detail.

European Union

One of the most comprehensive initiatives is the European Union (EU) General Data Protection Regulation (GDPR), approved by the EU Parliament in 2016, with an effective enforcement date of May 2108. The GDPR is designed to harmonize data privacy laws across Europe, to protect and empower the data privacy of all EU citizens, and to reshape the way organizations, both public and private, across the region approach data privacy.

The presentation "10 Key Facts Businesses Need to Note About the GDPR" from the 2016 *European Identity & Cloud Conference* [KINA16] summarizes important aspects of GDPR that organizations that do business in Europe need to be aware of:

- The GDPR applies to all companies worldwide that process personal data of EU residents, both EU citizens and non-citizens. Any company that works with information relating to EU residents must comply with the requirements of the GDPR, making it the first global data protection law. This aspect alone is contributing significantly to all companies around the world taking data privacy more seriously.

- The GDPR widens the definition of personal data compared to prior regulations by EU member states. As a result, parts of IT that have been unaffected by data protection laws in the past will need attention from businesses to ensure their compliance with the new regulation.

- The GDPR tightens the rules for obtaining valid consent to using personal information. Having the ability to prove valid consent for using personal information is likely to be one of the biggest challenges presented by the GDPR. The GDPR states that the consent of the data subject means any freely given, specific, informed, and unambiguous indication of his or her wishes by which the data subject, either by a statement or by a clear affirmative action, signifies agreement to personal data relating to him or her being processed.

- The GDPR requires public authorities processing personal information to appoint a data protection officer (DPO), as well as other entities, when core activities require regular and systematic monitoring of data subjects on a large scale or consist of processing on a large scale of special categories of data.

- The GDPR mandates data protection impact assessments. Data controllers must conduct assessments where privacy breach risks are high in order to minimize risks to data subjects. This means before organizations can implement projects involving personal information, they must conduct a privacy risk assessment and work with the DPO to ensure that they are in compliance as projects progress. Chapter 11 covers data protection impact assessments in detail.

- The GDPR requires organizations to notify the local data protection authority of a data breach within 72 hours of discovering it. This means organizations need to ensure that they have technologies and processes in place that will enable them to detect and respond to a data breach.

- The GDPR introduces the right to be forgotten. Also known as *data erasure*, the right to be forgotten entitles the data subject to have the data controller erase his/her personal data, cease further dissemination of the data, and potentially have third parties halt processing of the data. The conditions for erasure include the data no longer being relevant to original purposes for processing or a data subject withdrawing consent. This means organizations will have to get fresh consent before they can alter the way they are using the data they have collected. It also means organizations have to ensure that they have the processes and technologies in place to delete data in response to requests from data subjects.

- The GDPR requires that privacy be included in systems and processes by design. At its core, privacy by design—referred to as *data protection by design* in the GDPR—calls for the inclusion of data protection from the onset of the designing of systems rather than an addition.

The GDPR is an important landmark in the evolving integration of privacy in cybersecurity. Even organizations unaffected by this regulation should be aware of its provision and consider them in designing their own privacy controls. Chapter 14 examines the GDPR in detail.

U.S. Privacy Laws and Regulations

There is no single law or regulation covering privacy in the United States. Rather, a collection of federal privacy laws cover various aspects of privacy. Some U.S. privacy laws apply only to federal agencies and contractor companies working under federal contract. Others impose mandates on private organizations as well as government agencies and departments. These include:

- **The Privacy Act of 1974:** Specifies the rules that a federal agency must follow to collect, use, transfer, and disclose an individual's PII.

- **The Fair and Accurate Credit Transaction Act of 2003 (FACTA):** Requires entities engaged in certain kinds of consumer financial transactions (predominantly credit transactions) to be aware of the warning signs of identity theft and to take steps to respond to suspected incidents of identity theft.

- **The Health Insurance Portability and Accountability Act of 1996 (HIPAA):** Requires covered entities (typically medical and health insurance providers and their associates) to protect the security and privacy of health records.

- **The Family Educational Rights and Privacy Act of 1974 (FERPA):** Protects students and their families by ensuring the privacy of student educational records.

- **The Gramm Leach Bliley Act of 1999 (GLBA):** Imposes privacy and information security provisions on financial institutions; designed to protect consumer financial data.

- **Federal Policy for the Protection of Human Subjects:** Published in 1991 and codified in separate regulations by 15 federal departments and agencies, outlines the basic ethical principles (including privacy and confidentiality) in research involving human subjects.

- **The Children's Online Privacy Protection Act (COPPA):** Governs the online collection of personal information from children under the age of 13.

- **The Electronic Communications Privacy Act:** Generally, prohibits unauthorized and intentional interception of wire and electronic communications during the transmission phase and unauthorized accessing of electronically stored wire and electronic communications.

In addition, there are numerous state laws and regulations that impact business. By far, the most important of these is the California Consumer Privacy Act (CCPA). Chapter 15 examines the most important federal privacy laws as well as the CCPA.

3.5 Privacy Standards

The management, design, and implementation of privacy safeguards in information systems is complex and difficult. A wide variety of technologies are involved. These include cybersecurity mechanisms, such as cryptography, network security protocols, operating system mechanisms, database security schemes, and malware identification, which are discussed in Part III, "Technical Security Controls for Privacy." Also included are privacy-specific mechanisms, which are described in Part IV, "Privacy Enhancing Technologies." The areas of concern are broad, including stored data, data communications, human factors, physical asset and property security, and legal and regulatory concerns. And there is the ongoing need to maintain high confidence in the privacy protections in the face of evolving IT systems, relationships with outside parties, personnel turnover, changes to the physical plant, and the ever-evolving threat landscape.

Because effective information privacy is difficult, an attempt to develop an ad hoc, grow-your-own approach to cybersecurity is to invite failure. The good news is that a great deal of thought, experimentation, and implementation experience has gone into the development of policies, procedures, and overall guidance to the information privacy management team. The most important source of guidance of organizations are internationally-recognized standards. The dominant sources for such standards are the International Organization for Standardization (ISO) and the U.S. National Institute of Standards and Technology (NIST). Although NIST is a national organization, its standards and guidance documents have worldwide influence. This section provides an overview of ISO and NIST work in the area of privacy.

In addition, a number of organizations, based on wide professional input, have developed best practices types of documents for implementing and evaluating information privacy. Section 3.6 discusses best practices.

International Organization for Standardization (ISO)

ISO is an international agency that develops standards on a wide range of subjects. It is a voluntary, nontreaty organization whose members are designated standards bodies of participating nations, as well as nonvoting observer organizations. Although ISO is not a government body, more than 70% of ISO member bodies are government standards institutions or organizations incorporated by public law. Most of the remainder have close links with the public administrations in their own countries.

In the areas of data communications, networking, and security, ISO standards are developed in a joint effort with another standards body, the International Electrotechnical Commission (IEC). IEC is primarily concerned with electrical and electronics engineering standards. In the area of information technology, the interests of the two groups overlap, with IEC emphasizing hardware and ISO focusing on software. In 1987, the two groups formed the Joint Technical Committee 1 (JTC 1). This committee is responsible for developing the documents that ultimately become ISO (and IEC) standards in the area of information technology.

> **Note**
>
> Throughout the book, for brevity, ISO/IEC standards are simply designated with ISO.

ISO has been at the forefront of developing standards for information security. Perhaps the most important set of standards for cybersecurity is the ISO 27000 suite of standards that deal with information security management systems (ISMS). An ISMS consists of the policies, procedures, guidelines, and associated resources and activities that are collectively managed by an organization in the pursuit of protecting its information assets. This suite includes requirements documents, which are normative standards that define requirements for an ISMS and for those certifying such systems; and guidelines documents, which provide direct support, detailed guidance, and/or interpretation for the overall process to establish, implement, maintain, and improve an ISMS. The most noteworthy standards are:

- **ISO 27001:** *ISMS Requirements.* A normative standard that provides a mandatory set of steps as part of an Information Security Management System (ISMS), against which an organization can certify its security arrangements (e.g., define target environment, assess risks, and select appropriate controls).

- **ISO 27002:** *Code of Practice for Information Security Controls.* An informative standard that provides a framework of security controls that can be used to help select the controls required in an ISMS.

- **ISO 27005:** *Information Security Risk Management System Implementation Guidance.* A standard that provides information security risk management system implementation guidance, including advice on risk assessment, risk treatment, risk acceptance, risk reporting, risk monitoring, and risk review. The standard also includes examples of risk assessment methodologies.

ISO 27001 and 27002 are of great importance to organizations because they have become the universally accepted means of achieving security certification. Certification is the provision by an independent body of written assurance (a certificate) that the product, service, or system in question meets specific requirements. Certification can be a useful tool to add credibility, by demonstrating that a product or service meets the expectations of an organization's customers. In the case of security certification using ISO 27001, it is a way for executives to be assured that the security capability that has been funded and implemented meets the security requirements of the organization. For some industries, certification is a legal or contractual requirement. A number of independent certification bodies provide this service, and tens of thousands of organizations have been 27001/2 certified.

More recently, ISO has begun developing privacy standards that serve as companions to the requirements and guidelines standards in the 27000 series. ISO has added the following to the 27000 series:

- **ISO 27701:** *Extension to ISO/IEC 27001 and ISO/IEC 27002 for privacy information management—Requirements and guidelines.* Specifies the requirements for and provides guidance for establishing, implementing, maintaining, and continually improving a PIMS (privacy information management system) based on the requirements, control objectives and controls in ISO 27001 and 27002, and extended by a set of privacy-specific requirements, control objectives, and controls.

- **ISO 27018:** *Code of Practice for Protection of Personally Identifiable Information (PII) in Public Clouds as PII processors.* Specifies guidelines based on ISO/IEC 27002, taking into consideration the regulatory requirements for the protection of PII, which can be applicable within the context of the information security risk environment(s) of a provider of public cloud services.

ISO 27701 is particularly significant because of the potential for certification. Certification bodies are likely to add ISO 27701 certification to their offerings. As pointed out in [BRAC19], ISO 27701 gives privacy a visibility that wasn't there before. It ties risks to solutions within organizations, gives structure to accountability, promotes cross-team work between the security and privacy teams, and helps justify expenses for the privacy office.

In addition, ISO has developed a 29100 series of documents that provide specific guidance in implementing privacy protections:

- **ISO 29100:** *Privacy framework.* Provides a high-level framework for the protection of personally identifiable information (PII) within information and communication technology (ICT) systems. It is general in nature and places organizational, technical, and procedural aspects in an overall privacy framework.

- **ISO 29134:** *Guidelines for Privacy Impact Assessment.* Provides guidance on a process for performing privacy impact assessments and a structure and content of a Privacy Impact Assessment (PIA) report.

- **ISO 29151:** *Code of practice for personally identifiable information protection.* Offers guidance for PII controllers on a broad range of information security and PII protection controls that are commonly applied in many different organizations that deal with protection of PII.

- **DIS 29184:** *Guidelines for online privacy notices and consent.* This draft international standard provides general requirements and recommendation for online notice. It includes a list of requirements for providing notice, recommended contents of notice, and recommendations for providing for consent.

Figure 3.3 illustrates the relationship between the 27000 and 29100 series of documents.

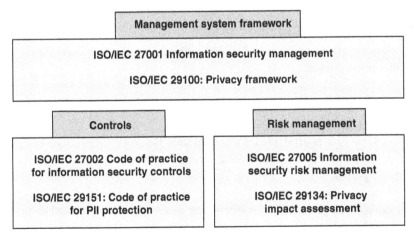

FIGURE 3.3   Relationships of ISO Security and Privacy Standards

One other noteworthy standard, not part of either series, is the following:

- **ISO 20889:** *Privacy enhancing data de-identification terminology and classification of techniques.* Focuses on commonly used techniques for de-identification of structured datasets as well as on datasets containing information about data principals that can be represented logically in the form of a table.

All these ISO standards are referenced in later chapters.

The heart of ISO 27701 are the following clauses:

- Clause 5 gives PIMS-specific requirements and other information regarding the information security requirements in ISO/IEC 27001 appropriate to an organization acting as either a PII controller or a PII processor.
- Clause 6 gives PIMS-specific guidance and other information regarding the information security controls in ISO/IEC 27002 and PIMS-specific guidance for an organization acting as either a PII controller or a PII processor.
- Clause 7 gives additional ISO/IEC 27002 guidance for PII controllers.
- Clause 8 gives additional ISO/IEC 27002 guidance for PII processors.

ISO 27701 is structured according to the clauses in 27001 and 27002, in the following ways:

- **Application of security clauses as is:** The clause applies as it is. Therefore, the clause is not repeated, but only referred to.
- **Refinement of security clauses:** The clauses are refined to include references to privacy. Typically, this simply means that wherever the term *security* appears in a clause, it is replaced by the term *security and privacy.*
- **Additions to security clauses:** The referring clause applies with additional privacy-specific requirements or implementation guidance.

Privacy Framework

The ISO 29100 privacy framework is a general model that indicates the key parties involved in protecting PII and the privacy principles that an organization should implement to achieve privacy goals. This framework serves two purposes:

- It provides high-level guidance to organizations for identifying, assessing, managing, and communicating about privacy risks and solutions.
- It serves to introduce and define the key elements and considerations that lead to other standards in the 29100 series.

ISO 29100 defines 11 privacy principles, shown in Table 3.3. These are similar to the OECD FIPPs. ISO views the privacy principles as a set of shared values governing the privacy protection of PII. The organization, and specifically the PII controller, should ensure adherence to these principles during the storage, processing, and transmission of PII under the organization's control by implementing the necessary privacy controls.

TABLE 3.3 ISO Privacy Principles

Principle	Objective
Consent and choice	Enable PII principal (person to whom the PII relates) to exercise consent to collection and use of PII and provide opt-out/opt-in choice.
Purpose legitimacy and specification	Ensure that the purpose(s) for processing of PII complies with applicable laws and relies on a permissible legal ground. Define purposes for which PII can be used, with clear specification to the PII principal.
Collection limitation	Limit the collection of PII to that which is within the bounds of applicable law and strictly necessary for the specified purpose(s).
Data minimization	Minimize the PII that is processed to what is strictly necessary for the legitimate interests pursued by the PII controller, and limit the disclosure of PII to a minimum number of privacy stakeholders.
Use, retention, and disclosure limitation	Limit the use, retention, and disclosure (including transfer) of PII to that which is necessary in order to fulfill specific, explicit, and legitimate purposes.
Accuracy and quality	Ensure that the PII is accurate and obtained from a reliable and verified source, and provide period checks of information integrity.
Openness, transparency, and notice	Provide PII principals with clear and easily accessible information about the PII controller's policies, procedures, and practices with respect to the processing of PII.
PII participation and access	Give PII principals the ability to access their PII, challenge its accuracy, and provide amendments or removals.
Accountability	Adopt concrete and practical measures for PII protection. Establish and perform, as necessary, a PIA.
Information security	Protect PII under the authority of the organization with appropriate controls at the operational, functional, and strategic levels to ensure the integrity, confidentiality, and availability of the PII; and protect it against risks such as unauthorized access, destruction, use, modification, disclosure, or loss throughout the whole of its life cycle.
Privacy compliance	Verify and demonstrate that the processing meets data protection and privacy safeguarding requirements by periodically conducting audits using internal auditors or trusted third-party auditors.

ISO 29100 also provides a narrative of the basic elements that comprise a privacy framework. Topics covered in a general way include:

- Actors and roles
- Interactions
- PII
- Privacy safeguarding requirements
- Privacy policies
- Privacy controls

A key aspect of the standard is the identification of the actors involved in the processing of PII and their interaction, which consist of:

- **PII principal:** A natural person to whom the PII relates; also referred to as a *data subject*.
- **Privacy stakeholder:** A person, an agency, or an organization that can affect or be affected by activity related to PII processing. More generally, the term *stakeholder* refers to a person, a group, or an organization that has interest or concern in an organization. Some examples of key stakeholders are managers, employees, creditors, directors, government (and its agencies), owners (shareholders), suppliers, unions, and the community from which the organization draws its resources.
- **PII controller:** A privacy stakeholder who determines the purposes and means for PII.
- **PII processor:** A privacy stakeholder who processes PII on behalf of and in accordance with the instructions of a PII controller. The PII controller and the PII processor may be the same entity.
- **Third party:** A privacy stakeholder other than the PII principal, the PII controller, or the PII processor.

Figure 3.4 shows the ways in which the privacy actors interact. The arrowed lines indicate a flow of PII. A PII principal can provide its PII to a PII controller—as, for example, when registering for a service provided by the controller. A PII principal can also provide PII directly to a PII processor, perhaps subsequent to registering with a PII controller. The controller can provide PII to a processor to perform authorized processing of the PII. The PII principal can request relevant PII from the controller, which can then be delivered by the controller or by the processor, as directed by the controller. A PII controller can also provide PII to a third party, as long as the transfer is governed by the privacy principles, or can direct the process to provide PII to a third party. This model is very general but serves to delimit the areas of concern that an organization must address in protecting PII.

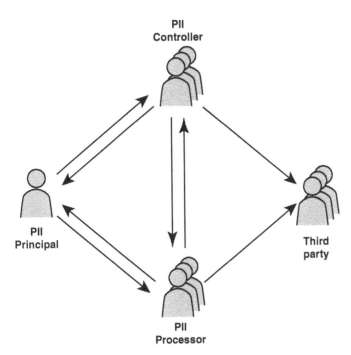

FIGURE 3.4   Roles and Interactions in the ISO Privacy Framework

Code of Practice for PII Protection

ISO 29151 complements and extends ISO 27002 to encompass privacy. It provides guidelines for organizational information security standards and information security management practices including the selection, implementation, and management of controls, taking into consideration the organization's information privacy risk environment(s).

ISO 29151 consists of two parts. The first part has the identical structure to ISO 27002, listing the same set of controls. As shown in Table 3.4, the two standards list 14 control categories and a total of 34 subcategories of controls. As discussed in Chapter 2, there are areas where existing security risk models and security-focused guidance also apply to privacy concerns. Thus, in ISO 29151, for many of the categories and subcategories of security controls, the standard simply says that the guidance in ISO 27002 applies. For some subcategories, ISO 29151 provides additional implementation guidance relevant to the protection of PII.

TABLE 3.4   ISO 29151 Privacy Controls for the Protection of PII

Control Category	Privacy Controls
Information security policies	Management direction for information security
Organization of information security	Internal organization Mobile devices and teleworking
Human resource security	Prior to employment During employment Termination and change of employment
Asset management	Responsibility for assets Information classification Media handling
Access control	Business requirements of access control User access management User responsibilities System and application access control
Cryptography	Cryptographic controls
Physical and environmental security	Secure areas Equipment
Operations security	Operational procedures and responsibilities Protection from malware Backup Logging and monitoring Control of operational software Technical vulnerability management Information systems audit considerations
Communications security	Network security management Information transfer
System acquisition, development, and maintenance	Security requirements of information systems Security in development and support processes Test data
Supplier relationships	Information security in supplier relationships
Information security incident management	Management of information security incidents and improvements
Information security aspects of business continuity management	Information security continuity Redundancies
Compliance	Compliance with legal and contractual requirements Information security reviews

The lesson to be drawn from the first part of ISO 29151 is that a substantial portion of the work needed to protect PII is already provided for in the design and implementation of security controls to manage security risk.

The second part of ISO 29151 contains a set of PII protection-specific controls that supplement those given in ISO/IEC 27002. These new PII protection controls, with their associated guidance, are divided into 12 categories. The first category indicates the topics that a privacy policy should cover. The remaining 11 categories correspond to the 11 privacy principles of ISO 29100 (refer to Table 3.3). For each privacy principle, ISO 29151 provides a detailed list of privacy controls.

It is not intended for an organization to be required to implement all of the privacy controls defined in ISO 29151. Rather, the standard attempts to provide a rather comprehensive set of controls, and an organization should implement those that are appropriate, based on its privacy impact assessment.

National Institute of Standards and Technology

NIST is a U.S. federal agency that deals with measurement science, standards, and technology related to U.S. government use and to the promotion of U.S. private sector innovation. Despite its national scope, NIST Federal Information Processing Standards (FIPS), Special Publications (SP), and Internal Reports (NISTIR) have worldwide impact. In the area of information security, the NIST Computer Security Resource Center (CSRC) is the source of a vast collection of documents that are widely used in industry.

As part of its ongoing development of standards and guidelines for information security, the CSRC has extended its concern to information privacy. The documents produced by the CSRC fall into three broad categories: privacy controls, privacy engineering, and a privacy framework.

Privacy Controls

To counter privacy threats and comply with government laws and regulations, organizations need a set of privacy controls that encompass their privacy requirements and that respond to legal requirements. Two NIST documents are invaluable:

- **SP 800-53:** *Security and Privacy Controls for Information Systems and Organizations*. This document provides a very detailed and comprehensive set of privacy controls. SP 800-53 was updated in 2019 to provide more comprehensive coverage of privacy controls.

- **SP 800-53A:** *Assessing Security and Privacy Controls in Federal Information Systems and Organizations*. This document provides a set of procedures for conducting assessments of the security controls and privacy controls defined in SP 800-53. SP 800-53A is scheduled to be updated in 2020 to match the revised version of SP 800-53.

The SP 800-53 controls are organized into 20 families, each family defining one or more controls related to the specific topic of the family. For each control, the document provides a description of the control, supplemental guidance on implementation, a description of control enhancements, and references to other documents.

Two of the families are concerned only with privacy requirements (see Table 3.5). Fifteen of the families, designated as joint, include controls that address only security requirements, controls that address only privacy requirements, and/or controls that address both security and privacy requirements.

TABLE 3.5   NIST Privacy and Joint Control Families

ID	Family	Number of Privacy Controls
Privacy-Specific Controls		
IP	Individual Participation	6
PA	Privacy Authorization	4
Joint Privacy/Security Controls		
AC	Access Control	3
AT	Awareness and Training	4
AU	Audit and Accountability	4
CA	Assessment, Authorization, and Monitoring	4
CM	Configuration Management	4
CP	Contingency Planning	4
IA	Identification and Authentication	3
IR	Incident Response	9
MP	Media Protection	1
PL	Planning	5
PM	Program Management	23
RA	Risk Assessment	4
SA	System and Services Acquisition	11
SC	System and Communications Protection	4
SI	System and Information Integrity	8

Table 3.6 lists the privacy-specific families, described as follows:

- **Individual participation:** Addresses the need to make individuals active participants in the decision-making process regarding the collection and use of their PII. By providing individuals with access to PII and the ability to have their PII corrected or amended, as appropriate, the controls in this family enhance public confidence in organizational decisions made based on the PII.

- **Privacy authorization:** Ensures that organizations identify the legal bases that authorize a particular PII collection or activity that impacts privacy and specify in their notices the purpose(s) for which PII is collected. These controls would be embodied in a policy statement.

TABLE 3.6 NIST Privacy-Specific Controls

ID	Name
Individual Participation (IP)	
IP-1	Individual Participation Policy and Procedures
IP-2	Consent
IP-2(1)	Attribute Management
IP-2(2)	Just-in-Time Notice of Consent
IP-3	Redress
IP-3(1)	Notice of Correction or Amendment
IP-3(2)	Appeal
IP-4	Privacy Notice
IP-4(1)	Just-in-Time Notice of Privacy Authorization
IP-5	Privacy Act Statements
IP-6	Individual Access
Privacy Authorization (PA)	
PA-1	Privacy Authorization Policy and Procedures
PA-2	Authority to Collect
PA-3	Purpose Specification
PA-3(1)	Usage restrictions of PII
PA-3(2)	Automation
PA-4	Information Sharing with External Parties

The joint families are:

- **Access control:** Controls that determine the setting used for limiting access to systems and information stored on the systems.

- **Awareness and training:** Controls related to developing policies and procedures for user awareness and operator training.

- **Audit and accountability:** Controls to record policy violations and related activities. The family also provides guidance on log retention policies and configurations.

- **Assessment, authorization, and monitoring:** Controls for assessing and monitoring the implementation of security controls and for specifying authorization procedures for control use.

- **Configuration management:** Focuses on baseline establishment and identifying the minimal software installations. Many of the important details concerning change control and configuration management are described in this family.

- **Contingency planning:** Controls define auditable settings for backup and recovery of systems.

- **Identification and authentication:** Focuses on the configuration settings concerned with authentication systems. The controls provide detailed guidance on tracking users employed by the organization, as well as for guests, contractors, shared accounts, and service accounts.

- **Incident response:** Identifies auditable settings to support incident response efforts.

- **Media protection:** Provides information on how to maintain the security of digital media. By offering guidance on how to configure media controls, classification markings, storage policies, and usage, this family can assist an organization in using digital media more securely.

- **Planning:** Provides guidance on information security architecture and describes the overall philosophy, requirements, and approach organizations take with regard to protecting the security and privacy of information.

- **Program management:** Provides guidance on facilitating compliance with applicable laws, policies, regulations, and standards. In addition, the audits in this family provide a vehicle for the organization to document all of the security controls in a central repository.

- **Risk assessment:** Provides guidance on the requirements to perform risk assessments.

- **System and services acquisition:** Provides guidance on using service-based software.

- **System and communications protection:** Provides guidance on how to implement protected communications for a system.

- **System and information integrity:** Provides guidance on monitoring information systems affected by announced software vulnerabilities, email vulnerabilities (spam), error handling, memory protection, output filtering, and many other areas of security.

Thus, SP 800-53 provides a collection of more than 100 well-defined and specific controls from which an organization can select and implement those that meet its privacy policy requirements. For example, Figure 3.5 shows the privacy control definition of IP-2. The control section prescribes specific security-related activities or actions to be carried out by organizations or by information systems. The supplemental guidance section provides non-prescriptive additional information for a specific security control. Organizations can apply the supplemental guidance as appropriate. The security control enhancements section provides statements of security capability to (1) add functionality/specificity to a control and/or (2) increase the strength of a control. In both cases, control enhancements are used in information systems and environments of operation requiring greater protection than provided by the base control due to the potential adverse organizational impacts or when organizations seek additions to the base control functionality/specificity based on organizational assessments of risk.

IP-2 CONSENT	
Control:	
Implement [Assignment: organization-defined tools or mechanisms] for users to authorize the processing of their PII prior to its collection that:	
IP-2(a)	Use plain language and provide examples to illustrate the potential privacy risks of the authorization.
IP-(2b)	Provide a means for users to decline the authorization.

Supplemental Guidance:

This control transfers risk that arises from the processing of PII from the organization to an individual. It is only selected as required by law or regulation or when individuals can be reasonably expected to understand and accept any privacy risks arising from their authorization. Organizations consider whether other controls may more effectively mitigate privacy risk either alone or in conjunction with consent.

To help users understand the risks being accepted when providing consent, organizations write materials in plain language and avoid technical jargon. The examples required in IP-2(a) focus on key points necessary for user decision-making. When developing or purchasing consent tools, organizations consider the application of good information design procedures in all user-facing consent materials; use of active voice and conversational style; logical sequencing of main points; consistent use of the same word (rather than synonyms) to avoid confusion; the use of bullets, numbers, and formatting where appropriate to aid readability; and legibility of text, such as font style, size, color, and contrast with surrounding background. Related controls: AT-2, AT-3, AT-4, CP-2, CP-4, CP-8, IR-2, IR-4, IR-9.

Control Enhancements:

(1) CONSENT | ATTRIBUTE MANAGEMENT

Allow data subjects to tailor use permissions to selected attributes.

Supplemental Guidance: Allowing individuals to select how specific data attributes may be further used or disclosed beyond the original use may help reduce privacy risk arising from the most sensitive of the data attributes while maintaining utility of the data

(2) CONSENT | JUST-IN-TIME NOTICE OF CONSENT

Present authorizations to process personally identifiable information in conjunction with the data action or [Assignment: organization-defined frequency].

Supplemental Guidance: If the circumstances under which an individual gave consent have changed or a significant amount of time has passed since an individual gave consent for the processing of his or her personally identifiable information, the data subject's assumption about how the information is being processed might no longer be accurate or reliable. Just-in-time notice can help maintain individual satisfaction with how the personally identifiable information is being processed

References:

NIST Special Publication 800-50. NIST Interagency Report 8062.

FIGURE 3.5 Privacy Control IP-2 in SP 800-53

In addition, SP 800-53A provides guidance, in the form of an assessment template, for assessing each of the controls defined in SP 800-53. The current revision of SP 800-53A does not include those controls that are unique to privacy but only those controls that overlap both security and privacy. A newer revision will incorporate the remaining controls. As an example, Table 3.8 shows the assessment template for CP-3 that is defined in SP 800-53A. The shaded portion of Figure 3.6 is not part of the template but provides an example of an assessment using the template.

CP-3 CONTINGENCY TRAINING		
ASSESSMENT OBJECTIVE:		
Determine if the organization provides contingency training to information system users consistent with assigned roles and responsibilities:		
CP-3(a)	CP-3(a)[1]	within the organization-defined time period of assuming a contingency role or responsibility; (S)
	CP-3(a)[2]	defines a time period within which contingency training is to be provided to information system users assuming a contingency role or responsibility; (S)
CP-3(b)	when required by information system changes; (O)	
CP-3(c)	CP-3(c)[1]	thereafter, in accordance with the organization-defined frequency; (S)
	CP-3(c)[2]	defines the frequency for contingency training. (S)
Potential Assessment Methods and Objects:		
Examine: [SELECT FROM: Contingency planning policy; procedures addressing contingency training; contingency plan; contingency training curriculum; contingency training material; security plan; contingency training records; other relevant documents or records].		
Interview: [SELECT FROM: Organizational personnel with contingency planning, plan implementation, and training responsibilities; organizational personnel with information security responsibilities].		
Test: [SELECT FROM: Organizational processes for contingency training].		
Comments and Recommendations:		
CP-3(b) is marked as other than satisfied because assessors could not find evidence that the organization provided contingency training to information system users consistent with their assigned roles and responsibilities when there were significant changes to the system.		

* Each determination statement contained within an assessment procedure executed by an assessor produces one of the following findings: (i) *satisfied* (S); or (ii) *other than satisfied* (O).

FIGURE 3.6   Example Assessment Findings for Control CP-3 Using Template from SP 800-53A

Privacy Engineering

NIST has produced a set of documents that provide guidance to privacy engineers. NISTIR 8062 defines three privacy engineering objectives (refer to Figure 2.5 in Chapter 2) that serve to complement the traditional security objectives. The privacy engineering objectives are intended to provide a degree of precision to encourage the implementation of measurable controls for managing privacy risk. System designers and engineers, working with policy teams, can use the objectives to help bridge the gap between high-level privacy principles and their implementation within systems. The three objectives are:

- **Predictability:** Enables individuals to have confidence in the manner of use of PII, both their own PII and that of others. Achieving predictability is essential to building trust; the goal is to design systems so that stakeholders are not surprised by the way in which personal information is handled. Predictability enables data controllers and system administrators to assess the impact of any changes in an information system and implement appropriate controls. Even in a system that may create unpredictable or previously unknown results—such as a large data analysis or research effort—predictability can provide a valuable set of insights about how to control privacy risks that may arise. For example, if the results of a study are inherently unpredictable, operators can implement controls to restrict access to or use of those results.

- **Manageability:** Enables fine-grained administration of PII, including alteration, deletion, and selective disclosure. Manageability is not an absolute right but rather a system property that allows individuals to control their information while minimizing potential conflicts in system functionality. Consider a system in which fraud detection is a concern. In such a system, manageability might limit the ability of individuals to be able to edit or delete information themselves while enabling an appropriately privileged actor to administer changes to maintain accuracy and fair treatment of individuals.

- **Disassociability:** Enables a data system to process PII or events without associating the information with individuals or devices beyond the system's operational requirements. Some interactions—such as providing health care services or processing credit card transactions—rely on privacy but also require identification. Unlike confidentiality, which is focused on preventing unauthorized access to information, disassociability recognizes that privacy risks can result from exposures even when access is authorized or as a by-product of a transaction. The principle allows system designers to deliberately weigh identification needs against privacy risks at each stage of design.

These three privacy engineering objectives are intended to provide a degree of precision and measurability so that system designers and engineers, working with policy teams, can use them to bridge the gap between high-level principles and practical implementation within a functional system. Table 3.7 indicates which objectives relate to each of the OECD FIPPs.

TABLE 3.7 Alignment of the Privacy Engineering Objectives to the OECD FIPPs

OECD FIPP	Predictability	Manageability	Disassociability
Collection limitation		✓	✓
Data quality		✓	
Purpose specification	✓		
Use limitation	✓		
Security safeguards			
Openness	✓		
Individual participation		✓	
Accountability	✓	✓	✓

The following are additional NIST documents related to privacy engineering:

- **SP 800-122:** *Guide to Protecting the Confidentiality of Personally Identifiable Information.* Provides practical, context-based guidance for identifying PII and determining what level of protection is appropriate for each instance of PII. The document also suggests safeguards that may offer appropriate levels of protection for PII and provides recommendations for developing response plans for incidents involving PII.

- **SP 800-188:** *De-Identifying Government Datasets.* Provides guidance regarding the selection, use, and evaluation of de-identification techniques.

- **NISTIR 8053:** *De-Identification of Personal Information.* Summarizes the main aspects of de-identification and re-identification.

NIST Cybersecurity and Privacy Frameworks

The NIST Privacy Framework is a voluntary tool that organizations can use to better identify, assess, manage, and communicate about privacy risks so that individuals can enjoy the benefits of innovative technologies with greater confidence and trust. Further, the privacy framework is designed to provide high-level alignment with the NIST Cybersecurity Framework. This section provides an introduction to both frameworks.

In response to the growing number of cyber intrusions at U.S. federal agencies, Executive Order 13636, *Improving Critical Infrastructure Cybersecurity* [EO13], directed the NIST to work with stakeholders to develop a voluntary framework for reducing cyber risks to critical infrastructure. The resulting *NIST Cybersecurity Framework* [NIST18] includes leading practices that a variety of standards bodies have deemed successful. Thus, the framework is a collection of best practices—practices that improve efficiency and protect constituents. Although provided for federal agencies, the document is of use for nongovernment organizations.

The NIST Cybersecurity Framework consists of three components:

- **Core:** Provides a set of cybersecurity activities, desired outcomes, and applicable references that are common across critical infrastructure sectors

- **Implementation tiers:** Provide context on how an organization views cybersecurity risk and the processes in place to manage that risk

- **Profiles:** Represent the outcomes based on business needs that an organization has selected from the core categories and subcategories

The framework's core identifies 5 key functions that comprise an organization's cybersecurity risk management approach (see Table 3.8). Each function is divided into a number of specific categories, each of which in turn is divided into a number of more detailed subcategories, for a total of 23 categories and 106 subcategories. The 5 functions provide a high-level view of the elements that comprise risk management for the organization. The categories are groups of cybersecurity outcomes that are closely tied to programmatic needs and particular activities. Each category is further divided into specific outcomes of technical and/or management activities. These subcategories provide results that, while not exhaustive, help support achievement of the outcomes in each category. Tied to each subcategory is a list of informative references, each of which is a specific section of standards, guidelines, and practices that are common among critical infrastructure sectors and that illustrate a method to achieve the outcomes associated with each subcategory.

TABLE 3.8 NIST Cybersecurity Framework Functions and Categories

Function	Description	Category
Identify	Develop the organizational understanding to manage cybersecurity risk to systems, assets, data, and capabilities.	Asset Management
		Business Environment
		Governance
		Risk Assessment
		Risk Management Strategy
		Supply Chain Risk Management
Protect	Develop and implement the appropriate safeguards to ensure delivery of critical infrastructure services.	Access Control
		Awareness and Training
		Data Security
		Information Protection Processes and Procedures
		Maintenance
		Protective Technology
Detect	Develop and implement the appropriate activities to identify the occurrence of a cybersecurity event.	Anomalies and Events
		Security Continuous Monitoring
		Detection Processes
Respond	Develop and implement the appropriate activities to take action regarding a detected cybersecurity event.	Response Planning
		Communications
		Analysis
		Mitigation
		Improvements
Recover	Develop and implement the appropriate activities to maintain plans for resilience and to restore any capabilities or services that were impaired due to a cybersecurity event.	Recovery Planning

The framework's core is intended not so much as a checklist of actions to be performed but as a planning tool that enables decision makers to more clearly appreciate what goes into effective risk management and to develop policies that emphasize those specific activities that are appropriate for the security goals of the organization.

The tiers defined in the framework document help an organization define the priority that is to be given to cybersecurity and the level of commitment that the organization intends to make. The tiers range from Partial (Tier 1) to Adaptive (Tier 4) and describe an increasing degree of rigor and sophistication in cybersecurity risk management practices and the extent to which cybersecurity risk management is informed by business needs and is integrated into an organization's overall risk management practices.

Once an organization has clarity on the degree of commitment to risk management (tiers) and an understanding of the actions that can be taken to match that commitment, security policies and plans can be put in place, as reflected in a framework profile. In essence, a profile is a selection of categories and subcategories from the framework's core. A current profile reflects the cybersecurity posture of the organization. Based on a risk assessment, an organization can define a target profile and then categories and subcategories from the framework's core to reach the target. This definition of current and target profiles enables management to determine what has been done, what needs to be maintained, and what new cybersecurity measures need to be implemented to manage risk. The referenced guidelines, standards, and practices for each subcategory provide a concrete description of the work needed to meet the target profile.

The NIST Privacy Framework [NIST19] is designed to help organizations consider:

- How their systems, products, and services affect individuals
- How to integrate privacy practices into their organizational processes that result in effective solutions to mitigate these impacts and protect individuals' privacy

As with the NIST Cybersecurity Framework, the NIST Privacy Framework comprises a core, profiles, and implementation tiers. Table 3.9 shows the five key functions that comprise the framework's core and the functional categories for each function. The framework offers dozens of actions that a company can take to investigate, mitigate, and communicate its privacy risks to both users and executives within the company.

TABLE 3.9   NIST Privacy Framework Functions and Categories

Function	Description	Category
Identify	Develop the organizational understanding to manage privacy risk for individuals arising from data processing or their interactions with system, products, or services.	Inventor and Mapping
		Business Environment
		Governance
		Risk Assessment
		Risk Management Strategy
		Supply Chain Risk Management

Function	Description	Category
Protect	Develop and implement appropriate data processing safeguards.	Identity Management, Authentication, and Access Control
		Awareness and Training
		Data Security
		Data Protection Processes and Procedures
		Maintenance
		Protective Technology
		Protected Processing
Control	Develop and implement appropriate activities to enable organizations or individuals to manage data with sufficient granularity to manage privacy risks.	Data Management Processes and Procedures
		Data Management
Inform	Develop and implement appropriate activities to enable organizations and individuals to have a reliable understanding about how data are processed.	Transparency Processes and Procedures
		Data Processing Awareness
Respond	Develop and implement appropriate activities to take action regarding a privacy breach or event.	Response Planning
		Communications
		Analysis
		Mitigation
		Improvements
		Redress

Figure 3.7 illustrates how the functions in the two frameworks relate to each other [NIST19]. The two frameworks have been structured in such a way as to provide guidance on how to perform security and privacy risk management in an integrated and coordinated fashion.

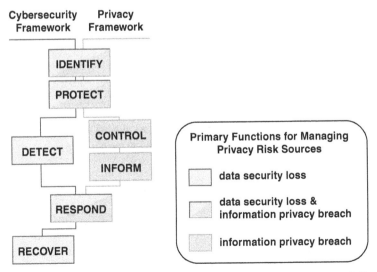

FIGURE 3.7 Cybersecurity Framework and Privacy Framework Functions Relationship

3.6   Privacy Best Practices

In addition to regulation and standards documents, there are a number of professional and industry groups that have produced best practices documents and guidelines that information privacy designers and implementers will find useful. The most important such document is the *Standard of Good Practice for Information Security*, produced by the Information Security Forum (ISF). This 300+-page document provides a wide range of best practices that are the consensus of industry and government organizations. One section of this document is devoted to privacy. In this regard, another important source of information is the Cloud Security Alliance (CSA), which, as the name suggests, is devoted to security measures for cloud providers. However, many of the best practices for cloud providers apply in other contexts. This section provides an overview of ISF and CSA documents related to privacy.

Information Security Forum (ISF)

ISF is an independent, not-for-profit association of leading organizations from around the world. Through ISF, its members fund and cooperate in the development of a practical research program in information security. It is dedicated to investigating, clarifying, and resolving key issues in cyber-security, information security, and risk management and to developing best practice methodologies, processes, and solutions that meet the business needs of its members. ISF members benefit from harnessing and sharing in-depth knowledge and practical experience drawn from within their organizations and developed through an extensive research and work program.

The most significant activity of ISF is the ongoing development of the *Standard of Good Practice for Information Security* (SGP); the current version of the SGP was issued in 2018. This document is a business-focused, comprehensive guide to identifying and managing information security risks in organizations and their supply chains. The breadth of the consensus in developing the SGP is unmatched. It is based on research projects and input from its members, as well as analysis of the leading standards on cybersecurity, information security, and risk management. The goal is the development of best practice methodologies, processes, and solutions that meet the needs of ISF members, including large and small business organizations, government agencies, and nonprofit organizations.

The SGP provides a detailed checklist for each topic that is covered. For the information privacy topic, the SGP provides guidance and recommendations in the following areas:

- **High-level working group:** The organization should establish a high-level working group responsible for managing information privacy issues and overseeing the information privacy program. This group should:
  - Appoint a chief privacy officer or data protection manager to coordinate information privacy activity
  - Appoint other individuals to monitor and advise on privacy-related matters and manage privacy-related implementation
  - Be aware of privacy-related regulations, the location(s) of PII within the organization, and the use purpose for all PII

- **Information privacy program:** The organization's information privacy program should:

    - Identify and protect PII throughout its life cycle (creation, storage, processing, transmission, destruction)

    - Develop a privacy awareness program

    - Perform privacy assessments as needed

    - Perform privacy audits as needed

- **Information privacy policy:** The organization should publish an information privacy policy that covers:

    - Acceptable use of PII

    - Requirements for protecting different types of PII

    - Rights of individuals whose PII is held

    - Requirements for privacy assessments, awareness programs, and compliance programs

    - Deployment of privacy-related technical controls

    - Specific policies and procedures for managing PII throughout its life cycle

- **Individual participation:** The organization should facilitate individual participation in the storage and use of their PII, in accordance with FIPP.

- **Technical controls:** The organization should select and implement technical controls, including:

    - Encryption and encryption key management

    - Data masking, such as via pseudonymization, data obfuscation, data de-identification, or data scrambling), which involves concealing parts of information when being stored or transmitted

    - Tokenization, which replaces valid information (e.g., database fields or records) with random information and provides authorized access to this information via the use of tokens

    - Protecting privacy-related metadata, such as document attributes or descriptive information that may contain personal information such as the name of the person who last updated a file

- **Data privacy breaches:** The organization should establish a method of dealing with data privacy breaches, including identifying breaches, responding to breaches, and notifying relevant parties.

Cloud Security Alliance (CSA)

CSA is dedicated to defining and raising awareness of best practices to help ensure a secure cloud computing environment. CSA draws on the subject matter expertise of industry practitioners, associations, governments, and its corporate and individual members.

Two privacy-related documents from CSA are noteworthy:

■ *Privacy Level Agreement [V2]: A Compliance Tool for Providing Cloud Services in the European Union*

■ *Code of Conduct for GDPR Compliance*

Although both documents address concerns related to the EU, the documents are useful and informative for all regulatory environments worldwide. The *Privacy Level Agreement* (PLA) document offers a structured way to communicate the level of personal data protection offered by a cloud service provider (CSP) to customers and potential customers. The document provides suggestion for content in the following clauses of a PLA:

■ Identity of the CSP, its role, and contact information for data protection inquiries

■ Ways in which the data will be processed

■ Data transfer

■ Data security measures

■ Monitoring

■ Personal breach notification

■ Data portability, migration, and transfer assistance

■ Data retention, restitution, and deletion

■ Accountability

■ Cooperation

■ Legally required disclosure

The *Code of Conduct for GDPR Compliance* also addresses the PLA. In addition, it provides detailed guidance for information privacy governance. Topics covered include:

■ Certification and code of ethics

■ Governance bodies, roles, and responsibilities

■ Governance process and related activities

3.7   Key Terms and Review Questions

Key Terms

accountability	Organisation for Economic Co-operation and Development (OECD)
aggregated information	personal data
anonymous information	personally identifiable information (PII)
best practices	PII controller
collection limitation	PII principal
data controller	PII processor
data quality	predictability
de-identified personal information	privacy framework
disassociability	privacy stakeholder
fair information practice principles (FIPP)	purpose specification
General Data Protection Regulation (GDPR)	regulations
individual participation	re-identification
linkable information	security safeguards
linked information	standards
manageability	technical controls
natural person	third party
openness	use limitation

Review Questions

1. What are the GDPR definition of *personal data*?

2. Explain the distinction between sensitive PII and non-sensitive PII.

3. Describe four categories of information that may relate to individuals.

4. What is re-identification, and how is it accomplished?

5. Describe the FIPPs defined by OECD.

6. Give a brief overview of GDPR.

7. List some of the major privacy-related laws in the United States.

8. What role does NIST play with respect to information privacy?

9. What contribution has ISO made to privacy standards?

10. Explain the purpose of the ISF Standard of *Good Practice for Information Security.*

3.8 References

ALFE12: Al-Fedaghi, S., and AL Azmi, A. "Experimentation with Personal Identifiable Information." *Intelligent Information Management*, July 2012.

BRAC19: Bracy, J. "World's first global privacy management standard hits the mainstream. IAPP Privacy Blog, August 20, 2019. https://iapp.org/news/a/worlds-first-global-privacy-management-standard-hits-the-mainstream/

DHS17: U.S. Department of Homeland Security. *Handbook for Safeguarding Sensitive PII.* Privacy Policy Directive 047-01-007, Revision 3. December 4, 2017

DOC17: U.S. Department of Commerce. *Privacy Program Plan.* September 2017. http://osec.doc.gov/opog/privacy/default.html

ENIS14: European Union Agency for Network and Information Security. *Privacy and Data Protection by Design—From Policy to Engineering.* December 2014. enisa.europa.eu

EO13: Executive Order 13636, "Improving Critical Infrastructure Cybersecurity." *Federal Register*, February 19, 2013. http://www.gpo.gov/fdsys/pkg/FR-2013-02-19/pdf/2013-03915.pdf

HEW73: U.S. Department of Health, Education, and Welfare. *Records, Computers and the Rights of Citizens, Report of the Secretary's Advisory Committee on Automated Personal Data Systems.* July 1973. https://epic.org/privacy/hew1973report/

KINA16: Kinast, K. "10 Key Facts Businesses Need to Note About the GDPR." *European Identity & Cloud Conference*, 2016.

NIST18: National Institute of Standards and Technology. *Framework for Improving Critical Infrastructure Cybersecurity, Version 1.1.* April 16, 2018. https://doi.org/10.6028/NIST.CSWP.04162018

NIST19: National Institute of Standards and Technology. *NIST Privacy Framework: An Enterprise Risk Management Tool.* April 30, 2019. https://www.nist.gov/privacy-framework

OECD80: Organisation for Economic Co-operation and Development. *OECD Guidelines on the Protection of Privacy and Transborder Flows of Personal Data.* 1980. http://www.oecd.org/sti/ieconomy/oecdguidelinesontheprotectionofprivacyandtransborderflowsofpersonaldata.htm

OECD13: Organisation for Economic Co-operation and Development. *The OECD Privacy Framework.* 2013. https://www.oecd-ilibrary.org/

SCHW14: Schwartz, P., and Solove, D. "Reconciling Personal Information in the United States and European Union." *California Law Review*, Vol. 102, No. 4, August 2014.

SOLO06: Solove, D. *A Taxonomy of Privacy.* GWU Law School Public Law Research Paper No. 129, 2006. http://scholarship.law.gwu.edu/faculty_publications/921/

Chapter 4

Information Privacy Threats and Vulnerabilities

Learning Objectives

After studying this chapter, you should be able to:

- Understand how changes in information technology have increased the threats to privacy
- Make a presentation on the types of privacy threats that individuals and organizations face
- List and discuss the various categories of privacy vulnerabilities
- Explain the purpose of the National Vulnerability Database and how organizations can use it

Chapter 3, "Information Privacy Requirements and Guidelines," discusses the requirements that drive the information privacy design and implementation process. These requirements derive from a number of sources, the most important of which are:

- **Fair information practice principles (FIPPs):** These principles, such as those defined by OECD (in Table 3.2), define overall design goals for information privacy.

- **Privacy laws and regulations:** Prominent recent examples are the EU General Data Protection Regulation (GDPR) and the California Consumer Privacy Act (CCPA). These laws are regulations that spell out specific requirements for the protection that must be provided to personally identifiable information (PII) and, in some cases, dictate management practices.

- **Standards:** Prominent in this category are the ISO and NIST privacy-related standards. These provide specific guidance to organizations and a means of certifying compliance.

- **Best practices:** These documents, such as the Standard of Good Practice for Information Security (SGP), recommend policies, procedures, and controls that have been found to be effective in protecting PII (personally identifiable information).

With the privacy requirements in mind, a fundamental exercise for an organization is to identify the privacy threats and the privacy vulnerabilities that are relevant to the organization and its use and storage of PII. It is useful at this point to repeat some definitions from Chapter 2, "Information Privacy Concepts":

- **Privacy threat:** A potential for violation of privacy, which exists when there is a circumstance, a capability, an action, or an event that could violate privacy and cause harm to an individual. That is, a threat is a possible danger that might exploit vulnerability.

- **Threat action:** Also referred to as a *threat event*, is a realization of a threat—that is, an occurrence in which a vulnerability is exploited as a result of either an accidental event or an intentional act.

- **Privacy vulnerability:** A flaw or weakness in a system's design, implementation, or operation and management that could be exploited by a threat to violate the system's privacy policy and compromise PII.

The first five sections of this chapter deal with privacy threats. Section 4.1 discusses the ways in which technological changes have increased the threats to privacy. Sections 4.2 and 4.3 present two different ways of categorizing threats, which serve as useful checklists for an organization to ensure that it has not overlooked any threat types. Section 4.4 provides a different perspective, classifying threats in terms of source. Section 4.5 provides some guidance on identifying threats. Section 4.6 discusses privacy vulnerabilities.

4.1 The Evolving Threat Environment

Advances in information technologies have created pressures that increasingly limit privacy and make the task of protecting information privacy significantly more difficult. This section, based on a discussion in *Engaging Privacy and Information Technology in a Digital Age* from the National Research Council, covers developments that are especially significant [NRC07].

Overall Impact of Advances in Technology

Advances in information technology, especially in the areas of information security and cryptography, have led to the creation of new tools and methods for protecting privacy. However, the overall impact of advancing technology has been to compromise privacy. Consider the following examples:

- **Decreasing data storage costs:** Data storage, particularly data storage, is so inexpensive that once PII is collected, it is easy to maintain it for the duration and beyond the lifetime of the individual. Organizations generally find it less expensive to retain data than to go through a process of deciding what data to destroy and when. Thus, the amount of PII available on an individual grows over time.

- **The Internet of Things:** The term Internet of Things (IoT) refers to a wireless-networked interconnection of smart devices, such as sensors. Interconnected IoT devices collect and transmit a variety of information, from home automation and security systems, automobile-based devices, municipal services devices, and more. The growth of IoT systems leads to the growing potential for collecting PII. Chapter 9, "Other PET Topics," examines some of the aspects of privacy in an IoT environment.

- **Always on or mostly on personal devices:** Smartphones, smart watches, and fitness trackers generate a considerable amount of personal information that is often accessible wirelessly.

- **Cloud computing:** When an organization outsources data and applications to a cloud service provider, the organization can no longer implement its own privacy controls and must rely on the privacy controls implemented by the cloud service provider. There are a number of issues in this regard, such as the complexity of the cloud environment compared to a typical organization's data center, the increased risks of a multitenant environment, and the risks associated with Internet-facing services. Chapter 9 examines cloud privacy issues.

- **Digitization of paper records:** Many records traditionally stored in paper form are now maintained in databases that are often accessible over the Internet. For example, many municipalities make property tax records readily available on a website, making it much more convenient for others to obtain ownership and property value information.

Repurposing Collected Data

While an organization might collect PII for one specific purpose, both the collecting organization and other entities increasingly find value in using this PII for other purposes. General examples include the following:

- **Businesses:** Businesses want to use PII to direct targeted product offerings to consumers, hire and place employees in the most cost-effective manner, and reduce economic risk through better understanding of demand.

- **Researchers:** Researchers in a variety of fields desire to use PII from one or more sources to derive statistical information such as current status and trends.

- **Government agencies:** Agencies seek sources of PII to provide services, administer benefits, and enhance security.

Data collected for one purpose can easily be used for a different purpose in the future unless use restrictions are built into database management and access system, especially because data can be retained indefinitely for little cost. Many of the privacy concerns cited in *Engaging Privacy and Information Technology in a Digital Age* from the National Research Council involve cases in which PII gathered for one purpose is used for another purpose, with neither notification nor consent [NRC07].

Means of Collection of PII

Businesses, government agencies, and even private individuals continue to develop new mechanisms and methods, both voluntary and involuntary, for obtaining PII. The following categories indicate the scope of the privacy exposure for individuals:

- **Mandatory disclosure:** There are a number of contexts in which individuals are required to provide PII, such as on tax returns and disclosures by convicted felons (e.g., fingerprints, DNA).

- **Incentivized disclosure:** An organization may provide an incentive to an individual to disclose information. For example, a retail business might offer a loyalty card, which entitles the user to discounts but enables the business to track purchases.

- **Conditioned disclosure:** This is similar to an incentivized disclosure and refers to the case in which, in order to obtain some important good or service, an individual must supply PII. Examples are driving an automobile, traveling on an airplane, voting, and gaining employment. In all these cases, the individual must supply some PII.

- **Entirely voluntary disclosure:** For example, people may disclose personal information on social media.

- **Unannounced acquisition of information:** This category covers cases in which an individual discloses PII without being aware of it. An example is the use of cookies on web browsers.

Thus, there are numerous occasions in which PII is gathered, adding to the volume of PII maintained on any given individual.

4.2 Privacy Threat Taxonomy

To understand the requirements for privacy, the threats must first be identified. One of the most comprehensive lists of privacy threats has been developed as a taxonomy in *A Taxonomy of Privacy* from the George Washington University Law School [SOLO06]. The taxonomy describes the different kinds of activities that impinge on privacy. It consists of four basic groups of potentially harmful activities: information collection, information processing, information dissemination, and invasion (see Figure 4.1 [SOLO06]). Each of these groups consists of different related subgroups of harmful activities.

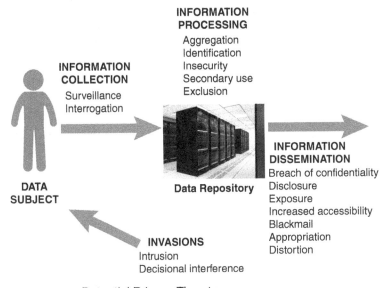

FIGURE 4.1 Potential Privacy Threats

Information Collection

Information collection is not necessarily harmful but can in some cases constitute a privacy threat. Two types of threat actions can occur:

- **Surveillance:** The watching, listening to, or recording of an individual's activities. Surveillance can be problematic and a violation of the right to privacy, especially if the surveillance is unknown to the individual.

- **Interrogation:** The pressuring of individuals to divulge information. If certain fields in a form or in an online registration process are required in order to proceed, the individual is compelled, or at least pressured, to divulge information that she would prefer not to.

Information Processing

Information processing refers to the use, storage, and manipulation of data that have been collected. Privacy issues related to information processing arise from how data that have already been collected are handled and the ability by processing to link the results back to the individuals to whom it pertains. Potential sources of privacy threat in this area include the following:

- **Aggregation:** Aggregation of data about an individual in various databases allows anyone with access to the aggregated data to learn more about an individual than could be learned from separate, and separately protected, dataset.

- **Identification:** It is possible, with sufficient data, to be able to aggregate data from various sources and use that to identify persons who are not otherwise identified in the dataset.

- **Insecurity:** Insecurity refers to the improper protection and handling of PII. Identity theft is one potential consequence. Another possible consequence is the dissemination of false information about a person, based on alteration of that person's record.

- **Secondary use:** Information about a person obtained for one purpose may be used or made available for other purposes without consent; this is referred to as *secondary use*.

- **Exclusion:** This is the failure to provide individuals with notice and input about their records.

Information Dissemination

The area of information dissemination encompasses the revelation of personal information or the threat of such revelation. Potential sources of privacy threats in this area include the following:

- **Disclosure:** Disclosure refers to the release of true information about a person. The potential harm is damage to reputation or position in some form. For example, many websites have a privacy link at the bottom of their main page that goes to a page that states their privacy policy, which is focused on disclosure issues. Typical sections of a policy include information collected; use of information; disclosure of information; cookies, web beacons and other tracking technologies; and user choice.

- **Breach of confidentiality:** *A Taxonomy of Privacy* distinguishes between disclosure and breach of confidentiality, defining the latter as a disclosure that involves the violation of trust in a relationship [SOLO06]. Thus, even if the disclosure itself is not harmful, the source of the disclosure is an entity that the person has a specific expectation of trust with. An example is the unauthorized release of medical information to a third party.

- **Exposure:** Exposure involves the exposing to others of certain physical and emotional attributes about a person, such as nude photographs or a video of a surgical operation.

- **Increased accessibility:** Increased accessibility means that information that is already publicly available is made easier to access. Increased accessibility does not create a new harm but does increase the likelihood and therefore the risk.

- **Blackmail:** Blackmail involves the threat of disclosure. Ransomware is an example of blackmail in the cybersecurity context.

- **Appropriation:** Appropriation involves the use of a person's identity or personality for the purpose of another person. This is not identity theft, in that the offender is not claiming to be the victim. Rather, the offender makes use of the image or other identifying characteristic for some purpose, such as advertising, that is not authorized by the victim.

- **Distortion:** Distortion is the manipulation of the way a person is perceived and judged by others and involves the victim being inaccurately exposed to the public. Distortion can be achieved by modifying records associated with an individual.

Invasions

The fourth area of privacy threats is referred to as *invasions*, and it involves impingements directly on the individual. Potential sources of privacy threat in this area include the following:

- **Intrusion:** In general terms, intrusion involves incursions into one's life or personal space. In the context of cybersecurity, intrusion relates to penetrating a network or a computer system and achieving some degree of access privilege. Intrusion is a part of a variety of security threats but can also cause a privacy threat. For example, the actual intrusion, or threat of intrusion, into a personal computer can disrupt the activities or peace of mind of the personal computer user.

- **Decisional interference:** This is a broad legal concept. In terms of the present discussion, it involves the individual's interest in avoiding certain types of disclosure. To the extent that certain actions, such as registering for a government benefit, might generate data that could potentially be disclosed, the decision to perform those actions is deterred.

This list of potential threats is comprehensive, and it is unlikely that any organization's set of privacy controls will attempt to address all of these threats. However, it is useful to have such a list in order to determine priorities for selecting privacy controls.

4.3   NIST Threat Model

The universally accepted method of performing information risk analysis involves identifying potential threats to an information system and the vulnerabilities of information systems to given threats. NISTIR 8062 proposes a different threat model that may be more directly useful in a privacy risk model. To justify this, NISTIR gives the example of smart meters. Smart meters are able to collect, record, and distribute highly granular information about household electrical use. Such information could be used, for example, to learn when a house is occupied and what appliances are running. A report from the NIST Smart Grid Cybersecurity Committee, published in NISTIR 7628, concluded that while much of the information accessible through the smart grid is not new, there is now the possibility that other parties will have access to that information. Further, the consolidation of this information allows many new uses for and ways to analyze the collected data, which may raise substantial privacy concerns. However, because this data collection is an authorized functioning of the system, it may not be obvious to a risk analyst that this activity should be classified as a threat.

The NIST threat model uses a privacy characterization presented in the *National Privacy Research Strategy* [NSTC16]. Figure 4.2, from the NSTC report, illustrates the key concepts that characterize information privacy concerns:

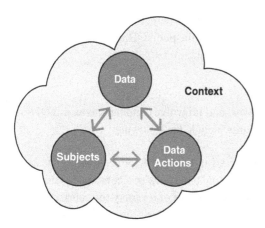

FIGURE 4.2   Privacy Characterization

- **Subjects:** Encompasses an individual or a group of individuals, the identity of individuals and groups, and their rights, autonomy, and privacy desires.

- **Data:** Encompasses the data and derived information about these individuals and groups.

- **Data actions:** Any system operations that process PII. These include the various data collection, processing, analysis, and retention practices; controls that constrain such practices; and impacts (negative and positive) of the collection and use of data on individuals, groups, and society.

- **Context:** The circumstances surrounding a system's processing of PII.

The need to consider context considerably complicates the task of ensuring information privacy. For example, individuals routinely share medical status with health care professionals, financial status with financial planners, and trip plans with travel agents and employers. But when information shared within one community shows up in another, outside the intended context, there is a privacy violation. The challenge for designers of privacy protection systems and controls is that individuals consider privacy from varied viewpoints, may use diverse terminologies to express their privacy concerns, perceive privacy-related harms differently, and vary their privacy requirements with circumstances. Existing models and best practices for information security do not capture these requirements well.

Table 4.1, based on NISTIR 8062, is an illustrative set of contextual factors that assist in determining privacy threats and performing a privacy risk assessment.

TABLE 4.1 Catalog of Contextual Factors

Category	Contextual Factors to Consider
Organizational	■ The nature of the organizations engaged in the system, such as public sector, private sector, or regulated industry, and how this factor might impact the data actions being taken by the system(s) ■ The public perception about participating organizations with respect to privacy ■ The nature and history of user relationships with the organizations participating in the system(s)
System	■ The degree of connections to external systems and the nature of the data actions being conducted by those external systems, such as retention, disclosure, or secondary use ■ Any intended public exposure of personal information and the degree of granularity ■ The nature and history of user interactions with the system(s) ■ The degree of similarity between the operational purpose (e.g., goods or services being offered) of the system and other systems that users have interacted with at participating organizations
Individuals	■ What is known about the privacy interests of the individuals whose information is being processed by the system ■ The individuals' degree of information technology experience/understanding ■ Any demographic factors that would influence the understanding or behavior of individuals with respect to the data actions being taken by the system(s)
Data action	■ The duration or frequency of the data actions being taken by the system(s) ■ How visible the data actions are to the individual ■ The relationship between data actions being taken by the system(s) and the operational purpose (e.g., in what manner or to what degree is the personal information being collected or generated contributing to the operational purpose?) ■ The degree of sensitivity of the personal information, including particular pieces or the bundle as a whole

NISTIR 8062 proposes the use of the terms illustrated in Figure 4.3 and described in the lists that follow:

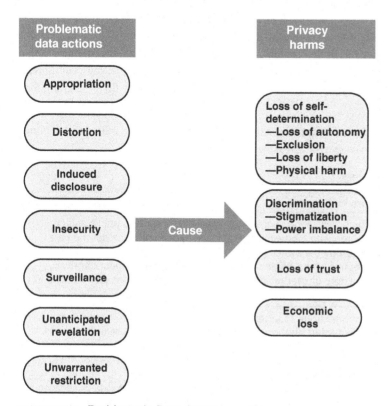

FIGURE 4.3   Problematic Data Actions and Harms

- **Problematic data action:** A *data action* that causes an adverse effect, or problem, for individuals.

- **Privacy harm:** An adverse experience for an individual resulting from the processing of his or her PII.

Problematic data actions include the following:

- **Appropriation:** Use of PII in ways that exceed an individual's expectation or authorization. Appropriation occurs when personal information is used in ways that an individual would object to or would have expected additional value for.

- **Distortion:** The use or dissemination of inaccurate or misleadingly incomplete personal information. Distortion can present users in an inaccurate, unflattering, or disparaging manner.

- **Induced disclosure:** Pressure to divulge personal information. Induced disclosure can occur when users feel compelled to provide information disproportionate to the purpose or outcome of the transaction. Induced disclosure can include leveraging access or privilege to an essential (or perceived essential) service.

- **Insecurity:** Lapses in data security.

- **Surveillance:** Tracking or monitoring of personal information that is disproportionate to the purpose or outcome of the service. The difference between the data action of monitoring and the problematic data action of surveillance can be very narrow. Tracking user behavior, transactions, or personal information may be conducted for operational purposes such as protection from cyber threats or to provide better services, but it becomes surveillance when it leads to privacy harms.

- **Unanticipated revelation:** Non-contextual use of data that reveals or exposes an individual or facets of an individual in unexpected ways. Unanticipated revelation can arise from aggregation and analysis of large and/or diverse dataset.

- **Unwarranted restriction:** Blocking tangible access to PII and limiting awareness of the existence of the information within the system or the uses of such information.

Privacy harms can be grouped into four categories:

- **Loss of self-determination:** The loss of an individual's personal sovereignty or ability to freely make choices. This includes the following categories:

  - **Loss of autonomy:** A loss that involves needless changes in behavior, including self-imposed restrictions on freedom of expression or assembly.

  - **Exclusion:** Lack of knowledge about or access to PII. When individuals do not know what information an entity collects or can make use of, or they do not have the opportunity to participate in such decision making, it diminishes accountability about whether the information is appropriate for the entity to possess or the information will be used in a fair or equitable manner.

  - **Loss of liberty:** Improper exposure to arrest or detainment. Even in democratic societies, incomplete or inaccurate information can lead to arrest, or improper exposure or use of information can contribute to instances of abuse of governmental power. More life-threatening situations can arise in non-democratic societies.

  - **Physical harm:** Actual physical harm to a person. For example, if an individual's PII is used to locate and gain access to cyber–physical systems that interact with the individual, harms may include the generation of inaccurate medical device sensor readings, the automated delivery of incorrect medication dosages via a compromised insulin pump, or the malfunctioning of critical smart car controls, such as braking and acceleration.

- **Discrimination:** The unfair or unequal treatment of individuals. This includes the following categories:
  - **Stigmatization:** The linking of PII to an actual identity in such a way as to create a stigma that can cause embarrassment, emotional distress, or discrimination. For example, sensitive information such as health data or criminal records or access to certain services such as food stamps or unemployment benefits may attach to individuals, creating inferences about them.
  - **Power imbalance:** Acquisition of PII that creates an inappropriate power imbalance or takes unfair advantage of or abuses a power imbalance between an acquirer and the individual. For example, collection of attributes or analysis of behavior or transactions about individuals can lead to various forms of discrimination or disparate impact, including differential pricing or redlining.
- **Loss of trust:** Breach of implicit or explicit expectations or agreements about the handling of personal information. For example, the disclosure of personal or other sensitive data to an entity is accompanied by a number of expectations for how those data are used, secured, transmitted, shared, and so on. Breaches can leave individuals reluctant to engage in further transactions.
- **Economic loss:** Direct financial losses resulting from identity theft as well as failure to receive fair value in a transaction involving personal information.

Figure 4.4 indicates which privacy threats have the potential to cause the various privacy harms.

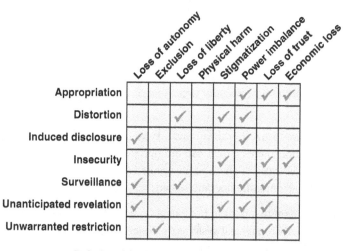

FIGURE 4.4   Relationship Between Privacy Threats and Potential Privacy Harms

4.4 Threat Sources

The nature of threats depends to a great extent on the type of source. NIST SP 800-30 (*Guide for Conducting Risk Assessments*) defines a threat source as either of the following:

- The intent and method targeted at the intentional exploitation of a vulnerability
- A situation and method that may accidentally trigger a vulnerability

SP 800-30 categorizes threat sources as follows:

- **Adversarial:** Individuals, groups, organizations, or states that seek to exploit the organization's dependence on cyber resources (i.e., information in electronic form, information and communications technologies, and the communications and information-handling capabilities provided by those technologies)
- **Accidental:** Erroneous actions taken by individuals in the course of executing their everyday responsibilities
- **Environmental:** Natural disasters and failures of critical infrastructures on which the organization depends but that are outside the control of the organization
- **Structural:** Failures of equipment, environmental controls, or software due to aging, resource depletion, or other circumstances that exceed expected operating parameters

For example, the 2018 Information Security Forum (ISF) *Standard of Good Practice for Information Security* defines a number of threats in the first three categories from the preceding list; these are listed in Table 4.2. This is not an exhaustive list but covers many threat categories. Although ISF lists these as information security threats, if a threat affects PII, it is also a privacy threat.

TABLE 4.2 Threats Defined in the *Standard of Good Practice for Information Security*

Adversarial Threats	Accidental Threats
Session hijacking	User error (accidental)
Unauthorized access to legitimate authentication credentials	Mishandling of critical and/or sensitive information by authorized users
Exploit vulnerable authorization mechanisms	User error (negligence)
Unauthorized monitoring and/or modification of communications	Loss of information systems
	Undesirable effects of change
Denial-of-service (DoS) attack	Resource depletion
Exploit insecure disposal of an organization's information assets	Misconfiguration
	Maintenance error
Introduce malware to information systems	Software malfunction (internally produced software)
Exploit misconfigured organizational information systems	Software malfunction (externally acquired software)
	Accidental physical damage

Adversarial Threats	Environmental Threats
Exploit design or configuration issues in an organization's remote access service	Pathogen (e.g., disease outbreak)
Exploit poorly designed network architecture	Storm (hail, thunder, blizzard)
Misuse of information systems	Hurricane
Unauthorized physical access to information systems	Tornado
Physical damage to or tampering with information systems	Earthquake
Theft of information system hardware	Volcanic eruption
Conduct physical attacks on organizational facilities or their supporting infrastructure	Flooding
Unauthorized network scanning and/or probing	Tsunami
Gather publicly available information about an organization	Fire
Phishing	Power failure or fluctuation
Insert subversive individuals into organizations	Damage to or loss of external communications
Interpersonal manipulation	Failure of environmental control systems
Exploit vulnerabilities in an organization's information systems	Hardware malfunction or failure
Introduce unauthorized code into applications or software	
Compromise supplier or business partner of target organization	

4.5 Identifying Threats

Information on environmental threats is typically available from a variety of government and trade groups. Accidental or structural threats are less easily documented but still generally can be predicted with reasonable accuracy. With respect to adversarial threats, organizations find it difficult to get reliable information on past events and to assess future trends for a variety of reasons, including the following:

- Organizations are often reluctant to report security events in an effort to save corporate image, avoid liability costs, and, in the case of responsible management and security personnel, avoid career damage.

- Some attacks may be carried out or at least attempted without being detected by the victim until much later, if ever.

- Threats continue to evolve as adversaries adapt to new security controls and discover new techniques.

Thus, keeping informed on adversarial threats is a never-ending battle. The following discussion examines three important categories of threat information sources: in-house experience, security alert services, and global threat surveys.

An important source of information on threats is the experience an organization has already had in identifying attempted and successful attacks on its assets. The organization can obtain this information through an effective security monitoring and improvement function; however, this information is of more value for threat and incident management (described in Chapter 13, "Event Monitoring, Auditing, and Incident Response") than for risk assessment. That is, detected attacks should prompt immediate remedial action rather than be folded into long-range actions.

Security alert services are concerned with detecting threats as they develop to enable organizations to patch code, change practices, or otherwise react to prevent a threat from being realized. Again, this category of information is of more value for threat and incident management. Two useful sources in this regard are:

- **Computer emergency response teams (CERTs):** Also called a computer emergency readiness teams, these cooperative ventures collect information about system vulnerabilities and known threats and disseminates it to systems managers. Hackers also routinely read CERT reports. Thus, it is important for system administrators to quickly verify and apply all software patches to discovered vulnerabilities. One of the most useful of these organizations is the U.S. Cybersecurity and Infrastructure Security Agency (CISA), which is a partnership between the U.S. Department of Homeland Security and the public and private sectors, intended to coordinate the response to security threats from the Internet (https://www.us-cert.gov). Another excellent resource is the CERT Coordination Center, which grew from the computer emergency response team formed by the Defense Advanced Research Projects Agency (https://www.sei.cmu.edu/about/divisions/cert/index.cfm). The CERT Coordination Center website provides good information on Internet security threats, vulnerabilities, and attack statistics.

- **Information sharing analysis centers (ISACs):** An ISAC is a nonprofit organization, generally sector specific, that provides a central resource for gathering information on cyber threats to critical infrastructure and providing two-way sharing of information between the private and public sectors. In the United States, the National Council of ISACs is a central home for 25 ISACs (https://www.nationalisacs.org). Although they are U.S.-based, these ISACs generally have global significance.

Of great value for threat identification are the various global threat surveys that are readily available. Some of the most important of these are the following:

- **Verizon *Data Breach Investigations Report* (DBIR):** This authoritative and highly respected report is based on data on security and privacy incidents systematically collected from a wide variety of organizations. See https://enterprise.verizon.com/resources/reports/dbir/.

- **Threat Horizon Report**: A useful complement to the DBIR is the annual *Threat Horizon Report* from ISF. It differs from the DBIR in two ways. First, it is a more broad-brush treatment, identifying key threat trends rather than detailed threats and detailed target profiles. Second, the *Threat Horizon Report* attempts to project the likely major threats over the next two years. See https://www.securityforum.org/research/.

- **ENISA *Threat Landscape Report***: This report, from the European Union Agency for Network and Information Security, provides a thorough look at current global privacy and security threats. See https://www.enisa.europa.eu/publications.

- **Trustwave *Global Security Report***: The Trustwave *Global Security Report* is a well-regarded annual survey of the cyberthreat landscape. The report is based on findings from extensive data sources, including breach investigations, global threat intelligence, product telemetry, and a number of research sources. Trustwave operates a number of security operations centers (SOCs) as a managed security service and from these logs billions of security and compliance events each day, examines data from tens of millions of network vulnerability scans, and conducts thousands of penetration tests. The infographic style makes the report easy to follow, yet it contains an extraordinary amount of detailed information that can assist in threat assessment and risk treatment. See https://www.trustwave.com/en-us/resources/library/.

- **Cisco *Annual Cybersecurity Report***: The Cisco *Annual Cybersecurity Report* is another excellent source of threat information. The report provides a detailed description of current attacker behavior patterns and highlights coming vulnerabilities. See https://www.cisco.com/c/en/us/products/security/security-reports.html.

- **Fortinet *Threat Landscape Report***: The findings in this report represent the collective intelligence of FortiGuard Labs, drawn from Fortinet's vast array of network devices/sensors within production environments. This report includes billions of threat events and incidents observed in live production environments around the world, reported quarterly. See https://secure.fortinet.com/LP=5681.

4.6   Privacy Vulnerabilities

In order to effectively design and implement privacy controls, an organization must identify the vulnerabilities that can be exploited by threats to cause privacy violations.

This section first develops categories of vulnerabilities, then discusses approaches to identifying and documenting vulnerabilities, and finally discusses the use of the National Vulnerability Database.

Vulnerability Categories

Vulnerabilities can occur in the following areas:

- **Technical vulnerabilities:** Flaws in the design, implementation, and/or configuration of software and/or hardware components, including application software, system software, communications software, computing equipment, communications equipment, and embedded devices.

- **Human resource vulnerabilities:** Key person dependencies, gaps in awareness and training, gaps in discipline, and improper termination of access.

- **Physical and environmental vulnerabilities:** Insufficient physical access controls, poor siting of equipment, inadequate temperature/humidity controls, and inadequately conditioned electrical power.

- **Operational vulnerabilities:** Lack of change management; inadequate separation of duties; lack of control over software installation, lack of control over media handling and storage; lack of control over system communications; inadequate access control or weaknesses in access control procedures; inadequate recording and/or review of system activity records; inadequate control over encryption keys; inadequate reporting, handling, and/or resolution of security incidents; and inadequate monitoring and evaluation of the effectiveness of security controls.

- **Business continuity and compliance vulnerabilities:** Misplaced, missing, or inadequate processes for appropriate management of business risks, inadequate business continuity/contingency planning, and inadequate monitoring and evaluation for compliance with governing policies and regulations.

- **Policy and procedure vulnerabilities:** Privacy policies and procedures that are inadequate to fully protect PII, including conformance with FIPPs.

- **Dataset vulnerabilities:** Weaknesses in de-identification measures, inadequate masking of PII in statistical dataset, and inadequate protection against discovery of PII by analysis of multiple dataset.

Technical privacy vulnerabilities overlap to a considerable extent with technical security vulnerabilities. Means of identifying technical privacy vulnerabilities are discussed later in this section.

In many of the areas of the preceding list, vulnerability identification depends critically on management initiative and follow-through. Techniques such as interviews, questionnaires, review of previous risk assessments and audit reports, and checklists can all contribute to developing a good picture of the vulnerability landscape.

Location of Privacy Vulnerabilities

Figure 4.5 illustrates the potential locations of privacy vulnerabilities for PII stored and processed by an organization, with each location indicated by a starburst image. The possibilities include:

- External transfer of PII, including to and from:

  - The PII principal

  - A third-party individual or organization

  - A cloud service provider

  - An IoT

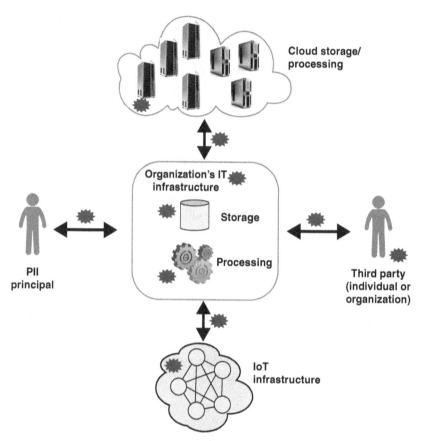

FIGURE 4.5 Location of Privacy Vulnerabilities

- Storage and processing of the PII within the organization's IT infrastructure

- Organizational vulnerabilities, such as human resource, physical, operational, business continuity, policy and procedure, and dataset vulnerabilities

- If the organization offloads some storage and processing functions to an external cloud service provider, possible privacy vulnerabilities at the cloud site

- If the organization maintains an IoT that extends beyond the organization premises, possible privacy vulnerabilities within the IoT network

National Vulnerability Database and Common Vulnerability Scoring System

In the area of technical vulnerabilities, it is possible to be quite precise and exhaustive. An outstanding resource is the NIST National Vulnerability Database (NVD) and the related Common Vulnerability Scoring System (CVSS) [FIRS15], described in NISTIR 7946 (*CVSS Implementation Guidance*). The NVD is a comprehensive list of known technical vulnerabilities in systems, hardware, and software; it covers both security and privacy vulnerabilities. The CVSS provides an open framework for communicating the characteristics of vulnerabilities. The CVSS defines a vulnerability as a bug, a flaw, a weakness, or an exposure of an application, a system device, or a service that could lead to a failure of confidentiality, integrity, or availability. The CVSS model attempts to ensure repeatable and accurate measurement while enabling users to view the underlying vulnerability characteristics used to generate numerical scores. The CVSS provides a common measurement system for industries, organizations, and governments requiring accurate and consistent vulnerability exploit and impact scores.

It is worthwhile to gain an understanding of the CVSS in order to understand the wide range of vulnerabilities that can affect systems. In addition, the systematic scheme for evaluating vulnerabilities in the CVSS is useful in guiding the development of a similar systematic approach to other vulnerabilities, such as those related to organization issues, policies and procedures, and the physical infrastructure. CVSS is widely accepted and used.

Figure 4.6 provides an example of one of the vulnerability entries in the NVD. Each entry includes:

Current Description
libcurl 7.1 through 7.57.0 might accidentally leak authentication data to third parties. When asked to send custom headers in its HTTP requests, libcurl will send that set of headers first to the host in the initial URL but also, if asked to follow redirects and a 30X HTTP response code is returned, to the host mentioned in URL in the 'Location:' response header value. Sending the same set of headers to subsequent hosts is in particular a problem for applications that pass on custom 'Authorization:' headers, as this header often contains privacy-sensitive information or data that could allow others to impersonate the libcurl-using client's request.
Source: MITRE **Last Modified:** 11/16/2018 View Analysis Description

CVSS v3.0 Severity:
Base Score: 9.8 Critical
Vector: AV:N/AC:L/PR:N/UI:N/S: U/C:H/I:H/A:H
Impact Score: 5.9
Exploitability Score: 3.9

CVSS Version 3 Metrics:
Attack Vector (AV): Network
Attack Complexity (AC): Low
Privileges Required (PR): None
User Interaction (UI): None
Scope (S): Unchanged
Confidentiality (C): High
Integrity (I): High
Availability (A): High

i QUICK INFO
CVE Dictionary Entry: CVE-2018-1000007
Original release date: 01/24/2018
Last modified: 11/16/2018

FIGURE 4.6 NVD Scoring Example

- The unique Common Vulnerabilities and Exposure (CVE) dictionary identifier
- A description of the vulnerability
- Links to websites and other references with information related to the vulnerability
- CVSS metrics from among the 14 metrics in 3 groups (discussed later in this section)

Table 4.3 lists the individual metrics and shows the levels defined for each. In each case, the levels are listed from highest to lowest security concern. In essence, the scoring is done as follows. For each identified vulnerability, the NVD provides a level for each metric in the base group, based on the characteristics of the vulnerability. For example, the attack vector metric indicates whether the attack can be launched remotely over a network or the Internet, is launched only across the immediate network to which both the attack source and the target system are attached, must be done by a local login, or requires physical access to the machine. The more remote the attack can be, the more attack sources are possible, and therefore the more serious is the vulnerability. This information is invaluable in enabling users to understand the characteristics of the vulnerability.

TABLE 4.3   CVSS Metrics

Base Metric Group		Temporal Metric Group	Environmental Metric Group
Exploitability	**Impact**		
Attack Vector ■ Network ■ Adjacent ■ Local ■ Physical **Attack Complexity** ■ Low ■ High **Privileges Required** ■ None ■ Low ■ High **User Interaction** ■ None ■ Required	**Confidentiality Impact** ■ High ■ Low ■ None **Integrity Impact** ■ High ■ Low ■ None **Availability Impact** ■ High ■ Low ■ None	**Exploit Code Maturity** ■ Not defined ■ High ■ Functional ■ Proof-of-concept ■ Unproven **Remediation Level** ■ Not defined ■ Workaround ■ Temporary fix ■ Official Fix **Report Confidence** ■ Not defined ■ Confirmed ■ Reasonable ■ Unknown	**Confidentiality Requirement** ■ Not defined ■ High ■ Medium ■ Low **Integrity Requirement** ■ Not defined ■ High ■ Medium ■ Low **Availability Requirement** ■ Not defined ■ High ■ Medium ■ Low
Scope ■ Unchanged ■ Changed			

As Table 4.3 shows, each level of a metric has a descriptive name. In addition, the CVSS assigns a numerical value on a scale of 0.0 to 10.0, with 10.0 being the most severe security issue. The numerical scores for the metrics in the base metric group are input to an equation defined in the CVSS that produces an aggregate base security score ranging from 0.0 to 10.0 (see Figure 4.6).

The base metric group represents the intrinsic characteristics of a vulnerability that are constant over time and across user environments. It consists of three sets of metrics:

- **Exploitability:** These metrics reflect the ease and technical means by which the vulnerability can be exploited. The metrics are:

  - **Attack vector:** As mentioned, this metric is a measure of how remote an attacker can be from the vulnerable component.

  - **Attack complexity:** Conveys the level of difficulty required for an attacker to exploit a vulnerability once the target component is identified. The complexity is rated high if the attacker cannot accomplish the attack at will but must invest some measurable amount of effort in preparation or execution.

  - **Privileges required:** Measures the access an attacker requires to exploit a vulnerability. The values are none (no privileged access required), low (basic user privileges), and high (administrative-level privileges).

  - **User interaction:** Indicates whether a user other than the attacker must participate for an attack to be successful.

- **Impact:** These metrics indicate the degree of impact on the primary security objectives of confidentiality, integrity, and availability. In each of these cases, the score reflects the worst outcome if more than one component is affected (scope = changed). For each of the three objectives, the values are high (total loss of confidentiality, integrity, or availability), low (some loss), and none.

- **Scope:** This metric is grouped within the base metric group, although it is somewhat independent of the remainder of the group. It refers to the ability for a vulnerability in one software component to impact resources beyond its means or privileges. An example is a vulnerability in a virtual machine that enables an attacker to delete files on the host OS. An unchanged value of this metric means that the vulnerability can only affect resources managed by the same authority.

Generally, the base and temporal metrics are specified by vulnerability bulletin analysts, security product vendors, or application vendors because they typically have better information about the characteristics of a vulnerability than do users. The environmental metrics, however, are specified by users because they are best able to assess the potential impact of a vulnerability within their own environments.

The temporal metric group represents the characteristics of a vulnerability that change over time but not among user environments. It consists of three metrics. In each case, the value *not defined* indicates that this metric should be skipped in the scoring equation:

- **Exploit code maturity:** This metric measures the current state of exploit techniques or code availability. Public availability of easy-to-use exploit code increases the number of potential attackers by including those who are unskilled, thereby increasing the severity of the vulnerability. The levels reflect the degree to which the exploit is available and usable for exploiting the vulnerability.

- **Remediation level:** Measures the degree to which remediation is available.

- **Report confidence:** Measures the degree of confidence in the existence of the vulnerability and the credibility of the known technical details.

The environmental metric group captures the characteristics of a vulnerability that are associated with a user's IT environment. It enables the analyst to customize the CVSS score depending on the importance of the affected IT asset to a user's organization, measured in terms of confidentiality, integrity, and availability.

4.7   Key Terms and Review Questions

Key Terms

accidental	environmental
adversarial	exclusion
aggregation	exploit code maturity
appropriation	exploitability
blackmail	exposure
breach of confidentiality	human resource vulnerabilities
business continuity and compliance vulnerabilities	identification
	impact
Common Vulnerability Scoring System (CVSS)	incentivized disclosure
	increased accessibility
conditioned disclosure	induced disclosure
context	insecurity
data	interrogation
data actions	intrusion
dataset vulnerabilities	loss of autonomy
decisional interference	loss of liberty
disclosure	loss of self-determination
discrimination	loss of trust
distortion	mandatory disclosure
economic loss	National Vulnerability Database (NVD)
entirely voluntary disclosure	operational vulnerabilities

physical and environmental vulnerabilities	scope
physical harm	secondary use
policy and procedure vulnerabilities	stigmatization
power imbalance	structural
privacy harm	subjects
privacy threat	surveillance
privacy vulnerability	technical vulnerabilities
problematic data action	unannounced acquisition of information
remediation level	unanticipated revelation
report confidence	unwarranted restriction

Review Questions

1. What is meant by the term *repurposing* collected data?
2. Describe the different means of collecting PII.
3. Describe each of the threats listed in the threat taxonomy of Figure 4.1.
4. Explain the NIST privacy threat model.
5. Explain the difference between privacy threat, problematic data action, and privacy harm.
6. List examples of problematic data actions.
7. Describe the categories of privacy harms.
8. What are the general sources of privacy threats?
9. Describe the categories of privacy vulnerabilities.
10. Where might privacy vulnerabilities be located in an IT infrastructure?
11. What are the National Vulnerability Database and the Common Vulnerability Scoring System?

4.8 References

FIRS15: FIRST.org, Inc. *Common Vulnerability Scoring System v3.0: Specification Document.* 2015. https://first.org/cvss/specification-document

NRC07: National Research Council. *Engaging Privacy and Information Technology in a Digital Age.* The National Academies Press, 2007.

NSTC16: National Science and Technology Council. *National Privacy Research Strategy.* Networking and Information Technology Research and Development Program. https://www.nitrd.gov/PUBS/NationalPrivacyResearchStrategy.pdf

SOLO06: Solove, D. *A Taxonomy of Privacy.* GWU Law School Public Law Research Paper No. 129, 2006. http://scholarship.law.gwu.edu/faculty_publications/921/

PART III

Technical Security Controls for Privacy

Chapter 5

System Access

Learning Objectives

After studying this chapter, you should be able to:

- Discuss the three general means of authenticating a user's identity
- Explain the mechanism by which hashed passwords are used for user authentication
- Present an overview of password-based user authentication
- Present an overview of hardware token-based user authentication
- Present an overview of biometric user authentication
- Summarize some of the key security issues for user authentication
- Understand the different types of access control
- Present an overview of identity and access management concepts

This chapter and Chapter 6, "Malicious Software and Intruders," provide an overview of technical measures that have been developed to meet the objectives of information security (e.g., confidentiality, integrity, availability) but are also essential for information privacy. This chapter specifically deals with issues related to system access.

One of the principal privacy concerns of organizations is protecting personally identifiable information (PII) that is stored in databases, such as health information databases. One means of doing this is to encrypt that PII. Doing so protects the data from adversaries who are able to gain unauthorized access to the system hosting the PII but do not possess the necessary decryption key. However, ultimately, the PII must be decrypted to be used. Accordingly, the organization seeks to restrict access to only those individuals who are authorized to access the PII and to restrict their use of the PII to only those functions they are authorized to perform. Further, the organization must ensure that any individual claiming to be an authorized user authentic—that is, that the user is who he or she claims to be.

Section 5.1 provides an overview of system access concepts. Sections 5.2 through 5.4 look at the major components of system access: authorization, authentication, and access control. Section 5.5 examines the related topic of identity and access management.

5.1 System Access Concepts

The Information Security Forum (ISF) 2018 *Standard of Good Practice for Information Security* (SGP) characterizes system access in terms of the following:

- **Principle:** Access control arrangements should be established to restrict access to business applications, systems, networks, and computing devices by all types of users, who should be assigned specific privileges to restrict them to particular information or systems.

- **Objective:** The objective is to ensure that only authorized individuals gain access to business applications, information systems, networks, and computing devices; to ensure individual accountability; and to provide authorized users with access privileges that are sufficient to enable them to perform their duties but not to exceed their authority.

- **Mechanism:** Require users to be granted access privileges in line with their roles, authenticated using access control mechanisms (e.g., password, token, or biometric), and subject to a rigorous sign-on process before being provided with approved levels of access.

Privileges

The term *privilege* refers to the actions a user is permitted to perform. From an information security perspective, the following concerns come into play:

- The level of access to basic system functions and databases. Examples include ordinary user access, root privileges on a Linux or Unix system, and administrator access on Windows systems.

- The functions that a user can perform on a particular database or file, such as read-only, read/write, add files, and delete files.

For privacy considerations, an organization can define a finer-grained set of privileges, including the following:

- **Read privileges:** These could include the following hierarchy of levels of access:

  - **Aggregate query:** The user is only allowed to query for information that is aggregated from a set of PII records (e.g., the average age of all heart disease patients in a hospital).

  - **Individual query:** The user may submit a name or an identifier and retrieve the PII corresponding to that individual.

  - **Total file read:** The user has access to the entire file.

- **Write privileges:** These could include the following:

  - **Personal update:** The user can update his or her own PII record.

  - **General update:** The user has permission to update any record in a PII database.

- **Share privileges:** The user can transmit the file or a portion of the file to another party.

System Access Functions

Figure 5.1 illustrates the relationship between the three distinct functions that comprise access control, described in more detail in the list that follows:

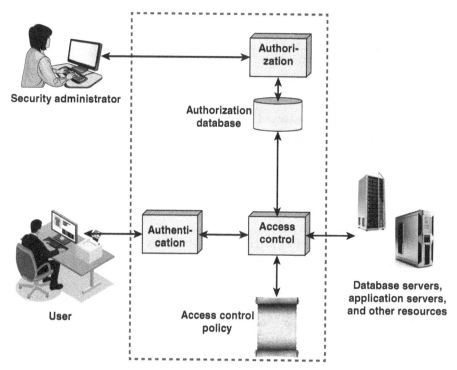

FIGURE 5.1   System Access Functions

- **Authorization:** Authorization is the process of deciding what an individual or a process ought to be allowed to do. In the context of system access, authorization is granting of specific rights to a user, program, or process to access system resources and perform specific functions. Authorization defines what an individual or a program can do after successful authentication.

- **Authentication:** Authentication is the process of establishing an understood level of confidence that an identifier presented to a system refers to a specific user, process, or device.

Authentication is often a prerequisite to allowing access to resources in an information system. This function is typically referred to as ***user authentication***, to distinguish it from message authentication or data authentication.

- **Access control:** The process of granting or denying specific requests (1) for accessing and using information and related information processing services and (2) to enter specific physical facilities. Access control ensures that access to assets is authorized and restricted based on business and security requirements.

In the literature, all of the elements depicted within the dashed lines in Figure 5.1 are referred to as *system access* or, simply, *access control*. To make clear that all of the functions are related, the ISF SGP uses the term *system access* to refer to the service provided by authorization, authentication, and access control working together.

System access is concerned with denying access to unauthorized users and limiting the activities of legitimate users to only those actions they are authorized to perform on system resources. The access control function mediates attempted access to an object in the system by a user or a program executing on behalf of that user. The authentication function establishes the identity of the user. The authorization function maintains an authorization database that defines the access privileges for each user. The access control function consults the authorization database and uses an access control policy that specifies how a user's privileges are to be mapped into allowable actions for specific data items or other resources.

Two principles typically determine the decision to authorize a user to access a given resource:

- **Need-to-know:** You are only granted access to the information you need to perform your tasks. (Different tasks/roles mean a different need-to-know and hence different access profile.)

- **Need-to-use:** You are only granted access to the information processing facilities (IT equipment, applications, procedures, rooms) you need to perform your task/job/role.

Privacy Considerations for System Access

The requirements for information security have dictated the development of policies and controls for authorization, authentication, and access control. These policies and controls also provide protection for PII. The perspective for information privacy is nonetheless somewhat different from that of information security. In dealing with PII, an organization needs to be concerned with who is authorized to access the PII, to control its processing, and to control its distribution. In this context, the organization needs to consider the effects of access, processing, and distribution on the privacy of PII.

The following are key privacy considerations for system access:

- **PII principal:** A privacy objective defined in ISO 29151 (*Code of Practice for Personally Identifiable Information Protection*) is to give PII principals the ability to access and review their PII. For PII principals who are not employees and do not otherwise need access to the organization's IT resources, the organization should strictly limit the access permissions to being able to read the principal's PII. PII principals who are employees might also need to access other IT resources, and the organization of course must control that access. ISO 29151 also advises that where identification and authentication of requestors is required, the organization should request only the minimum information to ensure correct identification.

- **Purpose specification:** In accordance with the OECD fair information practice principles (FIPPs), the organization must clearly specify the purpose(s) for which PII is collected. The organization should identify the PII that is useful to different applications or processes and logically separate the PII accordingly. ISO 29151 indicates that an organization must manage the different access rights according to the applications and processes and establish a dedicated IT environment for systems that process the most sensitive PII.

- **Information sharing with external parties:** The organization needs to set up authorization, authentication, and access control procedures to ensure that only authorized third parties have access to specific PII data sets.

- **Minimization:** A privacy objective defined in ISO 29151 to minimize the PII that is processed to what is strictly necessary for the legitimate interests pursued by the PII controller and to limit the disclosure of PII to a minimum number of privacy stakeholders. The organization should implement appropriate authorization and access control procedures to support this objective.

- **Use of query language:** Powerful query languages such as SQL enable a user to retrieve and manipulate large amounts of PII from one or more databases. ISO 29151 recommends limiting access to query language capabilities, consistent with protection requirements. This may involve limiting the number of individuals with access to the query language capability and limiting the use of query language to a small number of predefined fields of PII records.

5.2 Authorization

A designated security administrator is responsible for creating and maintaining the authorization database. The administrator sets authorizations on the basis of the security policy of the organization and the roles and responsibilities of individual employees. The process for authorizing users should include the following:

- Associate access privileges with uniquely defined individuals, such as by using unique identifiers, such as user IDs.

- Maintain a central record of access rights granted to a user ID to access information systems and services.

- Obtain authorization from the owner of the information system or service for the use of the information system or service; separate approval for access rights from management may also be appropriate.

- Apply the principle of least privilege to give each person the minimum access necessary to do his or her job.

- Assign access privileges for an individual for individual resources based on information security levels and classification of information.

- In addition to information resources, such as files and databases, ensure that authorization specifies which networks and networked services may be accessed.

- Define requirements for expiration of privileged access rights.

- Ensure that identifiers are not reused. That is, authorizations associated with a user ID should be deleted when the individual assigned that user ID changes roles or leaves the organization.

In addition to having the normal security protections used to protect databases, the authorization database should be reviewed on a regular basis to ensure that access privileges remain appropriate and that obsolete authorizations have been deleted.

Privacy Authorization

SP 800-53 (*Security and Privacy Controls for Information Systems and Organizations*) includes the Privacy Authorization (PA) control family. The controls in this family are primarily management rather than technical controls, but this is a convenient place to summarize them.

Policies and Procedures

Control PA-1 addresses the establishment of policy and procedures for the effective implementation of the controls and control enhancements in the PA family. It consists of the following management controls:

1. Develop, document, and disseminate to appropriate stakeholders a privacy authorization policy that defines roles and responsibilities, as well as procedures for implementing the policy.

2. Designate an official, such as a data protection officer (DPO) or chief privacy officer (CPO), to manage the privacy authorization policy and procedure.

3. Periodically review and update the privacy authorization policy and procedure.

4. Ensure that the privacy authorization procedures implement the privacy authorization policy and controls.

5. Develop, document, and implement remediation actions for violations of the privacy authorization policy.

Authority to Collect

Control PA-2 deals with the need for an organization to determine that it has the legal authority to collect, use, maintain, and share PII and to determine the scope of PII that falls within that authority.

Purpose Specification

Control PA-3 deals with the need to identify and document the purpose(s) for which PII is collected, used, maintained, and shared. In addition to clearly documenting the purpose(s), an organization should ensure that it restricts the use of PII to only the authorized purpose(s).

PA-3 also suggests that an organization employ automated mechanisms to support records management of authorizing policies and procedures for PII. Automated mechanisms augment verification that organization policies and procedures are enforced for the management and tracking of PII within an organization's systems.

Information Sharing with External Parties

Control PA-4 provides guidance for sharing PII with external parties. The CPO or DPO must review and approve each instance of such sharing. The following management controls support the objective of PA-4:

1. Develop, document, and disseminate guidelines for sharing PII to appropriate stakeholders.

2. Evaluate each proposed new instance of sharing to determine if it is authorized.

3. Develop and enforce specific agreements with external parties for each instance of PII sharing.

4. Monitor and audit the sharing of PII with external parties.

5.3 User Authentication

User authentication is one of the most complex and challenging security functions. There are a wide variety of methods of authentication, with associated threats, risks, and countermeasures. This section provides an overview.

User authentication is the process of determining whether some user or some application or process acting on behalf of a user is, in fact, who or what it declares itself to be. Authentication technology provides access control for systems by checking to see if a user's credentials match the credentials in a database of authorized users or in a data authentication server. Authentication enables organizations to keep their networks secure by permitting only authenticated users (or processes) to access its protected resources, which may include computer systems, networks, databases, websites, and other network-based applications or services.

In most computer security contexts, user authentication is the fundamental building block and the primary line of defense. User authentication is the basis for most types of access control and for user accountability. User authentication encompasses two functions:

- **Identification step:** Presenting an identifier to the security system. (Identifiers should be assigned carefully because authenticated identities are the basis for other security services, such as access control service.)

- **Verification step:** Presenting or generating authentication information that corroborates the binding between the entity and the identifier.

For example, user Alice Toklas could have the user identifier ABTOKLAS. This information needs to be stored on any server or computer system that Alice wishes to use and could be known to system administrators and other users. A typical item of authentication information associated with this user ID is a password, which is kept secret (known only to Alice and to the system). If no one is able to obtain or guess Alice's password, then the combination of Alice's user ID and password enables administrators to set up Alice's access permissions and audit her activity. Because Alice's ID is not secret, system users can send her email, but because her password is secret, no one can pretend to be Alice.

In essence, identification is the means by which a user provides a claimed identity to the system; user authentication is the means of establishing the validity of the claim.

Means of Authentication

There are three general means of authenticating a user's identity, and these *authentication factors* can be used alone or in combination:

- **Knowledge factor (something the individual knows):** Requires the user to demonstrate knowledge of secret information. Routinely used in single-layer authentication processes, knowledge factors can come in the form of passwords, passphrases, personal identification numbers (PINs), or answers to secret questions.

- **Possession factor (something the individual possesses):** Requires a physical entity possessed by the authorized user to connect to the client computer or portal. This type of authenticator used to be referred to as a *token*, but that term is now deprecated. The term *hardware token* is a preferable alternative. Possession factors fall into two categories:

  - **Connected hardware tokens:** Items that connect to a computer logically (e.g., via wireless) or physically in order to authenticate identity. Items such as smart cards, wireless tags, and USB tokens are common connected tokens used to serve as a possession factor.

  - **Disconnected hardware tokens:** Items that do not directly connect to the client computer, instead requiring input from the individual attempting to sign in. Typically, a disconnected hardware token device uses a built-in screen to display authentication data that are then utilized by the user to sign in when prompted.

- **Inherence factor (something the individual is or does):** Refers to characteristics, called *biometrics*, that are unique or almost unique to the individual. These include static biometrics, such as fingerprint, retina, and face; and dynamic biometrics, such as voice, handwriting, and typing rhythm.

The specific items used during authentication, such as a password or hardware token, are referred to as *authenticators*. All of these methods, properly implemented and used, can provide secure user authentication. However, each method has problems (see Table 5.1). An adversary might be able to guess or steal a password. Similarly, an adversary might be able to forge or steal a card. A user may forget a password or lose a card. A user might share a password or card with a colleague. Furthermore, there is significant administrative overhead associated with managing password and card information on systems and securing such information on systems. With respect to biometric authenticators, there are a variety of problems, including dealing with false positives and false negatives, user acceptance, cost, security of the sensor itself, and convenience. *Effective Cybersecurity: A Guide to Using Best Practices and Standards* provides a detailed discussion of authentication methods [STAL19].

TABLE 5.1 Authentication Factors

Factor	Examples	Properties
Knowledge	User ID Password PIN	Can be shared May be easy to guess Can be forgotten
Possession	Smart card Electronic badge Electronic key	Can be shared Can be duplicated (cloned) Can be lost or stolen
Inherence	Fingerprint Face Iris Voice print	Not possible to share False positives and false negatives possible Forging difficult, especially for some types

Multifactor Authentication

Multifactor authentication refers to the use of more than one of the authentication means in the preceding list (see Figure 5.2). Typically, this strategy involves the use of authentication technologies from two of the classes of factors described in the preceding section, such as a PIN plus a hardware token (knowledge factor plus possession factor) or a PIN and a biometric factor (knowledge factor plus inherence factor). Multifactor authentication is generally more secure than single-single authentication because the failure modes for different factors are largely independent. So, for example, a hardware token might be lost or stolen, but the PIN required for use with the token would not be lost or stolen at the same time. This assumption is not always true, however. For example, a PIN attached to a hardware token is compromised at the same time that the token is lost or stolen. Nevertheless, multifactor authentication is an important means of reducing vulnerability.

An example of two-factor authentication is commonly used for web-based services, including online banking, PayPal, and Facebook. Typically, the user provides a password. Then a six-digit code is sent as a text message to the user's cellphone, and the user must enter the code to complete the login.

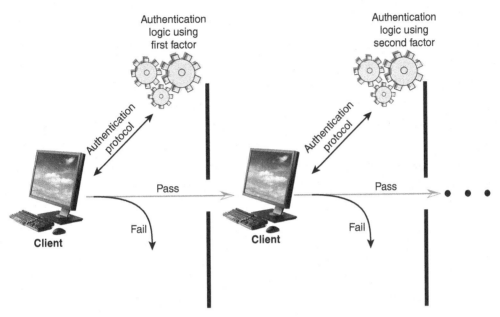

Multifactor Authentication

A Model for Electronic User Authentication

NIST SP 800-63 (*Digital Identity Guidelines*) defines a general model for user authentication that involves a number of entities and procedures, as shown in Figure 5.3.

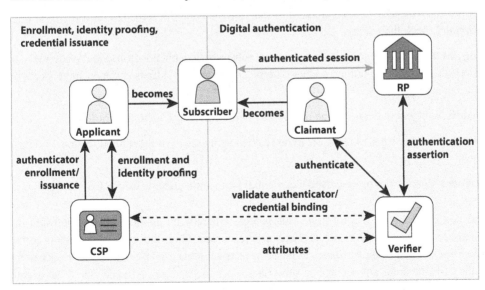

CSP = credential service provider
RP = relying party

FIGURE 5.3 The NIST 800-63 Digital Identity Model

Three concepts are important in understanding this model:

- **Digital identity:** The unique representation of an individual, generally referred to as a subject, engaged in an online transaction. The representation consists of an attribute or a set of attributes that uniquely describe a subject within a given context of a digital service but do not necessarily uniquely identify the subject in all contexts.

- **Identity proofing:** The process of establishing that a subject is who they claim to be to a stated level of certitude. This process involves collecting, validating, and verifying information about a person.

- **Digital authentication:** The process of determining the validity of one or more authenticators used to claim a digital identity. Authentication establishes that a subject attempting to access a digital service is in control of the technologies used for authentication. Successful authentication provides reasonable risk-based assurances that the subject accessing the service today is the same as the subject who previously accessed the service.

Six entities are defined in Figure 5.3:

- **Credential service provider (CSP):** A trusted entity that issues or registers subscriber authenticators. For this purpose, the CSP establishes a digital credential for each subscriber and issues electronic credentials to subscribers. A CSP may be an independent third party or may issue credentials for its own use.

- **Verifier:** An entity that verifies the claimant's identity by verifying the claimant's possession and control of one or two authenticators using an authentication protocol. To do this, the verifier may also need to validate credentials that link the authenticator(s) to the subscriber's identifier and check their status.

- **Relying party (RP):** An entity that relies on the subscriber's authenticator(s) and credentials or a verifier's assertion of a claimant's identity, typically to process a transaction or grant access to information or a system.

- **Applicant:** A subject undergoing the processes of enrollment and identity proofing.

- **Claimant:** A subject whose identity is to be verified using one or more authentication protocols.

- **Subscriber:** A party who has received a credential or an authenticator from a CSP.

The left-hand portion of Figure 5.3 illustrates the process whereby an applicant is enrolled into the system for purposes of accessing certain services and resources. First, the applicant presents to the CSP evidence of possession of the attributes to be associated with this digital identity. Upon successful proofing by the CSP, the applicant becomes a subscriber. Then, depending on the details of the overall authentication system, the CSP issues some sort of electronic credential to the subscriber. The *credential* is a data structure that authoritatively binds an identity and additional attributes to one or more authenticators possessed by a subscriber, and it can be verified when presented to the verifier in an authentication transaction. The authenticator could be an encryption key or an encrypted password that identifies the subscriber. The authenticator may be issued by the CSP, generated directly by the subscriber, or provided by a third party. The authenticator and credential may be used in subsequent authentication events.

Once a user is registered as a subscriber, the authentication process can take place between the subscriber and one or more systems that perform authentication (right-hand portion of Figure 5.3). The party to be authenticated is called a *claimant*, and the party verifying that identity is called a *verifier*. When a claimant successfully demonstrates possession and control of an authenticator to a verifier through an authentication protocol, the verifier can verify that the claimant is the subscriber named in the corresponding credential. The verifier passes on an assertion about the identity of the subscriber to the relying party (RP). That assertion includes identity information about a subscriber, such as the subscriber name, an identifier assigned at registration, or other subscriber attributes that were verified in the registration process. The RP can use the authenticated information provided by the verifier to make access control or authorization decisions.

In some cases, the verifier interacts with the CSP to access the credential that binds the subscriber's identity to his or her authenticator and to optionally obtain claimant attributes. In other cases, the verifier does not need to communicate in real time with the CSP to complete the authentication activity (e.g., with some uses of digital certificates). Therefore, the dashed line between the verifier and the CSP represents a logical link between the two entities.

An implemented system for authentication will differ from or be more complex than this simplified model, but this model illustrates the key roles and functions needed for a secure authentication system.

5.4 Access Control

This section provides an overview of important aspects of access control. It is useful to begin by defining the following terms:

- **Access:** The ability and means to communicate with or otherwise interact with a system, to use system resources to handle information, to gain knowledge of the information the system contains, or to control system components and functions.

- **Access control:** The process of granting or denying specific requests (1) for obtaining and using information and related information processing services and (2) to enter specific physical facilities.

- **Access control mechanism:** Security safeguards (i.e., hardware and software features, physical controls, operating procedures, management procedures, and various combinations of these) designed to detect and deny unauthorized access and permit authorized access to an information system.

- **Access control service:** A security service that protects against a system entity using a system resource in a way not authorized by the system's security policy.

Subjects, Objects, and Access Rights

The basic elements of access control are subject, object, and access rights. A *subject* is an entity capable of accessing objects. Generally, the concept of subject equates with that of process. Any user or application actually gains access to an object by means of a process that represents that user or application. The process takes on the attributes of the user, such as access rights.

A subject is typically held accountable for the actions he or she has initiated, and an audit trail may be used to record the association of a subject with security-relevant actions performed on an object by the subject.

Basic access control systems typically define three classes of subject, with different access rights for each class:

- **Owner:** This may be the creator of a resource, such as a file. For system resources, ownership may belong to a system administrator. For project resources, a project administrator or leader may be assigned ownership.

- **Group:** In addition to the privileges assigned to an owner, a named group of users may also be granted access rights, such that membership in the group is sufficient to exercise these access rights. In most schemes, a user may belong to multiple groups.

- **World:** The least amount of access is granted to users who are able to access the system but are not included in the categories owner and group for this resource.

An *object* is a resource to which access is controlled. In general, an object is an entity used to contain and/or receive information. Examples include records, blocks, pages, segments, files, portions of files, directories, directory trees, mailboxes, messages, and programs. Some access control systems also encompass bits, bytes, words, processors, communication ports, clocks, and network nodes.

The number and types of objects to be protected by an access control system depend on the environment in which access control operates and the desired trade-off between security on the one hand and complexity, processing burden, and ease of use on the other hand.

An *access right* describes the way in which a subject may access an object. Access rights could include the following:

- **Read:** User may view information in a system resource (e.g., a file, selected records in a file, selected fields within a record, some combination). Read access includes the ability to copy or print.

- **Write:** User may add, modify, or delete data in system resource (e.g., files, records, programs). Write access includes read access.

- **Execute:** User may execute specified programs.

- **Delete:** User may delete certain system resources, such as files or records.

- **Create:** User may create new files, records, or fields.
- **Search:** User may list the files in a directory or otherwise search the directory.

Access Control Policies

An access control policy dictates what types of access are permitted, under what circumstances, and by whom. Access control policies are generally grouped into the following categories:

- **Discretionary access control (DAC):** Access control based on the identity of the requestor and on access rules (authorizations) stating what requestors are (or are not) allowed to do. The controls are discretionary in the sense that a subject with a certain access permission is capable of passing that permission (perhaps indirectly) on to any other subject.

- **Mandatory access control (MAC):** Access control based on comparing security labels (which indicate how sensitive or critical system resources are) with security clearances (which indicate that system entities are eligible to access certain resources). This policy is termed *mandatory* because an entity that has clearance to access a resource may not, just by its own volition, enable another entity to access that resource.

- **Role-based access control (RBAC):** Access control based on user roles (i.e., a collection of access authorizations a user receives based on an explicit or implicit assumption of a given role). Role permissions may be inherited through a role hierarchy and typically reflect the permissions needed to perform defined functions within an organization. A given role may apply to a single individual or to several individuals.

- **Attribute-based access control (ABAC):** Access control based on attributes associated with and about subjects, objects, targets, initiators, resources, or the environment. An access control rule set defines the combination of attributes under which an access may take place.

DAC is the traditional method of implementing access control. MAC is a concept that evolved out of requirements for military information security. Both RBAC and ABAC have become increasingly popular.

These four policies are not mutually exclusive. An access control mechanism can employ two or even all four of these policies to cover different classes of system resources.

Discretionary Access Control

A general approach to DAC, as exercised by an operating system or a database management system, is an ***access matrix***. One dimension of the matrix consists of identified subjects that may attempt data access to the resources. Typically, this list consists of individual users or user groups, although access could be controlled for terminals, network equipment, hosts, or applications instead of or in addition to users. The other dimension lists the objects that may be accessed. At the greatest level of detail, objects may be individual data fields. More aggregate groupings, such as records, files, or even the entire database, may also be objects in the matrix. Each entry in the matrix indicates the access rights of a particular subject for a particular object.

Part a of Figure 5.4 shows a simple example of an access matrix. Thus, user A owns files 1 and 3 and has read and write access rights to those files. User B has read access rights to file 1, and so on.

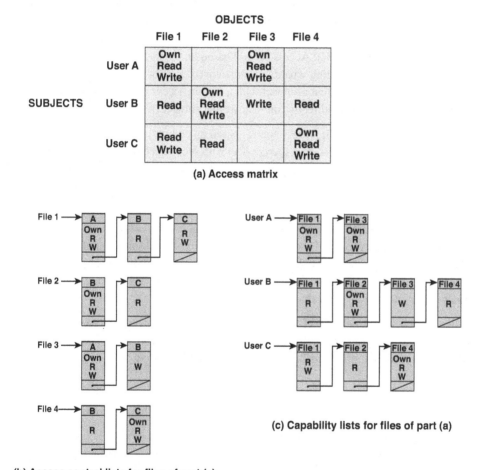

(a) Access matrix

(b) Access control lists for files of part (a)

(c) Capability lists for files of part (a)

FIGURE 5.4   Example of Access Control Structures

In practice, an access matrix is usually sparse and is implemented by decomposition in one of two ways. The matrix may be decomposed by columns, yielding *access control lists* (ACLs); see part b of Figure 5.4. For each object, an ACL lists users and their permitted access rights. The ACL may contain a default, or public, entry. This allows users who are not explicitly listed as having special rights to a default set of rights. The default set of rights should always follow the rule of least privilege or read-only access, whichever is applicable. Elements of the list may include individual users as well as groups of users.

When it is desired to determine which subjects have which access rights to a particular resource, ACLs are convenient because each ACL provides the information for a given resource. However, this data structure is not convenient for determining the access rights available to a specific user.

Decomposition by rows yields *capability tickets* (see part c of Figure 5.4). A capability ticket specifies authorized objects and operations for a particular user. Each user has a number of tickets and may be authorized to loan or give them to others. Because tickets may be dispersed around the system, they present a greater security problem than access control lists. The integrity of the ticket must be protected and guaranteed (usually by the operating system). In particular, the ticket must be unforgeable. One way to accomplish this is to have the operating system hold all tickets on behalf of users. These tickets would have to be held in a region of memory that is inaccessible to users. Another alternative is to include an unforgeable token in the capability. This could be a large random password or a crypto-graphic message authentication code. This value is verified by the relevant resource whenever access is requested. This form of capability ticket is appropriate for use in a distributed environment, when the security of its contents cannot be guaranteed.

The convenient and inconvenient aspects of capability tickets are the opposite of those for ACLs. It is easy to determine the set of access rights that a given user has, but it is more difficult to determine the list of users with specific access rights for a specific resource.

Role-Based Access Control

RBAC is based on the roles that users assume in a system rather than on the users' identities. Typically, RBAC models define a role as a job function within an organization. RBAC systems assign access rights to roles instead of to individual users. In turn, users are assigned to different roles, either stati-cally or dynamically, according to their responsibilities.

The relationship of users to roles is many to many, as is the relationship of roles to resources (i.e., system objects). The set of users changes—in some environments frequently—and the assignment of a user to one or more roles may also be dynamic. The set of roles in the system in most environments is relatively static, with only occasional additions or deletions. Each role has specific access rights to one or more resources. The set of resources and the specific access rights associated with a particular role are also likely to change infrequently.

We can use the access matrix representation to depict the key elements of an RBAC system in simple terms, as shown in Figure 5.5. The upper matrix relates individual users to roles. Typically, there are many more users than roles. Each matrix entry is either blank or marked, the latter indicating assignment to this role. Note that a single user may be assigned multiple roles (more than one mark in a row) and that multiple users may be assigned to a single role (more than one mark in a column). The lower matrix has the same structure as the DAC access control matrix, with roles as subjects. Typically, there are few roles and many objects, or resources. In this matrix, the entries are the specific access rights enjoyed by the roles. Note that a role can be treated as an object, allowing the definition of role hierarchies. The * symbol indicates the presence of a copy flag, which enables the user in the role designated by the row to transfer the right with or without the copy flag to another role.

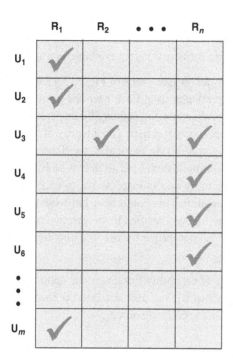

FIGURE 5.5   Access Control Matrix Representation of RBAC

OBJECTS

	R_1	R_2	R_n	F_1	F_1	P_1	P_2	D_1	D_2
R_1	control	owner	owner control	read *	read owner	wakeup	wakeup	seek	owner
R_2		control		write *	execute			owner	seek *
ROLES • • •									
R_n			control		write	stop			

RBAC lends itself to an effective implementation of the principle of least privilege. Each role should contain the minimum set of access rights needed for that role. A user is assigned to a role that enables him or her to perform only what is required for that role. Multiple users assigned to the same role enjoy the same minimal set of access rights.

Attribute-Based Access Control

An ABAC model can define authorizations that express conditions on properties of both the resource and the subject. For example, consider a configuration in which each resource has an attribute that identifies the subject that created the resource. Then, a single access rule can specify the ownership privilege for all the creators of every resource. The strength of the ABAC approach is its flexibility and expressive power.

Attributes are characteristics that define specific aspects of the subject, the object, environment conditions, and/or requested operations that are predefined and preassigned by an authority. Attributes contain information that indicates the class of information given by the attribute, a name, and a value (e.g., Class=HospitalRecordsAccess, Name=PatientInformationAccess, Value=MFBusinessHoursOnly).

The following are the three types of attributes in the ABAC model:

- **Subject attributes:** A subject is an active entity (e.g., user, application, process, or device) that causes information to flow among objects or changes the system state. Each subject has associated attributes that define the identity and characteristics of the subject. Such attributes may include the subject's identifier, name, organization, job title, and so on. A subject's role can also be viewed as an attribute.

- **Object attributes:** An object, also referred to as a *resource*, is a passive (in the context of the given request) information system–related entity (e.g., devices, files, records, tables, processes, programs, networks, domains) containing or receiving information. As with subjects, objects have attributes that can be leveraged to make access control decisions. A Microsoft Word document, for example, might have attributes such as title, subject, date, and author. Object attributes can often be extracted from the metadata of the object. In particular, a variety of web service metadata attributes may be relevant for access control purposes, such as ownership, service taxonomy, or even Quality of Service (QoS) attributes.

- **Environment attributes:** These attributes have so far been largely ignored in most access control policies. They describe the operational, technical, and even situational environment or context in which the information access occurs. For example, attributes such as current date and time, the current virus/hacker activities, and the network's security level (e.g., Internet versus intranet) are not associated with a particular subject or a resource but may nonetheless be relevant in applying an access control policy.

ABAC is a logical access control model that is distinguishable because it controls access to objects by evaluating rules against the attributes of entities (subject and object), operations, and the environment relevant to a request. ABAC relies on the evaluation of attributes of the subject, attributes of the object, and a formal relationship or access control rule that defines the allowable operations for subject/object attribute combinations in a given environment. All ABAC solutions contain these basic core capabilities to evaluate attributes and enforce rules or relationships between those attributes. ABAC systems are capable of enforcing DAC, RBAC, and MAC concepts. ABAC enables fine-grained access control, which allows for a higher number of discrete inputs into an access control decision, providing a bigger set of possible combinations of those variables to reflect a larger and more definitive set of possible rules, policies, or restrictions on access. Thus, ABAC allows an unlimited number of attributes to be combined to satisfy any access control rule. Moreover, ABAC systems can be implemented to satisfy a wide array of requirements from basic access control lists through advanced expressive policy models that fully leverage the flexibility of ABAC.

Figure 5.6 illustrates the essential components of an ABAC system in a logical architecture.

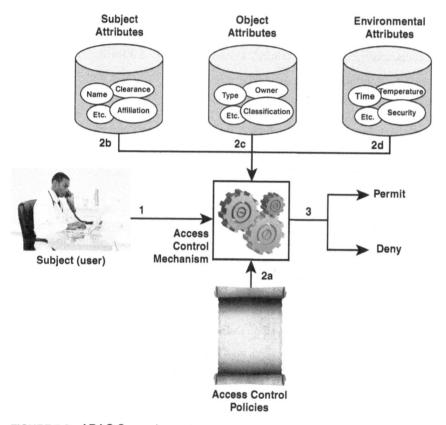

FIGURE 5.6 ABAC Scenario

As Figure 5.6 illustrates, access by a subject to an object proceeds according to the following steps:

1. A subject requests access to an object. This request is routed to an access control mechanism.

2. The access control mechanism is governed by a set of rules (2a) that are defined by a preconfigured access control policy. Based on these rules, the access control mechanism assesses the attributes of the subject (2b), the object (2c), and current environmental conditions (2d) to determine authorization.

3. The access control mechanism grants the subject access to the object if access is authorized and denies access if it is not authorized.

It is clear from the logical architecture that four independent sources of information are used for the access control decision. A system designer can decide which attributes are important for access control with respect to subjects, objects, and environmental conditions. The system designer or another authority can then define access control policies, in the form of rules, for any desired combination of attributes of subject, object, and environmental conditions. It should be evident that this approach is very powerful and flexible. However, the cost, both in terms of the complexity of the design and implementation and in terms of the performance impact, is likely to exceed that of other access control approaches. This is a trade-off that a system authority must make.

Attribute Privacy Considerations

SP 800-162 (*Guide to Attribute Based Access Control (ABAC) Definition and Considerations*) points out the risk in the use of subject attributes. Implementing attribute sharing capabilities may increase the risk of privacy violation of PII due to inadvertent exposure of attribute data to untrusted third parties or aggregation of sensitive information in environments less protected than the originator's. Thus, an organization must employ agreements to ensure the proper handling of PII and enforcement of PII regulations.

Attribute Metadata

It is useful to have a standardized means of characterizing attributes and their values. The benefits include the following:

- Obtain greater understanding of how the attribute and its value were obtained, determined, and vetted

- Have greater confidence in applying appropriate authorization decisions to subjects external to the domain of a protected system or data

- Develop more granular access control policies

- Make more effective authorization decisions

- Promote the use of attributes across multiple organizations, such as in federated identity schemes, discussed in Section 5.5

NISTIR 8112 (*Attribute Metadata*) provides such a standardized method. The document includes metadata definitions for both attribute metadata and attribute value metadata. Attribute metadata are for the attribute itself, not for the specific attribute's value. For example, this metadata may describe the format in which the attribute will be transmitted (e.g., height will always be recorded in inches). This schema provides a set of attribute metadata from which to choose when constructing an attribute sharing agreement (trust-time) and the rationale for their inclusion. The metadata items are as follows:

- **Description:** An informative description of the attribute

- **Allowed values:** A defined set of allowed values for the attribute

- **Format:** A defined format in which the attribute will be expressed

- **Verification frequency:** The frequency at which the attribute provider will reverify the attribute

Attribute value metadata consists of elements that focus on the asserted value for the attribute. Following the same example as above, the attribute value would be the actual height. A possible attribute value metadata for the height could be the name of the originating organization that provisioned the height, such as the DMV in the subject's home state. The NISTIR 8112 schema provides a set of attribute value metadata, proposed values for those metadata fields, and rationales for their inclusion. The metadata fall into the following categories:

- **Provenance:** Metadata relevant or pertaining to evaluating the source of the attribute's value

- **Accuracy:** Metadata relevant or pertaining to determining if the attribute's value is correct and belongs to a specific subject

- **Currency:** Metadata relevant or pertaining to determining the "freshness" of a given attribute's value

- **Privacy:** Metadata relevant or pertaining to privacy aspects of a given attribute's value

- **Classification:** Metadata relevant or pertaining to the security classification of a given attribute's value

Table 5.2 provides details about the individual metadata items.

TABLE 5.2   Attribute Value Metadata

Metadata Element	Description	Recommended Values
Provenance		
Origin	The legal name of the entity that issues or creates the initial attribute value	■ Origin's name ■ None
Provider	The legal name of the entity that is providing the attribute	■ Provider's name ■ None
Pedigree	Description of the attribute value's relationship to the authoritative source of the value	■ Authoritative ■ Sourced ■ Self-asserted ■ Derived
Accuracy		
Verifier	The entity that verified the attribute's value	■ Origin ■ Provider ■ Not verified
Verification method	The method by which the attribute value was verified as true and belonging to the specific individual	■ Document verification ■ Record verification ■ Document verification with record verification ■ Proof of possession ■ Not verified
Currency		
Last update	The date and time when the attribute was last updated	No restrictions
Expiration date	The date an attribute's value is considered to be no longer valid	No restrictions
Last verification	The date and time when the attribute value was last verified as being true and belonging to the specified individual	No restrictions

Metadata Element	Description	Recommended Values
Privacy		
Individual consented	Captures whether the user has expressly consented to providing the attribute value	■ Yes ■ No ■ Unknown
Date consented	The date on which express consent for release of the attribute value was acquired	No restrictions
Acceptable uses	Allowed uses for entities that receive attributes	■ Authorization ■ Secondary use ■ No further disclosure
Cache time to live	The length of time for which an attribute value may be cached	No restrictions
Data deletion date	The date a certain attribute should be deleted from records	No restrictions
Classification		
Classification	Security classification level of the attribute	Enterprise specific
Releasability	Restrictions regarding to whom an attribute value may be released	Enterprise specific

Resources

NIST has devoted considerable attention to ABAC. The following documents are useful for enterprises seeking to implement ABAC:

■ **SP 800-162:** *Guide to Attribute Based Access Control (ABAC) Definition and Considerations.* Provides good introduction to ABAC, plus guidance for using ABAC to improve information sharing within organizations and between organizations while maintaining control of that information.

■ **SP 800-178:** *A Comparison of Attribute Based Access Control (ABAC) Standards for Data Service Applications.* Describes two different ABAC standards: Extensible Access Control Markup Language (XACML) and Next Generation Access Control (NGAC). The document compares these standards with respect to five criteria. The goal of this publication is to help ABAC users and vendors make informed decisions when addressing future data service policy enforcement requirements.

■ **SP 1800-3:** *Attribute Based Access Control.* Develops an example of an advanced access control system to assist enterprises interested in deploying ABAC. This ABAC solution can manage access to networked resources more securely and efficiently and with greater granularity than traditional access management. It enables the appropriate permissions and limitations for the same information system for each user, based on individual attributes, and allows for permissions to multiple systems to be managed by a single platform, without a heavy administrative burden. The approach uses commercially available products that can be included alongside an enterprise's current products in its existing infrastructure. This example solution is packaged as a "how to" guide that demonstrates implementation of standards-based cybersecurity technologies in the real world. It can save organizations research and proof-of-concept costs for mitigating risk through the use of context for access decisions.

- **NISTIR 8112:** *Attribute Metadata*. Describes a schema for attribute metadata and attribute value metadata intended to convey information about a subject's attribute(s).

5.5   Identity and Access Management

Organizations increasingly are using some form of identity and access management facility to implement and manage system access. The 2018 ISF SGP defines identity and access management as follows:

Identity and access management (*IAM*) typically consists of several discrete activities that follow the stages of a user's life cycle within the organization. These activities fall into two categories:

- **Provisioning process:** Providing users with the accounts and access rights they require to access systems and applications

- **User access process:** Managing the actions performed each time a user attempts to access a new system, such as authentication and sign-on

IAM addresses the mission-critical need to ensure appropriate access to resources across increasingly heterogeneous technology environments and to meet increasingly rigorous compliance requirements. This security practice is a crucial undertaking for any enterprise. It is increasingly business aligned, and it requires business skills, not just technical expertise. Enterprises that develop mature IAM capabilities can reduce their identity management costs and, more importantly, become significantly more agile in supporting new business initiatives.

There are three deployment approaches for IAM:

- **Centralized:** All access decisions, provisioning, management, and technology are concentrated in a single physical or virtual location. Policies, standards, and operations are pushed out from this single location.

- **Decentralized:** Local, regional, or business units make the decisions for all access choices, provisioning, management, and technology. There may be enterprise-wide policies and standards, but they provide guidance for the decentralized provider.

- **Federated:** Each organization subscribes to a common set of policies, standards, and procedures for the provisioning and management of users. Alternatively, the organizations can buy a service from a supplier.

IAM Architecture

An architecture for identity and access management is a high-level model depicting the main elements and interrelationships of an IAM system. Figure 5.7 shows a typical architecture for an IAM system, whether centralized or decentralized. The list that follows describes the elements of an IAM system:

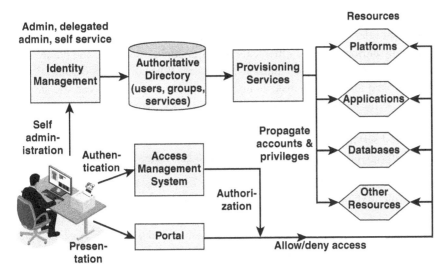

FIGURE 5.7 Identity and Access Management Infrastructure

- **Identity management service:** Defines an identity for each user (human or process), associates attributes with the identity, and enforces a means by which a user can verify identity. The central concept of an identity management system is the use of *single sign-on* (*SSO*). SSO is a security subsystem that enables a user identity to be authenticated at an identity provider (i.e., at a service that authenticates and asserts the user's identity), and then that authentication is honored by other service providers. SSO enables a user to access all network resources after a single authentication. The service implements facilities to enable user registration, change of status or other details, and deregistration. Identity management features enable creation, deletion, or modification of a user profile and change of the user's role or association with a function, business unit, or organization.

- **Directory:** Provides a central identity repository and reconciliation of identity details between application-specific directories. Among the items that could be stored for each user:

  - User credentials, such as user ID, password, and possibly certificates to enable authentication

  - Attributes, such as roles and groups that form a basis for authorization

  - User preferences to enable personalization

  - Access control policy defining access permissions for distinctive data entries

- **Access management system:** Implements user authentication.

- **Portal:** Provides a personalized interface for all user interaction with system resources.

- **Provisioning services:** Covers centralized user administration capabilities. Provisioning services serve to automate the task of changing users' rights and privileges across multiple enterprise applications. They enable fast creation of new employee accounts, and they augment existing security practices by allowing administrators to quickly cut off terminated accounts.

Federated Identity Management

Federated identity management refers to the agreements, standards, and technologies that enable the portability of identities, identity attributes, and entitlements across multiple enterprises and numerous applications and support many thousands, even millions, of users. When multiple organizations implement interoperable federated identity schemes, an employee in one organization can use single sign-on to access services across the federation with trust relationships associated with the identity. For example, an employee may log on to her corporate intranet and be authenticated to perform authorized functions and access authorized services on that intranet. The employee could then access her health benefits from an outside health care provider without having to reauthenticate.

Beyond SSO, federated identity management provides other capabilities. One is a standardized means of representing attributes. Increasingly, digital identities incorporate attributes other than simply an identifier and authentication information (e.g., passwords, biometric information). Examples of attributes include account numbers, organization roles, physical location, and file ownership. And a user may have multiple identifiers, such as identifiers associated with multiple roles, each with its own access permissions.

Another key function of federated identity management is identity mapping. Different security domains may represent identities and attributes differently. Further, the amount of information associated with an individual in one domain may be more than is necessary in another domain. The federated identity management protocols map identities and attributes of a user in one domain to the requirements of another domain.

Figure 5.8 illustrates entities and data flows in a generic federated identity management architecture.

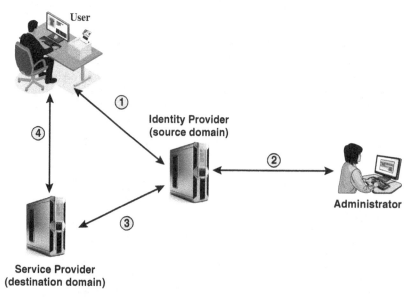

FIGURE 5.8 Federated Identity Operation

The numbered links in Figure 5.8 indicate the following actions:

1. The end user's browser or other application engages in an authentication dialogue with the identity provider in the same domain. The end user also provides attribute values associated with the user's identity.

2. Some attributes associated with an identity, such as allowable roles, may be provided by an administrator in the same domain.

3. A service provider in a remote domain, which the user wishes to access, obtains identity information, authentication information, and associated attributes from the identity provider in the source domain.

4. A service provider opens a session with a remote user and enforces access control restrictions based on the user's identity and attributes.

The identity provider acquires attribute information through dialogue and protocol exchanges with users and administrators. For example, a user needs to provide a shipping address each time an order is placed at a new web merchant, and this information needs to be revised when the user moves. Identity management enables the user to provide this information once, so that it is maintained in a single place and released to data consumers in accordance with authorization and privacy policies.

Service providers are entities that obtain and employ data maintained and provided by identity providers, often to support authorization decisions and to collect audit information. For example, a database server or file server is a data consumer that needs a client's credentials in order to know what access to provide to that client. A service provider can be in the same domain as the user and the identity provider. The power of this approach is for federated identity management, in which the service provider is in a different domain (e.g., a vendor or supplier network).

The goal is to share digital identities so a user can be authenticated once and then can access applications and resources across multiple domains, such as autonomous internal business units, external business partners, and other third-party applications and services. The cooperating organizations form a federation based on agreed standards and mutual levels of trust to securely share digital identities. Federated identity management reduces the number of authentications needed by the user.

5.6   Key Terms and Review Questions

Key Terms

access	environment attribute
access control	federated identity management
access control list	group
access control mechanism	identification
access control policy	identity and access management (IAM)
access control service	identity proofing
access matrix	inherence factor
access right	knowledge factor
applicant	mandatory access control (MAC)
attribute-based access control (ABAC)	multifactor authentication
attribute metadata	need-to-know
authentication	need-to-use
authentication factor	object
authenticator	object attribute
authorization	owner
biometrics	PII principal
capability ticket	possession factor
claimant	relying party (RP)
connected hardware token	resource
credential	role-based access control (RBAC)
credential service provider (CSP)	single sign-on (SSO)
digital authentication	subject
digital identity	subject attribute
disconnected hardware token	subscriber
discretionary access control (DAC)	system access

user authentication	verifier
verification	world

Review Questions

1. Explain the difference between authorization, authentication, and access control.
2. What is the difference between need-to-know and need-to-use?
3. Describe the process for authorizing users.
4. In the context of user authentication, what is the distinction between identification and verification?
5. Describe the functions of the various components in Figure 5.2.
6. Describe the three principal authentication factors.
7. What is multifactor authentication?
8. Describe four common access control policies.
9. What is the difference between an access control list and a capability ticket?
10. What is the difference between role-based access control and attribute-based access control?
11. What is identity and access management?
12. Describe three deployment approaches for identity and access management.
13. What is federated identity management?
14. What is meant by single sign-on?

5.7 Reference

STAL19: Stallings, W. *Effective Cybersecurity: A Guide to Using Best Practices and Standards.* Upper Saddle River, NJ: Pearson Addison Wesley, 2019.

Chapter | 6

Malicious Software and Intruders

Learning Objectives

After studying this chapter, you should be able to:

- Discuss malware protection strategies
- Understand the requirements for malware protection software
- Explain the role of firewalls as part of a computer and network security strategy
- List the key characteristics of firewalls
- Describe the principal approaches to intrusion detection

Chapter 5, "System Access," discussed the key ingredients of system access capabilities, including authorization, authentication, and access control. The purpose of system access capabilities is to regulate access to information and system resources from human users and programs. System access is an essential part of information security but also provides information privacy protection.

From both information security and information privacy perspectives, the general threat to a system access facility is the risk of intrusion from unauthorized software and users. Adversary techniques to overcome system access protection fall into two broad categories:

- **Malicious software (malware):** Software that exploits vulnerabilities in a computing system to create an attack. These malicious programs can perform a variety of different functions, such as stealing, encrypting or deleting sensitive data, altering or hijacking core computing functions, and monitoring users' computer activity without their permission.

- **Intrusion:** Unauthorized access to a computer system or network.

Both malware and intrusions constitute obvious security threats. Once malware or an intruder have achieved unauthorized access, it may be possible to compromise the confidentiality, integrity, or availability of system resources and data. Similarly, any form of unauthorized access to systems that collect, store, process, or distribute personally identifiable information (PII) constitutes a privacy threat.

This chapter looks at the common approaches to defending against malware and intrusion. Sections 6.1 and 6.2 discuss the nature of malicious software and examine approaches to protect systems from being infected with it. Section 6.3 describes firewalls, which are commonly used to protect networked IT systems from both malware and intrusions. Section 6.4 defines the concept of intrusion detection and looks at approaches to constructing and deploying intrusion detection systems.

6.1 Malware Protection Activities

Malicious software, commonly called *malware*, is perhaps the most significant security threat to organizations. NIST SP 800-83 (*Guide to Malware Incident Prevention and Handling for Desktops and Laptops*) defines malware as "a program that is covertly inserted into another program with the intent to destroy data, run destructive or intrusive programs, or otherwise compromise the confidentiality, integrity, or availability of the victim's data, applications, or operating system." Hence, malware can pose a threat to application programs; to utility programs, such as editors and compilers; and to kernel-level programs. Malware can also be used on compromised or malicious websites and servers, and in specially crafted spam emails or other messages that aim to trick users into revealing sensitive personal information.

Malware authors use a variety of means to spread software that infects devices and networks. Malware can be unknowingly downloaded from compromised or malicious websites and servers. Malware can be delivered in emails or other messages. Malware can be delivered over the Internet by programs that are able to bypass or compromise system access controls. And malware can be physically delivered with an infected USB drive.

This section begins with a brief survey of types of malware and then discusses best practices for malware protection.

Types of Malware

Although the terminology related to malware is not consistent, the following list provides a useful guide to the various types of malware:

- **Adware:** Advertising that is integrated into software. It can result in pop-up ads or redirection of a browser to a commercial site.

- **Auto-rooter:** A malicious hacker tool used to break into new machines remotely.

- **Bot:** Short for robot, a type of software application or script that performs tasks on command, allowing an attacker to take complete control remotely of an affected computer. The compromised machine may also be referred to as a *zombie*. A collection of these infected computers is known as a *botnet*.

- **Backdoor (trapdoor):** Any mechanism that bypasses a normal security check; it may allow unauthorized access to functionality.

- **Cryptojacking:** This involves taking over computing resources on an enterprise machine to mine cryptocurrency. The enterprise need not be involved in the use of cryptocurrency. The threat is the loss of processing and memory resources to the cryptojacker.

- **Downloader:** A program that installs other items on a machine that is under attack. Usually, a downloader is sent in an email message.

- **Dropper:** A malware installer that surreptitiously carries viruses, backdoors, and other malicious software to be executed on the compromised machine. Droppers don't cause harm directly but can deliver malware payloads onto target machines without detection.

- **Exploit:** Code specific to a single vulnerability or set of vulnerabilities.

- **Polymorphic dropper:** Also called a polymorphic packer, a software exploit tool that bundles several types of malware into a single package, such as an email attachment, and that can force its "signature" to mutate over time, making it difficult to detect and remove.

- **Flooder:** A tool used to attack networked computer systems with a large volume of traffic to carry out a denial-of-service (DoS) attack.

- **Keylogger:** A tool that captures keystrokes on a compromised system.

- **Kit (virus generator):** A set of tools for generating new viruses automatically.

- **Logic bomb:** A program inserted into software by an intruder that lies dormant until a predefined condition is met; the program then triggers an unauthorized act.

- **Malware as a service (MaaS):** Web-based provision of malware. MaaS may provide access to botnets, support hotlines, and servers that regularly update and test malware strains for efficacy.

- **Mobile code:** Software (e.g., script, macro, or other portable instruction) that can be shipped unchanged to a heterogeneous collection of platforms and executed with identical semantics.

- **Potentially unwanted program (PUP):** A program that may be unwanted, despite the possibility that users consented to download it. PUPs include spyware, adware, and dialers, and they are often downloaded in conjunction with programs that users want.

- **Ransomware:** A type of malware in which the data on a victim's computer is locked, typically by encryption, and payment is demanded before the ransomed data is decrypted and access returned to the victim.

- **Remote access Trojan (RAT):** A malware program that includes a backdoor for administrative control over the target computer. RATs are usually downloaded invisibly with a user-requested program (such as a game) or sent as an email attachment.

- **Rootkit:** A set of hacker tools used after an attacker has broken into a computer system and gained root-level access.

- **Scraper:** A simple program that searches a computer's memory for sequences of data that match particular patterns, such as credit card numbers. Point-of-sale terminals and other computers usually encrypt payment card data when storing and transmitting it, and attackers often use scrapers to locate card numbers in memory before they are encrypted or after they are decrypted for processing.

- **Spammer program:** A program that is used to send large volumes of unwanted email.

- **Spyware:** Software that collects information from a computer and transmits it to another system.

- **Trojan horse:** A computer program that appears to have a useful function but also has a hidden and potentially malicious function that evades security mechanisms, sometimes by exploiting legitimate authorizations of a system entity that invokes the Trojan horse program.

- **Virus:** Malware that, when executed, tries to replicate itself into other executable code; when it succeeds, the code is said to be *infected*. When the infected code is executed, the virus also executes.

- **Web drive-by:** An attack that infects a user system when the user visits a web page.

- **Worm:** A computer program that can run independently and can propagate a complete working version of itself onto other hosts on a network.

The Nature of the Malware Threat

The annual threat report from the European Union Agency for Network and Information Security [ENIS19] lists malware as the top cyber threat for 2017 and 2018. Key findings of the report include the following:

- Malware is the most frequently encountered cyberthreat and somehow involved in 30% of all data breach incidents reported.

- New types of malware attacks increasingly target IoT (Internet of Things) devices.

- Mobile malware threats increase year-over-year, and the continued use of older operating systems amplifies the problem. Major mobile threats include credential theft, mobile remote access trojans, and SIM card abuse/hijacking.

- Adversaries are moving from the use of ransomware to cryptojacking. The motivation is that cryptojacking is simpler, more profitable, and less risky to the adversary.

- **Clickless malware**, which is automated malware injection programs that do not require user action to activate, is presenting an increasing threat.

- There has been a rise in **fileless malware**, which is malware code that resides in RAM (random access memory) or propagates through the use of carefully crafted scripts, such as PowerShell, to infect its host.

- There has been growth in the use of open-source malware. Cyber-crime groups as well as cyber espionage groups have been extensively leveraging open source and publicly available tools for their campaigns. The goals of this approach are to make attribution efforts harder and to reduce their toolset development costs.

Practical Malware Protection

The battle against malware is never-ending. It is in effect an ongoing arms race between malware producers and defenders. As effective countermeasures are developed for existing malware threats, newer types and modifications of existing types of threats are developed. Malware can enter through a variety of attack surfaces, including end-user devices, email attachments, web pages, cloud services, user actions, and removable media. Malware can be designed to avoid, attack, or disable defenses. And malware is constantly evolving to stay ahead of existing defenses.

Given the complexity of the challenge, organizations need to automate anti-malware actions as much as possible. Figure 6.1, based on a figure from *The CIS Critical Security Controls for Effective Cyber Defense* [CIS18], indicates typical elements. Effective malware protection must be deployed at multiple potential points of attack. Enterprise endpoint security suites should provide administrative features to verify that all defenses are active and current on every managed system. There should be systems in place to collect ongoing incident results, with appropriate analysis and automated corrective action.

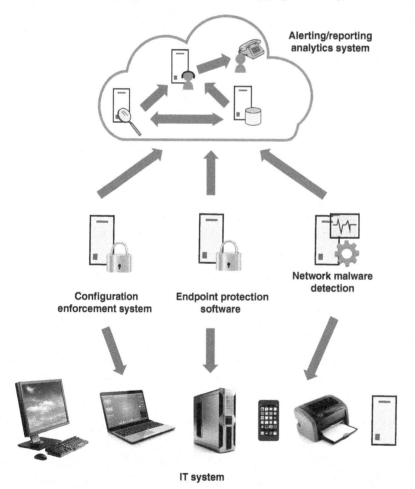

FIGURE 6.1   Malware Entity Relationship Diagram

IT management can implement a number of practical measures to provide the best possible protection at any given time, including the following:

- Define procedures and responsibilities to deal with malware protection on systems, training in their use, reporting, and recovering from malware attacks.

- Where practical, avoid granting administrative or root/superuser privileges to end users. This limits the damage that can be done by malware that is able to gain the status of an authenticated user on a system.

- Have a system and policies in place to keep track of where sensitive data is located, to erase data when no longer needed, and to concentrate security resources on systems containing sensitive data.

- Conduct regular reviews of the software and data content of systems supporting critical business processes; the presence of any unapproved files or unauthorized amendments should be formally investigated. Typically, most of this process is automated.

- Ensure that user and server platforms are well managed. This is especially important with Windows platforms, which continue to be a major target. Tasks include:

  - Install security updates as soon as available. Patch management software or outsourced services can help in this regard.

  - Enforce password selection policies to prevent password-guessing malware from infecting systems.

  - Monitor systems for new unexplained listening network ports. This includes not just servers, workstations, and mobile devices but also network devices such as routers and firewalls, as well as connected office equipment such as printers and fax machines.

- Ensure that key staff (e.g., information security specialists, IT personnel responsible for system and application software) regularly participate in security training and awareness events that cover malware.

- Establish a formal policy (as part of an acceptable use policy) prohibiting the use of unauthorized software.

- Install and appropriately maintain endpoint defenses. These could include:

  - Using centrally managed antivirus and anti-spyware software where appropriate. An example is Microsoft System Center Endpoint Protection.

  - Enabling and appropriately configuring host-based firewalls where practical.

  - Enabling and appropriately configuring host-based intrusion prevention where practical.

  - Where feasible, making available protection software that is licensed for personal use.

- Use DNS (Domain Name System)-based protection where practicable. Some malware allows attackers to hijack the DNS settings of PCs, home gateways, and applications. Armed with that information, the attackers can then mount man-in-the-middle attacks, overwriting DNS settings on the subscriber's computer or home gateway to new fraudulent or malicious targets. Such a change effectively allows the attacker to take over traffic (hijack) for the unsuspecting Internet broadband consumer [MAAW10].

- Use web filtering software, services, or appliances where practical. Examples of useful tools are the free Squid caching proxy, Forcepoint Web Security, and Microsoft Forefront Threat Management Gateway.

- Implement application whitelisting where practical. This allows systems to run software only if it is included on the whitelist and prevents execution of all other software on the system.

- Implement controls that prevent or detect the use of known or suspected malicious websites (e.g., blacklisting).

- Employ software or services that enable you to know where you are vulnerable. Examples are the Nmap, which is open source, and Metasploit, which has an open source version and a commercial version. Commercial tools include Nessus and Rapid7.

- Gather vulnerability and threat information from online sources, as discussed in Chapter 4, "Information Privacy Threats and Vulnerabilities." Additional resources include:

  - Google's hostmaster tools to scan your sites and report malware.

  - Dshield, a service of the Internet Storm Center, provides a variety of tools.

- Monitor available logs and network activity for indicators of malicious software. This includes:

  - Regularly checking antivirus logs.

  - Regularly checking DNS traffic for queries to known malware hosting domains.

  - Centralizing event log management and applying appropriate logic to identify out-of-spec results. An example of a tool that facilitates this is Microsoft System Center Operations Manager.

  - Subscribing to Shadowserver notifications for networks you manage. The Shadowserver Foundation is an all-volunteer, nonprofit, vendor-neutral organization that gathers, tracks, and reports on malicious software, botnet activity, and electronic fraud. It discovers the presence of compromised servers, malicious attackers, and the spread of malicious software. This reporting service is provided free of charge and is designed for organizations that directly own or control network space. It allows them to receive customized reports detailing detected malicious activity to assist in their detection and mitigation program.

- Have a backup strategy for your endpoints. Ensure that the backup stream is encrypted over the Internet and enterprise networks.

- Enable employees to report problems to IT security. In this regard, useful measures are:

    - All relevant points of contact should have current information in whois. This is an Internet program that allows users to query a database of people and other Internet entities, such as domains, networks, and hosts. The information stored includes a person's company name, address, phone number, and email address.

    - Use standard abuse reporting addresses, as specified in RFC 2142 (*Mailbox Names for Common Services, Roles and Functions*).

    - Make sure your domain or domains are available at the Network Abuse Clearinghouse, which enables targets to report the origin of an unwanted message.

6.2 Malware Protection Software

The term *malware protection software* refers to automated tools used to mitigate threats from a broad range of ever-evolving malware. This section first examines the types of capabilities that are desirable in malware protection software and then examines management issues.

Capabilities of Malware Protection Software

Numerous open source and commercial malware protection software packages are available for enterprise use, with similar capabilities. SP 800-83 lists the following as desired capabilities in malware protection software:

- Scanning critical host components such as startup files and boot records.

- Watching real-time activities on hosts to check for suspicious activity; a common example is scanning all email attachments for known malware as emails are sent and received. Anti-malware software should be configured to perform a real-time scan of each file as it is downloaded, opened, or executed; this is known as *on-access scanning*.

- Monitoring the behavior of common applications, such as email clients, web browsers, and instant messaging software. Anti-malware software should monitor activity involving the applications most likely to be used to infect hosts or spread malware to other hosts.

- Scanning files for known malware. Anti-malware software on hosts should be configured to scan all hard drives regularly to identify any file system infections and, optionally, depending on organization security needs, to scan removable media inserted into the host before allowing its use. Users should also be able to launch a scan manually as needed; this is known as *on-demand scanning*.

- Identifying common types of malware as well as attacker tools.

- ***Disinfecting*** files, which refers to removing malware from within a file, and ***quarantining*** files, which means that files containing malware are stored in isolation for future disinfection or examination. Disinfecting a file is generally preferable to quarantining it because the malware is removed and the original file restored; however, many infected files cannot be disinfected. Therefore, anti-malware software should be configured to attempt to disinfect infected files and to either quarantine or delete files that cannot be disinfected.

Malware protection software does not provide the same level of protection against previously unknown viruses or other malware as it does against known threats and attack signatures. Therefore, enterprises should also have in place other measures, including:

- Application sandboxing

- Intrusion detection software to scan for anomalous behavior (discussed later in this chapter)

- Awareness training providing guidance to users on malware incident prevention

- Firewalls that by default deny unexpected behavior patterns (discussed later in this chapter)

- Application whitelisting to prevent intrusion of unknown software

- Virtualization and container techniques to segregate applications or operating systems from each other

Managing Malware Protection Software

With any form of software installed on enterprise systems, including malware protection software, an organization should have specific management policies for the life cycle of the software. Management policy should dictate the following measures:

- Have documented procedures for selecting, installing, configuring, updating, and reviewing malware protection software

- Deploy malware protection software on all systems exposed to malware, including those that are connected to networks or the Internet, support the use of portable storage devices, or are accessed by multiple external suppliers

- Ensure that the installed suite of malware protection software protects against all forms of malware

- Maintain a schedule for automatic and timely distribution of malware protection software

- Configure malware protection software to be active at all times, provide notification when suspected malware is detected, and remove malware and any associated files immediately upon detection

- Regularly review devices to ensure that designated malware protection software is installed, enabled, and configured properly

6.3 Firewalls

A firewall is an important complement to host-based security services such as intrusion detection systems. Typically, a firewall is inserted between the premises network and the Internet to establish a controlled link and to erect an outer security wall or perimeter. The aim of this perimeter is to protect the premises network from Internet-based attacks and to provide a single choke point where security and auditing can be imposed. Firewalls are also deployed within an enterprise network to segregate portions of the network. A final deployment choice is a host-based firewall, which is a software module used to secure an individual host. Such modules are available in many operating systems or can be provided as add-on packages. Like conventional standalone firewalls, host-resident firewalls filter and restrict the flow of packets.

A firewall provides an additional layer of defense, insulating internal systems from external networks or other parts of the internal network. This follows the classic military doctrine of "defense in depth," which is just as applicable to IT security.

Firewall Characteristics

The article "Network Firewalls" from *IEEE Communications Magazine* [BELL94] lists the following design goals for a firewall:

- All traffic to and from the premises network must pass through the firewall. This is achieved by physically blocking all access to the local network except via the firewall. Various configurations are possible, as explained later in this chapter.

- Based on the local security policy, the firewall should permit only authorized traffic to pass. Various types of firewalls implement various types of security policies, as explained later in this chapter.

- The firewall itself must be secure. This implies the use of a hardened system with a secured operating system. Trusted computer systems are suitable for hosting a firewall and are often required in government applications.

In general terms, firewalls use four techniques to control access and enforce a site's security policy. Originally, firewalls focused primarily on service control, but they have since evolved to provide all four types of control:

- **Service control:** Determines the types of Internet services that can be accessed (inbound or outbound). The firewall may filter traffic on the basis of IP address, protocol, or port number; may provide proxy software that receives and interprets each service request before passing it on; or may host the server software itself, such as a web or mail service.

- **Direction control:** Determines the direction in which particular service requests may be initiated and allowed to flow through the firewall.

■ **User control:** Controls access to a service according to which user is attempting to access it. This feature is typically applied to users inside the firewall perimeter (local users). It may also be applied to incoming traffic from external users; the latter requires some form of secure authentication technology, such as is provided in IPsec.

■ **Behavior control:** Controls how particular services are used. For example, the firewall may filter email to eliminate spam, or it may enable external access to only a portion of the information on a local web server.

Before proceeding to the details of firewall types and configurations, it is best to summarize what you can expect from a firewall. The following capabilities are within the scope of a firewall:

■ A firewall defines a single choke point that keeps unauthorized users out of the protected network, prohibits potentially vulnerable services from entering or leaving the network, and provides protection from various kinds of IP spoofing and routing attacks. The use of a single choke point simplifies security management because security capabilities are consolidated on a single system or set of systems.

■ A firewall provides a location for monitoring security-related events. Audits and alarms can be implemented on the firewall system.

■ A firewall is a convenient platform for several Internet functions that are not security related. These include a network address translator, which maps local addresses to Internet addresses, and a network management function that audits or logs Internet usage.

■ A firewall can serve as the platform for implementing virtual private networks.

Firewalls have limitations, including the following:

■ A firewall cannot protect against attacks that bypass the firewall. Internal systems may have dial-out capability to connect to an ISP. An internal LAN may support a modem pool that provides dial-in capability for traveling employees and telecommuters.

■ A firewall may not protect fully against internal threats, such as disgruntled employees or employees who unwittingly cooperate with external attackers.

■ An improperly secured wireless LAN might be accessed from outside the organization. An internal firewall that separates portions of an enterprise network cannot guard against wireless communications between local systems on different sides of the internal firewall.

■ A laptop, mobile phone, or portable storage device might be used and infected outside the corporate network and then attached and used internally.

Types of Firewalls

A firewall can act as a packet filter. It can operate as a positive filter, allowing to pass only packets that meet specific criteria, or as a negative filter, rejecting any packets that meet certain criteria. Depending on the type of firewall, it might examine one or more protocol headers in each packet, the payload of each packet, or the pattern generated by a sequence of packets. In this section, we look at the principal types of firewalls.

Packet Filtering Firewall

A packet filtering firewall applies a set of rules to each incoming and outgoing IP packet and then forwards or discards the packet (see part b of Figure 6.2).

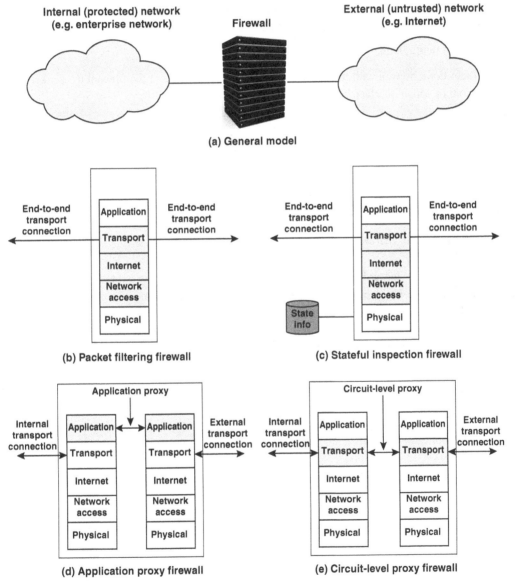

FIGURE 6.2 Types of Firewalls

A firewall is typically configured to filter packets going in both directions (from and to the internal network). Filtering rules are based on information contained in a network packet:

- **Source IP address:** The IP address of the system that originated the IP packet (e.g., 192.178.1.1)

- **Destination IP address:** The IP address of the system the IP packet is trying to reach (e.g., 192.168.1.2)

- **Source and destination transport-level address:** The transport-level (e.g., TCP or UDP) port number, which defines applications such as email and file transfer applications

- **IP protocol field:** Defines the transport protocol

- **Interface:** For a firewall with three or more ports, which interface of the firewall the packet came from or which interface of the firewall the packet is destined for

A packet filter is typically set up as a list of rules based on matches to fields in the IP header or TCP header. If there is a match to one of the rules, that rule is invoked to determine whether to forward or discard the packet. If there is no match to any rule, then a default action is taken. Two default policies are possible:

- **Default = discard:** That which is not expressly permitted is prohibited.

- **Default = forward:** That which is not expressly prohibited is permitted.

The first policy, default = discard, is more conservative. Initially, everything is blocked, and services must be added on a case-by-case basis. This policy is more visible to users, who are more likely to see the firewall as a hindrance. However, this is the policy likely to be preferred by businesses and government organizations. Further, visibility to users diminishes as rules are created. The default = forward policy increases ease of use for end users but provides reduced security; a security administrator must, in essence, react to each new security threat as it becomes known. This policy may be used by generally more open organizations, such as universities.

Table 6.1 gives some examples of packet filtering rule sets. In each set, the rules are applied top to bottom. The * in a field is a wildcard designator that matches everything. This table assumes that the default = discard policy is in force.

TABLE 6.1   Packet-Filtering Example

Rule Set A					
action	**ourhost**	**Port**	**theirhost**	**port**	**comment**
block	*	*	SPIGOT	*	we don't trust these people
allow	OUR-GW	25	*	*	connection to our SMTP port

Rule Set B					
action	**ourhost**	**port**	**theirhost**	**port**	**comment**
block	*	*	*	*	default

Rule Set C					
action	**ourhost**	**port**	**theirhost**	**port**	**comment**
allow	*	*	*	25	connection to their SMTP port

Rule Set D						
action	**src**	**port**	**dest**	**port**	**flags**	**comment**
allow	{our hosts}	*	*	25		our packets to their SMTP port
allow	*	25	*	*	ACK	their replies

Rule Set E						
action	**src**	**port**	**dest**	**port**	**flags**	**comment**
allow	{our hosts}	*	*	*		our outgoing calls
allow	*	*	*	*	ACK	replies to our calls
allow	*	*	*	>1024		traffic to nonservers

The rule sets in Table 6.1 are as follows:

- **Rule Set A:** Inbound mail is allowed (port 25 is for SMTP incoming) but only to a gateway host. However, packets from a particular external host, SPIGOT, are blocked because that host has a history of sending massive files in email messages.

- **Rule Set B:** This is an explicit statement of the default policy. All rule sets include this rule implicitly as the last rule.

- **Rule Set C:** This rule set is intended to specify that any inside host can send mail to the outside. A TCP packet with a destination port of 25 is routed to the SMTP server on the destination machine. The problem with this rule is that the use of port 25 for SMTP receipt is only a default; an outside machine could be configured to have some other application linked to port 25. As this rule is written, an attacker could gain access to internal machines by sending packets with a TCP source port number of 25.

■ **Rule Set D:** This rule set achieves the intended result that was not achieved in C. The rules take advantage of a feature of TCP connections: Once a connection is set up, the ACK flag of a TCP segment is set to acknowledge segments sent from the other side. Thus, this rule set states that it allows IP packets where the source IP address is one of a list of designated internal hosts and the destination TCP port number is 25. It also allows incoming packets with a source port number of 25 that include the ACK flag in the TCP segment. Note that we explicitly designate source and destination systems to define these rules explicitly.

■ **Rule Set E:** This rule set is one approach to handling FTP connections. With FTP, two TCP connections are used: a control connection to set up the file transfer and a data connection for the actual file transfer. The data connection uses a different port number that is dynamically assigned for the transfer. Most servers, and hence most attack targets, use low-numbered ports; most outgoing calls tend to use a higher-numbered port, typically above 1023. Thus, this rule set allows:

  ■ Packets that originate internally

  ■ Reply packets to a connection initiated by an internal machine

  ■ Packets destined for a high-numbered port on an internal machine

This scheme requires that the systems be configured so that only the appropriate port numbers are in use.

Rule set E points out the difficulty in dealing with applications at the packet filtering level. Another way to deal with FTP and similar applications is either stateful packet filters or an application-level gateway, both described later in this section.

One advantage of a packet filtering firewall is its simplicity. Also, packet filters typically are transparent to users and are very fast. However, packet filters have the following weaknesses:

■ Because packet filtering firewalls do not examine upper-layer data, they cannot prevent attacks that take advantage of application-specific vulnerabilities or functions. For example, if a packet filtering firewall cannot block specific application commands and if a packet filtering firewall allows a given application, all functions available within that application will be permitted.

■ Because of the limited information available to the firewall, the logging functionality present in packet filtering firewalls is limited. Packet filter logs normally contain the same information used to make access control decisions (source address, destination address, and traffic type).

■ Most packet filtering firewalls do not support advanced user authentication schemes. Once again, this limitation is mostly due to the firewall's lack of upper-layer functionality.

■ Packet filtering firewalls are generally vulnerable to attacks and exploits that take advantage of problems within the TCP/IP specification and protocol stack, such as *network layer address spoofing*. Many packet filtering firewalls cannot detect a network packet in which the IP addressing information has been altered. Spoofing attacks are generally employed by intruders to bypass the security controls implemented in a firewall platform.

- Finally, due to the small number of variables used in access control decisions, packet filtering firewalls are susceptible to security breaches caused by improper configurations. In other words, it is easy to accidentally configure a packet filtering firewall to allow traffic types, sources, and destinations that should be denied based on an organization's information security policy.

Some of the attacks that can be made on packet filtering firewalls and the appropriate countermeasures are as follows:

- **IP address spoofing:** The intruder transmits packets from the outside with a source IP address field containing an address of an internal host. The attacker hopes that the use of a spoofed address will allow penetration of systems that employ simple source address security, in which packets from specific trusted internal hosts are accepted. The countermeasure is to discard a packet with an inside source address if the packet arrives on an external interface. In fact, this countermeasure is often implemented at a router external to the firewall.

- **Source routing attacks:** The source station specifies the route that a packet should take as it crosses the Internet, in the hope of bypassing security measures that do not analyze the source routing information. The countermeasure is to discard all packets that use this option.

- **Tiny fragment attacks:** The intruder uses the IP fragmentation option to create extremely small fragments and force the TCP header information into a separate packet fragment. This attack is designed to circumvent filtering rules that depend on TCP header information. Typically, a packet filter makes a filtering decision on the first fragment of a packet. All subsequent fragments of that packet are filtered out solely on the basis that they are part of the packet whose first fragment was rejected. The attacker hopes that the filtering firewall examines only the first fragment and that the remaining fragments are passed through. A tiny fragment attack can be defeated by enforcing a rule that the first fragment of a packet must contain a predefined minimum amount of the transport header. If the first fragment is rejected, the filter can remember the packet and discard all subsequent fragments.

Stateful Inspection Firewalls

A traditional packet filter makes filtering decisions on an individual packet basis and does not take into consideration any higher-layer context. To understand what is meant by *context* and why a traditional packet filter is limited with regard to context, a little background is needed. Most standardized applications that run on top of TCP follow a client/server model. For example, with Simple Mail Transfer Protocol (SMTP), email is transmitted from a client system to a server system. The client system generates new email messages, typically from user input. The server system accepts incoming email messages and places them in the appropriate user mailboxes. SMTP operates by setting up a TCP connection between client and server, in which the TCP server port number, which identifies the SMTP server application, is 25. The TCP port number for the SMTP client is a number between 1024 and 65535 that is generated by the SMTP client.

In general, when an application that uses TCP creates a session with a remote host, it creates a TCP connection in which the TCP port number for the remote (server) application is a number less than 1024, and the TCP port number for the local (client) application is a number between 1024 and 65535. The numbers less than 1024 are the "well known" port numbers and are assigned permanently to particular applications (e.g., 25 for server SMTP). The numbers between 1024 and 65535 are generated dynamically and have temporary significance only for the lifetime of a TCP connection.

A simple packet filtering firewall must permit inbound network traffic on all these high-numbered ports for TCP-based traffic to occur. This creates a vulnerability that can be exploited by unauthorized users. A stateful inspection packet firewall tightens up the rules for TCP traffic by creating a directory of outbound TCP connections, as shown in Table 6.2. There is an entry for each currently established connection. The packet filter allows incoming traffic to high-numbered ports only for those packets that fit the profile of one of the entries in this directory.

TABLE 6.2   Stateful Firewall Connection State Table Example

Source Address	Source Port	Destination Address	Destination Port	Connection State
192.168.1.100	1030	210.9.88.29	80	Established
192.168.1.102	1031	216.32.42.123	80	Established
192.168.1.101	1033	173.66.32.122	25	Established
192.168.1.106	1035	177.231.32.12	79	Established
223.43.21.231	1990	192.168.1.6	80	Established
219.22.123.32	2112	192.168.1.6	80	Established
210.99.212.18	3321	192.168.1.6	80	Established
24.102.32.23	1025	192.168.1.6	80	Established
223.21.22.12	1046	192.168.1.6	80	Established

A stateful packet inspection firewall reviews the same packet information as a packet filtering firewall, but it also records information about TCP connections (refer to part c of Figure 6.2). Some stateful firewalls also keep track of TCP sequence numbers to prevent attacks that depend on the sequence number, such as session hijacking. Some even inspect limited amounts of application data for some well-known protocols like FTP, IM, and SIPS commands, in order to identify and track related connections.

Application-Level Gateway

An application-level gateway, also called an *application proxy*, acts as a relay of application-level traffic (refer to part d of Figure 6.2). The user contacts the gateway using a TCP/IP application, such as an email or file transfer application, and the gateway asks the user for the name of the remote host to be accessed. When the user responds and provides a valid user ID and authentication information, the gateway contacts the application on the remote host and relays TCP segments containing the application data between the two endpoints. If the gateway does not implement the proxy code for a specific application, the service is not supported and cannot be forwarded across the firewall. Further, the gateway can be configured to support only specific features of an application that the network administrator considers acceptable, while denying all other features.

Application-level gateways tend to be more secure than packet filters. Rather than trying to deal with the numerous possible combinations that are to be allowed and forbidden at the TCP and IP levels, an application-level gateway needs only scrutinize a few allowable applications. In addition, it is easy to log and audit all incoming traffic at the application level.

A prime disadvantage of this type of gateway is the additional processing overhead on each connection. In effect, there are two spliced connections between the end users, with the gateway at the splice point, and the gateway must examine and forward all traffic in both directions.

Circuit-Level Gateway

A circuit-level gateway or *circuit-level proxy* (refer to part e of Figure 6.2) can be a standalone system or a specialized function performed by an application-level gateway for certain applications. As with an application gateway, a circuit-level gateway does not permit an end-to-end TCP connection; rather, the gateway sets up two TCP connections—one between itself and a TCP user on an inner host and one between itself and a TCP user on an outside host. When the two connections are established, the gateway typically relays TCP segments from one connection to the other without examining the contents. The security function consists of determining which connections will be allowed.

A typical use of circuit-level gateways is a situation in which the system administrator trusts the internal users. The gateway can be configured to support application-level or proxy service on inbound connections and circuit-level functions for outbound connections. In this configuration, the gateway can incur the processing overhead of examining incoming application data for forbidden functions but does not incur that overhead on outgoing data.

Next-Generation Firewalls

Next-generation firewalls are a class of firewalls that are implemented in either software or hardware and are capable of detecting and blocking complicated attacks by enforcing security measures at the protocol, port, and application levels. The difference between a standard firewall and a next-generation firewall is that the latter performs more in-depth inspection and in smarter ways. Next-generation firewalls also provide additional features such as active directory integration support, SSH and SSL inspection, and malware filtering based on reputation.

The common functionalities present in traditional firewalls—such as state inspection, virtual private networking, and packet filtering—are also present in next-generation firewalls. Next-generation firewalls are more capable of detecting application-specific attacks than standard firewalls and thus can prevent more malicious intrusions. They do full-packet inspection by checking the signatures and payload of packets for any anomalies or malware.

DMZ Networks

Figure 6.3 illustrates the difference between an internal firewall and an external firewall. An external firewall is placed at the edge of a local or enterprise network, just inside the boundary router that connects to the Internet or some wide area network (WAN). One or more internal firewalls protect the bulk of the enterprise network. Between these two types of firewalls are one or more networked devices in a region referred to as a DMZ (demilitarized zone) network. Systems that are externally accessible but need some protections are usually located on DMZ networks. Typically, the systems in the DMZ require or foster external connectivity, such as to a corporate website, an email server, or a DNS server.

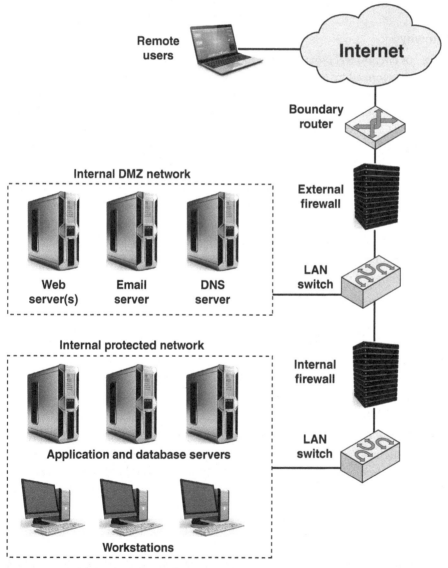

FIGURE 6.3   Example Firewall Configuration

The external firewall provides a measure of access control and protection for the DMZ systems consistent with the need for external connectivity. The external firewall also provides a basic level of protection for the remainder of the enterprise network. In this type of configuration, internal firewalls serve three purposes:

■ The internal firewall adds more stringent filtering capability compared to the external firewall in order to protect enterprise servers and workstations from external attack.

■ The internal firewall provides two-way protection with respect to the DMZ. First, the internal firewall protects the remainder of the network from attacks launched from DMZ systems. Such attacks might originate from worms, rootkits, bots, or other malware lodged in a DMZ system. Second, an internal firewall can protect the DMZ systems from attack from the internal protected network.

■ Multiple internal firewalls can be used to protect portions of the internal network from each other. For example, firewalls can be configured so that internal servers are protected from internal workstations and vice versa. A common practice is to place the DMZ on a different network interface on the external firewall from that used to access the internal networks.

The Modern IT Perimeter

Traditionally, the enterprise network perimeter was defined by the physical interface between network devices, such as routers, and external networks, such as the Internet and private WANs. For today's enterprise, the perimeter is better defined by each node on the network and not by the network itself. Key elements that can break traditional network perimeter security are the following:

■ **Wireless access points (APs):** Wi-Fi APs that are either unknowingly or maliciously deployed inside the enterprise network enable mobile devices on the premises or near the premises to gain access to resources on the enterprise network.

■ **Mobile devices:** Mobile devices create a host of security issues, many of which are addressed in Chapter 8, "Online Privacy." One issue specifically related to perimeter control is the ability of a mobile device to connect to the Internet via the cellular network. This makes it possible for a computer in the enterprise network to connect to the mobile device and through that device to the Internet, without going through perimeter firewalls.

The IBM redpaper *Understanding IT Perimeter Security* [BUEC08] suggests that the following elements should comprise network perimeter defense in a wireless environment:

■ The ability to globally enforce host-based security software deployed to the mobile systems known to access the enterprise network

■ Scanning for, discovering, and blocking unknown devices

■ Monitoring traffic patterns, communications, and transmitted data to discover how the enterprise network is being used and to uncover unwanted or threatening traffic from mobile devices

6.4   Intrusion Detection

The area of intrusion detection involves some specific terms:

- **Intrusion:** Violations of security policy, usually characterized as attempts to affect the confidentiality, integrity, or availability of a computer or network. These violations can come from attackers from a variety of internal and external sources, including accessing systems from the Internet or from internal authorized users of the systems attempting to overstep their legitimate authorization levels or using their legitimate access to the system to conduct unauthorized activity.

- **Intrusion detection:** The process of collecting information about events occurring in a computer system or network and analyzing them for signs of intrusions.

- **Intrusion detection system (IDS):** A hardware or software product that gathers and analyzes information from various areas within a computer or a network for the purpose of finding and providing real-time or near-real-time warning of attempts to access system resources in an unauthorized manner.

- **Intrusion prevention system (IPS):** An extension of an IDS that also includes the capability to attempt to block or prevent detected malicious activity. To a certain extent, an IPS can be viewed as a combination of an IDS and a firewall. A detailed discussion of IPSs is beyond the scope of this chapter.

Intrusion detection systems can be classified as follows:

- **Host-based IDS:** Monitors the characteristics of a single host and the events occurring within that host for suspicious activity. Host-based IDSs can determine exactly which processes and user accounts are involved in a particular attack on the OS. Furthermore, unlike network-based IDSs, host-based IDSs can more readily see the intended outcome of an attempted attack because they can directly access and monitor the data files and system processes usually targeted by attacks.

- **Network-based IDS:** Monitors network traffic for particular network segments or devices and analyzes network, transport, and application protocols to identify suspicious activity.

An IDS comprises three logical components:

- **Sensors:** Sensors are responsible for collecting data. The input for a sensor may be any part of a system that could contain evidence of an intrusion. Types of input to a sensor include network packets, log files, and system call traces. Sensors collect and forward this information to the analyzer.

- **Analyzers:** Analyzers receive input from one or more sensors or from other analyzers. An analyzer is responsible for determining if an intrusion has occurred. The output may include evidence supporting the conclusion that an intrusion occurred. The analyzer may provide guidance about what actions to take as a result of the intrusion.

- **User interface:** The user interface to an IDS enables a user to view output from the system or control the behavior of the system. In some systems, the user interface may equate to a manager, director, or console component.

Basic Intrusion Detection Principles

Authentication facilities, access control facilities, and firewalls all play roles in countering intrusions. Another line of defense is intrusion detection, and this has been the focus of much research in recent years. This interest is motivated by a number of considerations, including the following:

- If an intrusion is detected quickly enough, the intruder can be identified and ejected from the system before any damage is done or any data are compromised. Even if the detection is not sufficiently timely to preempt the intruder, the sooner that the intrusion is detected, the lower the amount of damage and the more quickly that recovery can be achieved.

- An effective IDS can serve as a deterrent, acting to prevent intrusions.

- Intrusion detection enables the collection of information about intrusion techniques that can be used to strengthen intrusion prevention measures.

Approaches to Intrusion Detection

Intrusion detection assumes that the behavior of the intruder differs from that of a legitimate user in ways that can be quantified. Of course, we cannot expect that there will be a crisp, exact distinction between an attack by an intruder and the normal use of resources by an authorized user. Rather, we must expect that there will be some overlap.

There are two general approaches to intrusion detection: misuse detection and anomaly detection (see Figure 6.4).

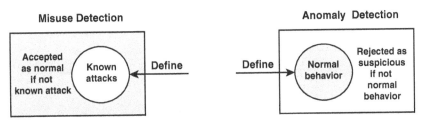

FIGURE 6.4 Approaches to Intrusion Detection

Misuse detection is based on rules that specify system events, sequences of events, or observable properties of a system that are believed to be symptomatic of security incidents. Misuse detectors use various pattern-matching algorithms, operating on large databases of attack patterns, or *signatures*. An advantage of misuse detection is that it is accurate and generates few false alarms. A disadvantage it that it cannot detect novel or unknown attacks.

Anomaly detection searches for activity that is different from the normal behavior of system entities and system resources. An advantage of anomaly detection is that it is able to detect previously unknown attacks based on an audit of activity. A disadvantage is that there is a significant tradeoff between false positives and false negatives. Figure 6.5 suggests, in abstract terms, the nature of the task confronting the designer of an anomaly detection system. Although the typical behavior of an intruder differs from the typical behavior of an authorized user, there is some overlap in these behaviors. Thus, a loose interpretation of intruder behavior, which will catch more intruders, will also lead to a number of *false positives*, or authorized users identified as intruders. On the other hand, an attempt to limit false positives by a tight interpretation of intruder behavior will lead to an increase in *false negatives*, or intruders not identified as intruders. Thus, there are elements of compromise and art in the practice of anomaly detection.

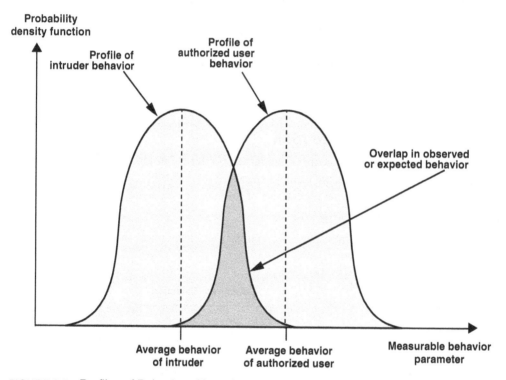

FIGURE 6.5 Profiles of Behavior of Intruders and Authorized Users

Table 6.3 clarifies the relationship between the terms false positive, true positive, false negative, and true negative.

TABLE 6.3 Test Outcomes

Test Result	Condition A Occurs	Condition A Does Not Occur
Test says "A"	True positive	False positive
Test says "NOT A"	False negative	True negative

Host-Based Intrusion Detection Techniques

Host-based IDSs add a specialized layer of security software to vulnerable or sensitive systems; examples include database servers and administrative systems. A host-based IDS monitors activity on a system in a variety of ways to detect suspicious behavior. In some cases, an IDS can halt an attack before any damage is done, but its primary purpose is to detect intrusions, log suspicious events, and send alerts.

The primary benefit of a host-based IDS is that it can detect both external and internal intrusions—something that is not possible with either network-based IDSs or firewalls.

Host-based IDSs use one or a combination of anomaly and misuse protection. For anomaly detection, two common strategies are:

- **Threshold detection:** This approach involves defining thresholds, independent of user, for the frequency of occurrence of various events.

- **Profile based:** A profile of the activity of each user is developed and used to detect changes in the behavior of individual accounts.

Network-Based Intrusion Detection Systems

A network-based ID (NIDS) monitors the traffic on its network segment as a data source. This is generally accomplished by placing the network interface card in promiscuous mode to capture all network traffic that crosses its network segment. Network traffic on other segments and traffic on other means of communication (like phone lines) can't be monitored by a single NIDS.

NIDS Function

Network-based intrusion detection involves looking at the packets on the network as they pass by some sensor. Packets are considered to be of interest if they match a signature. Three primary types of signatures are:

- **String signatures:** This type of signature looks for a text string that indicates a possible attack. An example of a string signature for Unix might be "cat "+ +" > /.rhosts", which, if successful, might cause a Unix system to become extremely vulnerable to network attack. To refine the string signature to reduce the number of false positives, it might be necessary to use a compound string signature. A compound string signature for a common webserver attack might be "cgi-bin" AND "aglimpse" AND "IFS".

- **Port signatures:** These signatures simply watch for connection attempts to well-known, frequently attacked ports. Examples of these ports include Telnet (TCP port 23), FTP (TCP port 21/20), SUNRPC (TCP/UDP port 111), and IMAP (TCP port 143). If any of these ports aren't used by the site, incoming packets to these ports are suspicious.

■ **Header signatures:** These signatures watch for dangerous or illogical combinations in packet headers. A famous example is WinNuke, where a packet is destined for a NetBIOS port and the urgent pointer or out-of-band pointer is set. This results in the "blue screen of death" for Windows systems. Another well-known header signature is a TCP packet with both the SYN and FIN flags set, signifying that the requestor wishes to start and stop a connection at the same time.

NIDS Placement

An NIDS sensor can only see the packets that happen to be carried on the network segment to which it is attached. Therefore, a NIDS deployment is typically set up as a number of sensors distributed on key network points to passively gather traffic data and feed information on potential threats to a central NIDS manager. Figure 6.6 illustrates examples of NIDS sensor placement.

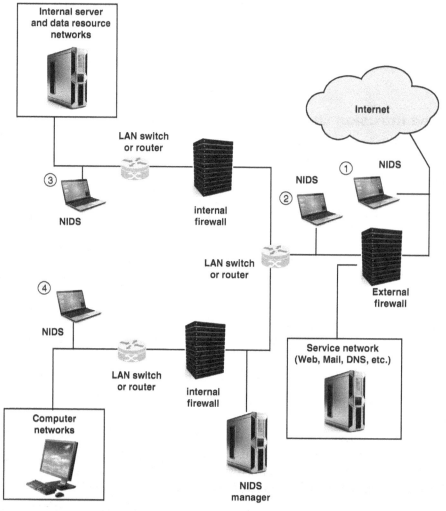

FIGURE 6.6   Example of NIDS Sensor Deployment

As shown in Figure 6.6, there are four types of locations for the sensors:

1. Outside the main enterprise firewall. This is useful for establishing the level of threat for a given enterprise network. Those responsible for winning management support for security efforts can find this placement valuable.

2. In the network DMZ (i.e., inside the main firewall but outside internal firewalls). This location can monitor for penetration attempts that target web and other services that are generally open to outsiders. The DMZ adds an additional layer of network security between the Internet and an organization's internal network so that external parties only have direct connections to devices in the DMZ rather than to the entire internal network. This provides external, untrusted sources with restricted access to releasable information while shielding the internal networks from outside attacks.

3. Behind internal firewalls, positioned to monitor major backbone networks, such as those that support internal servers and database resources.

4. Behind internal firewalls, positioned to monitor LANs that support user workstations and servers specific to a single department.

Locations 3 and 4 in Figure 6.6 can monitor for more specific attacks at network segments, as well as attacks originating from inside the organization.

IDS Best Practices

The following are some IDS suggestions that security managers might find helpful.

- Create a separate account for each IDS user or administrator.

- Restrict network access to IDS components.

- Ensure that IDS management communications are protected appropriately, such as by encrypting them or transmitting them over a physically or logically separate network.

- Back up IDS configuration settings periodically and before applying updates to ensure that existing settings are not inadvertently lost.

- Monitor and tune one IDS sensor at a time. This prevents security staff from being overwhelmed by alerts and false positives.

- Have alerts of a certain priority sent directly to a security administrator so attacks and other events that might require administration attention are quickly known. To reduce the noise, set alerts only to the risks the enterprise is most concerned about and don't rely on out-of-the box settings.

■ Use a log-and-alert correlation product in conjunction with the IDS. These correlation products can do several things. First, they can group alerts to reduce alert traffic so that batches of alerts or events arrive in more manageable increments. They also provide insight across multiple platforms, including network and host IDSs, firewalls, and syslog events from other systems. An example of such a product is Sguil, which is a free set of software packages.

A useful resource is SP 800-94 (*Guide to Intrusion Detection and Prevention Systems*). It contains a tutorial on IDS function and a range of recommendations related to the procurement and management of IDSs.

6.5 Key Terms and Review Questions

Key Terms

adware	false negative
analyzer	false positive
anomaly detection	flooder
application-level gateway	host-based intrusion detection system (HIDS)
auto-rooter	intrusion
backdoor	intrusion detection
behavior control	intrusion detection system (IDS)
bot	keylogger
circuit-level gateway	malware
clickless malware	logic bomb
direction control	malware as a service
downloaders	malware protection software
dropper	misuse detection
DMZ	mobile code
disinfect	network-based intrusion detection system (NIDS)
exploits	
fileless malware	next-generation firewall
firewall	packet filtering firewall

polymorphic dropper	spammer program
sensor	spyware
stateful inspection firewall	trapdoor
potentially unwanted program (PUP)	Trojan horse
quarantine	user control
ransomware	virus
remote access Trojan (RAT)	web drive-by
rootkit	worm
scraper	zombie
service control	

Review Questions

1. List some common types of malware.

2. With reference to SP 800-83, what are some desired capabilities of good malware protection software?

3. What is the difference between disinfecting and quarantining files?

4. Name all the techniques that firewalls use to control access and enforce a site's security policy.

5. What are some common types of firewalls?

6. What are some of the weaknesses of packet filters?

7. What is an intrusion detection system?

8. Describe the placement of intrusion detection systems.

9. What are two generic approaches to intrusion detection?

10. What is the difference between misuse detection and anomaly detection?

11. What are the typical locations for the sensors in network intrusion detection systems?

6.6 References

BELL94: Bellovin, S., and Cheswick, W. "Network Firewalls." *IEEE Communications Magazine*, September 1994.

BEUC09: Buecker, A., Andreas, P., and Paisley, S. *Understanding IT Perimeter Security*. IBM Redpaper REDP-4397-00, November 2009.

CIS18: Center for Internet Security. *The CIS Critical Security Controls for Effective Cyber Defense Version 7*. 2018. https://www.cisecurity.org

ENSI189: European Network and Information Security Agency. *ENISA Threat Landscape Report 2018*. January 2019. https://www.enisa.europa.eu

MAAW10: Messaging Anti-Abuse Working Group. *Overview of DNS Security - Port 53 Protection*. MAAWG Paper, June 2010. https://www.m3aawg.org

PART IV

Privacy Enhancing Technologies

Chapter | 7

Privacy in Databases

Learning Objectives

After studying this chapter, you should be able to:

- Explain the difference between summary tables and microdata tables
- Understand the concept of re-identification
- Present an overview of the types of re-identification attacks
- Explain the difference between anonymization and de-identification
- Discuss the importance of quasi-identifiers and how they pose a threat to privacy
- List and explain the basic techniques for privacy-preserving data publishing
- Explain and illustrate the concept of k-anonymity
- Discuss approaches to protecting frequency tables
- Discuss approaches to protecting magnitude tables
- Understand the nature of the privacy threat to queryable databases
- Discuss approaches to query restriction
- Discuss approaches to response perturbation
- Understand the concept of differential privacy

There are many instances in which an organization collects personally identifiable information (PII) and uses that information for authorized purposes. An example is an employee database that contains information about employees needed for paying wages, providing health insurance, and other applications related to human resources. Organizations may also use information about individuals in applications that do not require that the individuals be identified, such as actuarial or market research studies. In these latter cases, to preserve privacy, the organization providing the information transforms the PII in a dataset into summary information that is useful for the application but does not enable identification of individuals. Finally, organizations often maintain online query systems, either for accessing a database that contains PII or for accessing a database that contains summary information. In either case, the organization needs to be concerned about preserving privacy.

This chapter begins with a discussion in Section 7.1 of basic concepts related to privacy in databases. Section 7.2 then looks at the types of attacks and risks associated with databases containing personal information.

The remainder of the chapter addresses privacy concerns related to databases that contain PII or summary information derived from a database containing PII. The chapter covers the three main areas that involve the use of privacy-preserving techniques:

- Techniques that enable an organization to make available (publish) files consisting of records, with each record containing information on an individual. This type of file is known as a *microdata file*. Sections 7.3 through 7.5 describe these techniques.

- Techniques that enable an organization to publish files consisting of aggregate, or summary, statistics (e.g., means, counts). Section 7.6 covers these techniques.

- Techniques that allow online querying of microdata files that are otherwise not privacy protected. Section 7.7 covers these techniques.

The following standards and government documents are especially useful in understanding the range of techniques useful for protecting privacy in databases and for providing practical guidance on employing these techniques:

- **ISO 20889:** *Privacy Enhancing Data De-Identification Terminology and Classification of Techniques.* This 2018 document provides a good overview of basic concepts related to re-identification attacks. It also provides a thorough survey of de-identification techniques, including all of those covered in Sections 7.3 through 7.5 of this chapter.

- **NIST SP 800-188:** *De-Identifying Government Datasets.* This document provides specific guidance on the use of de-identification techniques.

- **NISTIR 8053:** *De-Identification of Personal Information.* This document provides a survey of de-identification techniques.

- **WP216:** *Opinion 05/2014 on Anonymisation Techniques.* This document, from the EU Data Protection Working Party, elaborates on the robustness of various anonymization and de-identification techniques.

- **SPWP22 – Statistical Policy Working Paper 22, Report on Statistical Disclosure Limitation Methodology:** This document from the U.S. Federal Committee on Statistical Methodology provides an overview of current practices in anonymization and de-identification.

7.1 Basic Concepts

Two terms that are commonly used in describing the obfuscation of PII for privacy purposes are *de-identification* and *anonymization*. Unfortunately, these terms are not consistently used in the literature. This chapter distinguishes between de-identification and anonymization in a way consistent with most standards and best practices documents.

The context for both de-identification and anonymization is the following: An organization collects PII on a group of individuals and stores it as a file of records, one per individual, often referred to as a *dataset*. Then, if the organization wants to use that dataset for an application or applications that do not require individual identification, the objective is to retain useful data while concealing information that identifies individuals and/or reducing the extent to which identifying information is able to be associated with individuals.

De-identification of PII has the following characteristics for each individual in the group:

- The remaining data do not suffice to associate identifying data to the PII principals to whom they relate.

- A re-identification parameter is associated with the de-identified data such that the combination of that parameter and the de-identified data enable identification of the associated PII principal.

- An adversary not in possession of the re-identification parameter cannot recover personal identities from the de-identified data by reasonable efforts.

Thus, de-identification retains the potential for recovering the identities associated with the de-identified data. Different data associated with the same re-identification parameter can be linked.

Anonymization of PII has the following characteristics for each individual in the group:

- The remaining data do not suffice to associate identifying data to the PII principals to whom they relate.

- An adversary cannot recover personal identities from the anonymized data by reasonable efforts.

Figure 7.1, from NISTIR 8053 (*De-Identification of Personal Information*), illustrates the de-identification or anonymization process. Data, including PII, are collected from data subjects (PII principals) and combined into a dataset that includes the PII of multiple individuals. De-identification or anonymization creates a new dataset that is assumed not to contain identifying data. Depending on the organizational context and mission, the organization may retain the original dataset for some applications, for which security and privacy controls are applied, or it may discard that dataset. In the latter case, the organization uses only the de-identified dataset to decrease privacy risk.

FIGURE 7.1   Data Collection, De-identification, and Use

The organization may use the de-identified data internally for specific applications. The organization may also make the dataset available to trusted data recipients who may be bound by additional controls such as data use agreements. The reason for the data use agreement, which limits the uses of the data by the recipients, is that even with de-identified or anonymized data, there is some residual risk of re-identification. For datasets for which the risk of re-identification is believed to be low or nonexistent, an organization might make the data broadly available to a larger number of unknown or unvetted data recipients.

Personal Data Attributes

Personal data consist of attributes related to individuals. With respect to privacy concerns, attributes can be classified as:

- **Direct identifier:** A variable that provides an explicit link to a data subject and can directly identify an individual. Examples of identifying variables include name, email address, home address, telephone number, health insurance number, and Social Security number. Direct identifiers are thus PII attributes.

- **Quasi-identifier (QI):** A QI by itself does not identify a specific individual, but QIs can be aggregated and linked with other information to identify data subjects. Examples of QIs include sex, marital status, postal code or other location information, a significant date (e.g., birth, death, hospital admission, discharge, autopsy, specimen collection, or visit), diagnostic information, profession, ethnic origin, visible minority status, and income. (An example in Section 7.2 of the re-identification of William Weld's medical records uses the QI's birthday, zip code, and sex.)

■ **Confidential attributes:** Attributes not in the PII or QI categories may contain sensitive data subject information (e.g., salary, religion, diagnosis).

■ **Non-confidential attributes:** Some attributes data subjects do not typically consider sensitive.

Types of Data Files

De-identification and anonymization are applicable to datasets that are released in some context to enable analysis by third parties and for which privacy concerns must be addressed.

The three most commonly used forms of data release are as follows:

■ **Microdata table:** A microdata table consists of individual records, each containing values of attributes for a single individual or other entity. Specifically, a microdata table X with s subjects and t attributes is an $s \times t$ matrix, where X_{ij} is the value of attribute j for data subject i.

■ **Summary table:** A summary table, also called a *macrodata table*, is typically two dimensional, with the rows and columns representing two different attributes. Thus, if the two attributes are A and B, the table can be expressed as A×B. A summary table contains aggregated data about individuals derived from microdata sources. For example, a table that presents counts of individuals by 5-year age categories and total annual income in increments of $10,000 is composed of statistical cells such as the cell (35–39 years of age, $40,000–$49,999 annual income). Summary tables are of two types:

　■ **Frequency table:** Presents the number of units of analysis (persons, households, establishments) in a table cell (an intersection of a table row and column). An example of this is a (race × sex) table in which the table cells show the counts of the people having these attributes for different attribute values. Equivalently, each cell may contain the percentage or fraction of the total population under study that fits in that cell.

　■ **Magnitude table:** Displays information on a numerical aggregate value in a table cell. An example of this is a (disease × town) table in which the table cells show the average age of patients having these attributes for different attribute values.

　Less common are one-dimensional or three-dimensional tables. These tables introduce no new privacy threats or countermeasures, and this chapter does not consider them.

■ **Queryable database:** Many organizations provide online query access to summary tables. Data users create their own tabulations with customized queries. In most of these systems, only data that have already had disclosure limitations applied are available to users. A query system that interfaces to an unprotected microdata file must automatically apply disclosure limitation rules to the requested tables. The concern with this approach is that users might be able to discern confidential data if they use a sequence of queries in which disclosure limitations are applied independently.

Figure 7.2 shows the relationship between the three concepts listed above. A microdata file with no privacy protection includes, for each individual record, direct identifiers, QIs, confidential attributes, and possibly non-confidential attributes. Anonymizing or de-identifying the unprotected file involves removing the direct identifiers and modifying the QIs (see Sections 7.3 through 7.5). Using aggregation, summary tables can be generated either from the unprotected microdata file or the protected microdata file. In the former case, aggregation includes algorithms for introducing privacy protection (see Section 7.6). Online querying of both protected microdata files and summary tables is common (see Section 7.7).

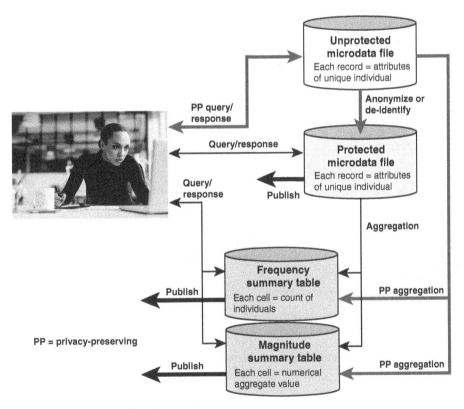

FIGURE 7.2   Releasable Datasets

Figure 7.3 illustrates the structure of microdata and summary tables.

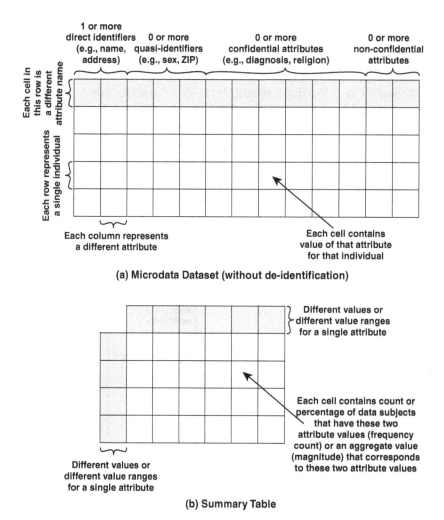

(a) Microdata Dataset (without de-identification)

(b) Summary Table

FIGURE 7.3   Search of Microdata Datasets and Summary Tables

Table 7.1 illustrates frequency and magnitude tables that contain measures computed over the attributes Sex and Diagnosis. Part a of Table 7.1 contains the number of males and females for each diagnosis over some total population of interest. Part b of Table 7.1 contains the percentage with each disease. The row totals in part b of Table 7.1 show the percentage of the total group that is male and female, respectively, and the column totals show the percentage of the total group that has each diagnosis. Part c of Table 7.1 shows the average number of days that males and females have spent in the hospital for each given disease. The row totals show the average number of days spent in the hospital, regardless of disease, for males and females. The column totals show the average stay for each disease.

TABLE 7.1 An Example of Frequency (Count and Percentage) and Magnitude Summary Tables

(a) Number of Individuals with a Disease(frequency table)

	Arthritis	Pneumonia	Diabetes	Heart Disease	TOTAL
M	10	18	19	12	59
F	19	17	1	6	43
TOTAL	29	35	20	18	102

(b) Percentage of Individuals with a Disease(frequency table)

	Arthritis	Pneumonia	Diabetes	Heart Disease	TOTAL
M	9.8	17.6	18.6	11.8	57.8
F	18.6	16.7	1.0	5.9	42.2
TOTAL	28.4	34.3	19.6	17.6	100

(c) Average Number of Days Spent in Hospital(magnitude table)

	Arthritis	Pneumonia	Diabetes	Heart Disease	AVERAGE
M	2	6.5	3.5	7	4.87
F	1	5.5	2	8	3.8
TOTAL	1.34	6.01	3.43	7.33	4.41

7.2 Re-Identification Attacks

As mentioned earlier in this chapter, even when a dataset has been de-identified or anonymized, there may remain some risk that an unauthorized party could re-identify that dataset. The threat of re-identification of de-identified or even anonymized data is a serious one. The document *Concerning the Re-Identification of Consumer Information*, from the Electronic Privacy Information Center [EPIC17], documents a number of examples of re-identification of de-identified or anonymized data, including the following:

- **Netflix study:** Netflix, an online video streaming service, publicly released 100 million records regarding how its users had rated movies over a six-year period. The records showed the movie, the rating the user had given, and the date the user had rated the movie. While identifying user-names had been removed, each user was given a unique identifying number. Researchers found that it was relatively easy to re-identify the individuals. According to the research, using only six movie ratings, one could identify the individual 84% of the time. With the six movie ratings and the approximate date of the ratings, one could identify the individual 99% of the time.

■ **AOL's release of user data:** In 2006, America Online (AOL) publicly posted 20 million search queries for 650,000 AOL search engine users. These queries summed up three months of activity. Before the data were released, AOL anonymized it by removing identifying information, such as the username and IP address. However, these identifiers were replaced with unique identification numbers so that researchers could still make use of the data. Even though the data were anonymized before the release, within a relatively short time, journalists were able to trace user queries to specific individuals. For example, many users made search queries that identified their city, or even neighborhood, their first and/or last name, and their age demographic. With such information, researchers were able to narrow down the population to the one individual responsible for the searches.

■ **Unique identification through zip code, sex, and birth date:** According to a study of census data by Latanya Sweeney [SWEE00], 87% of the American population has a unique combination of zip code, birth date, and sex. This means that the combination of these three pieces of information is enough to identify each of these individuals.

■ **Re-identifying health data:** Sweeney also illustrated the threat of re-identification of health data by gathering PII on William Weld, the governor of Massachusetts [SWEE02]. She combined data from two databases. One was a set of hospital data on state employees released to researchers by the Massachusetts Group Insurance Commission (GIC) for the purpose of improving health care and controlling costs. The hospital data provider removed names, addresses, Social Security numbers, and other identifying information in order to protect the privacy of these employees. The other dataset was publicly available voter registration rolls, which included the name, address, zip code, birth date, and sex of every voter. From GIC's databases, only six people in Cambridge were born on the same day as the governor, half of them were men, and the governor was the only one who lived in the zip code provided in the voter rolls. The information in the GIC database on the Massachusetts governor included prescriptions and diagnoses.

Thus, organizations that seek to de-identify or anonymize PII datasets must keep in mind the potential for re-identification either from the transformed dataset alone or in conjunction with other sources of data.

Types of Attacks

The upper part of Figure 7.4 illustrates the de-identification process and the general approaches to attacks that seek to identify individuals from a de-identified dataset. These attacks fall into two broad categories: security attacks and privacy attacks. In order for re-identification by authorized persons to be possible, there must be a link between re-identification parameters and individual identities. Security policy will dictate that only authorized persons have access to that linkage. Thus, an organization must implement security controls, such as system access controls, to limit re-identification to authorized persons. An adversary may attempt to overcome security controls in order to recover the linkage between re-identification parameters and individual identities.

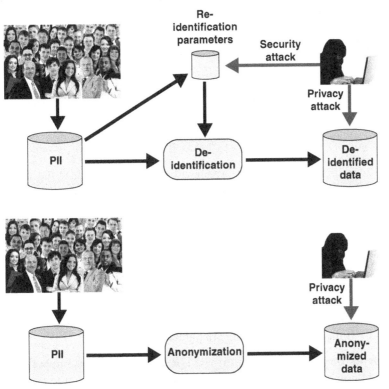

FIGURE 7.4   Types of Attacks on De-identified and Anonymized Data

An adversary may also attempt to re-identify data through an analysis of the de-identified data, perhaps with data from other datasets, such as publicly available datasets. Such attacks are privacy attacks that attempt to overcome the privacy controls used to de-identify the data.

The lower part of Figure 7.4 illustrates the anonymization process. In this case, there is no expectation that the anonymized data can be re-identified by the organization that performed the anonymization. Again, an adversary might attempt to re-identify the anonymized data through an analysis of those data and possibly related data.

Table 7.2 summarizes the privacy and security threats to PII.

TABLE 7.2   Threats to Personal Information

Type of Information	Authorized User	Adversary	
		Security Breach	**Privacy Breach**
PII	Controlled access	Defeat system access controls	Defeat privacy controls
De-identified personal information	Re-identify using re-identification parameters	Defeat access controls to re-identification parameters	Re-identify without re-identification parameters, possibly using multiple data sources
Anonymized data	Cannot re-identify	–	Re-identify using multiple data sources

Potential Attackers

In assessing the risk of a re-identification attack, an organization needs to consider the motivation of individuals who might attempt re-identification. NISTIR 8053 identifies the following categories:

- **To test the quality of the de-identification:** An organization may request that an internal or external auditor attempt re-identification as part of the overall privacy monitoring and auditing function.

- **To embarrass or harm the organization that performed the de-identification:** Demonstrating that inadequate privacy protection measures were employed can embarrass or harm an organization, especially if the de-identified data are publicly released.

- **To gain direct benefit from the re-identified data:** NISTIR 8053 gives the example that a marketing company might purchase de-identified health information and attempt to match up the information with identities so that the re-identified individuals can be sent targeted coupons for prescription medicines.

A responsible organization will allow the first category in the preceding list in order to ensure that the risks from the other two categories are minimized.

Disclosure Risks

In general terms, *disclosure* relates to inappropriate attribution of information to a data subject, whether an individual or an organization. The types of disclosure include the following:

- **Identity disclosure:** This type of disclosure occurs when a record in an anonymized or de-identified dataset can be linked with an individual identity. With identity disclosure, an adversary matches one or more records from a dataset of records on individuals to specific individuals. For example, an adversary might determine that the record with the label field 7 belongs to Mary Jones; this reveals that all the information in that record is associated with Mary Jones.

■ **Attribute disclosure:** This type of disclosure occurs when sensitive information about a data subject is revealed through a de-identified file. With attribute disclosure, an adversary obtains one or more attributes for a specific individual from a dataset of records on individuals, even though the adversary may not be able to obtain the full data record. For example, if a hospital releases information showing that all current female patients aged 56 to 60 have cancer, and if Alice Smith is a 56-year-old female who is known to be an inpatient at the hospital, then Alice Smith's diagnosis is revealed, even though her individual de-identified medical records cannot be distinguished from the others.

■ **Inferential disclosure:** With this type of disclosure, the released data make it possible to determine the value of some characteristic of an individual more accurately than otherwise would have been possible. For example, with a mathematical model, an intruder may be able to infer a subject sensitive income information by using attributes recorded in the data, leading to inferential disclosure. As a particular instance, the data may show a high correlation between income and purchase price of a home. Because the purchase price of a home is typically public information, a third party might use this information to infer the income of a data subject.

Applicability to Privacy Threats

Identity concealment, using anonymization or de-identification, is a type of privacy control. Such controls are applicable to a number of threat scenarios. Table 7.3, based on a table in [SHAP12], relates anonymization and de-identification to privacy risks, based on Solove's taxonomy (refer to Figure 4.1). Shaded rows indicate risks for which anonymization or de-identification can be used as a privacy control.

TABLE 7.3 Applicability of De-identification and Anonymization (Concealment) to Privacy Risks

Privacy Risk	Applicability
INFORMATION COLLECTION	
Surveillance	To the extent that the surveillance is information based (including digital photos/video), concealment could mitigate the risk.
Interrogation	The nature of this risk is such that it cannot be mitigated by concealment.
INFORMATION PROCESSING	
Aggregation	Anonymization can mitigate this risk by making it impossible to associate discrete pieces of information with the same individual. However, if aggregation per se must be performed, pseudonymity can maintain linkability of the information while still mitigating risk to the individual. Further mitigation might be obtained by reducing the information contained in the attributes being aggregated.
Identification	Concealment directly mitigates this risk.

Insecurity	Concealment can mitigate this risk by reducing the information being protected and/or the ability of others to associate the information with specific individuals.
Secondary use	Concealment can mitigate this risk by reducing the information being used and/or its linkage to an identifiable individual. However, substantial residual risk may remain regardless of the extent to which the data has been de-identified if secondary use may affect the individual as a member of an identifiable group.
Exclusion	Concealment can mitigate this risk. However, de-identification is seldom absolute; therefore, individuals likely will retain a stake in their information.
INFORMATION DISSEMINATION	
Breach of confidentiality	This risk is grounded in trust relationships; therefore, anonymization would not be a particularly effective mitigation.
Disclosure	Anonymization can mitigate this risk by reducing the information disclosed and/or the ability of others to associate the information with specific individuals.
Exposure	To the extent that the exposure is information based (including digital photos/video), anonymization could mitigate the risk.
Increased accessibility	Concealment can indirectly mitigate this risk by reducing the information being rendered more accessible.
Blackmail	Concealment can mitigate this risk by reducing the information available and/or its linkage to an identifiable individual.
Appropriation	This risk is grounded in identity; therefore, anonymization can mitigate the risk.
Distortion	Concealment can mitigate this risk by reducing the information being used and/or its linkage to an identifiable individual. However, because the harm arises in part from inaccuracy of the information, the mitigation obtained from information reduction may be very limited.
INVASIONS	
Intrusion	The nature of this risk is such that it cannot be mitigated by concealment.
Decision interference	The nature of this risk is such that it cannot be mitigated by concealment.

7.3   De-Identification of Direct Identifiers

This section examines techniques for de-identification related to direct identifiers. These same techniques can be used for anonymization if no re-identifying information is retained.

As an example, consider a dataset in which each record corresponds to a different individual, represented in Table 7.4 by one row per record. The first two fields of a record, Name and Address, are sufficient to identify a unique individual. The next three fields are QIs that are sufficient in some contexts to enable re-identification.

TABLE 7.4   Examples of Direct Identifiers and Quasi-Identifiers

Direct Identifiers		Quasi-identifiers			Other Attributes			
Name	Address	Birthday	Postal Code	Sex	Weight	Diagnosis	...	...

NISTIR 8053 lists the following methods of de-identification when dealing with direct identifiers:

- Remove the direct identifiers.

- Replace direct identifiers with either category names or data that are obviously generic. For example, names can be replaced with the phrase PERSON NAME, addresses with the phrase 123 ANY ROAD, ANY TOWN, USA, and so on.

- Replace direct identifiers with symbols such as ***** or XXXXX.

- Replace direct identifiers with random values such that if the same identity appears twice, it receives two different values. This preserves the form of the original data, allowing for some kinds of testing, but makes it harder to re-associate the data with individuals. This is sometimes called a *transaction pseudonym*.

- Replace direct identifiers with pseudonyms, allowing records referencing the same individual to be matched. This process is called *pseudonymization* and is also known as *tokenization*.

Anonymization

The first four techniques in the prior list anonymize the dataset. This is done if there is no need for authorized re-identification. The removal of the direct identifier does not by itself assure against re-identification. Anonymization must also consider QIs, discussed in Sections 7.3 and 7.4.

Pseudonymization

Figure 7.5 illustrates the pseudonymization of a database containing PII. The process replaces each direct identifier—in this case, the name—with a random number. A separate table maps the pseudonym to the direct identifier. Best practice dictates that the lookup table be stored on a physically separate database server from the pseudonymized database. Then, if to the pseudonymized database is compromised, an adversary is unable to look up the pseudonym, or token, and identify individual data subjects.

Original Database

Name	Age	Sex	Weight	Diagnosis
Chris Adams	47	M	210	Heart disease
John Blain	45	M	176	Prostate cancer
Anita Demato	18	F	120	Breast cancer
James Jones	39	M	135	Diabetes
Alex Li	39	M	155	Heart disease
Alice Lincoln	34	F	160	Breast cancer

Psuedonymized Databases

Pseudonym	Age	Sex	Weight	Diagnosis
10959333	34	F	160	Breast cancer
11849264	39	M	135	Diabetes
49319745	47	M	210	Heart disease
54966173	39	M	155	Heart disease
84866952	18	F	120	Breast cancer
88786769	45	M	176	Prostate cancer

Re-identification File

Pseudonym	Name
10959333	Alice Lincoln
11849264	James Jones
49319745	Chris Adams
54966173	Alex Li
84866952	Anita Demato
88786769	John Blain

FIGURE 7.5   Pseudonymization

Apple Pay, Samsung Pay, and Android Pay use tokenization to prevent payment card fraud, storing a token value on each smart phone instead of a payment card number. For a smartphone card payment, the smartphone app sends the token; a secured data center matches the token to the stored payment card details held within the data center, where the payment is processed.

7.4   De-Identification of Quasi-Identifiers in Microdata Files

As discussed in Section 7.1, a quasi-identifier or set of quasi-identifiers is one or more attributes that have the following characteristics:

- The attribute or attributes are not sufficient to directly identify an individual.

- It is possible to combine the attribute(s) with information from another dataset so that individuals can be identified.

Re-identification involves what a *linkage attack*, illustrated in Figure 7.6. In a linkage attack, an adversary links records in the de-identified dataset with similar records in a second dataset that contains both the same QIs and the identity of the data subject, resulting in re-identification of at least some of the records. Typically, the second dataset is one that is publicly available. As Figure 7.6 indicates, the first step is to select from both datasets only those records with a unique set of QI values. If two or more records in either of the datasets have identical values, then an adversary cannot, from the QIs, identify a unique individual. Once the adversary reduces both datasets to records, each of which has a unique set of QIs, the adversary can then look for records in the two datasets that have the same QI values.

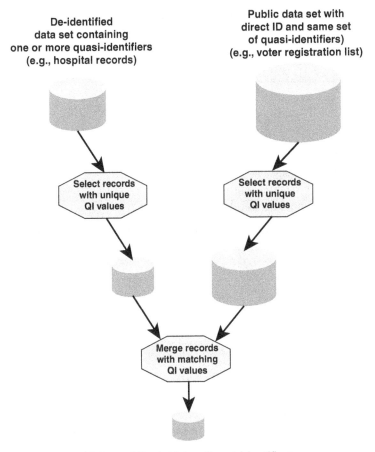

FIGURE 7.6   Linkage Attack Using Quasi-identifiers

Figure 7.7 provides a simple example. In this example, an organization has made available a dataset, perhaps for research or insurance purposes, that includes certain information about a set of individuals, together with medical diagnoses, but the direct identifier of each individual is suppressed. In this case, the attributes age, sex, and postal (zip) code are QIs in the dataset. An adversary may be able to combine this dataset with a public database, such as voter registration rolls. The adversary would look for an entry in the public database whose QIs match those in the published dataset and that are unique in both datasets. This constitutes a linkage and allows identification of the corresponding entry in the published dataset. In this example, of the six items in the published dataset, the adversary can determine the identities for four entries.

Public Database

Name	Age	Sex	ZIP
Chris Adams	47	M	12211
John Blain	45	M	12244
Anita Demato	18	F	12245
James Jones	19	M	12377
Alex Li	19	M	12377
Alice Lincoln	34	F	12391

Published Database

Age	Sex	ZIP	Diagnosis
47	M	12211	Heart disease
45	M	12244	Prostate cancer
18	F	12245	Breast cancer
19	M	12377	Diabetes
27	M	12377	Heart disease
34	F	12391	Breast cancer

Result of Linkage Attack

Name	Age	Sex	ZIP	Diagnosis
Chris Adams	47	M	12211	Heart disease
John Blain	45	M	12244	Prostate cancer
Anita Demato	18	F	12245	Breast cancer
Alice Lincoln	34	F	12391	Breast cancer

FIGURE 7.7   Linkage Attack Example

A number of techniques can be used to protect data in a de-identified dataset from re-identification. All of these techniques involve obfuscating or suppressing some QI value. These techniques are discussed later in this section and in Section 7.5.

Privacy-Preserving Data Publishing

The de-identification of microdata files, often referred to as *privacy-preserving data publishing* (*PPDP*), involves removing direct identifiers and modifying QIs. To express this symbolically, consider an unprotected microdata file UM represented as:

UM{Direct_Identifiers, Quasi-Identifiers, Confidential_Attributes, Non-confidential_Attributes}

That is, the unprotected microdata file consists of a set of records for individuals, and each record contains one or more direct identifiers, one or more QIs, one or more confidential attributes, and perhaps additional non-confidential attributes.

An organization wishing to publish (make available) this dataset for various purposes de-identifies or anonymizes the dataset to produce a privacy-protected dataset PM:

PM{QI*, Confidential_Attributes, Non-confidential_Attributes}

where QI* is the set of QIs transformed to preserve privacy.

Disclosure Risk Versus Data Utility

In considering PPDP techniques, an organization needs to be mindful of the trade-off between disclosure risk and data utility.

Chapter 2, "Information Privacy Concepts," discusses the general trade-off between privacy and utility. The same sort of consideration applies to de-identification of datasets with QIs. In this context, the trade-off is between the following concepts:

- **Maximizing data utility:** For a given application, the de-identified data should be faithful to the original data in critical ways. That is, the application or analysis should be able to produce meaningful results despite the obfuscation of QIs.

- **Minimizing disclosure risk:** Disclosure refers to the revelation of information that relates to the identity of a data subject. Disclosure risk relates to the probability of disclosure under a given set of circumstances.

For example, if a de-identification process substitutes age groups for exact ages, there will be a calculable margin of error when calculating the average age across the dataset. Increasing the size of the age groups reduces disclosure risk, but it also increases the margin of erroring in calculating average age, thus reducing utility.

Data utility is a subjective measure made by management that depends on the nature of the application and the degree of accuracy and completeness required. Determination of disclosure risk is difficult and can, at best, be estimated. For example, the Federal Committee on Statistical Methodology [FCSM05] indicates that the disclosure risk of an individual being identified from a microdata file and a public records file depends on the following factors:

- The probability that the individual for whom an adversary is looking is represented on both the microdata file and some matchable file

- The probability that the matching variables are recorded identically on the microdata file and on the matchable file

- The probability that the individual for whom the adversary is looking is unique in the population for the matchable variables

- The degree of confidence of the adversary that he or she has correctly identified a unique individual

Figure 7.8 illustrates the trade-off between data utility and disclosure risk. The upper-right circle represents a dataset with the direct identifier removed but all QIs retained. For any application that makes use of one or more of the quasi-identifiers, this dataset has the highest utility. At the same time, the disclosure risk is the highest. The lower-left circle represents a dataset with the direct identifier and all quasi-identifiers removed. In this case, the disclosure risk is very small or zero, but the data utility is also minimal. The other circles in Figure 7.8 represent various techniques for de-identification, with obfuscation increasing toward the left.

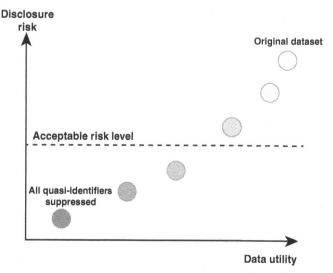

FIGURE 7.8   Disclosure Risk Versus Data Utility

The remainder of this section looks at common techniques for dealing with quasi-identifiers. These techniques are often referred to as privacy-preserving data publishing. See [CHEN09], [FUNG10], and [XU14] for more detail on the topics covered in this section and the next. Section 7.5 looks at some refinements on these techniques.

PPDP Techniques

Table 7.5 is used in the following discussion, and part a of Table 7.5 shows the original dataset.

Suppression

Suppression techniques are used to remove some of the QI values. The objective is to eliminate those QI values that have a higher risk of allowing re-identification of specific records. Examples of applying suppression include:

■ **Elimination of exceptional values:** This might be done, for example, if there are only one or two males in a large microdata file, or if there are files with outlier values, such as an unusually large or small number (such as age).

- **Elimination of an entire QI:** For example, an analyst might eliminate the zip code field if that information is considered too risky for re-identification.

- **Elimination of an individual record:** This can occur when the record is very distinctive (e.g., only one individual within a county has a salary above a certain level).

Part b of Table 7.5 illustrates the suppression technique. (Tables 7.5 and 7.6 are from an Office of Civil Rights publication [OCR12].)

TABLE 7.5 Techniques for De-identifying Quasi-identifiers

(a) Example of protected information

Age	Sex	ZIP	Diagnosis
15	M	12210	Diabetes
21	F	12211	Prostate cancer
36	M	12220	Heart disease
91	F	12221	Breast cancer

(b) Version of (a) with suppressed values

Age	Sex	ZIP	Diagnosis
*	M	12210	Diabetes
21	F	12211	Prostate cancer
36	M	*	Heart disease
*	F	*	Breast cancer

(c) Version of (a) with generalized values

Age	Sex	ZIP	Diagnosis
Under 21	M	1221*	Diabetes
21–34	F	1221*	Prostate cancer
35–44	M	1222*	Heart disease
45 and over	F	1222*	Breast cancer

(d) Version of (a) with randomized values

Age	Sex	ZIP	Diagnosis
16	M	12212	Diabetes
20	F	12210	Prostate cancer
34	M	12220	Heart disease
93	F	12223	Breast cancer

Suppression might reduce the utility of the microdata dataset as it is more difficult to draw conclusions. However, in the case of eliminating numerical outliers, suppression might have minimal effects on utility.

Generalization

Generalization involves transforming some QIs into less precise representations. Part c of Table 7.5 shows two examples (shaded cells): transforming specific ages into age ranges and generalizing a five-digit zip code to a four-digit zip code. Generalization can result in one or both of the following:

- It can reduce the number of records in a microdata file with a unique set of QI values.

- For any remaining unique microdata records, it can reduce the probability that there will be a unique match in the matchable file.

Whether generalization decreases the utility of a microdata dataset depends on the application. It is likely that for health data, especially for large datasets, generalization does not significantly reduce utility.

Perturbation

Perturbation, also known as randomization, involves replacing specific QI values with equally specific but different values. For example, the algorithm may replace an age value with a random value within a five-year window of the actual age. Part d of Table 7.5 illustrates perturbation (shaded cells). In this example, every age is within +/– 2 years of the original age, and the final digit in each zip code is within +/– 2 of the original.

One advantage of perturbation is that it significantly decreases the probability of finding a unique match in a matchable file. If the adversary knows which QI fields have been disturbed, then the adversary must work with only the unperturbed fields, which greatly reduces the chance of finding a unique match. If the adversary does not know which fields have been perturbed, then he or she is unable to use a matching algorithm.

Another advantage of perturbation is that it maintains statistical properties about the original data, such as mean or variance. For many applications, the result is that utility is not significantly lessened.

Swapping

Swapping involves exchanging QI values between records. Swapping must be handled with care if it is necessary to preserve statistical properties. As an example, consider a health dataset such as the ones in the preceding examples. If there are multiple records with the same diagnosis, then swapping zip code, sex, and age between two such records would not alter statistical properties.

7.5 *K*-Anonymity, *L*-Diversity, and *T*-Closeness

This section examines three techniques for de-identifying microdata intended to maintain a high level of utility while reducing privacy risk.

K-Anonymity

K-anonymity, first proposed in [SWEE02], is a formal model for privacy protection. A dataset provides *k*-anonymity protection if the information for each person contained in the dataset cannot be distinguished from at least $k - 1$ individuals whose information also appears in the dataset. This criterion ensures that there are at least *k* records in the dataset that have the same values on the quasi-identifiers for every combination of values present in the dataset.

For example, consider part a of Table 7.6, which shows a dataset that contains the confidential attribute *diagnosis*. The dataset has been de-identified to the extent of removing all direct identifiers. A 2-anonymous version of this dataset (see part b of Table 7.6) results from a combination of suppression and generalization. In this version, every unique combination of QIs that is present includes at least two records. Part c of Table 7.6 shows a portion of a public database. An adversary using this database and the 2-anonymous dataset can only conclude that the individual Corbin matches two of the records from the dataset and obtains no confidential attribute information.

TABLE 7.6   Example of 2-Anonymization

(a) Example of protected information

Age	Sex	ZIP	Diagnosis
18	M	46801	Arthritis
19	M	46814	Prostate cancer
27	M	46815	Heart disease
27	M	46909	Asthma
27	F	46909	Arthritis
34	F	46943	Diabetes
45	F	46943	Asthma

(b) 2-anonymous version of (a)

Age	Sex	ZIP	Diagnosis
18-19	M	468**	Arthritis
18-19	M	468**	Prostate cancer
27	*	*	Heart disease
27	*	*	Asthma
27	*	*	Arthritis
>30	F	46943	Diabetes
>30	F	46943	Asthma

(c) Portion of public database

Name	Age	Sex	ZIP
Corbin	18	M	46801
Mike	20	M	46611

(d) Attempt at disclosure

Name	Age	Sex	Zip	Diagnosis
Corbin?	18-19	M	468**	Arthritis
Corbin?	18-19	M	468**	Prostate cancer

The risk with the *k*-anonymization approach is that more than one record with the same QIs may have the same confidential attribute values. Table 7.7 illustrates this. This is an example of 3-anonymization. Three records in the 3-anonymized dataset with the same QI values also have the same value for the diagnosis attribute. An adversary is able to find a unique record in the public database with the same QI values. In this case, the adversary can deduce that Corbin has heart disease. This is an example of attribute disclosure. However, the anonymized dataset may contain more attributes not shown in part b of Table 7.7. The adversary cannot determine which of the three records corresponds to Corbin, so this is not a case of identity disclosure.

TABLE 7.7   Example of Attribute Disclosure

(a) Example of protected information

Age	Sex	ZIP	Diagnosis
18	M	46801	Heart disease
19	M	46814	Heart disease
19	M	46815	Heart disease
27	M	46815	Prostate cancer
27	F	46909	Arthritis
27	F	46909	Diabetes
34	F	46943	Breast cancer
45	F	46943	Asthma
47	M	46943	Asthma

(b) 3-anonymous version of (a)

Age	Sex	ZIP	Diagnosis
18-19	M	468**	Heart disease
18-19	M	468**	Heart disease
18-19	M	468**	Heart disease
27	*	46***	Prostate cancer
27	*	46***	Arthritis
27	*	46***	Diabetes
>30	*	46943	Breast cancer
>30	*	46943	Asthma
>30	*	46943	Asthma

(c) Portion of public database

Name	Age	Sex	ZIP
Corbin	18	M	46801
Mike	20	M	46611

(d) Attribute disclosure but not Identity disclosure

Name	Age	Sex	ZIP	Diagnosis
Corbin?	18	M	46801	Heart disease
Corbin?	18	M	46801	Heart disease
Corbin?	18	M	46801	Heart disease

The critical parameter in using k-anonymity is the value of k. The higher the value of k, the stronger the privacy guarantee. This is true for two reasons:

- Larger values of k imply that more has been done to obfuscate the QIs in order to create larger sets with the same QI values. But this also means that a corresponding public dataset is less likely to have any records with a unique set of QI values matching one of the sets in the de-identified dataset.

- With larger values of k, the probability that the k individuals in a set share the same confidential attribute value, allowing for an attribute disclosure, is lower.

At the same time, a higher value of k indicates that the QIs are more obfuscated, which may reduce utility. Thus, it is hard to optimally select k.

L-Diversity

The preceding discussion demonstrates that while k-anonymity is able to prevent identity disclosure (a record in a k-anonymized dataset cannot be mapped back to the corresponding record in the original dataset), in general it may fail to protect against attribute disclosure. Researchers have proposed several extensions to *k*-anonymity to mitigate this weakness, with *l*-diversity being one of the more prominent [MACH06].

A *k*-anonymous dataset satisfies *l*-diversity if, for each group of records sharing QI values, there are at least *l* distinct values for each confidential attribute. The *l*-diversity technique can help protect against inferential disclosure by assuring that each group of records matching a specific criterion has a certain amount of diversity. The disadvantage of this technique is that it lessens the fidelity of the de-identified data to the original dataset, reducing utility.

T-Closeness

T-closeness is a further refinement on *l*-diversity [LI07]. A *k*-anonymous dataset satisfies *t*-closeness if, for each group of records sharing QI values, the distance between the distribution of each confidential attribute within the group and the distribution of the attribute in the whole dataset is no more than a threshold *t*. *T*-closeness creates equivalent classes that resemble the initial distribution of attributes in the table prior to de-identification. This technique is useful when it is important to keep the data as close as possible to the original. *T*-closeness adds the constraint that not only at least *l* different values should exist within each equivalence class, but also each value is represented as many times as necessary to mirror the initial distribution of each attribute.

T-closeness guards against a privacy weakness in *l*-diversity that can be illustrated with the following example: Consider a patient dataset in which 95% of records have flu and 5% of records have HIV. Suppose that a QI group has 50% of flu and 50% of HIV and, therefore, satisfies 2-diversity. However, this group presents a serious privacy threat because any record owner in the group could be inferred as having HIV with 50% confidence, compared to 5% in the overall table.

A disadvantage of *t*-closeness is that it greatly degrades the data utility because it requires the distribution of sensitive values to be the same in all QI groups. This would significantly damage the correlation between QI values and confidential attributes.

7.6 Summary Table Protection

Section 7.1 defines summary tables as containing aggregated data about individuals derived from microdata sources. A summary table may be either a frequency count table or a magnitude table. A certain level of privacy protection is inherent in summary tables because the data in a summary table is aggregate and so does not contain any records that correspond to an individual but rather provides data that refer to a number of individuals.

The following types of attacks are possible on summary tables [ENIS14]:

- **External attack:** As an example of an external attack, consider a frequency table Ethnicity × Town that contains a single subject for ethnicity Ei and town Ti. Then if a magnitude table is released with the average blood pressure for each ethnicity and each town, the exact blood pressure of the only subject with ethnicity Ei in town Ti is publicly disclosed.

- **Internal attack:** If there are only two subjects for ethnicity Ei and town Ti, the blood pressure of each of them is disclosed to the other.

- **Dominance attack:** If one or a few respondents dominate in the contribution to a cell in a magnitude table, the dominant subject(s) can upper-bound the contributions of the rest. For example, if the table displays the cumulative earnings for each job type and town, and one individual contributes 90% of a certain cell value, that individual knows his or her colleagues in the town are not doing very well.

It is possible to deal with these types of attacks in two ways:

- Derive the summary table that is de-identified with respect to QIs, using one or more of the methods defined in Sections 7.4 and 7.5.

- Identify sensitive cells in the summary table and modify them to limit disclosure. A *sensitive cell* is a cell in which the number is considered to represent an unacceptable disclosure risk (e.g., a cell in which the number of individuals represented is less than some specified threshold).

This section deals with identifying and modifying sensitive cells, looking at frequency and magnitude table types separately. For the interested reader, the Federal Committee on Statistical Methodology's *Statistical Policy Working Paper 22: Report on Statistical Disclosure Limitation Methodology* [FCSM05] contains a detailed technical and mathematical discussion of the methods described in this section.

Frequency Tables

A frequency table shows a count, or frequency (percentage), of individuals by category. The most common method for defining a cell as sensitive is the threshold rule, which defines a cell as sensitive if the count is less than some specified number. U.S. government agencies typically use a threshold value in the range of 3 to 5 [FCSM05].

For cells defined as sensitive, methods that can limit disclosure include suppression, random rounding, controlled rounding, and controlled tabular adjustment. To illustrate these techniques, this section uses an example from the Federal Committee on Statistical Methodology [FCSM05], shown in Table 7.8, with part a of Table 7.8 showing the original dataset. Note that, as is typical with summary tables, the table include marginal (row and column) totals. The shaded cells fit a typical definition of sensitive.

TABLE 7.8 Example of Disclosure Limitation for Sensitive Cells in a Frequency Table

(a) With Disclosure

County	Low	Medium	High	Very High	TOTAL
Alpha	15	1	3	1	20
Beta	20	10	10	15	55
Gamma	3	19	10	2	25
Delta	12	14	7	2	35
TOTAL	50	35	30	20	135

(b) Ineffective Use of Suppression

County	Low	Medium	High	Very High	TOTAL
Alpha	15	S1	S2	S3	20
Beta	20	S4	S5	15	55
Gamma	S6	19	10	S7	25
Delta	S8	14	7	S9	35
TOTAL	50	35	30	20	135

(c) Effective Use of Suppression

County	Low	Medium	High	Very High	TOTAL
Alpha	15	S	S	S	20
Beta	20	10	10	15	55
Gamma	S	S	10	S	25
Delta	S	14	S	S	35
TOTAL	50	35	30	20	135

(d) Random Rounding

County	Low	Medium	High	Very High	TOTAL
Alpha	15	0	0	0	20
Beta	20	10	10	15	55
Gamma	5	10	10	0	25
Delta	15	15	10	0	35
TOTAL	50	35	30	20	135

(e) Controlled Rounding

County	Low	Medium	High	Very High	TOTAL
Alpha	15	0	5	0	20
Beta	20	10	10	15	55
Gamma	5	10	10	0	25
Delta	10	15	5	5	35
TOTAL	50	35	30	20	135

(f) Controlled Tabular Adjustment

County	Low	Medium	High	Very High	TOTAL
Alpha	15	1−1=0	3	1+2=3	20+1=21
Beta	20	10	10	15	55
Gamma	3	19	10	2−2=0	25−2=23
Delta	12	14	7	2+1=3	35+1=36
TOTAL	50	35−1=34	30	20+1=21	135

Suppression

Cell suppression involves two steps:

1. Suppress all cells that meet the definition of sensitive (below the threshold). These are primary suppressions.

2. Suppress additional cells to prevent recovery of primary suppressions from marginal totals. These are secondary suppressions.

Cell suppression must be done carefully. Part b of Table 7.8 shows an ineffective use of cell suppression on the example table that has at least two suppressed cells in each row and column. The secondary suppressions are highlighted in lighter shading. Consider the following calculation:

$$(15 + S1 + S2 + S3) + (20 + S4 + S5 + 15) - (S1 + S4 + 10 + 14) - (S2 + S5 + 10 + 7) = 20 + 55 - 35 - 30$$

which reduces to:

$$(S1 + S2 + S3) + (S4 + S5) - (S1 + S4 + 10) - (S2 + S5) = 20 + 55 - 35 - 30 - 15 - 35 + 24 + 17 = 1$$

which reduces to $S3 = 1$. Thus, the value of one of the suppressed cells is recovered.

Linear programming techniques can ensure that cell suppression is effective. Part c of Table 7.8 uses cell suppression and provides adequate protection for the sensitive cells. It also illustrates one of the problems with suppression. In this case, 9 of the 16 cells are suppressed.

Random Rounding

Random rounding is a technique that affects every cell in a table (other than row and column totals). Random rounding of each cell is done to a multiple of some nonnegative base value. In part d of Table 7.8, the base value is 5. With random rounding, the algorithm makes a random decision whether to round up or round down. For this example, express each cell count value X in the form:

$$X = 5q + r$$

where q is a nonnegative integer, and r is the remainder ($0 \leq r \leq 4$). Round the cell count up to $5(q + 1)$ with probability $r / 5$ and down to $5q$ with probability $\left(1 - \frac{r}{5}\right)$. Part d of Table 7.8 shows a possible result.

A disadvantage of random rounding is that the rows and columns do not necessarily add to the published row and column totals. Generally, a releasing organization would not want to change the total values because these values are important independent of the individual cell values. But without such an adjustment, the public could lose confidence in the numbers.

Controlled Rounding

Controlled rounding involves random rounding followed by an adjustment to some of the cell values so that all rows and columns add to the original row and column totals. Linear programming techniques are used to adjust the rounding values to preserve totals. The U.S. Social Security Administration uses controlled rounding in published frequency tables. Part e of Table 7.8 is an example of controlled rounding.

Controlled Tabular Adjustment

Controlled tabular adjustment (CTA) involves modifying the values in a table to prevent inference of sensitive cell values within a prescribed protection interval. CTA attempts to find the closest table to the original one that protects all sensitive cells. CTA optimization is typically based on mixed linear integer programming and entails less information loss than CS.

CTA adjusts each sensitive cell to be either 0 or the threshold value and then minimally adjusts non-sensitive cell values to ensure that the row and column totals are satisfied. Alternatively, non-sensitive cells can be left unchanged, and the marginal total can be adjusted to account for the internal changes. Whether it is important to maintain the original marginal values depends on the application. Part f of Table 7.8 is an example.

Magnitude Tables

Magnitude tables display a numerical aggregate value in a table cell, rather than a count of individuals. Typically, magnitude tables contain the results of surveys of organizations or establishments, in which the items published are aggregates of nonnegative reported values. For such surveys, the values reported by subjects may vary widely, with some extremely large values and some small values. The privacy problem relates to ensuring that a person cannot use the published total and other publicly available data to estimate an individual subject's value too closely.

Thus, the disclosure limitation objective for magnitude tables is to ensure that the published data cannot be used to estimate within too close of a range the values reported by the largest, most highly visible subject.

Defining Sensitive Cells

The most common methods for defining the sensitivity of a magnitude cell are linear sensitivity rules. Examples of sensitivity rules for primary suppressions are:

- **(n, k)-dominance:** A cell is sensitive if n or fewer subjects contribute more than a fraction k of the cell value.

- **pq-rule:** If subjects' contributions to the cell can be estimated within $q\%$ before seeing the cell and within $p\%$ after seeing the cell, the cell is sensitive.

- **$p\%$-rule:** This is a special case of the pq-rule with $q = 100$.

The objective with all these rules is to make it difficult to estimate too closely the value corresponding to a single individual. The largest reported individual value contributing to a cell is the most likely to be estimated accurately.

Protecting Sensitive Cells

Three options exist for protecting sensitive cells in magnitude tables:

- Restructure the table and collapse cells until no sensitive cells remain. You can achieve this by merging two rows or two columns to reduce sensitivity. For example, if rows refer to age, and adjacent rows have the attribute values 20–29 and 30–39, you can merge the two rows for an attribute value of 20–39. Merging rows or columns dilutes the contribution of any one individual to a cell.

- Apply cell suppression. This is the same technique as used for frequency tables and again requires suppression of secondary cells.

- Apply controlled tabular adjustment. For magnitude data, CTA alters the value of a sensitive cell by the amount needed so that the linear sensitivity rule would classify the cell as not sensitive.

As with frequency tables, methods used to protect magnitude tables raise the issue of privacy versus utility.

7.7   Privacy in Queryable Databases

This section deals with databases that can be accessed by an online query system. For databases that contain personal data or data derived from personal data, individuals use online query systems to obtain aggregate information about the individuals represented in the database.

Figure 7.2 in Section 7.1 depicts three categories of online query of databases:

- **Queries to summary tables:** The responsible organization (e.g., a health care provider) generates summary tables from either:

  - **An unprotected microdata file:** In this case, the techniques discussed in Section 7.6 provide privacy protection.

  - **An anonymized or de-identified microdata file:** In this case, the techniques discussed in Sections 7.3 through 7.5 provide privacy protection, which in turn extends to the summary tables generated from the protected microdata file.

- **Queries to protected microdata files:** The files are anonymized or de-identified, providing privacy protection.

- **Queries to unprotected microdata files:** These are the original files that contain PII and QI attributes for individuals, with no privacy protection.

The techniques used to provide privacy protection in the first two categories enable organizations to publish the resulting tables. Therefore, the use of an online query system does not introduce any new privacy concerns. An organization may permit online access to the original microdata files for applications that require full or at least a high degree of accuracy; this is the third category listed above. This section therefore deals with privacy protection for online query systems for unprotected microdata files.

Privacy Threats

The privacy concerns related to online query systems can be stated as follows: An organization (e.g., health care provider, government agency) maintains a microdata database containing information on a number—typically a large number—of individuals. The database owner wishes to allow researchers to use this database to obtain statistical information (e.g., count, median) for groups of individuals with certain attribute values. An example is a query for the average age of females making insurance claims related to heart attack. But the database owner also must provide privacy protection by preventing a user from determining information about any one individual. The database owner faces two specific challenges:

- A user might possess either public (e.g., age, sex, marital status) or confidential (e.g., salary) information about certain individuals and use this knowledge in framing queries to obtain confidential information about those individuals or other individuals.

- A user could present a number of apparently "safe" queries and deduce confidential information from the set of responses.

Consider the following series of examples for a database at a company and suppose you know that Alicia's age is 32, that she works in the legal department, and that she has a law degree:

- **Example 1:** What is the average year-end bonus for last year of all persons who are 32 years old, work in the legal department, and have a law degree? If you know that Alicia is the only person in the database who satisfies these conditions, then this query reveals her bonus.

- **Example 2:** One countermeasure to the problem posed by example 1 is to restrict the size of the response sets (e.g., to require that the response to a query involves information from at least five individuals). But consider the following queries: What is the total year-end bonus for last year of all persons who are 32–60 years old, work in the legal department, and have a law degree? What is the total year-end bonus for last year of all persons who are 33–60 years old, work in the legal department, and have a law degree? Both queries might satisfy the query set size restriction. However, you could easily deduce Alicia's bonus from the responses.

- **Example 3:** Suppose that the query of example 1 resulted in a response set size of two. Alicia, and anyone else who knows Alicia's bonus, could easily determine the name of the other person with the same age and education, as well as that person's bonus.

- **Example 4:** Suppose you did not know whether Alicia was the only one in the legal department who was age 32 and had a law degree. Consider the following queries: How many individuals are 32–60 years old, work in the legal department, have a law degree, and received a bonus of $30,000 to $35,000? How many individuals are 32–60 years old, work in the legal department, have a law degree, and received a bonus of $30,000 to $35,000? If the answers to these queries differ, you have discovered that Alicia's bonus is between $30,000 to $35,000.

In each of these examples, you have been able to obtain information about Alicia without mentioning her name.

Protecting Queryable Databases

There are two overall approaches for protecting queryable databases (see Figure 7.9):

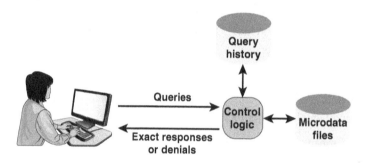

(a) Query restriction approach

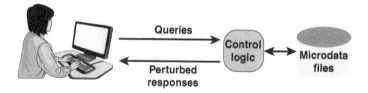

(b) Query perturbation approach

FIGURE 7.9   Disclosure Limitation Approaches for Online Query Systems

- **Query restriction:** Control logic associated with the database blocks answers to certain queries. The database may block some queries based on characteristics associated with the query, such as the response set size being too small. The database may block other queries based on how they may be used in conjunction with previous queries.

- **Response perturbation:** This technique involves changing the answer that would have been returned if there were no intervention, with an answer that is modified in some way. Two approaches are possible. Input perturbation is applied to the microdata records on which a query is computed. Output perturbation is applied to the result that is computed from the original data.

Query Restriction

Query restriction is the appropriate approach if the query application requires deterministically correct answers, and these numbers must be exact. To protect against disclosure when exact answers are provided, query restriction denies queries that risk disclosure.

With query restriction, each query must pass through a series of filters that apply various disclosure limitation rules. It should be pointed out at the outset of this discussion that the main challenges of query restriction are:

- The database can be repeatedly queried. Each individual query may be innocuous, but the sequential queries may be sufficient to compromise the database. This particular problem is an area of ongoing research.

- As a consequence of the preceding problem, the computational burden of keeping track of previous queries can be significant.

- Collusion attacks can circumvent the query limit.

[ADAM89] identifies five methods of query restriction, and a database will typically implement more than one of these methods:

- Query set size control

- Query set overlap control

- Auditing

- Partitioning

- Cell suppression

The following sections examine each of these in turn.

Query Set Size Control

Query set size control rejects queries that contain too few or too many records. Specifically, queries are rejected if they do not satisfy the following:

$$k \leq |C| \leq N - k, \text{ with } k \leq N/2$$

where:

- N = total number of records in the microdata database.

- k = parameter set by the administrator.

- C = characteristic formula that defines the query. For example, AVERAGE(Age < 50; Weight) requests the average weight of all individuals in the dataset whose age is under 50.

- $|C|$ = number of records included in the response to the query.

Results in the literature show that with query set size control alone, a database can be easily compromised with four or five queries for modest values of k, and a large value of k rejects too many queries.

Query Set Overlap Control

Many compromises use query sets that have a large number of overlapping records. Query set overlap control allows only queries that have small overlap with previously answered queries. For successive queries C and D, the restriction is:

$$S(C) \cap S(D) \leq r$$

where S(C) is the set of records returned for C. Thus, r is the maximum number of overlapping records allowed between pairs of queries.

Query set overlap tends to be costly, both in terms of storage and processing. Further, it is open to attack by a sequence of queries. Thus, although of theoretical interest, this technique is not typically used.

Auditing

Auditing involves keeping current logs of all queries made by each user and checking for possible compromise when a new query is issued. Auditing minimizes the number of query denials that a database must issue. One of the major drawbacks of auditing, however, is the excessive processing time and storage requirements to store and process the accumulated logs. [ADAM89] notes a number of efforts to provide more efficient versions of auditing.

Partitioning

Partitioning involves separating a dataset into disjoint subsets of individual records. With this technique, records are stored in groups of some minimum size; queries may refer to any group or set of groups but never to subsets of records within a group. This prevents a user from isolating a record with overlapping queries. However, the formation of such groups may severely obscure useful statistical information in the database. In addition, the revision of groupings as records are added and deleted may be costly.

Cell Suppression

Cell suppression in online query systems is the same concept discussed in Section 7.4 for de-identification of quasi-identifiers. While cell suppression is a worthwhile technique in the static case of creating a de-identified microdata file, it presents difficulties for responding to online queries.

[DENN82] shows that cell suppression becomes impractical if arbitrarily complex queries are allowed. If the query syntax is restricted to certain simple queries of the form:

$$(A_1 = v_1) \text{ AND } (A_2 = v_2) \dots \text{ AND } \dots (A_m = v_m)$$

where the set of attributes in the microdata file is $\{A_1, A_2, \dots, A_m\}$ and v_i is an allowable value for attribute A_i ($1 < i \leq m$), then cell suppression has practical value.

Response Perturbation

Response perturbation involves modifying the response values to user queries while leaving the data in the microdata file untouched. Common methods of response perturbation are:

- Random sample queries
- Rounding
- Differential privacy

Random Sample Queries

A random sample query works as follows: A user issues a request C, which is satisfied by $|C|$ records. For each record i in the response set, the system applies a selection function $f(C, i)$ to determine whether this entity is to be included in the sampled query set. The function $f(C, i)$ is such that there is a probability P that the record is included in the sampled query set. The system then answers the query through a calculation performed only over the sampled records rather than all records that satisfy C. The system should produce a relatively large sample, such as with P in the range 80% to 90%. This results in fairly accurate statistics. Results show that small relative errors in the answers to queries may be obtained while providing a low risk of compromise [DENN82].

Rounding

Output perturbation produced by rounding results in an answer that is rounded up or down to the nearest multiple of a given base b. Section 7.6 discusses various types of rounding. Studies of output perturbation make use of systematic, random, and controlled rounding. Each of these methods has strengths and weaknesses [DENN82].

Differential Privacy

Differential privacy involves adding noise, or small random values, to response values [DWOR11]. Differential privacy determines how much noise to add, and in what form, to get the necessary privacy guarantees.

Differential privacy's mathematical definition holds that the result of an analysis of a dataset should be roughly the same before and after the addition or removal of a single data record (which is usually taken to be the data from a single individual). This works because the amount of noise added masks the contribution of any individual. The degree of sameness is defined by the parameter ε (epsilon). The smaller the parameter ε, the more noise is added, and the more difficult it is to distinguish the contribution of a single record. The result is increased privacy for all of the data subjects.

A detailed discussion of differential privacy is beyond the scope of this chapter. What follows is a brief discussion of the mathematical model. Define the following:

- $D1, D2$ = two microdata datasets that differ by one record; specifically, D2 is D1 with any one record missing

- $F(D)$ = a randomized function applied to dataset D

- Range(F) = set of possible outputs of F

- S = a subset of the possible outputs of F; that is, a subset of Range (F)

Then, F ensures ε-differential privacy for all datasets D1 and D2 differing on one record:

$$Pr(F(D1) \in S) \le e^{\varepsilon} \times Pr(F(D2) \in S) \text{ for all } S \in Range(F)$$

[DWOR11] suggests that values of ε that provide good privacy would be in the range of 0.01 to 0.1. For example, for $\varepsilon = 0.01$, $e^{\varepsilon} = 1.01$. In this case, the probability that the function F produces a value in any given S for a dataset containing a particular individual's record is no greater than 1.10 times the probability that F produces a value in S for the dataset without that record. So, the smaller the value of ε, the more difficult it is to learn anything significant about the record in question. Put another way, the smaller the parameter ε, the more noise is added, and the more difficult it is to distinguish the contribution of a single record.

The objective with differential privacy is to provide a quantitative measure that the risk to an individual's privacy should not substantially (as bounded by ε) increase as a result of participating in a statistical database. Thus, an attacker should not be able to learn any information about any participant that he or she could not learn if the participant had opted out of the database. You could then state with some confidence that there is a low risk of any individual's privacy being compromised as a result of his or her participation in the database.

The key to using differential privacy is to select a function F for which the above inequality holds. One common method is to add random noise to the result of a query that conforms to the Laplace statistical distribution. The Laplace distribution centered on 0 has only a single parameter, which is directly proportional to its standard deviation, or noisiness. How much randomness, or noisiness, to apply depends on the privacy parameter, ε. It should also depend on the nature of the query itself and, more specifically, the risk to the most different individual of having their private information teased out of the data. This latter risk, known as the sensitivity of the data, is defined as follows:

$$\Delta f = \max_{D1,D2} \| f(D1) - f(D2) \|$$

This can be expressed in words that Δf is the maximum difference in the values that the query f may take on a pair of databases that differ in only one row. It can be shown that by adding a random Laplace ($\Delta f / \varepsilon$) variable to a query, ε-differential privacy is guaranteed.

With differential privacy, it is important to limit the number of identical queries. Otherwise, an adversary can arrive at an accurate average value with sufficient requests.

7.8 Key Terms and Review Questions

Key Terms

anonymization	magnitude table
attribute	microdata table
attribute disclosure	non-confidential attribute
auditing	partitioning
cell suppression	perturbation
confidential attribute	privacy-preserving data publishing (PPDP)
controlled rounding	pseudonymization
controlled tabular adjustment	quasi-identifier (QI)
dataset	query restriction
de-identification	query set overlap control
differential privacy	query set size control
direct identifier	queryable database
disclosure	random rounding
dominance attack	random sample queries
external attack	re-identification
frequency table	response perturbation
generalization	rounding
identity disclosure	sensitive cell
inferential disclosure	swapping
internal attack	summary table
k-anonymity	suppression
l-diversity	t-closeness
microdata table	tokenization

Review Questions

1. List and define the four types of attributes that may be present in a microdata file.

2. Explain the differences between microdata tables, frequency tables, and magnitude tables.

3. What is a re-identification attack?

4. List and define three types of disclosure risk.

5. Explain the differences between pseudonymization, anonymization, and de-identification.

6. List and define approaches to privacy-preserving data publishing.

7. Explain the differences between k-anonymity, l-diversity, and t-closeness.

8. What types of attacks are possible on summary tables?

9. List and define approaches to protecting privacy in frequency tables.

10. List and define approaches to protecting privacy in online queryable databases.

11. What is differential privacy?

7.9 References

ADAM89: Adam, N., and Wortmann, J. "Security-Control Methods for Statistical Databases: A Comparative Study." *ACM Computing Surveys.* December 1989.

CHEN09: Chen, B., et al. "Privacy-Preserving Data Publishing." *Foundations and Trends in Databases.* January 2009.

DENN82: Denning, D. *Cryptography and Data Security.* Reading, MA: Addison-Wesley, 1982.

DWOR11: Dwork, C. "A Firm Foundation for Private Data Analysis." *Communications of the ACM,* January 2011.

ENIS14: European Union Agency for Network and Information Security. *Privacy and Data Protection by Design—From Policy to Engineering.* December 2014. enisa.europa.eu

EPIC17: Electronic Privacy Information Center. *Concerning the Re-Identification of Consumer Information.* 2017 https://epic.org/privacy/reidentification/

FCSM05: Federal Committee on Statistical Methodology. *Statistical Policy Working Paper 22: Report on Statistical Disclosure Limitation Methodology.* U.S. Office of Management and Budget. 2005. https://www.hhs.gov/sites/default/files/spwp22.pdf

FUNG10: Fung, B., et al. "Privacy-Preserving Data Publishing: A Survey of Recent Developments." *ACM Computing Surveys.* June 2010.

LI07: Li, N., and Venkatasubramanian, S. "*t*-Closeness: Privacy Beyond *k*-Anonymity and *l*-Diversity." *IEEE 23rd International Conference on Data Engineering*, 2007.

MACH06: Machanavajjhala, A., et al. "*l*-Diversity: Privacy Beyond *k*-Anonymity." *22nd International Conference on Data Engineering*, 2006.

OCR12: Office of Civil Rights. *Guidance Regarding Methods for De-identification of Protected Health Information in Accordance with the Health Insurance Portability and Accountability Act (HIPAA) Privacy Rule.* U.S. Department of Health and Human Services. November 26, 2012. https://www.hhs.gov/hipaa/for-professionals/privacy/special-topics/de-identification/index.html

SHAP12: Shapiro, S. "Situating Anonymization Within a Privacy Risk Model." *2012 IEEE International Systems Conference*, 2012.

SWEE00: Sweeney, L. *Simple Demographics Often Identify People Uniquely.* Carnegie Mellon University, School of Computer Science, Data Privacy Laboratory, Technical Report LIDAP-WP4, Pittsburgh, PA: 2000. https://dataprivacylab.org/projects/identifiability/paper1.pdf

SWEE02: Sweeney, L. "*k*-Anonymity: A Model for Protecting Privacy." *International Journal on Uncertainty, Fuzziness and Knowledge-Based Systems.* Vol. 10, No. 5, 2002.

XU14: Xu, Y., et al. "A Survey of Privacy Preserving Data Publishing Using Generalization and Suppression." *Applied Mathematics & Information Sciences.* Vol 8, No. 3, 2014.

Chapter | **8**

Online Privacy

Learning Objectives

After studying this chapter, you should be able to:

- Discuss key considerations related to web security
- Discuss key considerations related to mobile app security
- Understand the nature of privacy threats related to web access and the use of mobile apps
- Present an overview of the FTC online privacy framework
- Discuss the design of privacy notices for both the web and mobile app environments
- Understand the privacy threats posed by tracking

A unique area of privacy—and one of the most challenging areas—is online privacy. This chapter uses the term *online privacy* to refer to privacy concerns related to user interaction with Internet services through web servers and mobile apps. This is a quite distinct topic from online access to queryable databases, discussed in Section 7.7 of Chapter 7, "Privacy in Databases." Organizations need to be concerned about online privacy in two contexts:

- Organizations need to maintain the privacy of personal information that they collect, directly or indirectly, from online activity of users.

- Organizations need to be concerned about privacy protection for employees who engage in online activity with services outside the organization.

This chapter covers a variety of topics related to online security and privacy. Sections 8.1 through 8.3 provide a survey of security approaches for online web access and the use of mobile apps. These approaches provide some privacy protection but are inadequate by themselves to address all privacy concerns. Section 8.4 discusses online privacy threats. Then, Section 8.5 looks at online privacy requirements and a framework for responding to these requirements. Sections 8.6 and 8.7 look in more detail at two specific online privacy issues: privacy notices and tracking.

8.1   The Online Ecosystem for Personal Data

The World Wide Web (WWW) has rapidly expanded since its introduction in the 1990s to become a near-essential infrastructure for businesses, consumers, and other users. Users access services on the web, including purchasing goods and service, online financial transactions, search engines, web-based email, and forums. But the convenience brings privacy-related concerns. Websites collect personal information explicitly through a variety of means, including registration pages, user surveys, and online contests, application forms, and order forms. Websites also collect personal information through means that are not obvious to consumers, such as cookies and other tracking technologies.

The recent explosive growth in the number of mobile apps raises similar privacy concerns. Apps connect users to services that, as part of their operation, collect a substantial amount of personal information on the users.

Figure 8.1 illustrates the many players involved in the online collection and use of personal data [FTC12].

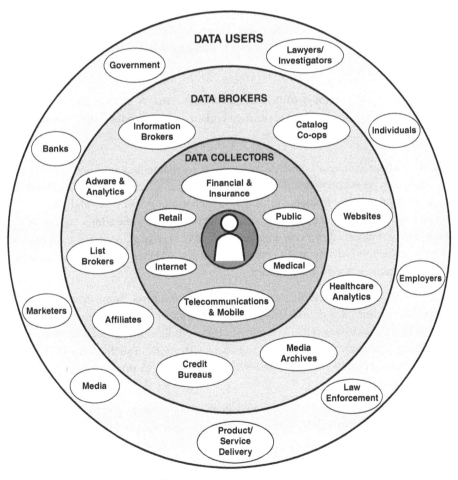

FIGURE 8.1   Personal Data Ecosystem

Figure 8.1 shows three categories of organizations involved:

- *Data collectors* collect information directly from their customers, audience, or other types of users of their services.

- *Data brokers* compile large amounts of personal data from a number of data collectors and other data brokers, without having direct online contact with the individuals whose information is in the collected data. Data brokers repackage and sell the collected information to various data users, typically without the permission or input of the individuals involved. Because consumers generally do not directly interact with data brokers, they have no means of knowing the extent and nature of information that data brokers collect about them and share with others for their own financial gain. Data brokers can collect information about consumers from a variety of public and nonpublic sources, including courthouse records, website cookies, and loyalty card programs. Typically, brokers create profiles of individuals for marketing purposes and sell them to data users.

- The *data users* category encompasses a broad range. One type of data user is a business that wants to target its advertisements and special offers. Other uses are fraud prevention and credit risk assessment.

This privacy data ecosystem raises a number of privacy-related concerns. A 2013 report to the U.S. Senate [OOI13] made the following observations about data brokers involved in the collection and sale of consumer data specifically for marketing purposes:

- Data brokers collect a huge volume of detailed information on hundreds of millions of consumers, including consumers' personal characteristics and preferences as well as health and financial information. Beyond publicly available information such as home addresses and phone numbers, data brokers maintain data as specific as whether consumers view a high volume of YouTube videos, the type of cars they drive, ailments they may have (e.g., depression, diabetes), whether they are hunters, what types of pets they have, and whether they have purchased a particular shampoo product in the past six months.

- Data brokers sell products that identify financially vulnerable consumers. Some brokers compile and sell consumer profiles that define consumers in categories, without consumer permission or knowledge of the underlying data. A number of these products focus on consumers' financial vulnerability. The names, descriptions, and characterizations in such products likely appeal to companies that sell high-cost loans and other financially risky products to populations that are likely to need quick cash.

- Data broker products provide information about consumer offline behavior to tailor online outreach by marketers. While historically marketers used consumer data to locate consumers to send catalogs and other marketing promotions through the mail or contact via telephone, increasingly the information data brokers sell marketers about consumers is provided digitally. Data brokers provide customers digital products that target online outreach to a consumer based on the dossier of offline data collected about the consumer.

- Data brokers operate behind a veil of secrecy. Data brokers typically amass data without direct interaction with consumers, and a number of brokers perpetuate this secrecy by contractually limiting customers from disclosing their data sources. Brokers' privacy policies vary widely regarding consumer access and correction rights regarding their own data.

Thus, organizations that are data brokers need to have privacy policies and technical mechanisms to ensure the privacy of data collected directly from individuals.

8.2   Web Security and Privacy

The WWW is fundamentally a client/server application running over the Internet. The use of the Web presents a number of security challenges:

- The Web is vulnerable to attacks on web servers over the Internet.

- Web browsers are very easy to use, web servers are relatively easy to configure and manage, and Web content is increasingly easy to develop, but the underlying software is extraordinarily complex. This complex software may hide many potential security flaws. The short history of the Web is replete with examples of new and upgraded systems, properly installed, that are vulnerable to a variety of security attacks.

- A web server can be exploited as a launching pad into a corporation's or an agency's entire computer complex. Once a web server is subverted, an attacker may be able to gain access to data and systems not part of the Web itself but connected to the server at the local site.

- Casual and untrained (in security matters) users are common clients for web-based services. Such users are not necessarily aware of the security risks that exist and do not have the tools or knowledge to take effective countermeasures.

A useful way of breaking down the issues involved is to consider the following classification of security and privacy issues:

- **Web server security and privacy:** Concerned with the vulnerabilities and threats associated with the platform that hosts a website, including the operating system (OS), file and database systems, and network traffic

- **Web application security and privacy:** Concerned with web software, including any applications accessible via the Web

- **Web browser security and privacy:** Concerned with the browser used from a client system to access a web server

Web Server Security and Privacy

A web server is a platform that hosts one or more websites for an organization. Often, the organization uses one or more dedicated servers for this purpose. If the resource demands for the website do not require a dedicated server, the system design may employ a virtual machine or container architecture that partitions off part of a server's resources for the website.

OS Concerns

If an adversary is able to obtain privileged access to the server OS (higher access than that of the ordinary user), the adversary may be able to compromise the confidentiality, integrity, or availability of the system. In addition, the adversary may be able to access personally identifiable information (PII) files or databases or to observe ingoing or outgoing traffic containing PII. The threats may be in the form of malware or intrusions. Thus, the system access methods discussed in Chapter 5, "System Access," are the primary means of defending a web server from unwanted access, just as they are applicable to any type of platform used for any purpose. These include authorization, user authentication, and access control mechanisms.

File and Database Concerns

Beyond the system access controls, there may be other countermeasures and defenses associated with files and databases containing data that need to be protected, including PII. Encryption is one form of defense. Additional access controls associated with stored data, such as with a database management system (DBMS), are another form. Data loss prevention (DLP) techniques, discussed in Chapter 9, "Other PET Topics," are also relevant for detecting access to PII.

Network Concerns

The protections applied to any server or other system in an organization against network-based threats apply to web servers. These systems include firewalls and intrusion detection systems. As shown in Figure 6.3 in Chapter 6, "Malicious Software and Intruders," an organization might choose to position a web server in a DMZ to allow a greater level of access from external users than is allowed for other IT resources.

Virtually all websites also employ a secure data transfer protocol to provide a number of security services. This secure protocol is based on *Hypertext Transfer Protocol* (*HTTP*), which is the foundation protocol of the WWW and can be used in any client/server application involving hypertext. The name is somewhat misleading in that HTTP is not a protocol for transferring hypertext; rather, it is a protocol for transmitting information with the efficiency necessary for making hypertext jumps. The data transferred by the protocol can be plaintext, hypertext, audio, images, or any other Internet-accessible information.

HyperText Transfer Protocol Secure (*HTTPS*) is the secure version of HTTP. HTTPS encrypts all communications between a browser and the website. Web browsers such as Safari, Firefox, and

Chrome display a padlock icon in the address bar to visually indicate that an HTTPS connection is in effect.

Data sent using HTTPS provides three important areas of protection:

- **Encryption:** Encrypts the exchanged data to keep it secure from eavesdroppers. The encryption covers the URL of the requested document, the contents of the document, the contents of browser forms (filled in by the browser user), the cookies sent from browser to server and from server to browser, and the contents of the HTTP header.

- **Data integrity:** Ensures that data cannot be modified or corrupted during transfer, intentionally or otherwise, without being detected.

- **Authentication:** Proves that your users communicate with the intended website. It protects against man-in-the-middle attacks and builds user trust, which translates into other business benefits.

Web Application Security and Privacy

As enterprises move applications online, both for internal use and for external users, such as customers and vendors, web application security and privacy become an increasing concern.

Web Application Security Risks

Web applications, by their nature, are at risk from a wide variety of threats. The applications are hosted on a server available over the Internet or other networks, usually using HTTPS. Any given application may exhibit internal weaknesses, weaknesses associated with the server OS, or connection-based weaknesses. The top 10 list of risks maintained by the Open Web Application Security Project (OWASP) provides a useful guide to the most serious risks. Table 8.1 shows the 2017 version of the list, which was compiled with the input of a wide range of organizations.

TABLE 8.1   OWASP Top 10 Application Security Risks, 2017

Risk	Description
Injection	Injection flaws, such as SQL, OS, and LDAP injection, occur when untrusted data are sent to an interpreter as part of a command or query. The hostile data can trick the interpreter into executing unintended commands or accessing data without proper authorization.
Broken authentication	Application functions related to authentication and session management are often implemented incorrectly, allowing attackers to compromise passwords, keys, or session tokens or to exploit other implementation flaws to assume other users' identities.
Sensitive data exposure	Many web applications and APIs do not properly protect sensitive data. Attackers may steal or modify such weakly protected data. Sensitive data deserves extra protection, such as encryption at rest or in transit, as well as special precautions when exchanged with the browser.

Risk	Description
XML external entity	This type of attack parses XML input. This attack occurs when XML input containing a reference to an external entity is processed by a weakly configured XML parser. This attack may lead to the disclosure of confidential data, denial of service, server-side request forgery, port scanning from the perspective of the machine where the parser is located, and other system impacts.
Broken access control	Restrictions on what authenticated users are allowed to do are not properly enforced. Attackers can exploit these flaws to access unauthorized functionality and/or data, such as access other users' accounts, view sensitive files, modify other users' data, and change access rights.
Security misconfiguration	Security misconfiguration is the most common issue in the data, which is due in part to manual or ad hoc configuration, insecure default configurations, open S3 buckets, misconfigured HTTP headers, error messages containing sensitive information, and not patching or upgrading systems, frameworks, dependencies, and components in a timely fashion.
Cross-site scripting (XSS)	XSS flaws occur whenever an application includes untrusted data in a new web page without proper validation or escaping, or when it updates an existing web page with user-supplied data using a browser API that can create JavaScript. XSS allows attackers to execute scripts in the victim's browser, which can hijack user sessions, deface websites, or redirect the user to malicious sites.
Insecure deserialization	Insecure deserialization flaws occur when an application receives hostile serialized objects, which can lead to remote code execution. Even if deserialization flaws do not result in remote code execution, serialized objects can be replayed, tampered, or deleted to spoof users, conduct injection attacks, and elevate privileges.
Using components with known vulnerabilities	Components, such as libraries, frameworks, and other software modules, run with the same privileges as the application. If a vulnerable component is exploited, such an attack can facilitate serious data loss or server takeover. Applications and APIs using components with known vulnerabilities may undermine application defenses and enable various attacks and impacts.
Insufficient logging and monitoring	Insufficient logging and monitoring, coupled with missing or ineffective integration with incident response, allows attackers to further attack systems, maintain persistence, pivot to more systems, and tamper, extract, or destroy data. Breach studies show that the time to detect a breach is over 200 days, and detection is typically based on the work by external parties rather than internal processes or monitoring.

Web Application Firewall

The most important tool in countering web application threats is a web application firewall. A *web application firewall* (*WAF*) is a firewall that monitors, filters, or blocks data packets as they travel to and from a web application. Running as a network appliance, server plugin, or cloud service, a WAF inspects each packet and uses a rule base to analyze web application logic and filter out potentially harmful traffic. Chapter 6 provides an overview of firewalls.

A WAF is placed logically between an application and users such that all traffic to and from the application goes through the WAF. Figure 8.2 depicts this logical context.

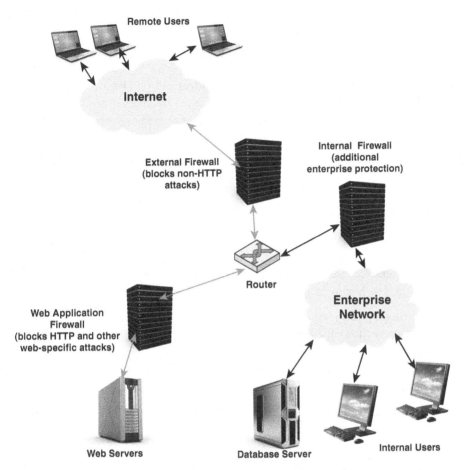

FIGURE 8.2 Context for Web Application Firewall

There are a number of hosting options for WAFs, including the following:

- **Network-based:** A network-based firewall is a hardware firewall installed at the edge of an enterprise network that acts as a filter to all traffic to and from network devices, including web-based application servers. Because there may be a variety of web applications on a number of servers, this approach can be complex to maintain. In addition, a network-based firewall may not be placed so as to catch internal traffic.

- **Local hardware:** A local hardware firewall is placed between the application server and its network connection or connections. This type of firewall is much simpler than a network-based firewall because it only has to have logic for filtering traffic specific to the local server.

- **Local software:** A software firewall is built on the server host operating system or virtual machine operating system. This approach can be as effective as a local hardware firewall and is easier to configure and modify.

An example of a WAF is ModSecurity, an open source software WAF. It is cross-platform capable, enables web application defenders to gain visibility into HTTPS traffic, and provides a language and an API to implement monitoring, logging, and access control. Key features of ModSecurity include:

- **Real-time application security monitoring and access control:** All HTTP traffic in both directions passes through ModSecurity, where it can be inspected and filtered. ModSecurity also has a persistent storage mechanism, which enables tracking of events over time to perform event correlation.

- **Virtual patching:** This is the ability to apply web application patching without making changes directly to the application. Virtual patching is applicable to applications that use any communication protocol, but it is particularly useful with HTTP because the traffic can generally be well understood by an intermediary device.

- **Full HTTP traffic logging:** Web servers traditionally do very little when it comes to logging for security purposes. ModSecurity provides the ability to log events, including raw transaction data, which is essential for forensics. In addition, the system manager gets to choose which transactions are logged, which parts of a transaction are logged, and which parts are sanitized.

- **Web application hardening:** This is a method of attack surface reduction, in which the system manager selectively narrows down the HTTP features that will be accepted (e.g., request methods, request headers, content types).

ModSecurity can be deployed as an embedded software package on the same server as the web applications. It can also be deployed on a separate server that can protect a number of web servers from one central location. This provides complete isolation and dedicated resources to the firewall function.

Web Browser Security and Privacy

Web browsers on user systems provide an entry point for malware and a variety of privacy violations. This is of concern to all users, whether at home or in the workplace. For organizations, the particular concern is that malware or other threat actions may gain entry to the organization's IT resources via a web browser on an employee system.

A number of factors come into play:

- Users do not know how to configure their web browsers securely.

- Users click on links without considering the risks of their actions.

- Web addresses can be disguised or take a user to an unexpected site.

- Websites require that users enable certain features or install more software, putting the computer at additional risk.

- Vendors configure web browsers for increased functionality at the cost of decreased security.

- Vendors discover new security vulnerabilities after the software is configured and packaged.

- Vendors bundle computer systems and software packages with additional software, which increases the number of vulnerabilities.

- Third-party software does not have a mechanism for receiving security updates.

As a result, exploiting vulnerabilities in web browsers has become a popular way for attackers to compromise computer systems. According to the F-Secure Labs article "Securing the Web Browser" [FSEC19], the following are the most common threat actions:

- **Connections to online resources (e.g., DNS servers, websites):** To fetch content from a site for viewing, a web browser normally communicates with a DNS server that directs it to the correct site; the site then provides the desired content to the browser. Various attacks subvert and intercept this communication. The actual interception can happen at various points and usually ends in redirecting the browser to a malicious site, where it and the user are exposed to unsolicited content, drive-by downloads, and exploit kits.

- **Plugins installed on the browser:** Attackers can target vulnerabilities in third-party plugins that users install on their browser to either hijack the browser's web traffic, snoop on it (particularly for sensitive finance-related data), or perform harmful actions on the device, such as installing malware.

- **Vulnerabilities in the browser itself:** Attackers often leverage flaws in a browser to either snoop on sensitive data transmitted via the web browser (e.g., when entered in forms on a web page) or to perform harmful actions on the device.

Organizations should ensure that employees have updated their browsers to the latest version. A web browser should have basic user access with no administrator privileges. The organization should require use of a browser with strong security features, including:

- **Anti-phishing:** Evaluates and filters suspect links in search results or on a website

- **Anti-malware:** Scans and blocks suspect files from being downloaded

- **Plugin security:** Evaluates and blocks insecure plugins

- **Sandbox:** Isolates the web browser's processes so that it doesn't affect the operating system

Users should be trained to set the security and privacy settings of a browser to the highest levels possible and allow only certain actions, such as the use of JavaScript, on trusted sites.

8.3 Mobile App Security

A *mobile device* is any portable technology running an operating system optimized or designed for mobile computing, such as Android or Apple's iOS. The definition excludes technology running traditional/classic or more general-purpose operating systems, such as any of the Microsoft Windows desktop or server operating systems, versions of macOS, or Linux.

Mobile devices have become an essential element for organizations as part of the overall network infrastructure. Mobile devices provide increased convenience for individuals as well as the potential for increased productivity in the workplace. Because of the widespread use and unique characteristics of mobile devices, security for the devices is a pressing and complex issue. In essence, an organization needs to implement a security policy through a combination of security features built into the mobile devices and additional security controls provided by network components that regulate the use of the mobile devices.

Just as users access remote services via web browsers on computers that link to web servers, users access remote services via apps on their mobile device that link to remote servers. The focus in this case is on the security of the apps.

Mobile Ecosystem

The execution of mobile applications on a mobile device may involve communication across a number of networks and interaction with a number of systems owned and operated by a variety of parties. This ecosystem makes the achievement of effective security challenging.

Figure 8.3 illustrates the main elements in the ecosystem within which mobile device applications function.

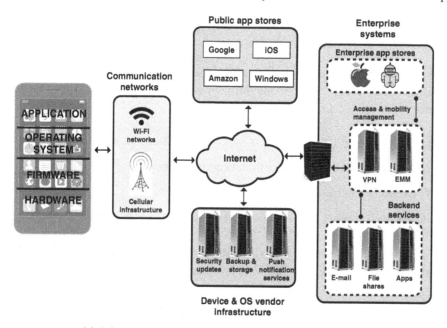

FIGURE 8.3   Mobile Ecosystem

Figure 8.3 shows the following elements in the ecosystem within which mobile device applications function:

- **Cellular and Wi-Fi infrastructure:** Modern mobile devices are typically equipped with the capability to use cellular and Wi-Fi networks to access the Internet and to place telephone calls. Cellular network cores also rely upon authentication servers to use and store customer authentication information.

- **Public application stores (public app stores):** Public app stores include native app stores; these are digital distribution services operated and developed by mobile OS vendors. For Android, the official app store is Google Play, and for iOS, it is simply called the App Store. These stores invest considerable effort in detecting and thwarting malware and ensuring that the apps do not cause unwanted behavior on mobile devices. In addition, there are numerous third-party app stores. The danger with third-party stores is uncertainty about what level of trust the user or the enterprise should have that the apps are free of malware.

- **Private application stores (private app stores):** Many enterprises maintain their own app stores that offer applications of specific utility to the enterprise, for Android, for iOS, or for both.

- **Device and OS vendor infrastructure:** Mobile device and OS vendors host servers to provide updates and patches to the OS and apps. Other cloud-based services may be offered, such as storing user data and wiping a missing device.

- **Enterprise mobility management systems:** Enterprise mobility management (EMM) is a general term that refers to everything involved in managing mobile devices and related components (e.g., wireless networks). EMM is much broader than just information security; it includes mobile application management, inventory management, and cost management. Although EMM is not directly classified as a security technology, it can help in deploying policies to an enterprise's device pool and monitoring a device's state.

- **Enterprise mobile services:** These backend services—including email, file sharing, and other applications—are accessible from authorized users' mobile devices.

Mobile Device Vulnerabilities

Mobile devices need additional, specialized protection measures beyond those implemented for other client devices, such as desktop and laptop devices that are used only within the organization's facilities and on the organization's networks. SP 800-124 (*Guidelines for Managing and Securing Mobile Devices in the Enterprise*) lists seven major security concerns for mobile devices, which the following paragraphs summarize.

Lack of Physical Security Controls

Mobile devices, which are typically under the complete control of the user, are used and kept in a variety of locations outside the organization's control, including off premises. Even if a device is required to remain on premises, the user may move the device within the organization between secure and non-secured locations. Thus, theft and tampering are realistic threats.

A security policy for mobile devices must assume that any mobile device may be stolen or at least accessed by a malicious party. The threat is twofold: A malicious party may attempt to recover sensitive data from the device itself or may use the device to gain access to the organization's resources.

Use of Untrusted Mobile Devices

In addition to company-issued and company-controlled mobile devices, virtually all employees have personal smartphones and/or tablets. An organization must assume that these devices are not trustworthy. That is, the devices may not employ encryption, and either the user or a third party may have installed a bypass to the built-in restrictions on security, operating system use, and so on. A policy that allows employees, business partners, and other users to utilize a personally selected and purchased client device to execute enterprise applications and access data and the corporate network is known as a *bring-your-own-device* (**BYOD**) policy. Typically, it spans smartphones and tablets, but the strategy may also be used for laptops.

Measures for dealing with BYOD are discussed later in this section.

Use of Untrusted Networks

If a mobile device is used on premises, it can connect to organization resources over the organization's own in-house wireless networks. However, for off-premises use, the user will typically access organizational resources via Wi-Fi or cellular access to the Internet and from the Internet to the organization. Thus, traffic that includes an off-premises segment is potentially susceptible to eavesdropping or man-in-the-middle types of attacks. Thus, the security policy must assume that the networks between the mobile device and the organization are not trustworthy.

A good mechanism for dealing with untrusted networks is to use a virtual private network (VPN). A VPN is a restricted-use, logical (i.e., artificial or simulated) computer network that is constructed from the system resources of a relatively public physical (i.e., real) network (e.g., the Internet), often using encryption (located at hosts or gateways) and authentication. The endpoints of the virtual network are said to be *tunneled* through the larger network. An external user can in effect log on to the VPN and then communicate with enterprise servers.

Use of Applications Created by Unknown Parties

By design, it is easy to find and install third-party applications on mobile devices. This poses the obvious risk of installing malicious software. An organization has several options for dealing with this threat, as described subsequently.

Interaction with Other Systems

A common feature on smartphones and tablets is the ability to automatically synchronize data, apps, contacts, photos, and so on with other computing devices and with cloud-based storage. Unless an organization has control of all the devices involved in synchronization, there is considerable risk of the organization's data being stored in an unsecured location—as well as a risk that malware will be introduced.

Use of Untrusted Content

Mobile devices may access and use content that other computing devices do not encounter. An example is the Quick Response (QR) code, which is a two-dimensional barcode. QR codes are designed to be captured by a mobile device camera and used by the mobile device. The QR code translates to a URL, so that a malicious QR code could direct the mobile device to malicious websites.

Use of Location Services

The GPS capability on mobile devices can be used to maintain a knowledge of the physical location of the device. While this feature might be useful to an organization as part of a presence service, it creates security risks. An attacker can use the location information to determine where the device and user are located, which may be of use to the attacker.

BYOD Policies

A number of organizations supply mobile devices for employee use and preconfigure those devices to conform to the enterprise security policy. However, many organizations find it convenient or even necessary to adopt a bring-your-own-device (BYOD) policy that allows the personal mobile devices of employees to have access to corporate resources. IT managers should be able to inspect each device before allowing network access. IT should establish configuration guidelines for operating systems and applications. For example, it may say that rooted or jailbroken devices are not permitted on the network, and mobile devices cannot store corporate contacts on local storage. The BYOD policy generally also prohibits sideloading. Whether a device is owned by the organization or an employee, the organization should configure the device with security controls, including the following:

Rooting is the process of removing a restricted mode of operation. For example, rooting may enable content with digital rights to be used on any computer, or it may allow enhanced third-party operating systems or applications to be used on a mobile device. While rooting is the term used for Android devices, jailbreaking is the equivalent term used for Apple's devices.

Sideloading is the act of downloading an app to a device via links or websites, without going through the official App Store. While enterprises often use sideloading as a method for distributing homegrown apps, malicious actors also use sideloading (via enterprise certificates in many cases bought on the black market) to distribute their malware.

- Enable auto-lock, which causes the device to lock if it has not been used for a given amount of time, requiring the user to re-enter a PIN or a password to re-activate the device.

- Enable password or PIN protection. The PIN or password is needed to unlock the device. In addition, it can be configured so that email and other data on the device are encrypted using the PIN or password and can only be retrieved with the PIN or password.

- Avoid using auto-complete features that remember usernames or passwords.

- Enable remote wipe.

- Ensure that TLS protection is enabled, if available.

- Make sure that software, including operating systems and applications, is up to date.

- Install antivirus software as it becomes available.

- Either prohibit sensitive data from being stored on the mobile device or require that it be encrypted.

- Ensure that IT staff have the ability to remotely access devices, wipe the device of all data, and then disable the device in the event of loss or theft.

- Prohibit all installation of third-party applications, implement whitelisting to prohibit installation of all unapproved applications, or implement a secure sandbox that isolates the organization's data and applications from all other data and applications on the mobile device. Any application that is on an approved list should be accompanied by a digital signature and a public-key certificate from an approved authority.

- Implement and enforce restrictions on what devices can synchronize and on the use of cloud-based storage.

- To deal with the threat of untrusted content, train personnel on the risks inherent in untrusted content and disabling camera use on corporate mobile devices.

- To counter the threat of malicious use of location services, require that these services be disabled on all mobile devices.

Organizations can also enforce the use of a device's permission options, which are designed to protect privacy. In the case of Android OS, no app, by default, has permission to perform any operations that would adversely impact other apps, the OS, or the user. This includes reading or writing the user's private data (such as contacts or emails), reading or writing another app's files, performing network access, keeping the device awake, and so on. An app must publicize the permissions it requires by including a notice known as a *manifest*. If an app lists normal permissions in its manifest (i.e., permissions that don't pose much risk to the user's privacy or the device's operation), the system automatically grants those permissions to the app. If an app lists dangerous permissions in its manifest (i.e., permissions that could potentially affect the user's privacy or the device's normal operation), the user must explicitly agree to grant those permissions.

An Android user can manage all app permissions by opening the list of apps and selecting App Permissions. Android displays a list of different categories of permissions, along with the number of apps installed that have access to that permission. Categories include Body Sensors, Calendar, Camera, Contacts, Location, Microphone, Phone, SMS, and Storage. The user can see a list of which apps have which permission or go to a specific app and see what permissions it has and change the allowable permissions.

Apple's iOS, for iPhone and iPad, has a similar permissions capability.

Mobile Application Vetting

Millions of apps are available from the two major stores, Apple App Store and Google Play, and millions more from other public app stores. The reliability and security of apps may vary widely, and the vetting process may be opaque or insufficiently robust, particularly for apps from outside the two major stores.

Regardless of the source of an app, an enterprise should perform its own evaluation of the security of an app to determine if it conforms to an organization's security requirements. The requirements should specify how data used by an app should be secured, the environment in which an app will be deployed, and the acceptable level of risk for an app.

The process of evaluation and approval or rejection of apps within an organization, referred to as *app vetting* in NIST SP 800-163 (*Vetting the Security of Mobile Applications*), is illustrated in Figure 8.4. The vetting process begins when an app is acquired from a public or enterprise store or submitted by an in-house or third-party developer. An administrator is a member of the organization who is responsible for deploying, maintaining, and securing the organization's mobile devices as well as ensuring that deployed devices and their installed apps conform to the organization's security requirements. The administrator submits the app to an app testing facility in the organization that employs automated and/ or human analyzers to evaluate the security characteristics of an app, including searching for malware, identifying vulnerabilities, and assessing risks. The resulting security report and risk assessment are conveyed to an auditor or auditors.

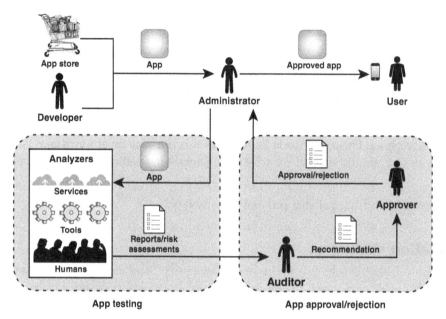

FIGURE 8.4   App Vetting Process

The role of an auditor is to inspect reports and risk assessments from one or more analyzers to ensure that an app meets the security requirements of the organization. The auditor also evaluates additional criteria to determine if the app violates any organization-specific security requirements that could not be ascertained by the analyzers. The auditor then makes recommendation to someone in the organization who has the authority to approve or reject an app for deployment on mobile devices. If the approver approves an app, the administrator can then deploy the app on the organization's mobile devices.

The U.S. Department of Homeland Security offers a tool, AppVet, that provides automated management support of the app testing and app approval/rejection activities.

Resources for Mobile Device Security

A number of documents from U.S. agencies are valuable resources for any organization planning for mobile device security. The following are particularly useful:

- **[DHS17]:** *Study on Mobile Device Security.* Develops a threat model consisting of six areas that provides a detailed summary of the greatest threats in each area as well as current mitigations and defenses.

- **NISTIR 8144:** *Assessing Threats to Mobile Devices & Infrastructure.* Provides a detailed description of the threats related to mobile devices and the enterprise.

- **SP 800-124:** *Guidelines for Managing and Securing Mobile Devices in the Enterprise.* Provides recommendations for selecting, implementing, and using centralized management technologies and explains the security concerns inherent in mobile device use and provides recommendations for securing mobile devices throughout their life cycles.

- **SP 800-163:** *Vetting the Security of Mobile Applications.* (Describes in detail app vetting and app approval/rejection activities.

- **SP 800-164:** *Guidelines on Hardware-Rooted Security in Mobile Devices.* Focuses on defining the fundamental security primitives and capabilities needed to securely enable mobile devices.

- **SP 1800-4:** *Mobile Device Security: Cloud and Hybrid Builds.* Contains reference architectures; demonstrates implementation of standards-based, commercially available cybersecurity technologies; and helps organizations use technologies to reduce the risk of intrusion via mobile devices.

8.4 Online Privacy Threats

As with any other area of privacy, the first step in developing privacy by design and privacy engineering solutions for online privacy is to define the threats to online privacy. This section looks at these threats in the two areas covered by this chapter: web application privacy and mobile app privacy.

Web Application Privacy

The Open Web Application Security Project (OWASP) Top 10 Privacy Risks Project provides a list of the top privacy risks in web applications. The goal of the project is to identify the most important technical and organizational privacy risks for web applications, from the perspectives of both the user (data subject) and the provider (data owner). The risks are:

- **Web application vulnerabilities:** Failing to suitably design and implement an application, detect a problem, or promptly apply a fix (patch), which is likely to result in a privacy breach. Vulnerability is a key problem in any system that guards or operates on sensitive user data.

- **User-side data leakage:** Failing to prevent the leakage of any information containing or related to user data, or the data itself, to any unauthorized party resulting in loss of data confidentiality. Leakage may be introduced due to either intentional malicious breach or unintentional mistake (e.g., caused by insufficient access management controls, insecure storage, duplication of data, or a lack of awareness).

- **Insufficient data breach response:** Not informing the affected persons (data subjects) about a possible breach or data leak, resulting either from intentional or unintentional events; failure to remedy the situation by fixing the cause; not attempting to limit the leaks.

- **Insufficient deletion of personal data:** Failing to delete personal data effectively and/or in a timely fashion after termination of the specified purpose or upon request.

- **Non-transparent policies, terms, and conditions:** Not providing sufficient information describing how data are processed, such as their collection, storage, and processing. Failure to make this information easily accessible and understandable for non-lawyers.

- **Collection of data not required for the primary purpose:** Collecting descriptive, demographic, or any other user-related data that are not needed for the purposes of the system. Applies also to data for which the user did not provide consent.

- **Sharing of data with third party:** Providing user data to a third party without obtaining the user's consent. Sharing results either due to transfer or exchanging for monetary compensation or otherwise due to inappropriate use of third-party resources included in websites, such as widgets (e.g., maps, social networking buttons), analytics, or web bugs (e.g., beacons).

- **Outdated personal data:** Using outdated, incorrect, or bogus user data and failing to update or correct the data.

- **Missing or insufficient session expiration:** Failing to effectively enforce session termination. May result in collection of additional user data without the user's consent or awareness.

- **Insecure data transfer:** Failing to provide data transfers over encrypted and secured channels, excluding the possibility of data leakage. Failing to enforce mechanisms that limit the leak surface (e.g., allowing to infer any user data out of the mechanics of web application operation).

Table 8.2 shows the results of an OWASP survey of privacy and security experts that estimates the frequency and impact of each of the 10 privacy risks.

TABLE 8.2   Web Application Privacy Risks

Privacy Risk	Frequency	Impact
Web application vulnerabilities	High	Very high
Operator-sided data leakage	High	Very high
Insufficient data breach response	High	Very high
Insufficient deletion of personal data	Very high	High
Non-transparent policies, terms, and conditions	Very high	High
Collection of data not required for the primary purpose	Very high	High
Sharing of data with third party	High	High
Outdated personal data	High	Very high
Missing or insufficient session expiration	Medium	Very high
Insecure data transfer	Medium	Very high

Mobile App Privacy

Privacy threats related to mobile apps fall into two categories: threats that exploit vulnerabilities in apps that are not themselves malicious and threats related to the installation of malicious apps.

Threats Against Vulnerable Applications

Legitimate mobile apps may be vulnerable to a number of privacy and security threats, typically due to poor coding practices used in app development or underlying vulnerabilities in the mobile device operating system. Consider the following threats against vulnerable applications, encompassing both privacy and security threats [DHS17]:

- **Insecure network communications:** Network traffic needs to be securely encrypted to prevent an adversary from eavesdropping. Apps need to properly authenticate the remote server when connecting to prevent man-in-the-middle attacks and connection to malicious servers.

- **Web browser vulnerabilities:** Adversaries can exploit vulnerabilities in mobile device web browser applications as an entry point to gain access to a mobile device.

- **Vulnerabilities in third-party libraries:** Third-party software libraries are reusable components that may be distributed freely or offered for a fee to other software vendors. Software development by component or modules may be more efficient, and third-party libraries are routinely used across the industry. However, a flawed library can introduce vulnerabilities in any app that includes or makes use of that library. Depending on the pervasiveness of the library, its use can potentially affect thousands of apps and millions of users.

- **Cryptographic vulnerabilities:** Cryptographic vulnerabilities can occur due to failure to use cryptographic protections for sensitive data, due to the improper implementation of a secure cryptographic algorithm, or due to the use of a proprietary cryptographic technique that can be more easily cracked than those validated and recommended for use by NIST.

Threats from Potentially Harmful Applications

Harmful applications are designed to gather or compromise sensitive information. Consider the following examples [DHS17]:

- **Apps that gather privacy-sensitive information:** These are malicious apps that can collect information such as device persistent identifiers, device location, list of installed applications, contact lists, call logs, calendar data, or text messages without adequate consent of the user.

- **Surreptitious eavesdropping:** These apps access device sensors to eavesdrop or photograph the user or others.

- **Exploiting vulnerabilities:** Apps may be designed to take advantage of vulnerabilities in other apps, the operating system, or other device components, despite the isolation capabilities of the mobile OS.

- **Manipulation of trusted apps:** These apps masquerade as benign (and often popular) applications. Downloaded unwittingly by a user, such an app then performs any number of malicious activities without the user's awareness. Some effectively mimic the real app's behavior on the surface, making it difficult for users to recognize the risks to which they are exposed.

- **Sharing of data between trusted apps:** Apps may share data with external resources, such as Dropbox, without the user's awareness.

A useful source of information on both threats against vulnerable apps and threats from potentially harmful apps is the Mobile Threat Catalogue maintained by NIST (https://pages.nist.gov/mobile-threat-catalogue).

8.5 Online Privacy Requirements

This section follows the method used in Chapter 3, "Information Privacy Requirements and Guidelines," to arrive at online privacy requirements. The first part of this section presents several different categorizations of principles for online privacy. The second part of this section discusses an online privacy framework developed by the U.S. Federal Trade Commission (FTC), which is based on the FTC's statement of principles.

Online Privacy Principles

The FTC defines a set of fair information practice principles (FIPPs) appropriate for specifying online privacy requirements [FTC98]. The FTC derives these principles from the privacy FIPPs developed by the OECD and other organizations, as described in Chapter 3. The principles are:

- **Notice/awareness:** Ensuring that consumers are notified or made aware of an organization's information practices before any information is actually collected from them (e.g., an organization's privacy policy). Such notification or awareness should include:

    — Identification of the entity collecting the data

    — Identification of the uses to which the data will be put

    — Identification of any potential recipients of the data

    — Nature of the data collected

    — Whether the provision of the requested data is voluntary or required and the consequences of a refusal to provide the requested information

    — Steps taken by the data collector to ensure the confidentiality, integrity, and quality of the data

- **Choice/consent:** Ensuring that consumers are given the option to decide how personal information collected about them is to be used and whether it may be used for secondary purposes.

- **Access/participation:** Ensuring an individual's ability both to access data and to contest that data's accuracy and completeness.

- **Integrity/security:** Ensuring that data are both accurate and secure. Security and accuracy come from both the consumer and the organization collecting the PII.

- **Enforcement/redress:** Ensuring that mechanisms are in place to enforce privacy.

A proposed consumer privacy bill of rights from the U.S. government [OWH12] develops a more detailed list of principles, which is useful in understanding the range of requirements that should guide implementation of online privacy:

- **Individual control:** Consumers have a right to exercise control over what personal data companies collect from them and how they use it. Companies should provide consumers appropriate control over the personal data that consumers share with others and over how companies collect, use, or disclose personal data. Companies should enable these choices by providing consumers with easily used and accessible mechanisms that reflect the scale, scope, and sensitivity of the personal data that they collect, use, or disclose, as well as the sensitivity of the uses they make of personal data. Companies should offer consumers clear and simple choices, presented at times and in ways that enable consumers to make meaningful decisions about personal data collection, use, and disclosure. Companies should offer consumers means to withdraw or limit consent that are as accessible and easily used as the methods for granting consent in the first place.

- **Transparency:** Consumers have a right to easily understandable and accessible information about privacy and security practices. At times and in places that are most useful to enabling consumers to gain a meaningful understanding of privacy risks and the ability to exercise individual control, companies should provide clear descriptions of what personal data they collect, why they need the data, how they will use it, when they will delete the data or de-identify it, and whether and for what purposes they may share personal data with third parties.

- **Respect for context:** Consumers have a right to expect that companies will collect, use, and disclose personal data in ways that are consistent with the context in which consumers provide the data. Companies should limit their use and disclosure of personal data to purposes that are consistent with both the relationship they have with consumers and the context in which consumers originally disclosed the data, unless required by law to do otherwise. If companies use or disclose personal data for other purposes, they should provide heightened transparency and individual control by disclosing these other purposes in a manner that is prominent and easily actionable by consumers at the time of data collection. If, subsequent to collection, companies decide to use or disclose personal data for purposes that are inconsistent with the context in which the data was disclosed, they must provide heightened measures of transparency and individual choice. Finally, the age and familiarity with technology of consumers who engage with a company are important elements of context. Companies should fulfill the obligations under this principle in ways that are appropriate for the age and sophistication of consumers. Helen Nissenbaum's work in this area is particularly interesting [NISS11].

- **Security:** Consumers have a right to secure and responsible handling of personal data. Companies should assess the privacy and security risks associated with their personal data practices and maintain reasonable safeguards to control risks such as loss; unauthorized access, use, destruction, or modification; and improper disclosure.

■ **Access and accuracy:** Consumers have a right to access and correct personal data in usable formats in a manner that is appropriate to the sensitivity of the data and the risk of adverse consequences to consumers if the data is inaccurate. Companies should use reasonable measures to ensure that they maintain accurate personal data. Companies also should provide consumers with reasonable access to personal data that they collect or maintain about them, as well as the appropriate means and opportunity to correct inaccurate data or request its deletion or use limitation. Companies that handle personal data should construe this principle in a manner consistent with freedom of expression and freedom of the press. In determining what measures they may use to maintain accuracy and to provide access, correction, deletion, or suppression capabilities to consumers, companies may also consider the scale, scope, and sensitivity of the personal data that they collect or maintain and the likelihood that its use may expose consumers to financial, physical, or other material harm.

■ **Focused collection:** Consumers have a right to reasonable limits on the personal data that companies collect and retain. Companies should collect only as much personal data as they need to accomplish purposes specified under the respect for context principle. Companies should securely dispose of or de-identify personal data when they no longer need it, unless they are under a legal obligation to do otherwise.

■ **Accountability:** Consumers have a right to have personal data handled by companies with appropriate measures in place to ensure that they adhere to the Consumer Privacy Bill of Rights. Companies should be accountable to enforcement authorities and consumers for adhering to these principles. Companies also should hold employees responsible for adhering to these principles. To achieve this end, companies should train their employees as appropriate to handle personal data consistently with these principles and regularly evaluate their performance in this regard. Where appropriate, companies should conduct full audits. Companies that disclose personal data to third parties should at a minimum ensure that the recipients are under enforceable contractual obligations to adhere to these principles, unless they are required by law to do otherwise.

Online Privacy Framework

The FTC presents an online privacy framework that is a useful guide to best practices for implementing online privacy policies and mechanisms [FTC12]. The framework consists of three elements, as shown in Figure 8.5 and described in the list that follows:

■ **Privacy by design:** Build in privacy at every stage of product development.

- **Simplified choice for businesses and consumers:** Give consumers the ability to make decisions about their data at a relevant time and in a relevant context, including through a "do not track" mechanism, while reducing the burden on businesses of providing unnecessary choices.

- **Greater transparency:** Make information collection and use practices transparent.

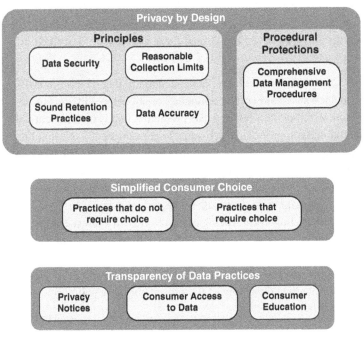

FIGURE 8.5 FTC Online Privacy Network

Privacy by Design

As described in Chapter 2, "Information Privacy Concepts," privacy by design (PbD) dictates that privacy requirements be considered at the time of designing a new system, subsystem, application, or other component of the IT infrastructure of an organization. The intent is to design privacy engineering mechanisms and techniques that can be incorporated in a holistic fashion during the implementation and deployment of a system.

The PbD element of the online privacy framework defines two components. First, companies should incorporate substantive privacy protections into their actions, referred to as PbD principles. Second, companies should maintain comprehensive data management procedures throughout the life cycle of their products and services.

The relevant PbD principles are as follows:

- **Data security:** Effective security for PII involves both management practices and technical controls. Organizations can obtain guidance in this area from a number of private sector sources, such as the Payment Card Institute Data Security Standard for payment card data, the SANS Institute's security policy templates, and standards and best practices guidelines for the financial services industry provided by BITS, the technology policy division of the Financial Services Roundtable. Standards organizations, such as NIST and ISO, also provide useful guidance for all types of organizations; these sources are described in Chapter 3.

- **Reasonable collection limits:** Companies should limit data collection to that which is consistent with the context of a particular transaction or the consumer's relationship with the business, or as required or specifically authorized by law. For any data collection that is inconsistent with these contexts, companies should make appropriate disclosures to consumers at a relevant time and in a prominent manner—outside of a privacy policy or other legal document. The FTC cites one example of a company innovating around the concept of privacy by design through collection limitation [FTC12]. The Graduate Management Admission Council (GMAC) previously collected fingerprints from individuals taking the Graduate Management Admission Test. After concerns were raised about individuals' fingerprints being cross-referenced against criminal databases, GMAC developed a palm vein recognition system that could be used solely for test-taking purposes [CLIN10]. GMAC found this system more stable over time than fingerprinting, more accurate than facial recognition, and less invasive than iris or retinal scanning. It is less susceptible to function creep over time than the taking of fingerprints because palm prints are not widely used as a common identifier.

- **Sound retention practices:** Companies should implement reasonable restrictions on the retention of data and should dispose of the data when they have outlived the legitimate purpose for which they were collected. In some contexts, companies could retain data after de-identification.

- **Data accuracy:** Companies should take reasonable steps to ensure the accuracy of the data they collect and maintain, particularly if such data could cause significant harm or be used to deny consumers services.

Procedural Protections

The other aspect of PbD in the privacy framework is procedural protections. In essence, this means that companies should maintain comprehensive data management procedures throughout the life cycle of their products and services.

To understand the scope that is intended by the term *procedural protections*, it is useful to look at a settlement between the FTC and Google [FTC11]. The privacy programs that the settlement mandates must, at a minimum, contain certain controls and procedures, including:

- The designation of personnel responsible for the privacy program.

- A risk assessment that, at a minimum, addresses employee training and management and product design and development. The privacy risk assessment should include consideration of risks in each area of relevant operation, including but not limited to (1) employee training and management, including training on the requirements of this order, and (2) product design, development, and research.

- The implementation of controls designed to address the risks identified, together with regular testing or monitoring of the effectiveness of those privacy controls.

- Appropriate oversight of service providers.

- Evaluation and adjustment of the privacy program in light of regular testing and monitoring.

A 2016 independent assessor's report [PROM16] found that Google had implemented the mandated privacy program, including the following controls:

- Privacy program staffing and subject matter expertise

- Employee privacy training and awareness

- Internal and external policies, procedures, and guidelines

- Privacy risk assessment activities

- Product launch reviews for privacy considerations

- Privacy code audits

- End user privacy tools and settings

- Complaint and feedback processes and mechanisms

- Periodic internal and external privacy program assessments

- Coordination with, and support of, the Google information security program

- Third-party service provider oversight

- Incident reporting and response procedures

Of particular interest are the end user privacy tools and settings. Table 8.3 indicates the privacy settings, guides, and tools for users to control how Google collects, uses, and protects their data. The Google privacy program is a good example of a set of online privacy policies and procedures and can serve as a guide for other companies.

TABLE 8.3   Google End User Privacy Settings and Tools

Setting/Tool Type	Name	Description
Account management tools	My Account	Serves as the central hub of security, privacy, and general account settings, tools, and guides for each user
	Dashboard	Provides an "at-a-glance" view of the user's recent activity (e.g., how many documents and emails the user has saved) and lets the user manage product settings directly
	Activity Controls	Displays settings to manage, edit, and delete activity and data use associated with a user's account, including the user's searches and browsing activity
	Account Permissions for Connected Apps	Shows the applications and external websites connected to a user's Google account and allows the user to manage those permissions and remove applications as desired
	Inactive Account Manager	Allows the user to choose what happens to account data if an account becomes inactive for a length of time that the user specifies, including deleting the account or nominating a trusted contact who may access the account data when the account becomes inactive
	Account and Service Deletion	Allows the user to delete certain Google products (e.g., Gmail) or delete the user's entire Google account
Product settings	Ads Settings	Allows the user to control the types of ads received by adjusting the user's interests and demographic details and removing unwanted ads or to opt out of personalized ads altogether
	Search Settings	Allows the user to control search settings such as the use of SafeSearch filters and whether private results are included in search results
	Analytics Opt-Out	Allows the user to control whether the user's data will be used by Google Analytics
Privacy tools and guides	Privacy Checkup	Facilitates a walkthrough of a user's products and services that allows the user to adjust privacy settings
	Product Privacy Guide	Contains links to articles with information about how Google's products work and how a user can manage his or her data within products
	Incognito Mode	Allows use of Google's Chrome browser without Chrome saving the pages viewed in Incognito windows

Setting/Tool Type	Name	Description
Security tools and guides	Security Checkup	Facilitates a walkthrough of a user's products and services that allows the user to adjust security settings, including the user's recovery information, recent security events, connected devices, and account permissions
	2-Step Verification	Allows the user to enable a stronger security sign-on process for the user's Google accounts that requires two forms of authentication (e.g., password and verification code)
	Device Activity and Notifications	Allows the user to review which devices have accessed the user's accounts and control how to receive alerts if Google detects potentially suspicious activity
	Service Encryption	Provides information about service encryption, which is available for several Google products, including Search, Maps, YouTube, and Gmail
	Chrome Safe Browsing	Provides warning messages about websites that could contain malware, unwanted software, and phishing schemes designed to steal personal information
Data export	Download Your Data	Allows the user to download and export data from his or her Google accounts

Simplified Consumer Choice

The FTC considers the handling of personal data to fall into two categories [FTC12]:

- **Practices that do not require choice:** Companies do not need to provide choice before collecting and using consumer data for practices that are consistent with the context of the transaction or the company's relationship with the consumer or that are required or specifically authorized by law.

- **Practices that require choice:** For practices requiring choice, companies should offer the choice at a time and in a context in which the consumer is deciding about his or her data. Companies should obtain affirmative express consent before (1) using consumer data in a materially different manner than claimed when the data was collected or (2) collecting sensitive data for certain purposes.

Transparency of Data Practices

Users need to be aware of the privacy risks inherent in sharing information with particular companies. The FTC lists three principles that should guide companies in providing customers and other uses with privacy information [FTC12]:

- **Privacy notices:** Privacy notices should be clear, short, and standardized to enable better comprehension and comparison of privacy practices.

- **Access:** Companies should provide reasonable access to the consumer data they maintain; the extent of access should be proportionate to the sensitivity of the data and the nature of their use.

- **Consumer education:** All stakeholders should expand their efforts to educate consumers about commercial data privacy practices.

8.6   Privacy Notices

The most fundamental requirement for users to be able to make informed online privacy decisions is that they need to be aware of and understand the data practices of the service or company, including what personal information is collected, used, retained, and shared. The principal vehicle by which companies provide this information is the privacy notice. For web-based services, virtually all web pages have a privacy link at the bottom of their main page that goes to a page that states the privacy policy, which is focused on disclosure issues.

For mobile apps, this type of privacy information is generally less available. Comparatively smaller screens and other device restrictions constrain how users can be given notice about and control over data practices.

A number of studies have demonstrated that most current privacy notices are ineffective at informing users and providing choice, although recent regulations such as GDPR are tending to correct this. These studies cite a number of factors as likely reasons for the ineffectiveness of current privacy notices [SCHA17]:

- **Conflating requirements:** Companies are faced with a number of requirements in the design of their online privacy notices. Users want clear, easy-to-understand, and brief statements about a company's privacy practices and privacy controls. Companies need to comply with legal and regulatory requirements concerning the content of the privacy notice, such as defined in Europe's General Data Protection Regulation (GDPR), the U.S. Health Insurance Portability and Accountability Act (HIPAA), and the California Online Privacy Protection Act (CalOPPA). In addition, companies use privacy notices to demonstrate compliance with privacy laws and regulations other than those related to the privacy notice itself and in an attempt to limit liability by promising more than they are legally required to promise.

- **Lacking choices:** Most privacy notices offer little choice, especially for mobile apps and IoT devices. Many websites and apps interpret user access as consent to use, regardless of whether the user has seen, read, or understood the privacy policy.

- **High burden/low utility:** Most users are not willing to invest the time required to read and understand all of the privacy notices they routinely encounter, much less take the time to make choices via user controls. This problem is compounded by the lack of user-friendliness and the lack of choices.

- **Decoupled notices:** Privacy notices are generally separate from normal user interaction. Websites only link to a privacy policy at the bottom of the page; mobile apps link to a privacy policy in the app store or in some app submenu; privacy policies for IoT devices are only available on the manufacturer's website.

Notice Requirements

ISO 29184 (*Online Privacy Notices and Consent*) provides a list of requirements that an organization should satisfy in developing a notice policy, consisting of the following:

- **Obligation to provide notice:** The organization must determine what circumstances require that notice be provided to PII principals. This includes conforming to regulatory and legal requirements, contractual obligations, and concerns with corporate image.

- **Appropriate expression:** The notice should be clear and easy to understand by the targeted PII principals.

- **Multilingual notice:** The notice should be provided in the language(s) most appropriate to the context.

- **Appropriate timing:** Typically, organizations should provide notice just prior to the collection of PII.

- **Appropriate locations:** It should be easy for PII principals to find and access privacy notices.

- **Appropriate form:** The notice structure should be clear and appropriate for the context, taking into account the means by which PII principals access notice information. For example, a mobile phone presents a limited interface and may call for a different structure of notice compared to access via a PC. Notice structure is discussed subsequently.

- **Ongoing reference:** Organizations should retain versions of notices for as long as they are associated with retained PII.

- **Accessibility:** Organizations should accommodate PII principals who have accessibility issues (e.g., vision-impaired or blind individuals).

Notice Content

There is broad agreement among a number of organizations about the required topic coverage of a privacy notice. See for example [CDOJ14], [MUNU12], [OECD06], and [BBC19].

Table 8.4 lists the topics covered by three representative policies: those of Google, which provides a variety of online applications and services (see https://policies.google.com/privacy?hl=en&gl=us); JPMorgan Chase Bank, which provides online banking services (see https://www.chase.com/digital/resources/privacy-security/privacy/online-privacy-policy); and the International Association of Privacy Professionals (IAPP), which is a membership organization (see https://iapp.org/about/privacy-notice/).

TABLE 8.4   Privacy Notice Topics

Google	JPMorgan Chase Bank	IAPP
Introduction Information Google Collects Why Google Collects Data Your Privacy Controls Sharing Your Information Keeping Your Information Secure Exporting and Deleting Your Information Compliance and Cooperation with Regulators About This Policy Related Privacy Practices Data Transfer Frameworks Key Terms Partners	Overview Use of Information Disclosure of Information Understanding Cookies, Web Beacons, and Other Tracking Technologies Opting Out of Online Behavioral Advertising Linking to Third-Party Websites Updating Your Information Changes to This Online Privacy Policy	Introduction Data Protection Officer How We Collect and Use (Process) Your Personal Information Use of the iapp.org Website When and How We Share Information with Others Transferring Personal Data from the EU to the US Data Subject Rights Security of Your Information Data Storage and Retention Changes and Updates to the Privacy Notice Questions, Concerns, or Complaints

The California Department of Justice has developed one of the clearest statements of what topics to cover in an online privacy notice [CDOJ14]. Its recommendation covers the following topics:

- **Data collection:** Describe how you collect PII, including other sources and technologies, such as cookies. Describe the kind of PII you collect.

- **Online tracking/do not track:** Make it easy for the user to find the section of your policy that relates to online tracking. Describe how you respond to a do not track (DNT) signal or similar mechanism. Disclose the presence of other parties that collect PII on your site or service, if any.

- **Data use and sharing:** Explain how you use and share PII, including:

  - Explain the uses of PII beyond what is necessary for fulfilling a customer transaction or for the basic functionality of an online service.

  - Explain your practices regarding the sharing of PII with other entities, including affiliates and marketing partners.

  - At a minimum, list the different types or categories of companies with which you share customer PII.

  - Whenever possible, provide a link to the privacy policies of third parties with whom you share PII.

  - Provide the retention period for each type or category of PII collected.

- **Individual choice and access:** Describe the choices a consumer has regarding the collection, use, and sharing of his or her PII. Consider offering your customers the opportunity to review and correct their PII.

- **Security safeguards:** Explain how you protect your customers' PII from unauthorized or illegal access, modification, use or destruction.

- **Effective date:** Give the effective date of your privacy policy.

- **Accountability:** Tell your customers whom they can contact with questions or concerns about your privacy policy and practices.

ISO 29184 includes the following, more comprehensive, list:

- **Collection purpose:** The organization should provide the following information relevant to the purpose of collection of PII:

  - The purpose(s) for which the PII is collected.

  - Information about the plausible risk to the PII principal from the processing of the PII.

  - If different purposes apply to different items of collected PII, the organization should make this clear to the PII principal.

- **PII controller:** The organization should provide the identity and contact details for the PII controller. Typically, this is not an individual, but a department or office within the organization.

- **Specific PII elements:** The organization should indicate what specific PII is being collected (e.g., name, address, and telephone number). It may be appropriate to display the actual value of an item to the principal prior to its collection.

- **Collection method:** The PII principal should understand how his or her PII is being collected. Possibilities include:

  - Directly collected from the PII principal, such as through a web form.

  - Indirectly collected. For example, the organization may collect information from a third party, such as a credit agency, and combine that with PII collected directly.

  - Observed by the PII controller. Examples include browser fingerprint and browser history.

- **Timing and location of collection:** For PII that is not directly collected, the notice should inform the principal of the timing and location of the collection.

- **Method of use:** The organization shall indicate how the PII will be used. ISO 29184 gives the following examples:

  - Used as is

  - Used after some processing (e.g., derivation, inference, de-identification, or combining with other data)

  - Combined with other data (e.g., geo-localized, via the use of cookies, from third parties)

  - Used by automated decision-making techniques (e.g., profiling, classification)

- **Geo-location and jurisdiction:** The organization should indicate where PII will be stored and processed and the legal jurisdiction(s) that govern the handling of the data.

- **Third party transfer:** The organization should provide detailed information about any transfer of the PII to a third party.

- **Retention period:** The organization should indicate how long the PII will be retained and its disposal schedule.

- **Participation of the PII principal:** The organization should indicate what rights the PII principal has with respect to collected PII, including consent, access to the PII, ability to correct PII, and ability to revoke permission.

- **Inquiry and complaint:** The organization should inform the PII principal about how to exercise his or her rights and how to file a complaint.

- **Accessing the choices for consent:** The organization should provide a means for a PII principal to review what permissions he or she has granted.

- **Basis for processing:** The organization shall provide information about the basis by which the PII will be processed, which may be by consent, contractual requirements, or legal/regulatory obligations.

- **Risks:** The organization should provide specific information about plausible risks to PII principals, where the impact to privacy and likelihood of occurrence (after mitigations are considered) are high or those risks cannot be inferred from other information provided to the PII principal.

Notice Structure

The structure of a privacy notice is a key factor in its readability and usability. Traditionally, privacy notices have consisted of a single long document divided into sections to cover the various topics. The web privacy notice of JPMorgan Chase (at the time of this writing) is an example. Such a structure tends to discourage the reader and make it difficult to find anything useful. Increasingly, companies are opting for various types of layered privacy notices to provide users with a high-level summary of a privacy policy. One approach is to use short sections with "to learn more" links to more detailed information. The IAPP web privacy notice is of this type. Another approach is to display a list of tabs with descriptive titles, which the user can select for a description of each topic. The current TDBank web privacy notice is of this type (see https://www.td.com/us/en/personal-banking/privacy/).

Mobile App Privacy Notices

Readability and accessibility of privacy notices are significant challenges for mobile apps. The California Department of Justice makes the following recommendations [CDOJ14]:

- Post or link to the policy on the application's platform page so that users can review the policy before downloading the application.

- Link to the policy within the application (e.g., from the application configuration, "About," "Information," or settings page).

The Mobile Marketing Association has released the Mobile Application Privacy Policy Framework [MMA11], which serves as a recommended template for the contents of a privacy notice for mobile apps. It covers the following topics:

- The information the application obtains and how it is used. This includes user-provided information at the time of download and registration, plus automatically collected information, such as the type of mobile device you use, your mobile device's unique device ID, the IP address of your mobile device, your mobile operating system, the type of mobile Internet browsers you use, and information about the way you use the application.

- Whether the application collects precise real-time location information of the device.

- Whether third parties see and/or have access to information obtained by the application.

- Automatic data collection and advertising, such as whether the application is supported via advertising and collects data to help the application serve ads.

- Opt-out rights.

- Data retention policy and information management.

- Children. Avoiding soliciting data from or marketing to children under age 13.

- Security procedures.

- How users are informed of changes to the privacy policy.

- Consent to the processing of user-provided and automatically collected information as set forth in the privacy policy.

- Contact information.

This list is quite in line with recommended topics for web-based privacy notices. But organizations need to be concerned about effectively presenting this information on the small screens of mobile devices. To that end, the National Telecommunications and Information Administration has developed a recommended short form privacy notice [NTIA13]. The short form should provide brief information in the following categories: types of data collected, sharing of user-specific data, means of accessing a long form privacy notice, and the identity of the entity providing the app.

With respect to the types of data collected, the short form notice should state which of the following data categories the app collects:

- **Biometrics:** Information about your body, including fingerprints, facial recognition, signatures, and/or voice print

- **Browser history:** A list of websites visited

- **Phone or text log:** A list of calls or texts made or received

- **Contacts:** A list of contacts, social networking connections or their phone numbers, postal, email, and text addresses

- **Financial info:** Credit, bank, and consumer-specific financial information such as transaction data

- **Health, medical, or therapy info:** Health claims and other information used to measure health or wellness

- **Location:** Precise past or current location of a user

- **User files:** Files stored on the device that contain the user's content, such as calendar, photos, text, or video

The short form notice should state whether the app shares user-specific data with any third-party entity that falls within any of the following categories:

- **Ad networks:** Companies that display ads to you through apps

- **Carriers:** Companies that provide mobile connections

- **Consumer data resellers:** Companies that sell consumer information to other companies for multiple purposes, including offering products and services that may interest you

- **Data analytics providers:** Companies that collect and analyze your data

- **Government entities:** Any sharing with the government except where required by law or expressly permitted in an emergency

- **Operating systems and platforms:** Software companies that power your device, app stores, and companies that provide common tools and information for apps about app consumers

- **Other apps:** Other apps of companies that the consumer may not have a relationship with

- **Social networks:** Companies that connect individuals around common interests and facilitate sharing

The National Telecommunications and Information Administration also provides guidance concerning how and when to display this data [NTIA13].

Privacy Notice Design Space

The content of a privacy notice is only one aspect of good privacy notice design. The article "Designing Effective Privacy Notices and Controls" from *IEEE Internet Computing* [SCHA17] presents a design space for privacy notices that encompasses four dimensions: the notice's timing (when it is presented), channel (how it is presented), modality (communication model used), and control (how are the choices provided), as illustrated in Figure 8.6.

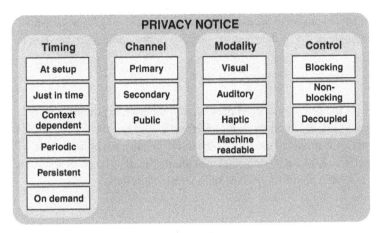

FIGURE 8.6   Privacy Notice Design Space

Timing

The effectiveness of a privacy notice depends a great deal on the timing of its presentation. If the web service or app presents the notice at a time that is inconvenient for the user, the user is apt to ignore it. "Designing Effective Privacy Notices and Controls," from *IEEE Internet Computing* [SCHA17] lists six timing opportunities:

- **At setup:** A mobile app can present the privacy notice once when the user is about to install the software. This enables the user to make an informed decision about purchasing the software. Typically, the app that uses this timing also provides a means for the user to review the privacy notice subsequently.

- **Just in time:** A mobile app or web service can show the privacy implications of a requested transaction. This has the advantage that the user need only be shown privacy information related to that transaction.

- **Context dependent:** A mobile app or web service can present a privacy notice triggered by certain aspects of the user's context, such as location (e.g., in proximity to a data-collecting sensor) or who will have access to the information, or can warn about potentially unintended settings.

- **Periodic:** A mobile app or web service may repeat a privacy notice periodically as a reminder. For example, iOS periodically reminds users of apps that access the phone's location in the background.

- **Persistent:** Persistent notices alert the user of ongoing data activity with privacy consequences. For instance, Android and iOS display a small icon in the status bar whenever an application accesses the user's location; if the icon is not shown, the user's location is not being accessed. Privacy browser plugins typically place an icon in the browser's toolbar to inform users about the data practices or third-party trackers of the website visited.

■ **On demand:** Systems should enable users to access particular portions or all of a privacy notice on demand. A simple example of this is the standard practice of providing a privacy link at the bottom of each web page.

Channel

The channel dimension refers to how the privacy notice is presented to the user. A primary channel is the one in which the privacy notice is presented on the same platform as the one the service itself is provided with. For example, if a service is provided through a web interface, then the policy notice will be integrated as part of the web interface. A secondary channel uses another method, such as email, and a public channel utilizes publicly available platforms such as billboards and posters.

Modality

Modality specifies the way in which the privacy notice is communicated to the user (e.g., visual, auditory, haptic [vibration], machine readable). For online services, the most common modalities are visual presentation of the policies as texts and graphics. The other modalities may represent a supplemental effort to ensure that the user is aware of the privacy implications of various actions. An example of the machine-readable modality is IoT devices that broadcast their machine-readable privacy notices to smartphones or other devices, which then use other modalities for presentation to the user.

Control

Control means providing users with decisions on possible control of their data. Options to opt in and opt out of data activity may be available to a user. A user might need to pause and make choices and therefore provide consent. Controls may wait for user action (blocking) or not (non-blocking), or they can be separate from the main notice (decoupled).

8.7 Tracking

Tracking refers to the capability of a web server or other online system to create a record of websites visited by a user over time. Tracking can also involve the ability to include in this history all of the web pages visited at each website by the user and what links on each web page the user selects. This data collection technique, particularly if it involves sharing information with third parties that can consolidate tracking information on a single user from multiple sources, raises substantial privacy concerns.

Tracking is a complex and ever-changing technology. This section provides an overview of common tracking technologies, as well as common countermeasures.

Cookies

A cookie is a short block of text that is sent from a web server to a web browser when the browser accesses the server's web page. The cookie is stored in the user space of the web browser user. The information stored in a cookie includes, at a minimum, the name of the cookie, a unique identification number, and its domain (URL). Typically, a website generates a unique ID number for each visitor and stores the ID number on each user's machine using a cookie file. When a browser requests a page from the server that sent it a cookie, the browser sends a copy of that cookie back to the server. A website can retrieve only the information that it has placed on the browser machine. It cannot retrieve information from other cookie files.

The method of cookie retrieval is as follows:

1. A user types the URL of a website or clicks a link to a website.

2. The browser sends an HTML message requesting a connection. If there are any cookies from that website, the browser sends those cookies along with the URL.

3. The web server receives the cookies and can use any information stored in those cookies.

Cookies are a convenience for both the user and the web service. Here are some examples:

- **Saved logon:** For example, if a user subscribes to a news site that is protected by a pay wall, the user must log on to access the site. This creates a cookie. Subsequently, the user can go to the news site without having to log on again because the website has the cookie information to say that the user has successfully logged on.

- **Aggregate visitor information:** Cookies enable sites to determine how many visitors arrive, how many are new versus repeat visitors, and how often a visitor has visited.

- **User preferences:** A site can store user preferences so that the site can have a customized appearance for each visitor.

- **Shopping carts:** A cookie contains an ID and lets the site keep track of you as you add different things to your cart. Each item you add to your shopping cart is stored in the site's database along with your ID value. When you check out, the site knows what is in your cart by retrieving all of your selections from the database. It would be impossible to implement a convenient shopping mechanism without cookies or something like them.

Note that most cookie information is stored on the web server. In most cases, all that is required in the user's cookie is the unique ID. Note that a user's removing a cookie does not necessarily remove potential personal data from the server.

Cookies can be characterized along three dimensions: identity, duration, and party (see Table 8.5). If a user visits a website without logging on to the website—such as a news site that does not have a logon requirement or a retail site for the purpose of browsing without shopping—the web server does not know the identity of the user. In this case, the only identifying information associated with the cookie is a unique ID assigned by the server; this is an ***unidentified cookie***. If the user does log on to the site, then typically the web server will associate the user ID with the cookie, either by storing the user ID in the cookie or by maintaining state information at the website that associates the user ID with the cookie ID; this is an *identified cookie*.

TABLE 8.5   Characteristics of Cookies

Characteristic	Types
Identity	Unidentified cookie: Does not contain user ID Identified cookie: Contains user ID entered at logon to website
Duration	Session cookie: Deleted when web session terminates. Persistent cookie: Deleted when time specified in cookie expires.
Party	First party: Contains URL of the website the user is visiting Third party: Contains URL of a third party

With respect to duration, cookies are either session or persistent cookies. A *session cookie* remains on the user system only while the user has on open window to that website. When the user closes all windows connected to that website or closes the browser, the browser deletes the cookie. Session cookies are useful for temporarily maintaining information about a user, such as for a shopping cart or a chat session.

A *persistent cookie* includes an expiration date. This means that, for the cookie's entire life span (which can be as long or as short as its creators want), its information will be transmitted to the server every time the user visits the website that it belongs to or every time the user views a resource belonging to that website from another website (e.g., an advertisement). A persistent identified cookie allows a user to revisit a website that requires a logon without having to go through the logon procedure again. A persistent unidentified cookie can also be useful to the web server, in that it allows the website to track the activity of a single user over multiple visits, even though that user is not identified. The site could use such anonymous information for a number of purposes. One purpose could be to improve the interface so that more frequently visited pages on the site are easier to find. Another possible use is price manipulation: If the same user visits a site multiple times and looks at the same item, this could indicate interest in the item but resistance to the price, and the site may lower the price for that user.

Cookies can also be first party or third party. A *first-party cookie* is set and read by the web server hosting the website the user is visiting. In this case, the domain portion of the cookie matches the domain that is shown in the web browser's address bar.

A *third-party cookie*, however, belongs to a domain different from the one shown in the address bar. This sort of cookie typically appears when web pages feature content from external websites, such as banner advertisements. This type of cookie opens up the potential for tracking a user's browsing history and is often used by advertisers in an effort to serve relevant advertisements to each user. A third-party cookie is placed on a user's computer to track the user's activity on different websites, creating a detailed profile of the user's behavior. Third-party cookies can only track user activity through pages related to a site's advertising; they cannot establish full surveillance capability through any website.

There are a number of mechanisms by which web servers can install third-party cookies on web browser machines, including requesting that the browser connect to the third-party website and the installation of a Java plugin.

Third-party cookies enable advertisers, analytics companies, and others to track user activity across multiple sites. For example, suppose a user visits nypost.com to get the news. This site will contain a number of advertisement images. Each advertiser can install a third-party cookie. If the user subsequently visits another site, such as an online clothing site, that has the same advertiser, the advertiser can retrieve its cookie and now knows the user is interested in the news plus in clothing, and possibly which types of clothing. Over time, the advertiser can build up a profile of the user, even if it does not know the identity of the user, and tailor ads for that user. Further, with sufficient information, the advertiser may be able to identify the user. This is where online tracking raises a privacy issue.

Various browsers offer a number of countermeasures to users, including blocking ads and blocking third-party cookies. Some of these techniques may disable certain sites for the user. In addition, third-party trackers are continually trying to come up with new ways to overcome the countermeasures.

Other Tracking Technologies

A *flash cookie* is a small file stored on a computer by a website that uses Adobe's Flash Player technology. Flash cookies use Adobe's Flash Player to store information about your online browsing activities. Flash cookies can be used to replace cookies used for tracking and advertising because they also can store your settings and preferences. Flash cookies are stored in a different location than HTTP cookies; thus users may not know what files to delete in order to eliminate them. In addition, they are stored so that different browsers and standalone Flash widgets installed on a given computer access the same persistent Flash cookies. Flash cookies are not controlled by the browser. Erasing HTTP cookies, clearing history, erasing the cache, or choosing a "delete private data" option within the browser does not affect flash cookies. As countermeasures to flash cookies, recent versions of Flash Player honor the privacy mode setting in modern browsers. In addition, some anti-malware software is able to detect and erase flash cookies.

Device fingerprinting can track devices over time, based on the browser's configurations and settings. The fingerprint is made up from information that can be gathered passively from web browsers, such as their version, user agent, screen resolution, language, installed plugins, and installed fonts. Because each browser is unique, device fingerprinting can identify your device without using cookies. Because device fingerprinting uses the characteristics of your browser configuration to track you, deleting cookies won't help. A countermeasure to fingerprinting is to make your device fingerprint anonymous. This approach is taken in a recent version of Safari on macOS, which makes all the Macs in the world look alike to trackers.

Do Not Track

All browsers allow the user to select a "do not track" option. This feature enables users to tell every website, their advertisers, and content providers that they do not want their browsing behavior tracked. When the "do not track" option is selected, the browser sends an identifier in the HTTP header field. Honoring this setting is voluntary; individual websites are not required to respect it. Websites that do honor this setting should automatically stop tracking the user's behavior without any further action from the user.

Many websites simply ignore the "do not track" field. Websites that listen to the request react to the request in different ways. Some simply disable targeted advertising, showing you generic advertisements instead of ones targeted to your interests, but use the data for other purposes. Some may disable tracking by other websites but still track how you use their websites for their own purposes. Some may disable all tracking. There's little agreement on how websites should react to "do not track."

8.8   Key Terms and Review Questions

Key Terms

cookies	mobile app vetting
data brokers	mobile device
data collectors	online privacy
data users	online tracking
device fingerprinting	persistent cookie
do not track	privacy notice
enterprise mobile services	private app store
enterprise mobility management	public app store
first-party cookie	session cookie
flash cookie	third-party cookie
HTTP	tracking
HTTPS	unidentified cookie
identified cookie	web application firewall (WAF)
mobile app	

Review Questions

1. What are the main elements of the online ecosystem for personal data?

2. What security features are built into HTTPS?

3. How does a web application firewall function?

4. What are the main elements of the mobile app ecosystem?

5. List major security concerns for mobile devices.

6. What is mobile app vetting?

7. List and briefly define major privacy risks for web applications.

8. What are some of the major privacy/security threats for the use of mobile apps?

9. What are the online privacy principles defined by the FTC?

10. What are the elements and subelements of the FTC online privacy framework?

11. List and briefly describe the main factors that contribute to the ineffectiveness of current web privacy notices.

12. List and briefly define the dimensions of a privacy notice design space.

13. Define the various types of cookies.

8.9 References

BBB19: Better Business Bureau. *Sample Privacy Policy*. 2019. https://www.bbb.org/greater-san-francisco/for-businesses/toolkits1/sample-privacy-policy/

CDOJ14: California Department of Justice. *Making Your Privacy Practices Public*. May 2014. https://oag.ca.gov/sites/all/files/agweb/pdfs/cybersecurity/making_your_privacy_practices_public.pdf

CLIN10: Cline, J. "GMAC: Navigating EU Approval for Advanced Biometrics." *Inside Privacy blog*, October 2010. https://iapp.org/news/a/2010-10-20-gmac-navigating-eu-approval-for-advanced-biometrics/

DHS17: U.S. Department of Homeland Security. *Study on Mobile Device Security*. DHS Report, April 2017.

FSEC19: F-Secure Labs. "Securing the Web Browser." *F-Secure blog*, 2019. https://www.f-secure.com/en/web/**labs_global/browser-security**

FTC11: Federal Trade Commission. *In the Matter of Google Inc., FTC Docket No. C-4336.* October 13, 2011. https://www.ftc.gov/sites/default/files/documents/cases/2011/10/111024googlebuzz do.pdf

FTC12: Federal Trade Commission. *Protecting Consumer Privacy in an Era of Rapid Change: Recommendations for Businesses and Policymakers.* U.S. Federal Trade Commission, March 2012.

FTC98: Federal Trade Commission. *Privacy Online: A Report to Congress.* U.S. Federal Trade Commission, June 1998.

MMA11: Mobile Marketing Association. *Mobile Application Privacy Policy Framework.* December 2011. https://www.mmaglobal.com

MUNU12: Munur, M., and Mrkobrad, M. "Best Practices in Drafting Plain-Language and Layered Privacy Policies." *Inside Privacy Blog.* September 2012. https://iapp.org/news/a/2012-09-13-best-practices-in-drafting-plain-language-and-layered-privacy/

NISS11: Nissenbaum, H. "A Contextual Approach to Privacy Online." *Daedalus.* Fall 2011. https://www.amacad.org/publication/contextual-approach-privacy-online

NTIA13: National Telecommunications and Information Administration. *Short Form Notice Code of Conduct to Promote Transparency in Mobile App Practices.* July 25, 2013. https://www.ntia. doc.gov/files/ntia/publications/july_25_code_draft.pdf

OECD06: Organisation for Economic Co-operation and Development. *Making Privacy Notices Simple.* OECD Digital Economy Papers No. 120. July 2006.

OOI13: Office of Oversight and Investigations. *A Review of the Data Broker Industry: Collection, Use, and Sale of Consumer Data for Marketing Purposes.* Majority Staff Report to the U. S. Senate Committee on Commerce, Science, and Transportation, 2013.

OWH12: Office of the White House. *Consumer Data Privacy in a Networked World: A Framework for Protecting Privacy and Promoting Innovation in the Global Digital Economy.* February 2012. https://obamawhitehouse.archives.gov/sites/default/files/privacy-final.pdf

PROM16: Promontory Financial Group, LLC. *Independent Assessor's Report on Google Inc.'s Privacy Program.* U.S. Federal Trade Commission, June 24, 2016. https://www.ftc.gov/about-ftc/foia/frequently-requested-records/foia-records/google/2018-00387-3

SCHA17: Schaub, F., Balebako, R., and Cranor, L. "Designing Effective Privacy Notices and Controls." *IEEE Internet Computing.* May/June 2017.

Chapter | 9

Other PET Topics

Learning Objectives

After studying this chapter, you should be able to:

- Understand the concept of data loss prevention
- Define the three data states in data loss prevention
- Explain the scope of the Internet of Things
- List and discuss the five principal components of IoT-enabled things
- Understand the relationship between cloud computing and the IoT
- Present an overview of cloud computing concepts
- List and define the principal cloud services
- List and define the cloud deployment models
- Understand the unique security and privacy issues related to cloud computing

This chapter begins with a discussion of data loss prevention and its applicability to privacy protection. Then the chapter provides an overview of the Internet of Things (IoT), followed by a discussion of privacy issues related to the IoT. The chapter concludes with an overview of cloud computing, followed by a discussion of privacy issues related to cloud computing.

9.1 Data Loss Prevention

Data loss is the intentional or unintentional release of information to an untrusted environment. *Data loss prevention* (**DLP**), also referred to as *data leakage prevention*, refers to a comprehensive approach covering people, processes, and systems that identify, monitor, and protect data in use (e.g., endpoint actions), data in motion (e.g., network actions), and data at rest (e.g., data storage) through deep content inspection and with a centralized management framework. The past several years have seen a noticeable shift in attention and investment from securing the network to securing systems within the network and securing the data itself. DLP controls are based on policy and include classifying sensitive data, discovering data across an enterprise, enforcing controls, and reporting and auditing to ensure policy compliance. Sensitive information that is at risk of leakage or that is actually leaked often includes shared and unencrypted content such as word processing documents, presentation files, and spreadsheets that could leave an organization via many different points or channels (e.g., via email, instant messaging, Internet browsing, or on portable storage devices).

DLP was developed to address security concerns, but it is also a vital technology for information privacy. DLP addresses the protection of sensitive data, including personally identifiable information (PII).

Data Classification and Identification

All sensitive data and PII within an enterprise need to be protected at all times and in all places. As a first step, an enterprise needs to define what is sensitive data and, if necessary, establish different levels of sensitive data. Then, there is a need to recognize sensitive data wherever it is encountered in the enterprise. Finally, there must be applications that can recognize sensitive data in real time. The following are common approaches to the recognition task [MOGU07]:

- **Rule based:** Regular expressions, keywords, and other basic pattern-matching techniques are best suited for basic structured data, such as credit card numbers and Social Security numbers. Rule-based matching can efficiently identify data blocks, files, database records, and so on that contain easily recognized sensitive data.

- **Database fingerprinting:** This technique searches for exact matches to data loaded from a database, which can include multiple-field combinations, such as name, credit card number, and CVV number. For example, a search could look only for credit card numbers in the customer base, thus ignoring employees buying online. This is a time-consuming technique, but it has a very low false positive rate.

- **Exact file matching:** This technique involves computing the hash value of a file and monitoring for any files that match that exact fingerprint. It is easy to implement and can check whether a file has been accidentally stored or transmitted in an unauthorized manner. However, unless a more time-consuming cryptographic hash function is used, evasion is trivial for an attacker.

- **Partial document matching:** This technique looks for a partial match on a protected document. It involves the use of multiple hashes on portions of the document, such that if a portion of the document is extracted and filed elsewhere or pasted into an email, it can be detected. This method is useful for protecting sensitive documents.

Data States

A key to effective DLP is to develop an understanding of the places and times at which data are vulnerable. A useful way of managing DLP is to categorize data into three states: data at rest, data in motion, and data in use. Table 9.1 defines these states and the DLP objectives corresponding to each state.

TABLE 9.1   Data States

Data State	Definition	DLP Objective	Examples
Data at rest	Data in a stable storage system that are not often updated, if at all; organizations often store such data in encrypted form	Locate and catalog sensitive information stored throughout the enterprise.	Corporate files stored on servers or cloud storage; relatively static databases; and reference or stable data on desktops and laptops
Data in motion	Data moving through any kind of internal or external network	Monitor and control the movement of sensitive information across enterprise networks.	Email attachments, web uploads/downloads, instant messages, transfers over local networks or to/from a cloud, and mobile device traffic
Data in use	Data that are in the process of being generated, updated, processed, erased, or viewed through various endpoint interfaces	Monitor and control the movement of sensitive information on end user systems.	Data processing by office applications, viewing/editing PDF files, database functions, cloud applications, and mobile applications

Data at Rest

The data at rest category presents significant risk for enterprises. A large enterprise might have millions of files and database records on drives and removable media. A particular set of data files or records might have a "home" location, but portions of that data may also migrate to other storage locations, and this situation, if not monitored and controlled, can quickly become unmanageable. One example of how data may be replicated and proliferated is file sharing. With networked computer systems, file sharing for collaborative projects is common, but it might mean that the owner or creator of a file has no idea of what happened to the file after sharing it. The same risk exists with the many web-based collaboration and document management platforms in common use.

The fundamental task of DLP for data at rest is to identify and log where specific types of information are stored throughout the enterprise. The DLP unit uses some sort of data discovery agent that performs the actions depicted in Figure 9.1 and described in the list that follows:

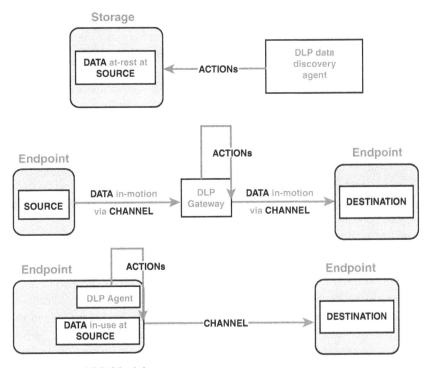

FIGURE 9.1 DLP Models

- Seek out and identify specific file types, such as spreadsheets, word processing documents, email files, and database records. The automated search activity encompasses files servers, storage area networks, network attached storage, and endpoint systems.

- Once files are found, the agent must be able to open each file to scan the content for specific types of information.

- The agent logs files that contain information of security relevance and may issue alerts if a security policy is violated. There needs to be a policy and mechanism for encrypted data, such that an entire encrypted block is labeled as sensitive or the agent is able to decrypt and determine sensitivity. Security for the log file is paramount because it would be a useful tool for an adversary.

Data in Motion

Data-in-motion solutions operate in one of two modes:

- **Passive monitoring:** Observes a copy of data packets as they move across a network link. This monitoring could be done by a port mirror on a switch (i.e., a cross-connection of two or more ports on a switch) or a network line tap. Packets or sequences of packets containing information of interest can be logged, and security violations can trigger an alert.

■ **Active monitoring:** Interposes a relay or gateway type of device on a network line to analyze and forward data packets (refer to Figure 9.1). An active monitor can log and issue alerts but can also be configured to block data flows that violate a security policy.

To inspect the information being sent across the network, the DLP solution must be able to monitor the network traffic, recognize the correct data streams to capture, assemble the collected packets, reconstruct the files carried in the data stream, and then perform the same analysis that is done on data at rest to determine whether any portion of the file contents is restricted by its rule set.

The advantages of passive monitoring are that it is non-intrusive and does not slow down the flow of traffic. This approach, when combined with instant alerts and fast incident response, can be quite effective. The advantage of active monitoring is that it can enforce a DLP policy proactively. This comes at the cost of increased network and computational demands.

Data in Use

Data-in-use solutions generally involve installing DLP agent software on endpoint systems. The agent can monitor, report, block, or quarantine the use of particular kinds of data files and/or the contents of a file itself. The agent can also maintain an inventory of files on the hard drives and removable media plugged in to the endpoint. The agent can allow or disallow certain types of removable media, such as requiring that a removable device support encryption.

DLP for Email

An example of applying DLP to emails is a policy promulgated by the U.S. Department of Commerce [DOC14]. The document defines a filtering standard used to determine whether an email contains sensitive PII or non-sensitive PII combined with other information, which, when combined, becomes sensitive PII. The following is the filtering hierarchy, in order:

1. Social Security number

2. Passport number

3. Driver's license/state identification number

4. Bank account/credit card number

5. Medical/HIPAA information

6. Date of birth

7. Mother's maiden name

For example, the passport number filter scans for the word "passport" in English or Spanish followed by a string of digits.

Egress Scanning

All outgoing messages from a network are subject to filtering for sensitive PII. The DLP system quarantines any email with a match and sends the email sender an auto-generated email message describing the possible violation, the quarantine of the email message, and the steps necessary to release the email message to the intended recipients. The options are encrypt the email, remove the sensitive data, or contact the privacy office. If the employee suspects the DLP quarantine is in error (false positive) and contacts the privacy office, another email message is sent, stating the results of the review.

If the sender does not act upon the quarantine notice within a predetermined period of time, the DLP system alerts the user that the email message and any attachments have been deleted and not sent.

Ingress Scanning

A DLP system also scans incoming email. The system blocks any incoming email message containing PII from entering the network. Its system sends an automated notification to the sender describing the policy prohibition, with instructions for using department-approved encryption software. In addition, the DLP system electronically notifies the intended recipient of the block message.

DLP Model

Ernst & Young [ERNS11] has developed a conceptual model that illustrates all the elements that contribute to a holistic view of data loss prevention (see Figure 9.2). There are three levels to the model. The first level of the model, data governance, ensures that DLP aligns with corporate goals and requirements, and it drives the development of DLP controls. An organization needs to develop a classification scheme for the specific types of personal data it holds in order to customize DLP controls for its needs. In the Ernst & Young model, part of governance is the identification of what sensitive data the organization stores and processes and where in the IT architecture (servers, data centers, cloud, workstations) data are held.

The next level of the model, DLP controls, applies to the two high-level ways data are stored within an organization:

- **Structured repositories:** These are databases, such as relational databases, that are typically supported and controlled by the IT organization.

- **Unstructured repositories:** This type of data is generally end user driven and stored in less controlled repositories such as network shares, SharePoint sites, and workstations.

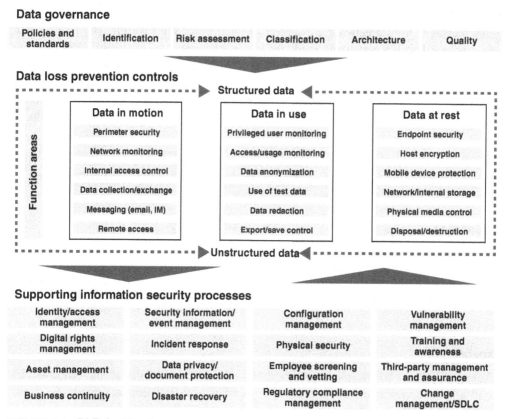

Data governance

Policies and standards	Identification	Risk assessment	Classification	Architecture	Quality

Data loss prevention controls

Structured data

Function areas

Data in motion	Data in use	Data at rest
Perimeter security	Privileged user monitoring	Endpoint security
Network monitoring	Access/usage monitoring	Host encryption
Internal access control	Data anonymization	Mobile device protection
Data collection/exchange	Use of test data	Network/internal storage
Messaging (email, IM)	Data redaction	Physical media control
Remote access	Export/save control	Disposal/destruction

Unstructured data

Supporting information security processes

Identity/access management	Security information/ event management	Configuration management	Vulnerability management
Digital rights management	Incident response	Physical security	Training and awareness
Asset management	Data privacy/ document protection	Employee screening and vetting	Third-party management and assurance
Business continuity	Disaster recovery	Regulatory compliance management	Change management/SDLC

FIGURE 9.2 DLP Architecture

For data in motion, the controls, with typical definition of objectives, are as follows:

- **Perimeter security:** Prevent unencrypted sensitive data from leaving the perimeter.

- **Network monitoring:** Log and monitor network traffic to identify and investigate inappropriate sensitive data transfers.

- **Internal access control:** Prevent users from accessing unauthorized sites or uploading data to the web through personal web mail, social media, online backup tools, and so on.

- **Data collection/exchange:** Ensure that data exchange with third parties occurs only through secure means.

- **Messaging:** Prevent file transfers to external parties through instant messaging and other non-web-based applications.

- **Remote access:** Ensure that remote access to the company network is secured, and control the data that can be saved through remote facilities such as Outlook Web Access.

For data in use, the controls are:

- **Privileged user monitoring:** Monitor the actions of privileged users who have the ability to override DLP controls, perform mass data extracts, and so on.

- **Access/usage monitoring:** Monitor access to and usage of high-risk data to identify potentially inappropriate usage.

- **Data anonymization:** Sanitize/anonymize sensitive data when they are not required for the intended use.

- **Use of test data:** Do not use or copy sensitive data into non-production systems. Sanitize data before moving into test systems when possible.

- **Data redaction:** Remove sensitive data elements from reports, interfaces, and extracts when they are not necessary for the intended use.

- **Export/save control:** Restrict users' ability to copy sensitive data into unapproved containers (e.g., email, web browsers), including controlling the ability to copy, paste, and print sections of documents.

For data at rest, the controls are:

- **Endpoint security:** Restrict access to local admin functions, such as the ability to install software and modify security settings. Prevent malware, viruses, spyware, and so on.

- **Host encryption:** Ensure that hard disks are encrypted on all servers, workstations, laptops, and mobile devices.

- **Mobile device protection:** Harden mobile device configurations and enable features such as password protection and remote wipe facilities.

- **Network/internal storage:** Govern access to network-based repositories containing sensitive data on a least-privilege basis.

- **Physical media control:** Prevent the copying of sensitive data to unapproved media. Ensure that authorized data extraction takes place only on encrypted media.

- **Disposal/destruction:** Ensure that all equipment with data storage capabilities are cleansed or destroyed as part of the equipment disposal process (including devices such as digital copiers and fax machines).

A number of information security processes support the implementation of the DLP controls. The lowest portion of Figure 9.2 depicts the most important of these.

9.2   The Internet of Things

The *Internet of Things* (*IoT*) is the latest development in the long and continuing revolution of computing and communications. Its size, ubiquity, and influence on everyday lives, business, and government dwarf those of any technical advance that has gone before. This section provides a brief overview of the IoT.

Things on the Internet of Things

The term *IoT* refers to the expanding interconnection of smart devices, ranging from appliances to tiny sensors. A dominant theme is the embedding of short-range mobile transceivers into a wide array of gadgets and everyday items, enabling new forms of communication between people and things and between things themselves. The Internet now supports the interconnection of billions of industrial and personal objects, typically through cloud systems. The objects deliver sensor information, act on their environment, and in some cases modify themselves to create overall management of a larger system, like a factory or city.

The IoT is primarily driven by **deeply embedded devices**. These devices are low-bandwidth, low-power, low-repetition data capture and low-bandwidth data usage appliances that communicate with each other and with higher-level devices, such as gateway devices that funnel information to cloud systems. Embedded appliances, such as high-resolution video security cameras, video VoIP phones, and a handful of others, require high-bandwidth streaming capabilities. Yet countless products simply require packets of data to be delivered intermittently.

The user interface for an IoT device may be tightly constrained by limited display size and functionality, or the device might only be able to be controlled via remote means. Thus, it might be difficult for individuals to know what data devices are collecting about them and how the information will be processed after collection.

Components of IoT-Enabled Things

Figure 9.3 illustrates the key components of an IoT-enabled device.

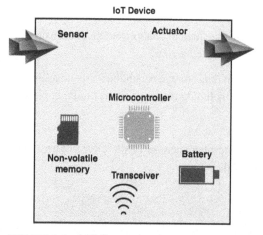

FIGURE 9.3   IoT Components

Figure 9.3 shows the following key components of an IoT-enabled device:

- **Sensor:** A sensor measures some parameter of a physical, chemical, or biological entity and delivers an electronic signal proportional to the observed characteristic, either in the form of an analog voltage level or a digital signal. In both cases, the sensor output is typically input to a microcontroller or other management element. Examples include temperature measurement, radiographic imaging, optical sensing, and audio sensing.

- **Actuator:** An actuator receives an electronic signal from a controller and responds by interacting with its environment to produce an effect on some parameter of a physical, chemical, or biological entity. Examples include heating coils, cardiac electric shock delivery mechanisms, electronic door locks, unmanned aerial vehicle operation, servo motors, and robotic arms.

- **Microcontroller:** The "smart" in a smart device is provided by a deeply embedded microcontroller.

- **Transceiver:** A transceiver contains the electronics needed to transmit and receive data. An IoT device typically contains a wireless transceiver, capable of communication using Wi-Fi, ZigBee, or some other wireless protocol. By means of the transceiver, IoT devices can interconnect with other IoT devices, with the Internet, and with gateway devices to cloud systems.

- **Power supply:** Typically, this is a battery.

An IoT device also typically contains a *radio-frequency identification* (*RFID*) component. RFID technology, which uses radio waves to identify items, is increasingly becoming an enabling technology for IoT. The main elements of an RFID system are tags and readers. RFID tags are small programmable devices used for object, animal, and human tracking. They come in a variety of shapes, sizes, functionalities, and costs. RFID readers acquire and sometimes rewrite information stored on RFID tags that come within operating range (a few inches up to several feet). Typically, RFID readers communicate with a computer system that records and formats the acquired information for further uses. RFID components on some devices can transmit considerable information about their devices, raising privacy issues.

IoT and Cloud Context

To better understand the function of the IoT, it is useful to view it in the context of a complete enterprise network that includes third-party networking and cloud computing elements. Figure 9.4 provides an overview illustration.

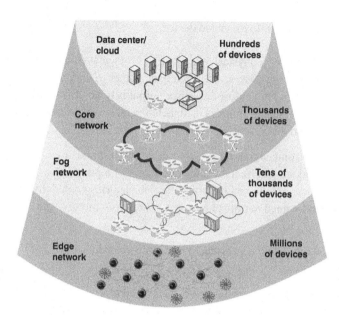

FIGURE 9.4   The IoT/Cloud Context

Edge

At the *edge* of a typical enterprise network is a network of IoT-enabled devices, consisting of sensors and perhaps actuators. These devices may communicate with one another. For example, a cluster of sensors may all transmit their data to one sensor that aggregates the data to be collected by a higher-level entity. At this level there might also be a number of gateways. A gateway interconnects the IoT-enabled devices with the higher-level communication networks. It performs the necessary translation between the protocols used in the communication networks and those used by devices. It might also perform a basic data aggregation function.

Fog

In many IoT deployments, massive amounts of data might be generated by a distributed network of sensors. For example, offshore oil fields and refineries can generate a terabyte of data per day. An airplane can create multiple terabytes of data per hour. Rather than store all of that data permanently (or at least for a long period) in central storage accessible to IoT applications, it is often desirable to do as much data processing close to the sensors as possible. Thus, the purpose of what is sometimes referred to as the *fog* computing level is to convert network data flows into information that is suitable for storage and higher-level processing. Processing elements at these levels may involve high volumes of data and data transformation operations that result in the storage of much lower volumes of data. The following are examples of fog computing operations:

- **Evaluation:** Evaluating data to determine whether they should be processed at a higher level
- **Formatting:** Reformatting data for consistent higher-level processing

- **Expanding/decoding:** Handling cryptic data with additional context (e.g., the origin)

- **Distillation/reduction:** Reducing and/or summarizing data to minimize the impact of data and traffic on the network and higher-level processing systems

- **Assessment:** Determining whether data represent a threshold or an alert; this could include redirecting data to additional destinations

Generally, fog computing devices are deployed physically near the edge of the IoT network—that is, near the sensors and other data-generating devices. Thus, some of the basic processing of large volumes of generated data is offloaded and outsourced from IoT application software located at the center.

Fog computing represents an opposite trend in modern networking from cloud computing. With cloud computing, massive, centralized storage and processing resources are made available to distributed customers over cloud networking facilities to a relatively small number of users. With fog computing, massive numbers of individual smart objects are interconnected with fog networking facilities that provide processing and storage resources close to the edge IoT devices. Fog computing addresses the challenges raised by the activity of thousands or millions of smart devices, including security, privacy, network capacity constraints, and latency requirements. The term *fog computing* is inspired by the fact that fog tends to hover low to the ground, whereas clouds are high in the sky.

Core

The core network, also referred to as a ***backbone network***, connects geographically dispersed fog networks and provides access to other networks that are not part of the enterprise network. Typically, the core network uses very high-performance routers, high-capacity transmission lines, and multiple interconnected routers for increased redundancy and capacity. The core network may also connect to high-performance, high-capacity servers, such as large database servers and private cloud facilities. Some of the core routers may be purely internal, providing redundancy and additional capacity without serving as edge routers.

Cloud

The cloud network provides storage and processing capabilities for the massive amounts of aggregated data that originate in IoT-enabled devices at the edge. Cloud servers also host the applications that interact with and manage the IoT devices and that analyze the IoT-generated data.

Table 9.2 compares cloud and fog computing.

TABLE 9.2   Comparison of Cloud and Fog Features

Factor	Cloud	Fog
Location of processing/storage resources	Center	Edge
Latency	High	Low
Access	Fixed or wireless	Mainly wireless
Support for mobility	Not applicable	Yes

Factor	Cloud	Fog
Control	Centralized/hierarchical (full control)	Distributed/hierarchical (partial control)
Service access	Through core	At the edge/on handheld device
Availability	99.99%	Highly volatile/highly redundant
Number of users/devices	Tens/hundreds of millions	Tens of billions
Main content generator	Human	Devices/sensors
Content generation	Central location	Anywhere
Content consumption	End device	Anywhere
Software virtual infrastructure	Central enterprise servers	User devices

9.3   IoT Security

As in any other area of information privacy, privacy for the IoT relies substantially on information security mechanisms. The IoT environment presents a number of specific security challenges. Thus, this section provides an overview of IoT security; Section 9.4 discusses IoT privacy.

IoT Device Capabilities

An IoT device is the basic element of an IoT system. Any given device will provide some collection of capabilities to meet specific application requirements. Figure 9.5, based on a figure in NISTIR 8228 (*Considerations for Managing Internet of Things (IoT) Cybersecurity and Privacy Risks*), illustrates the capabilities that are of primary interest in terms of vulnerability to security or privacy threats.

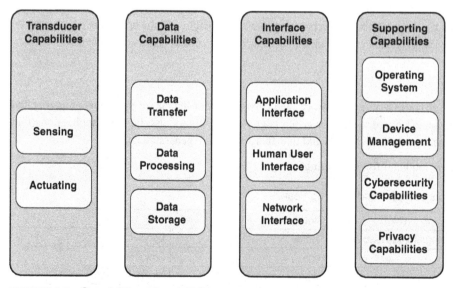

FIGURE 9.5   Capabilities of an IoT Component

The capabilities shown in Figure 9.5 fall into the following categories:

- **Transducer capabilities:** Transducers, including sensors and actuators, interact with the physical world. Every IoT device has at least one transducer capability.

- **Data capabilities:** These capabilities are directly involved in providing functionality to the system. Functions include storing and processing data that has been sensed and transferring data to actuators and to interfaces.

- **Interface capabilities:** These capabilities enable the device to interact with other devices and humans. The types of interface capabilities are:

  - **Application interface:** An application interface enables other devices to interact with an IoT device. A typical capability is an application programming interface (API).

  - **Human user interface:** Some but not all IoT devices enable human users to interact directly with the device. Examples include touchscreens, haptic devices, microphones, cameras, and speakers.

  - **Network interface:** The network interface comprises the hardware and software that enables a device to send and receive data across a communications network. Examples include Wi-Fi, Bluetooth, and ZigBee.

- **Supporting capabilities:** Supporting capabilities are underlying functions that enable applications on IoT devices and provide functionality for meeting system requirements. They include:

  - **Operating system:** The OS constitutes the software platform of the IoT device. Typically, the OS is minimal because of the limited resources of the device.

  - **Device management:** This includes I/O functions and device drivers.

  - **Cybersecurity capabilities:** These include cryptographic functions and security protocols.

  - **Privacy capabilities:** These include any additional functions specifically related to protecting privacy.

Security Challenges of the IoT Ecosystem

The European Union Agency for Network and Information Security (ENISA) *Baseline Security Recommendations for IoT* [ENIS17] lists the following issues that hinder the development of secure IoT ecosystems:

- **Very large attack surfaces:** An IoT ecosystem has a wide variety of points of vulnerability and a large variety of data that may be compromised.

- **Limited device resources:** IoT devices are typically constrained devices, with limited memory, processing power, and power supply. This makes it difficult to employ advanced security controls.

- **Complex ecosystem:** The IoT involves not only a large number of devices but interconnections, communications, and dependencies among them and with cloud elements. This makes the task of assessing security risk extremely complex.

- **Fragmentation of standards and regulations:** Comparatively little work has been done on security standards for IoT, and the best practices documentation is limited. Thus, there is a lack of comprehensive guidance for security managers and implementers.

- **Widespread deployment:** There is an ongoing rapid deployment of IoT arrangements in commercial environments and, more importantly, critical infrastructure environments. These deployments are attractive targets for security attacks, and the rapid deployment often occurs without comprehensive risk assessment and security planning.

- **Security integration:** IoT devices use a wide variety of communications protocols and, when implemented, authentication schemes. In addition, there may be contractor viewpoints and requirements from involved stakeholders. Integrating security into an interoperable scheme is thus extraordinarily challenging.

- **Safety aspects:** Because many IoT devices act on their physical environment, security threats can become safety threats, raising the bar for the effectiveness of security solutions.

- **Low cost:** IoT devices are manufactured, purchased, and deployed in the millions. This provides great incentive for all parties to minimize the cost of these devices. Manufacturers might be inclined to limit security features to maintain a low cost, and customers might be inclined to accept these limitations.

- **Lack of expertise:** The IoT is still a relatively new and rapidly evolving technology. A limited number of people have suitable cybersecurity training and experience.

- **Security updates:** Embedded devices are riddled with vulnerabilities, and there is no good way to patch them [SCHN14]. Chip manufacturers have strong incentives to produce their product with its firmware and software as quickly and cheaply as possible. Device manufacturers choose a chip based on price and features and do very little, if anything, to the chip software and firmware. Their focus is the functionality of the device. The end user may have no means of patching the system or little information about when and how to patch. As a result, the hundreds of millions of Internet-connected devices in the IoT are vulnerable to attack. This is certainly a problem with sensors, as attackers can use them to insert false data into the network. It is potentially a graver threat with actuators, where the attacker can affect the operation of machinery and other devices.

- **Insecure programming:** Effective cybersecurity practice requires the integration of security planning and design throughout the software development life cycle. But again, due to cost pressures, developers of IoT products have an incentive to place more emphasis on functionality and usability than on security.

- **Unclear liabilities:** A major IoT deployment involves a large and complex supply chain and complex interaction among numerous components. Because it is difficult under these circumstances to clearly assign liabilities, ambiguities and conflicts may arise in the event of a security incident.

These security issues also constitute privacy issues; IoT privacy is discussed in Section 9.4.

IoT Security Objectives

NISTIR 8200 (*Interagency Report on Status of International Cybersecurity Standardization for the Internet of Things*) lists the following security objectives for the IoT:

- **Restricting logical access to the IoT network:** This may include using unidirectional gateways, using firewalls to prevent network traffic from passing directly between the corporate and IoT networks, and having separate authentication mechanisms and credentials for users of the corporate and IoT networks. An IoT system should also use a network topology that has multiple layers, with the most critical communications occurring in the most secure and reliable layer.

- **Restricting physical access to the IoT network and components:** Physical access security can involve a combination of physical access controls, such as locks, card readers, and/or guards.

- **Protecting individual IoT components against exploitation:** This includes deploying security patches in an expeditious manner after testing them under field conditions; disabling all unused ports and services and ensuring that they remain disabled; restricting IoT user privileges to only those that are required for each person's role; tracking and monitoring audit trails; and using security controls such as antivirus software and file integrity checking software where technically feasible.

- **Preventing unauthorized modification of data:** This applies to data in transit (at least across the network boundaries) and at rest.

- **Detecting security events and incidents:** The goal is to detect security events early enough to break the attack chain before attackers attain their objectives. This includes the capability to detect failed IoT components, unavailable services, and exhausted resources that are important to providing proper and safe functioning of an IoT system.

- **Maintaining functionality during adverse conditions:** This involves designing IoT systems so that each critical component has a redundant counterpart. In addition, if a component fails, it should fail in a manner that does not generate unnecessary traffic on IoT or other networks or does not cause another problem elsewhere. IoT systems should also allow for graceful degradation, during which there is less automation and more operator involvement.

- **Restoring the system after an incident:** Incidents are inevitable, and an incident response plan is essential. A major characteristic of a good security program is that it enables the IoT system to be recovered quickly after an incident has occurred.

A discussion of security measures for IoT is beyond the scope of this chapter. See *Computer Security: Principles and Practice* [STAL18] for a discussion.

9.4 IoT Privacy

Many of the security challenges and issues related to IoT discussed in Section 9.2 also apply to providing information privacy. In addition, the IoT poses unique privacy risks. A Federal Trade Commission report [FTC15] noted that some of these risks involve the direct collection of sensitive personal information, such as precise geolocation information, financial account numbers, or health information—risks already presented by traditional Internet and mobile commerce. Other risks arise from the collection of personal information, habits, locations, and physical conditions over time, which may allow an entity that has not directly collected sensitive information to infer it. In addition, even a small network of IoT devices can generate a massive volume of data. Such a massive volume of granular data allows those with access to the data to perform analyses that would not be possible with less rich data sets. Yet another privacy risk is that a manufacturer or an intruder could eavesdrop remotely, intruding into an otherwise private space. In an office or factory environment, IoT data can reveal the location and movement of employees, perhaps correlated with office or factory functions or events.

IoT devices have penetrated into virtually all organizational environments. Thus, organizations need to be concerned for and act to protect the privacy of their employees in an IoT environment. In addition, organizations that manufacture or market IoT devices face regulatory, liability, and corporate image concerns related to the privacy of individuals in environments where these products are deployed.

Because of the distinct requirements of the IoT environment, it is useful to recast the definition of privacy into terms that relate to that environment. Ziegeldorf et al. [ZIEG13] define privacy in IoT as a threefold guarantee:

- Awareness of the privacy risks imposed by IoT devices and services. This awareness is achieved by means of transparent practices by the data controller (i.e., the entity that is providing IoT devices and/or services).

- Individual control over the collection and processing of personal information by IoT devices and services.

- Awareness and control of the subsequent use and dissemination of personal information by data controllers to any entity outside the subject's personal control sphere. This point implies that the data controller must be accountable for its actions on the personal information.

An IoT Model

Figure 9.6 depicts an IoT model that is useful in determining the various points of vulnerability and the potential threats in an IoT environment. The figure highlights important movements of data and processing operations with relevance to the privacy of any data subject that interacts with or is sensed by IoT devices.

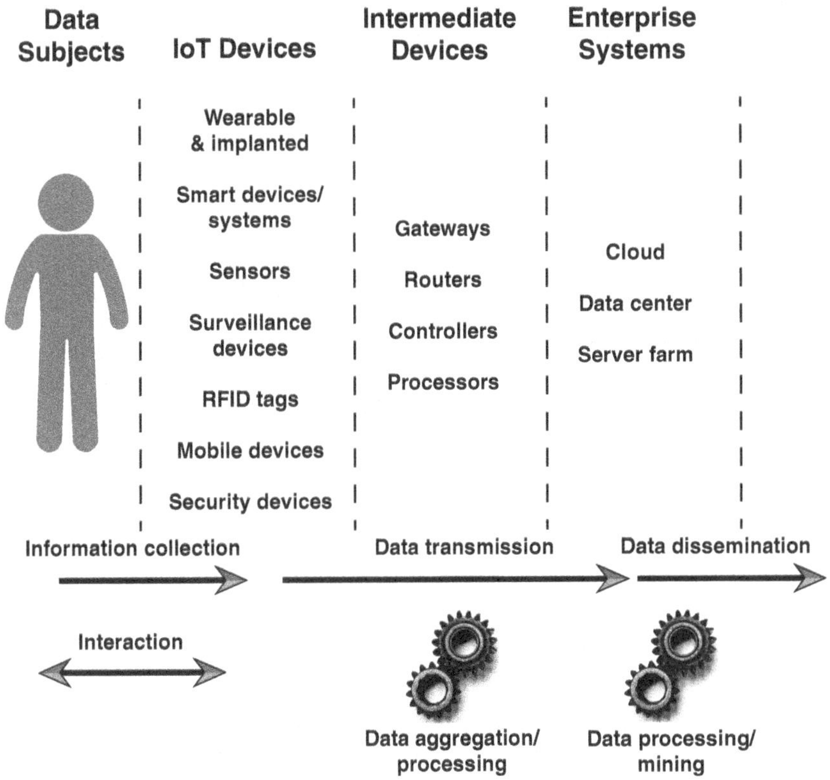

FIGURE 9.6   IoT Model

As shown in Figure 9.6, the IoT environment has three broad regions:

- **IoT devices:** A wide variety of IoT device types are capable of capturing personal information about individuals in the near environment. Among these are:

  - **Wearable and implanted devices:** These can collect highly personal information, including health-related information.

  - **Smart devices and systems:** An example is a smart home system, which can collect information about the residents' habits and preferences.

- **Sensors:** A variety of types of sensors can collect geolocation information and perhaps other information about individuals in the environment.

- **Surveillance devices:** For example, a facial recognition device can identify and record the presence of individuals at specific locations at specific times.

- **RFID tags:** Tags on devices carried by individuals can transmit information related to the individual in the presence of an RFID reader.

- **Mobile devices:** Smartphones and other mobile devices can provide personal information to data collection devices in the vicinity.

- **Security devices:** For example, biometric devices used for access control record information about the individual.

- **Intermediate devices:** Intermediate devices collect information from IoT devices. Devices such as gateways and other processors collect IoT data and transmit these data to enterprise systems. An intermediate device may also perform aggregation or other processing functions.

- **Enterprise systems:** At the enterprise level, which may be a cloud, an enterprise data center, or some other type of server farm or set of individual servers, personal data collected from the IoT are processed, stored, and potentially transmitted to other parties.

The privacy challenges presented at the level of intermediate devices and enterprise systems are essentially those for any system that handles personal data. The unique privacy challenges for IoT systems relate specifically to the environment of the IoT devices.

Privacy Engineering Objectives and Risks

Figure 2.4 in Chapter 2, "Information Privacy Concepts," defines three privacy engineering objectives:

- **Predictability:** Enabling reliable assumptions by individuals, owners, and operators about PII and its processing by an information system.

- **Manageability:** Providing the capability for granular administration of PII, including alteration, deletion, and selective disclosure.

- **Disassociability:** Enabling the processing of PII or events without association to individuals or devices beyond the operational requirements of the system.

Based on these objectives, a NIST document [NIST18] lists potential IoT data actions and the corresponding privacy harms for individuals. Table 9.3 summarizes them.

TABLE 9.3 IoT Privacy-Related Risks for Individuals

Privacy Engineering Objective	IoT Data Actions	Potential Harms
Predictability	■ Devices may collect a variety of data about an individual and the environment. ■ Decentralized data processing functions can contribute to complex automated systems and data flows. ■ IoT systems can act on human behavior directly. For example, traffic systems can influence or control where vehicles move. Environmental systems can influence behavior or movement in buildings.	It may be difficult for individuals to know what data devices are collecting about them and how the information will be processed after collection, especially if user interfaces are limited. This can create problems related to loss of self-determination: ■ Individuals may have difficulty participating in meaningful decisions about the use of their information. ■ This may create "chilling effects" on ordinary behavior and activity.
Manageability	■ The ubiquity of IoT sensors and devices in public and private environments can contribute to the aggregation and analysis of enormous amounts of data about individuals.	■ Even non-identifying information can become identifying when combined with other information. ■ Information can be deeply sensitive and provide detailed insights into individuals' lives in ways that individuals did not anticipate and do not find beneficial. ■ Decentralization can contribute to difficulty in ensuring the quality and management of data and could lead to inaccurate or damaging determinations about individuals or difficulty in providing redress.
Disassociability	■ Devices may collect information indiscriminately, even when information about individuals is not necessary for the purpose of the system. ■ Securing data is predominantly focused on data at rest in a system or data in motion between two known parties. ■ Decentralizing data processing may be complicated by the low power and low processing capabilities required by many sensor use cases.	■ Processing identifying information even when not operationally necessary can increase the capability for tracking and profiling individuals. ■ In a decentralized system, encryption that relies on known parties/devices (as opposed to just trusted parties/devices) can create information-rich data trails about individuals.

Challenges for Organizations

NISTIR 8228 provides guidance for mitigating the risk to individual's privacy in an IoT environment. The document defines five risk mitigation areas, which are aspects of privacy risk mitigation most significantly affected by the IoT environment. That is, the IoT environment presents unique challenges to organizations for privacy risk mitigation in these areas:

- **Disassociated data management:** Identifying authorized PII processing and determining how PII may be minimized or disassociated from individuals and IoT devices.

- **Informed decision making:** Enabling individuals to understand the effects of PII processing and interactions with the device, participating in decision making about the PII processing or interactions, and resolving problems.

- **PII processing permissions management:** Maintaining permissions for PII processing to prevent unpermitted PII processing.

- **Information flow management:** Maintaining a current, accurate mapping of the information life cycle of PII, including the type of data action, the elements of PII being processed by the data action, the party doing the processing, and any additional relevant contextual factors about the processing to use for privacy risk management purposes.

- **Privacy breach detection:** Monitoring and analyzing IoT device activity for signs of breaches involving individuals' privacy.

Table 9.4 lists specific challenges posed by the IoT environment and the implications for organizations.

TABLE 9.4 Challenges for Organizations in Protecting Individuals' Privacy

Challenges for Individual IoT Devices	Implications for the Organization
Disassociated Data Management	
An IoT device may contribute data that are used for identification and authentication, but the device does not participate in a traditional federated environment.	Techniques such as the use of identifier mapping tables and privacy-enhancing cryptographic techniques to blind credential service providers and relying parties from each other or to make identity attributes less visible to transmitting parties may not work outside a traditional federated environment.
Informed Decision Making	
An IoT device may lack interfaces that enable individuals to interact with it.	Individuals may not be able to provide consent for the processing of their PII or place conditions further processing of specific PII attributes.
Decentralized data processing functions and heterogenous ownership of IoT devices challenge traditional accountability processes.	Individuals may not be able to locate the source of inaccurate or otherwise problematic PII in order to correct it or fix the problem.
An IoT device may lack interfaces that enable individuals to read privacy notices.	Individuals may not be able to read or access privacy notices.

Challenges for Individual IoT Devices	Implications for the Organization
Informed Decision Making	
An IoT device may lack interfaces to enable access to PII, or PII may be stored in unknown locations.	Individuals may have difficulty accessing their PII, which curtails their ability to manage their PII and understand what is happening with their data and increases compliance risks.
Individuals may be unaware of the existence of some nearby IoT devices.	Individuals may be unaware that their PII is being collected.
PII Processing Permissions Management	
An IoT device may collect PII indiscriminately or analyze, share, or act upon the PII based on automated processes.	PII may be processed in ways that are out of compliance with regulatory requirements or an organization's policies.
IoT devices may be complex and dynamic, with sensors frequently added and removed.	PII may be hard to track such that individuals, as well as device owners/operators, may not have reliable assumptions about how PII is being processed, causing informed decision making to be more difficult.
An IoT device may be accessed remotely, allowing the sharing of PII outside the control of the administrator.	PII may be shared in ways that are out of compliance with regulatory requirements or an organization's policies.
Information Flow Management	
IoT devices may be complex and dynamic, with sensors frequently added and removed.	PII may be difficult to identify and track using traditional inventory methods.
IoT devices may not support standardized mechanisms for centralized data management, and the sheer number of IoT devices to manage may be overwhelming.	Application of PII processing rules intended to protect individuals' privacy may be disrupted.
An IoT device may not have the capability to support configurations such as remote activation prevention, limited data reporting, notice of collection, and data minimization.	Lack of direct privacy risk mitigation capabilities may require compensating controls and may impact an organization's ability to optimize the amount of privacy risk that can be reduced.
An IoT device may indiscriminately collect PII. Heterogenous ownership of devices challenges traditional data management techniques.	It is more likely that operationally unnecessary PII will be retained.
Decentralized data processing functions and heterogenous ownership of IoT devices challenge traditional data management processes with respect to checking for accuracy of data.	It is more likely that inaccurate PII will persist, with the potential to create problems for individuals.
Decentralized data processing functions and heterogenous ownership of IoT devices challenge traditional de-identification processes.	Aggregation of disparate data sets may lead to re-identification of PII.
Privacy Breach Detection	
An IoT device may lack the hardware/software capability, processing power, and/or data transfer capacity to provide detailed activity logs.	Privacy violations may occur that are difficult for the organization to monitor.

9.5 Cloud Computing

There is an increasingly prominent trend in many organizations to move a substantial portion or even all information technology (IT) operations to an Internet-connected infrastructure known as enterprise cloud computing. This section provides an overview of cloud computing.

Cloud Computing Elements

In NIST SP 800-145 (*The NIST Definition of Cloud Computing*), NIST defines ***cloud computing*** as follows:

> A model for enabling ubiquitous, convenient, on-demand network access to a shared pool of configurable computing resources (e.g., networks, servers, storage, applications, and services) that can be rapidly provisioned and released with minimal management effort or service provider interaction. This cloud model promotes availability and is composed of five essential characteristics, three service models, and four deployment models.

This definition refers to various models and characteristics, whose relationship is illustrated in Figure 9.7.

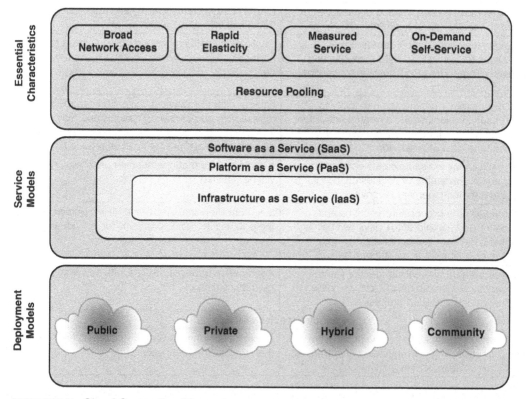

FIGURE 9.7   Cloud Computing Elements

The essential characteristics of cloud computing include the following:

- **Broad network access:** The cloud provides capabilities over the network, which are accessed through standard mechanisms that promote use by heterogeneous thin or thick client platforms (e.g., mobile phones, tablets, laptops).

- **Rapid elasticity:** Cloud computing provides the ability to expand and reduce resources according to the customer's specific service requirement. For example, the customer may need a large number of server resources for the duration of a specific task. The customer can release these resources upon completion of the task.

- **Measured service:** Cloud systems automatically control and optimize resource use by leveraging a metering capability at some level of abstraction appropriate to the type of service (e.g., storage, processing, bandwidth, active user accounts). Cloud systems enable resource usage to be monitored, controlled, and reported, providing transparency for both the provider and the consumer of the utilized service.

- **On-demand self-service:** A consumer can unilaterally provision computing capabilities, such as server time and network storage, as needed automatically without requiring human interaction with each *cloud service provider* (*CSP*). Because the service is on demand, the resources are not permanent parts of the consumer's IT infrastructure.

- **Resource pooling:** The CSP's computing resources are pooled to serve multiple consumers using a multitenant model, with different physical and virtual resources dynamically assigned and reassigned according to consumer demand. There is a degree of location independence in that the customer generally has no control or knowledge of the exact location of the provided resources but may be able to specify location at a higher level of abstraction (e.g., country, state, data center). Examples of resources include storage, processing, memory, network bandwidth, and virtual machines. Even private clouds tend to pool resources between different parts of the same organization.

NIST defines three *service models*, which can be viewed as nested service alternatives:

- **Software as a service (SaaS):** The capability provided to the consumer is to use the CSP's applications running on a cloud infrastructure. The applications are accessible from various client devices through a thin client interface such as a web browser. Instead of obtaining desktop and server licenses for software products it uses, an enterprise obtains the same functions from the cloud service. With SaaS, the customer does not have the complexity of software installation, maintenance, upgrades, and patches. Examples of SaaS include Google Gmail, Microsoft Office 365, Salesforce, Citrix GoToMeeting, and Cisco WebEx.

- **Platform as a service (PaaS):** The consumer can deploy onto the cloud infrastructure consumer-created or acquired applications created using programming languages and tools supported by the CSP. PaaS often provides middleware-style services such as database and component services for use by applications. In effect, PaaS is an operating system in the cloud. Google AppEngine, Engine Yard, Heroku, Microsoft Azure Cloud Services, and Apache Stratos are examples of PaaS.

- **Infrastructure as a service (IaaS):** The consumer can provision processing, storage, networks, and other fundamental computing resources where the consumer is able to deploy and run arbitrary software, which can include operating systems and applications. IaaS enables customers to combine basic computing services, such as number crunching and data storage, to build highly adaptable computer systems. Examples of IaaS are Amazon Elastic Compute Cloud (Amazon EC2), Microsoft Azure, Google Compute Engine (GCE), and Rackspace.

NIST defines four *deployment models*:

- **Public cloud:** The cloud infrastructure is made available to the general public or a large industry group and is owned by an organization selling cloud services. The CSP is responsible both for the cloud infrastructure and for the control of data and operations within the cloud.

- **Private cloud:** The cloud infrastructure is operated solely for an organization. It may be managed by the organization or a third party and may exist on premises or off premises. The CSP is responsible only for the infrastructure and not for the control.

- **Community cloud:** The cloud infrastructure is shared by several organizations and supports a specific community that has shared concerns (e.g., mission, security requirements, policy, compliance considerations). It may be managed by the organizations or a third party and may exist on premises or off premises.

- **Hybrid cloud:** The cloud infrastructure is a composition of two or more clouds (private, community, or public) that remain unique entities but are bound together by standardized or proprietary technology that enables data and application portability (e.g., cloud bursting for load balancing between clouds).

Figure 9.8 illustrates the two typical private cloud configurations. The private cloud consists of an interconnected collection of servers and data storage devices hosting enterprise applications and data. Local workstations have access to cloud resources from within the enterprise security perimeter. Remote users (e.g., from satellite offices) have access through a secure link, such as a virtual private network (VPN) connecting to a secure boundary access controller, such as a firewall. An enterprise may also choose to outsource the private cloud to a CSP. The CSP establishes and maintains the private cloud, consisting of dedicated infrastructure resources not shared with other CSP clients. Typically, a secure link between boundary controllers provides communications between enterprise client systems and the private cloud. This link might be a dedicated leased line or a VPN over the Internet.

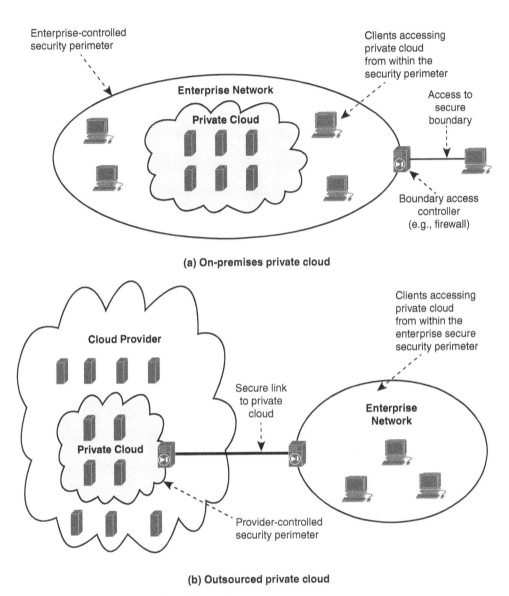

Enterprise-controlled
security perimeter

Clients accessing
private cloud
from within the
security perimeter

Enterprise Network

Private Cloud

Access to
secure
boundary

Boundary access
controller
(e.g., firewall)

(a) On-premises private cloud

Cloud Provider

Clients accessing
private cloud
from within the
enterprise secure
security perimeter

Secure link
to private
cloud

Enterprise
Network

Private Cloud

Provider-controlled
security perimeter

(b) Outsourced private cloud

FIGURE 9.8   Private Cloud Configurations

Figure 9.9 shows in general terms the context for a public cloud used to provide dedicated cloud services to an enterprise. The public CSP serves a diverse pool of clients. Any given enterprise's cloud resources are segregated from those used by other clients, but the degree of segregation varies among CSPs. For example, a CSP dedicates a number of virtual machines to a given customer, but a virtual machine for one customer may share the same hardware as virtual machines for other customers. The enterprise must enhance this link with cryptographic and authentication protocols to maintain security of traffic between the enterprise and the cloud.

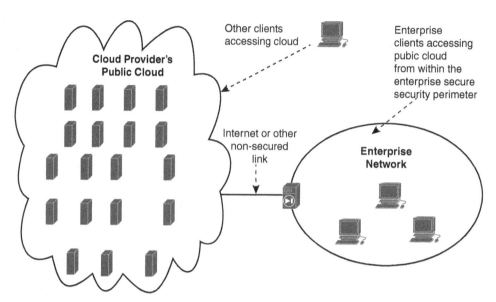

FIGURE 9.9   Public Cloud Configuration

Threats for Cloud Service Users

The use of cloud services and resources introduces a novel set of threats to enterprise cybersecurity. For example, a report issued by ITU-T [ITUT12a] lists the following threats for cloud service users:

- **Responsibility ambiguity:** The enterprise-owned system relies on services from the CSP. The level of the service provided (SaaS, PaaS, or IaaS) determines the magnitude of resources that are offloaded from IT systems to the cloud systems. Regardless of the level of service, it is difficult to define precisely the security responsibilities of the customer and those of the CSP. Any ambiguity complicates risk assessment, security control design, and incident response.

- **Loss of governance:** The migration of a part of the enterprise's IT resources to the cloud infrastructure gives partial management control to the CSP. The degree of loss of governance depends on the cloud service model (SaaS, PaaS, or IaaS). In any case, the enterprise no longer has complete governance and control of IT operations.

- **Loss of trust:** It is sometimes difficult for a cloud service user to assess the CSP's trust level due to the black-box nature of the cloud service. There is no way to obtain and share the CSP's security level in a formalized manner. Furthermore, the cloud service users are generally unable to evaluate the security implementation level achieved by the CSP. This makes it difficult for the customer to perform a realistic risk assessment.

- **Service provider lock-in:** A consequence of the loss of governance could be a lack of free-dom in terms of how to replace one CSP with another. An example of the difficulty in tran-sitioning would be a CSP relying on proprietary hypervisors or virtual machine image formats and not providing tools to convert virtual machines to a standardized format.

- **Non-secure cloud service user access:** Because most of the resource deliveries are through remote connections, unprotected APIs (mostly management APIs and PaaS services) are among the easiest attack vectors. Attack methods such as phishing, fraud, and exploitation of software vulnerabilities pose significant threats.

- **Lack of asset management:** A cloud service user may have difficulty assessing and moni-toring asset management by the CSP. Key elements of interest include location of sensitive asset/information, degree of physical control for data storage, reliability of data backup (data retention issues), and countermeasures for business continuity and disaster recovery. Further-more, cloud service users also have important concerns related to exposure of data to foreign governments and compliance with privacy laws.

- **Data loss and leakage:** This threat may be strongly related to the preceding item. However, loss of an encryption key or a privileged access code will bring serious problems to the cloud service users. Accordingly, lack of cryptographic management information (e.g., encryption keys, authentication codes, access privilege) leads to sensitive damages, such as data loss and unexpected leakage to the outside.

A discussion of security measures for cloud computing is beyond the scope of this chapter. See [STAL20] for a discussion.

9.6   Cloud Privacy

This section examines some of the risks and countermeasures related specifically to cloud privacy.

Several issues complicate consideration of privacy in the cloud. First, there is the distinction between SaaS, PaaS, and IaaS. For IaaS and PaaS, the CSP has little or no visibility into the nature of the data stored in the cloud or how it is processed. For the CSP, the responsibility is primarily security: to ensure the confidentiality, integrity, and availability of the customer's data, whether it includes PII or not. For SaaS, the CSP may need to incorporate specific privacy measures to ensure proper handling of PII. In general, the cloud customer has primary responsibility for the privacy of PII stored and processed in the cloud, whereas this may be a shared responsibility for SaaS.

A second consideration is the distinction between the data stored and processed in the cloud and the identity of individuals who access the cloud as cloud customers. Here, the CSP has a responsibility to provide mechanisms and policies to protect the PII of individuals who are accessing the cloud, regardless of whether they are accessing PII in the cloud.

ITU-T's *Privacy in Cloud Computing* [ITUT12b] examines the types of privacy protection measures that a cloud service provider should implement at each stage of the data life cycle, including collection, storage, sharing and processing, and deletion. Table 9.5 summarizes the concepts from this report. ITU-T makes use of a set of privacy principles that are similar to those defined by OECD (refer to Table 3.2 in Chapter 3, "Information Privacy Requirements and Guidelines") and the GDPR (refer to Table 3.3).

TABLE 9.5 Privacy Principles and Protection Measures in Cloud Computing

Data Life Cycle Stage	Privacy Principles	Privacy Protection Measures
Collection	Proportionality and purpose specification	Data minimization
Storage	Accountability and security	Encryption
Sharing and processing	Fairness, consent, and right of access	Data access control
Deletion	Openness and right to delete	Deletion and anonymization

Data Collection

A CSP is responsible for protecting the identity of persons who access cloud services. The customer should be able to access applications and data without revealing to the service provider more personal information than is strictly necessary to verify the customer's rights.

The anonymous credential is an example of a mechanism for protecting the privacy of cloud customers. This type of mechanism enables a user to obtain a credential from one organization and then later prove possession of the credential to another organization without revealing anything more. Anonymous credential systems also allow selective disclosure by permitting the user to reveal some credential attributes or prove that they satisfy some properties (e.g., age < 25) while hiding all the other credential attribute information.

Identity Mixer (https://www.zurich.ibm.com/identity_mixer/), developed by IBM, provides one means of implementing anonymous credentials. Identity Mixer is a generalization of a traditional identity management scheme. A traditional scheme encompasses the following basic steps:

1. An end user engages in an authentication dialogue with an identity provider and provides attribute values associated with the user's identity.

2. The user requests access to a service, using credentials supplied by the identity provider.

3. The service provider obtains identity information, authentication information, and associated attributes from the identity provider.

4. The service provider opens a session with the user and enforces access control restrictions based on the user's identity and attributes.

Identity Mixer enables the user to selectively disclose only those attributes that are required by the verifier and can do so without being linkable across their transactions. In essence, this scheme involves two techniques:

- **Flexible public keys:** Rather than being bound to a single public key, users can have many independent public keys, called pseudonyms, for the same secret key, so that they can use a different pseudonym for each verifier or even for each session.

- **Flexible credentials:** The credentials that certify the user's attributes can be transformed into valid tokens for any of the user's pseudonyms that contain only a subset of the attributes in the original credential. The transformed token remains verifiable under the issuer's public verification key.

Microsoft offers a different mechanism, called U-Prove, that has the same capability [PAQU13]. A U-Prove token is a new type of credential similar to a PKI certificate that can encode attributes of any type, but with two important differences:

- The issuance and presentation of a token is unlinkable due to the special type of public key and signature encoded in the token; the cryptographic "wrapping" of the attributes contains no correlation handles. This prevents unwanted tracking of users when they use their U-Prove tokens, even by colluding insiders.

- Users can minimally disclose information about what attributes are encoded in a token in response to dynamic verifier policies. As an example, a user may choose to disclose only a subset of the encoded attributes, prove that her undisclosed name does not appear on a blacklist, or prove that she is of age without disclosing her actual birth date.

Storage

The CSP has a duty to maintain the confidentiality of any personal data stored and processed in the cloud. As mentioned earlier, in many cases, the CSP does not know which data are personal data within a hosted customer database.

The primary mechanism by which the CSP protects all customer data, including PII, is encryption. The primary difficulty with database encryption is that online processing of the data becomes very challenging. A straightforward solution to the security problem in this context is to encrypt the entire database and not provide the encryption/decryption keys to the service provider. This solution by itself is inflexible. The user has little ability to access individual data items based on searches or indexing on key parameters but rather has to download entire tables from the database, decrypt the tables, and work with the results. To provide more flexibility, it must be possible to work with the database in its encrypted form.

Another option is to retrieve data from an encrypted but queryable database. Figure 9.10 shows a simple example of this approach.

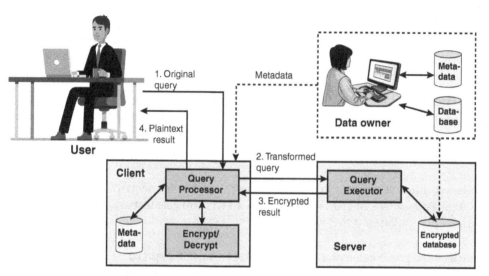

FIGURE 9.10   A Database Encryption Scheme

As Figure 9.10 shows, four entities are involved:

- **Data owner:** An organization that produces data to be made available for controlled release, either within the organization or to external users. The owner maintains the database and a set of metadata that provides indices into the database, such as primary or key fields.

- **User:** A human entity that presents requests (queries) to the system. The user could be an employee of the organization who is granted access to the database via the server or a user external to the organization who, after authentication, is granted access.

- **Client:** A front end that transforms user queries into queries on the encrypted data stored on the server.

- **Server:** An organization that receives the encrypted data from a data owner and makes the data available for distribution to clients. The server could in fact be owned by the data owner but, more typically, is a facility owned and maintained by an external provider, such as a CSP.

Suppose that each item in a database is encrypted separately but using the same encryption key. The encrypted database is stored at the server, but the server does not have the key, making the data secure at the server. Even if someone were able to hack into the server's system, all he or she would have access to is encrypted data. The client system does have a copy of the encryption key. A user at the client can retrieve a record from the database with the following sequence:

1. The user issues an SQL query for fields from one or more records with a specific value of the primary key.

2. The query processor at the client encrypts the primary key, modifies the SQL query accordingly, and transmits the query to the server.

3. The server processes the query using the encrypted value of the primary key and returns the appropriate record or records.

4. The query processor decrypts the data and returns the results.

For example, consider this query on an employee database:

```
SELECT Ename, Eid, Ephone
      FROM Employee
      WHERE Did = 15
```

Assume that the encryption key k is used and that the encrypted value of the department ID 15 is $E(k, 15) = 1000110111001110$. Then the query processor at the client could transform the preceding query into:

```
SELECT Ename, Eid, Ephone
      FROM Employee
      WHERE Did = 1000110111001110
```

This method is certainly straightforward but, as mentioned earlier, it lacks flexibility. For example, suppose the Employee table contains a salary attribute, and the user wishes to retrieve all records for salaries less than $70,000. There is no obvious way to do this because the attribute value for salary in each record is encrypted. The set of encrypted values does not preserve the ordering of values in the original attribute. You can find examples of more flexible versions of this approach in *Computer Security: Principles and Practice* [STAL18].

The article "Cryptographic Cloud Storage" [KAMA10] describes a more sophisticated scheme that enables multiple users to access portions of an encrypted cloud-based database without having possession of the encryption key. In essence, the architecture consists of four components:

- **Data processor:** Processes data before it is sent to the cloud; this includes encrypting the data and encrypting indices into rows or other blocks of data in the database.

- **Data verifier:** Checks whether the data in the cloud has been tampered with.

- **Token generator:** Generates tokens that enable the cloud storage provider to retrieve segments of customer data. For example, the token could be the encrypted value of an index; the CSP matches that with the encrypted index and returns the corresponding encrypted block.

- **Credential generator:** Implements an access control policy by issuing credentials to the various parties in the system. (These credentials will enable the parties to decrypt encrypted files according to the policy.)

Sharing and Processing

The possibility for a user to control his or her personal data as it is processed by applications is a fundamental right. To provide users with greater transparency and control over their own data, a CSP can implement a dashboard that can be used to summarize data used by applications and provide links to personal setting controls. An example of a standard for defining a policy language for expressing information system security policy is ITU-T X.1142 (*eXtensible Access Control Markup Language (XACML 2.0)*). With a dashboard solution based on XACML, a user can define preferences to control which entity (e.g., service provider) can access which data according to policies.

Deletion

At the end of the contractual relationship between a data subject and his or her cloud provider, the data subject has the right to request that the provider delete his or her data if there are no legitimate grounds for retaining them.

9.7   Key Terms and Review Questions

Key Terms

active monitoring	deeply embedded device
actuator	deployment model
cloud	disassociability
cloud computing	edge
community cloud	egress scanning
core	fog
data at rest	hybrid cloud
data in motion	infrastructure as a service (IaaS)
data in use	ingress scanning
data leakage prevention	Internet of Things (IoT)
data loss prevention (DLP)	manageability

microcontroller	public cloud
passive monitoring	radio-frequency identification (RFID)
platform as a service (PaaS)	sensor
power supply	service model
predictability	software as a service (SaaS)
private cloud	transceiver

Review Questions

1. Define *data loss prevention*.

2. Discriminate between data at rest, data in motion, and data in use.

3. Define *Internet of Things*.

4. List and briefly describe the principal components of an IoT-enabled thing.

5. Define *cloud computing*.

6. List and briefly describe three cloud service models.

7. List and briefly define four cloud deployment models.

8. Describe some of the main cloud-specific security threats.

9.8 References

DOC14: U.S. Department of Commerce. *Privacy Data Loss Prevention Working Group Recommendations.* December 17, 2014. http://osec.doc.gov/opog/privacy/Memorandums/DLP-Memo_04152016.pdf

ENIS17: European Union Agency For Network And Information Security. *Baseline Security Recommendations for IoT in the context of Critical Information Infrastructures.* November 2017. www.enisa.europa.eu

ERNS11: Ernst & Young. *Data Loss Prevention: Keeping Your Sensitive Data Out of the Public Domain.* October 2011. https://www.ey.com/Publication/vwLUAssets/EY_Data_Loss_Prevention/$FILE/EY_Data_Loss_Prevention.pdf

FTC15: U.S. Federal Trade Commission. *Internet of Things: Privacy & Security in a Connected World.* FTC Staff Report, January 2015.

ITUT12a: International Telecommunication Union Telecommunication Standardization Sector. *Focus Group on Cloud Computing Technical Report Part 5: Cloud Security.* FG Cloud Technical Report, February 2012.

ITUT12b: International Telecommunication Union Telecommunication Standardization Sector. *Privacy in Cloud Computing.* ITU-T Technology Watch Report, March 2012.

KAMA10: Kamara, S., and Lauter, K. "Cryptographic Cloud Storage." *Proceedings of Financial Cryptography Workshop on Real-Life Cryptographic Protocols and Standardization.* 2010.

MOGU07: Mogull, R. *Understanding and Selecting a Data Loss Prevention Solution.* SANS Institute whitepaper, December 3, 2007. https://securosis.com/assets/library/publications/DLP-Whitepaper.pdf

NIST18: National Institute of Standards and Technology. *NIST Cybersecurity for IoT Program.* March 29, 2018. https://www.nist.gov/sites/default/files/documents/2018/03/29/iot_roundtable_3.29.pdf

PAQU13: Paquin, C. *U-Prove Technology Overview V1.1.* Microsoft whitepaper, April 2013. https://www.microsoft.com/en-us/research/wp-content/uploads/2016/02/U-Prove20Technology20Overview20V1.120Revision202.pdf

SCHN14: Schneier, B. "The Internet of Things Is Wildly Insecure—and Often Unpatchable." *Wired,* January 6, 2014.

STAL18: Stallings, W., and Brown. L. *Computer Security: Principles and Practice.* New York: Pearson, 2018.

STAL20: Stallings, W. *Cryptography and Network Security: Principles and Practice.* New York: Pearson, 2020.

ZIEG13: Ziegeldorf, J., Morchon, O., and Wehrle, K. "Privacy in the Internet of Things: Threats and Challenges." *Security and Communication Networks.* 2013.

PART V

Information Privacy Management

Chapter 10

Information Privacy Governance and Management

Learning Objectives

After studying this chapter, you should be able to:

- Explain the concept of security governance and how it differs from security management
- Provide an overview of the key components of security governance
- Explain the roles and responsibilities that are part of security governance
- Explain the concept of security governance
- Explain the roles and responsibilities that are part of privacy governance
- Understand the key areas of privacy management
- Present an overview of the topics that should be addressed by a privacy program plan, a privacy plan, and a privacy policy
- Present an overview of the OASIS privacy management reference model

This chapter looks at the key concepts of information privacy governance and information privacy management. Section 10.1 provides an overview of information security governance, explaining the overall concept of governance and how it is realized with respect to information security. Section 10.2 then explores information privacy governance and, in particular, examines privacy roles and the privacy program. Section 10.3 examines information privacy management, including the concepts of privacy planning and the privacy policy. Section 10.4 describes a model that is useful to privacy managers in fulfilling their responsibilities: the OASIS privacy management reference model.

10.1 Information Security Governance

This section first introduces the concept of an information security management system (ISMS) and then examines information security governance as a component of an ISMS. *Effective Cybersecurity: A Guide to Using Best Practices and Standards* [STAL19] provides a more detailed description of these topics.

Information Security Management System

The International Organization for Standardization (ISO) has promulgated the ISO 27000 suite of information security standards that is the benchmark for the development of organizational information security policies and procedures. ISO 27000 provides the following definition of an ISMS:

> **Information Security Management System** consists of the policies, procedures, guidelines, and associated resources and activities, collectively managed by an organization, in the pursuit of protecting its information assets. An ISMS is a systematic approach for establishing, implementing, operating, monitoring, reviewing, maintaining and improving an organization's information security to achieve business objectives. It is based upon a risk assessment and the organization's risk acceptance levels designed to effectively treat and manage risks. Analyzing requirements for the protection of assets, as required, contributes to the successful implementation of an ISMS. The following fundamental principles also contribute to the successful implementation of an ISMS:
>
> a) awareness of the need for information security
>
> b) assignment of responsibility for information security
>
> c) incorporating management commitment and the interests of stakeholders
>
> d) enhancing societal values
>
> e) risk assessments determining appropriate controls to reach acceptable levels of risk
>
> f) security incorporated as an essential element of information networks and systems
>
> g) active prevention and detection of information security incidents
>
> h) ensuring a comprehensive approach to information security management
>
> i) continual reassessment of information security and making of modifications as appropriate

Information Security Governance Concepts

NIST SP 800-100 (*Information Security Handbook: A Guide for Managers*) defines *information security governance* as follows:

> The process of establishing and maintaining a framework and supporting management structure and processes to provide assurance that information security strategies are aligned

with and support business objectives, are consistent with applicable laws and regulations through adherence to policies and internal controls, and provide assignment of responsibility, all in an effort to manage risk.

ITU-T's X.1054 (*Governance of Information Security*) defines information security governance as the system by which an organization's information security–related activities are directed and controlled.

To better understand the role of security governance, it is useful to distinguish between information security governance (defined above), information security management, and information security implementation/operations. ISO 27000 defines *information security management* as follows:

> The supervision and making of decisions necessary to achieve business objectives through the protection of the organization's information assets. Management of information security is expressed through the formulation and use of information security policies, procedures and guidelines, which are then applied throughout the organization by all individuals associated with the organization.

Note

ISO is not an acronym (in which case it would be IOS), but a word, derived from the Greek *isos*, meaning "equal."

We can define *information security implementation/operations* in this fashion:

> The implementation, deployment, and ongoing operation of security controls defined within a cybersecurity framework.

Figure 10.1 suggests the hierarchical relationship between these three concepts. The *security governance* level communicates the mission priorities, available resources, and overall risk tolerance to the security management level. In essence, security governance is the process of developing a security program that adequately meets the strategic needs of the business. A *security program* encompasses the management, operational, and technical aspects of protecting information and information systems. It encompasses policies, procedures, and management structure and mechanisms for coordinating security activity. Thus, the security program defines the plans and requirements for security management and the implementation/operations level.

The *security management* level uses the information as inputs into the risk management process that realizes the security program. It then collaborates with the implementation/operations level to communicate security requirements and create a cybersecurity profile.

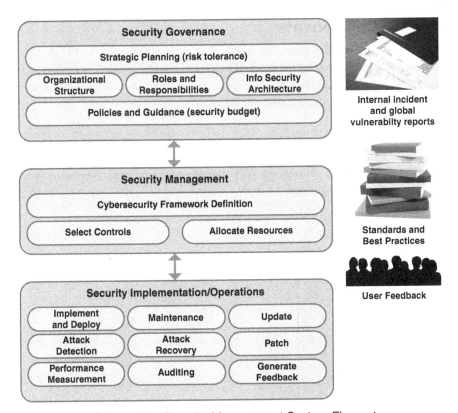

FIGURE 10.1 Information Security Management System Elements

The *implementation/operations level* integrates this profile into the system development life cycle and continuously monitors security performance. It executes or manages security-related processes relating to current infrastructure on a day-to-day basis. The security management level uses monitoring information to assess the current profile and reports the outcomes of that assessment to the governance level to inform the organization's overall risk management process.

Figure 10.1 illustrates the key elements at each level. As indicated, the three layers interact in the ongoing evolution of the ISMS. In addition, three supplemental factors play a role. Internal security incident reports and global vulnerability reports from various sources help to define the threat and level of risk that the organization faces in protecting its information assets. The numerous standards and best practices documents provide guidance on managing risk. User feedback comes from both internal users and external users who have access to the organization's information assets. This feedback helps improve the effectiveness of policies, procedures, and technical mechanisms. Depending on the organization and its cybersecurity approach, the three factors play roles to greater or lesser extents at each level.

Security Governance Components

NIST SP 800-100 lists the key activities that constitute effective security governances as (1) strategic planning, (2) organizational structure, (3) establishment of roles and responsibilities, (4) integration with the enterprise architecture, and (5) documentation of security objectives in policies and guidance (refer to Figure 10.1). This section examines each of these in turn.

Strategic Planning

It is useful for this discussion to define three hierarchically related aspects of strategic planning: enterprise strategic planning, information technology (IT) strategic planning, and cybersecurity or information security strategic planning (see Figure 10.2).

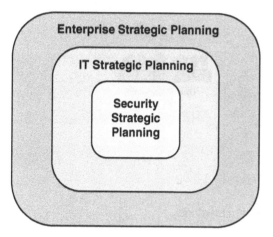

FIGURE 10.2   Strategic Planning

Enterprise strategic planning involves the definition of long-term goals and objectives for an organization (e.g., business enterprise, government agency, nonprofit organization) and the development of plans to achieve these goals and objectives. The Strategic Management Group's *Strategic Planning Basics* [SMG17] describes the management activity involved in enterprise strategic planning as an activity used to set priorities, focus energy and resources, strengthen operations, ensure that employees and other stakeholders are working toward common goals, establish agreement around intended outcomes/results, and assess and adjust the organization's direction in response to a changing environment. It involves the development of a strategic plan and the ongoing oversight of the implementation of that plan. The strategic plan is a document used to communicate with the organization the organization's goals, the actions needed to achieve those goals, and all the other critical elements developed during the planning exercise.

IT strategic planning involves the alignment of IT management and operation with enterprise strategic planning. The need to move beyond simply IT management and ensure that the IT planning process is integrated with enterprise strategic planning follows from two strategic factors: mission necessity and enterprise maturity [JUIZ15]. With many actors exploiting IT to maximize effectiveness, an organization must engage in strategic planning to ensure that investments in IT produce business value and that the assessment of risks is aligned with enterprise goals and objectives. This is necessary to support the overall enterprise mission. Further, as the IT infrastructure develops and matures, meeting enterprise strategic goals is likely to involve new arrangements with outside providers, such as cloud service providers, more use of mobile devices by employees and outside actors, and perhaps reliance on a variety of new hardware and software to develop Internet of Things (IoT) capability. These activities may create unintended barriers to flexibility and introduce whole new areas of risk; therefore, IT management must be guided by strategic planning.

Information security strategic planning is alignment of information security management and operation with enterprise and IT strategic planning. The pervasive use and value of IT within organizations has resulted in expanding the notion of IT's delivery of value to the organization to include mitigation of the organization's risk [ZIA15]. Therefore, IT security is a concern in all levels of an organization's governance and decision-making processes, and information security strategic planning is an essential component of strategic planning.

The information security strategic plan should be embodied in a document that is approved by the appropriate executives and committees and is regularly reviewed. Table 10.1 suggests an outline for such a document.

TABLE 10.1 Elements of an Information Security Strategic Plan Document

Section	Description
Definition	
Mission, Vision, and Objectives	Defines the strategy for aligning the information security program with organization goals and objectives, including the roles of individual security projects in enabling specific strategic initiatives.
Priorities	Describes factors that determine strategy and the priorities of objectives.
Success Criteria	Defines success criteria for the information security program. Includes risk management, resilience, and protection against adverse business impacts.
Integration	Spells out the strategy for integrating the security program with the organization's business and IT strategy.
Threat Defense	Describes how the security program will defend the organization against security threats.
Execution	
Operations Plan	Provides an annual plan to achieve agreed objectives that involve budgets, resources, tools, policies, and initiatives. This plan (a) can be used for monitoring progress and communicating with stakeholders and (b) ensures that information security is included from the outset within each relevant project.
Monitoring Plan	Provides a plan for maintaining a stakeholder feedback loop; measuring progress against objectives; and ensuring that strategic objectives remain valid and in line with business needs.
Adjustment Plan	Provides a plan to ensure that strategic objectives remain valid and in line with business needs and procedures to communicate the value.
Review	
Review Plan	Describes procedure and individuals/committees involved in regular review of information security strategy.

Organizational Structure

The organizational structure to deal with cybersecurity depends, in large part, on the size of the organization, its type (government agency, business, nonprofit), and the degree of dependence on IT. But the essential security governance functions to be performed are in essence the same. Figure 10.3, which is based on a figure in ITU-T's X.1054 (*Governance of Information Security*), illustrates these basic functions within a broader context, which comprises:

- **Direct:** Guiding security management from the point of view of enterprise strategies and risk management. This function involves developing an information security policy.

- **Monitor:** Monitoring the performance of security management with measurable indicators.

- **Evaluate:** Assessing and verifying the results of security performance monitoring in order to ensure that objectives are met and to determine future changes to the ISMS and its management.

- **Communicate:** Reporting enterprise security status to stakeholders and evaluating stakeholder requirements.

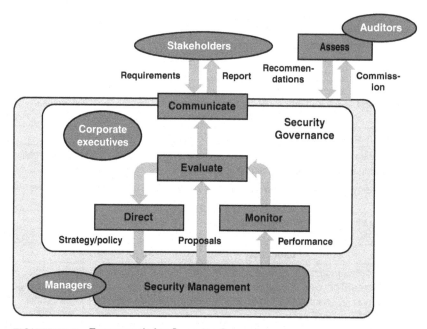

FIGURE 10.3 Framework for Security Governance

This framework includes the governing cycle to direct, monitor, and evaluate the ISMS. The evaluation incorporates both the results of the monitoring and proposals from security management to dictate changes and improvements. This cycle is in accordance with Requirement 4.4 in ISO 27001, which says that the organization shall establish, implement, maintain, and continually improve an ISMS.

The evaluate function triggers communication with stakeholders in the form of a report, which may be issued annually, more frequently, or based on a security incident.

ITU-T's X.1054 provides an example of information security status report structure that covers the following topics:

- **Introduction**
  - Scope (strategy, policies, standards), perimeter (geographic/organizational units) Period covered (month/quarter/six months/year)

- **Overall status**
  - Satisfactory/not yet satisfactory/unsatisfactory

- **Updates (as appropriate and relevant)**
  - Progress toward achieving the information security strategy
  - Elements completed/in-hand/planned
  - Changes in information security management system
  - ISMS policy revision, organizational structure to implement ISMS (including assignment of responsibilities)
  - Progress toward certification
  - ISMS (re)certification, certified information security audits
  - Budgeting/staffing/training
  - Financial situation, headcount adequacy, information security qualifications
  - Other information security activities
  - Business continuity management involvement, awareness campaigns, internal/external audit assistance

- **Significant issues (if any)**
  - Results of information security reviews (recommendations, management responses, action plans, target dates)
  - Progress in respect of major internal/external audit reports (recommendations, management responses, action plans, target dates)
  - Information security incidents (estimated impact, action plans, target dates)
  - Compliance (or noncompliance) with related legislation and regulations (estimated impact, action plans, target dates)

- **Decision(s) required (if any)**

  - Additional resources to enable information security to support business initiative(s)

This outline is particularly useful for organizations that expect to enhance their reputation by emphasizing their security (e.g., information and communications technology businesses). Transparency of the organization's approach to its security risk and appropriate disclosure is also effective in increasing trust. Common awareness can be shared among stakeholders through those activities. For example, public cloud service providers share considerable detail about the information security program and even go the extent that their customers can conduct audits and vulnerability testing with prior arrangement. Other service providers and organizations with business customers traditionally have not provided this level of transparency.

Finally, independent third-party auditors, commissioned by enterprise top management, perform the assess function depicted in Figure 10.3.

Roles and Responsibilities

A key aspect of security governance is defining the roles and responsibilities of executives related to information security. Typically, these are C-level executives. The term *C-level*, or *chief level*, refers to high-ranking executive titles within an organization. Officers who hold C-level positions set the company's strategy, make higher-stakes decisions, and ensure that day-to-day operations align with the company's strategic goals.

Examples of executive positions that may play roles in security governance include the following:

- **Chief executive officer (CEO):** Responsible for the success or failure of the organization, overseeing the entire operation at a high level.

- **Chief operating officer (COO):** Generally second in command to the CEO. Oversees the organization's day-to-day operations on behalf of the CEO, creating the policies and strategies that govern operations.

- **Chief information officer (CIO):** In charge of information technology (IT) strategy and the computer, network, and third-party (e.g., cloud) systems required to support the enterprise's objectives and goals.

- **Chief security officer (CSO) or chief information security officer (CISO):** Tasked with ensuring data and systems security. In some larger enterprises, the two roles are separate, with a CSO responsible for physical security and a CISO in charge of digital security.

- **Chief risk officer (CRO):** Charged with assessing and mitigating significant competitive, regulatory, and technological threats to an enterprise's capital and earnings. This role does not exist in most enterprises. It is most often found in financial service organizations. In enterprises in which a CRO is not present, organizational risk decisions may be made by the CEO or board of directors.

- **Chief privacy officer (CPO):** Charged with developing and implementing policies designed to protect employee and customer data from unauthorized access.

- **Chief counsel:** Also called general counsel or chief legal officer (CLO), the chief lawyer in the legal department, responsible for overseeing and identifying the legal issues in all departments.

Integration with Enterprise Architecture

A key element of security governance is the development of an information security architecture, which can be defined using the following terms:

- **Architecture:** The way in which the component parts of an entity are arranged, organized, and managed.

- **Enterprise architecture:** The systems, infrastructure, operations, and management of all information technology throughout an enterprise. The architecture is typically organized as high-level internally compatible representations of organizational business models, data, applications, and information technology infrastructure.

- **Information security architecture:** An embedded, integral part of the enterprise architecture that describes the structure and behavior for an enterprise's security processes, information security systems, personnel, and organizational sub-units, showing their alignment with the enterprise's mission and strategic plans.

The organization's information security architecture provides information on how security capabilities (e.g., identity and access management) are to be placed and used in the enterprise architecture. It allocates security requirements and controls to common services or infrastructures. It also provides a foundation for achieving risk-appropriate information system security, determining under what circumstances and which security controls apply to information systems.

Over the past 20 years, a number of enterprise architecture models have been developed and adopted by various organizations. A widely used governance resource for developing an information security architecture as part of an enterprise architecture (EA) is the Federal Enterprise Architecture Framework (FEAF) [OMB13]. The FEAF is the most comprehensive of all the enterprise architectures in use [SESS07], and this section provides an overview. Although developed for use by U.S. federal agencies, the FEAF can be used effectively as a governance tool by other government organizations, private enterprises, nonprofit groups, and other organizations.

The FEAF provides the following:

- A perspective on how enterprise architectures should be viewed in terms of sub-architecture domains
- Six reference models for describing different perspectives of the enterprise architecture
- A process for creating an enterprise architecture
- A transitional process for migrating from a pre-EA paradigm to a post-EA paradigm
- A taxonomy for cataloging assets that fall within the purview of the enterprise architecture
- An approach to measuring the success of using the EA to drive business value

The sub-architecture domains represent specific areas of the overall framework. The domains provide a standardized language and framework for describing and analyzing investments and operations. Each domain is defined in terms of a set of artifacts, which are essentially items of documentation that describe part or all of an architecture. There are three levels of artifacts:

- **High-level artifacts:** These artifacts document strategic plans and objectives, typically in the form of policy statements and diagrams.

- **Mid-level artifacts:** These artifacts document organizational procedures and operations, such as services, supply chain elements, information flows, and IT and network architecture. Typical artifacts at this level are narrative description, flowcharts, spreadsheets, and diagrams.

- **Low-level EA artifacts:** These artifacts document the specific resources, such as applications, interfaces, data dictionaries, hardware, and security controls. Typical artifacts at this level are detailed technical specifications and diagrams.

The use of these artifacts with the EA framework can greatly assist managers and planners in understanding the relationships among elements of the architecture. The various levels of scope and detail help clarify the six domains in the EA framework: strategy, business, data and information, enabling applications, host and infrastructure, and security. Corresponding to the six domains are six reference models that describe the artifacts in the corresponding domain (see Table 10.2). The list that follows describes the reference models in more detail:

TABLE 10.2 Enterprise Architecture Reference Models

Reference Model (RM)	Elements	Goals/Benefits
Performance (PRM)	Goals, measurement areas, and measurement categories	Improved organizational performance and governance and cost benefits
Business (BRM)	Mission sectors, functions, and services	Organization transformation, analysis, design, and reengineering
Data (DRM)	Domain, subject, and topic	Data quality/re-use, information sharing, and Agile development

Reference Model (RM)	Elements	Goals/Benefits
Application (ARM)	System, component, and interface	Application portfolio management and cost benefits
Infrastructure (IRM)	Platform, facility, and network	Asset management standardization and cost benefits
Security (SRM)	Purpose, risk, and control	Secure business/IT environment

- **Performance reference model (PRM):** Defines standard ways of describing the value delivered by enterprise architectures, linked to the strategy domain. An example of a PRM artifact for this domain is a *SWOT* analysis—a report that presents the *strengths, weaknesses/ limitations, opportunities, and threats* involved in a project or in a business venture, including risks and impacts.

- **Business reference model (BRM):** Describes an organization through a taxonomy of common mission and support service areas. The BRM provides guidance in defining functions and services in various mission sectors of the enterprise and is linked to the business services domain. An example of a BRM artifact for this domain is a use case narrative and diagram, which describes a set of possible sequences of interactions between systems and users in a particular environment and related to a particular goal.

- **Data reference model (DRM):** Facilitates discovery of existing data holdings residing in silos and enables understanding of the meaning of the data, how to access it, and how to leverage it to support performance results. The DRM is linked to the data and information domain. An example of a DRM artifact for this domain is a data dictionary, which is a centralized repository of information about data such as name, type, range of values, source, and authorization for access for each data element in the organization's files and databases.

- **Application reference model (ARM):** Categorizes the system- and application-related standards and technologies that support the delivery of service capabilities. The ARM provides guidance in developing a uniform scheme for documenting system, components, and interfaces and in application portfolio management. It is linked to the enabling applications domain. An example of an ARM artifact for this domain is a system/application evolution diagram. This artifact documents the planned incremental steps toward migrating a suite of systems and/or applications to a more efficient suite or toward evolving a current system or application to a future implementation.

- **Infrastructure reference model (IRM):** Categorizes the network/cloud-related standards and technologies to support and enable the delivery of voice, data, video, and mobile service components and capabilities. The ARM provides guidance in developing a uniform scheme for documenting platform, facility, and network elements and in asset management. It is linked to the host infrastructure domain. An example of an IRM artifact for this domain is a hosting concept of operations, which presents the high-level functional architecture, organization, roles, responsibilities, processes, metrics, and strategic plan for hosting and use of hosting services. Other artifacts provide detailed documentation of infrastructure elements.

■ **Security reference model (SRM):** Provides a common language and methodology for discussing security and privacy in the context of the organization's business and performance goals. The SRM provides guidance in risk-adjusted security/privacy protection and in the design and implementation of security controls. It is linked to the security domain. An example of an SRM artifact for this domain is a continuous monitoring plan, which describes the organization's process of monitoring and analyzing the security controls and reporting on their effectiveness.

Figure 10.4, based on a figure from the U.S. Office of Management and Budget and Federal Chief Information Officers Council [OMB13], illustrates the interactions among the reference models.

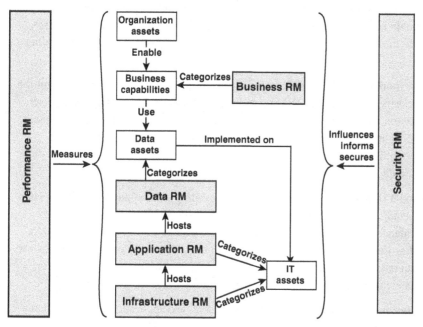

FIGURE 10.4   Relationship Between Reference Model (RM) Components

These models operate on four categories of assets:

■ **Organization assets:** These include investments, programs, processes, applications, infrastructures, and individuals.

■ **Business capabilities:** A business capability represents the ability of an organization to perform an activity that results in an outcome of value. A business capability can be viewed as an assembly of organization assets for a specific purpose.

■ **Data assets:** These assets include databases, files, and other data resources available to the organization.

■ **IT assets:** These assets include devices, peripherals, systems, applications, and IT capital investments.

Figure 10.5 shows in more detail the interaction between the security reference model and the other reference models.

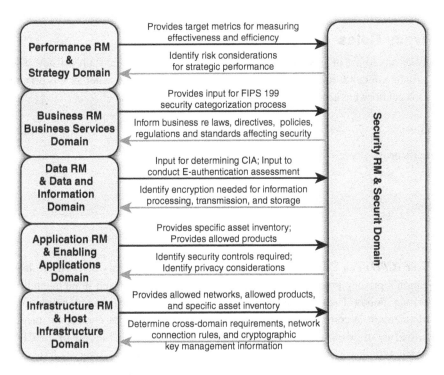

FIGURE 10.5   Interaction Between the Security Reference Model and Other Reference Models

An enterprise architecture is a powerful methodology for enabling enterprise and security governance and should be viewed as an essential element of governance.

Policies and Guidance

NIST SP 800-53 (*Security and Privacy Controls for Information Systems and Organizations*) defines an *information security policy* as an aggregate of directives, rules, and practices that prescribes how an organization manages, protects, and distributes information. It is an essential component of security governance that provides a concrete expression of the security goals and objectives of the organization. The policies, together with guidance documents on the implementation of the policies, are put into practice through the appropriate selection of controls to mitigate identified risks. The policies and guidance need to cover information security roles and responsibilities, a baseline of required security controls, and guidelines for rules of behavior for all users of data and IT assets.

10.2 Information Privacy Governance

This section provides an overview of key aspects of information privacy governance.

Information Privacy Roles

There is no universally accepted set of positions within an organization that deal with privacy. The privacy management structure depends in large part on the size of the organization, whether it is private or public sector, and its regulatory environment. Common privacy positions include:

- Chief privacy officer
- Data protection officer
- Privacy counsel
- Privacy champion
- Privacy leader

The *chief privacy officer* (*CPO*) is a C-level position. The CPO has the necessary authority to lead and direct the organization's privacy program, which involves the development and implementation of the organization's privacy policy. The CPO must be aware of relevant privacy laws and regulations and ensure that the organization is compliant. Typically, the CPO is the point of contact for media and other external inquiries about privacy-related matters. In many organizations, the role of the CPO has expanded to keep pace with the increasing importance of information privacy. A survey based on online job descriptions for CPOs that found the following as common responsibilities [LEAC14]:

- **Compliance duties/efforts:** Ensure that existing and new services comply with privacy obligations. Ensure that the organization maintains appropriate privacy and confidentiality consent, authorization forms and information notices, and materials reflecting current organization and legal practices and requirements.
- **Coordinate regulatory monitoring efforts:** Coordinate and liaise with regulatory entities to ensure compliance of programs, policies, and procedures.
- **Operationalize compliance efforts:** Maintain current knowledge of applicable privacy regulations and accreditation standards and monitor advancements in information privacy technologies to ensure organizational adaptation and compliance.
- **Intra-organizational collaboration:** Work with senior management, IT managers, IT security units, IT auditing and monitoring units, business units, and others to ensure that privacy is considered at all stages of system development, meets strategic corporate goals, and conforms to an information privacy program.
- **Employee training:** Develop privacy training and awareness materials and supervise ongoing privacy training and awareness activities.

- **Privacy public relations:** Work with organization administration, legal counsel, and other relevant parties to represent the organization's information privacy interests with external parties. Ensure that the organization's privacy policies are communicated externally as needed.

- **Employee management and oversight:** Direct and oversee privacy specialists and coordinate privacy and data security programs with senior executives globally to ensure consistency across the organization. Be responsible for employee compliance with the organization's privacy policy.

- **Build and improve the privacy program:** Ensure privacy by design and privacy engineering throughout the system development life cycle.

- **Data governance:** Supervise and monitor the use, collection, and disclosure of PII. Conduct periodic privacy impact assessments.

- **Third-party contracts:** Develop and manage procedures for ensuring that third-party relationships comply with the organization's privacy policy.

- **Incident response:** Develop, implement, and monitor privacy incident response.

A *data protection officer* (*DPO*) is responsible for highlighting any issues or concerns related to the organization's compliance with privacy regulations and laws. The DPO is typically responsible for performing internal audits and handling complaints. The DPO may be responsible for conducting a privacy impact assessment. Although the position of DPO predates the GDPR, there has been more interest in developing this position because the GDPR mandates it for certain situations. The GDPR lists the tasks of the DPO as the following:

- Inform and advise the controller or the processor (refer to Figure 3.4 in Chapter 3, "Information Privacy Requirements and Guidelines") and the employees who carry out processing of their obligations pursuant to the GDPR and to other union or member state data protection provisions.

- Monitor compliance with the GDPR, with other union or member state data protection provisions, and with the policies of the controller or processor in relation to the protection of personal data, including the assignment of responsibilities, awareness-raising and training of staff involved in processing operations, and the related audits.

- Provide advice where requested regarding the data protection impact assessment and monitor its performance.

- Cooperate with the supervisory authority.

- Act as the contact point for the supervisory authority on issues related to processing and to consult, where appropriate, with regard to any other matter.

The GDPR indicates that the DPO should be independent of others with information privacy responsibilities and should report to the highest levels of management. The DPO does not have operational responsibility for implementing privacy measures nor policy responsibility for deciding the level of privacy risk the organization will assume.

The *privacy counsel* is an attorney who deals with legal matters related to privacy. Duties typically include:

- Providing advice on data privacy and security legal requirements

- Advising on the incident response process and providing legal advice on responding to actual incidents

- Developing compliance mechanisms for new products and services

- Being actively involved in product development and drafting relevant customer-facing documentation

- Drafting and negotiating contractual provisions with customers, vendors, and partners

- Responding to third-party questionnaires and inquiries

- Actively monitoring and advising on local and global legal developments

The term *privacy leader* is becoming increasingly widespread. In general, a privacy leader is head of privacy compliance and operations and may be the most senior privacy official in the organization. In the U.S federal government, the equivalent term is *senior agency official for privacy* (*SAOP*). According to the U.S. Office of Management and Budget's *Managing Federal Information as a Strategic Resource* [OMB16], the privacy leader has responsibility and accountability for developing, implementing, and maintaining a privacy program to manage privacy risks, develop and evaluate privacy policy, and ensure compliance with all applicable statutes, regulations, and policies regarding the creation, collection, use, processing, storage, maintenance, dissemination, disclosure, and disposal of PII by programs and information systems. The privacy leader shall:

- Develop and maintain a privacy program plan.

- Develop and maintain a privacy continuous monitoring (PCM) strategy and PCM program to maintain ongoing awareness of privacy risks and assess privacy controls at a frequency sufficient to ensure compliance with applicable privacy requirements and manage privacy risks.

- Conduct and document the results of privacy control assessments to verify the continued effectiveness of all privacy controls selected and implemented.

- Identify assessment methodologies and metrics to determine whether privacy controls are implemented correctly, operating as intended, and sufficient to ensure compliance with applicable privacy requirements and manage privacy risks.

- Review IT capital investment plans and budgetary requests to ensure that privacy requirements (and associated privacy controls), as well as any associated costs, are explicitly identified and included, with respect to any IT resources that will be used to create, collect, use, process, store, maintain, disseminate, disclose, or dispose of PII.

- Review and approve the categorization of information systems that create, collect, use, process, store, maintain, disseminate, disclose, or dispose of PII in terms of risk and privacy impact.

- Review and approve the privacy plans for information systems.

- Coordinate with the CIO, the CISO, and other officials in implementation of these requirements.

There is considerable overlap between this list of duties and those of a CPO. In practice, in an organization with a CPO, the CPO is also the privacy leader. A recent global survey of privacy leaders also shows overlap with other privacy offices. Quite often, the privacy leader is also the DPO or the chief privacy counsel [IAPP18] (see Figure 10.6). Only rarely do privacy leaders also serve the function of CISO.

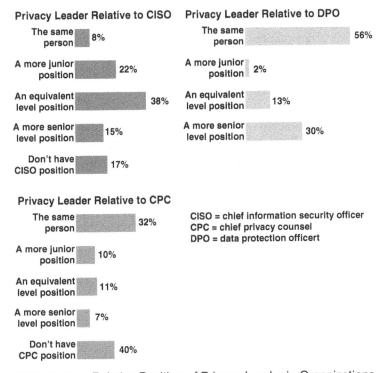

FIGURE 10.6   Relative Position of Privacy Leader in Organizations

In recent years, a number of enterprises have adopted the practice of designating a ***privacy champion***, either organization-wide or in each local environment (e.g., branch office). This can be a full-time job or part of the job of a privacy manager or another privacy professional. The role of privacy champion can also be combined with that of a security champion.

The role of privacy champion is to promote a culture of privacy throughout the organization. On the one hand, the champion acts as an ambassador for the privacy leader and the enterprise privacy manager to communicate privacy policy in the local environment. On the other hand, the champion acts as an advocate for a privacy culture, promoting awareness and working to ensure that privacy requirements are built into end user systems and software.

The Privacy Program Plan

An essential element of information privacy governance is the development of a privacy program plan. Two terms are important to this discussion:

- **Privacy program:** The management, operational, and technical aspects of protecting PII. It encompasses policies, procedures, and management structure and mechanisms for coordinating privacy activity.

- **Privacy program plan:** A formal document that provides an overview of an organization's privacy program. The program plan communicates, within the organization, the organization's privacy goals, the management structure and actions needed to achieve those goals, and all the other critical elements to ensuring PII privacy. This document should be approved and regularly reviewed by the appropriate executive committees.

The level of detail in the privacy program plan depends on the size of the organization and the amount of PII that it collects, stores, processes, and distributes. Table 10.3 lists the topics that might be covered in a privacy program plan, grouped into three areas: strategic, operational, and oversight.

TABLE 10.3   Elements of a Privacy Program Plan Document

Area	Topic
Strategic	Mission statement and strategic goals
	Fair information privacy practices
	Structure of privacy program
	Privacy roles
	Coordination among organizational entities
Operational	Managing PII
	Privacy controls
	Budget and acquisition
	Privacy impact assessment
	Workforce management
	Training and awareness
	Incident response
Oversight	Audit and monitoring
	Notice and redress
	Privacy reporting

The strategic area of the privacy program plan document could encompass the following topics:

- **Mission statement and strategic goals:** Defines the strategy for aligning the information security program with organization goals and objectives and describes the manner in which privacy objectives harmonize with security objectives.

- **Fair information privacy practices:** States that the program adheres to the fair information practice principles (FIPPs), which provide all stakeholders with an understanding of what the privacy program commits to enforcing. The OECD FIPPs (see Table 3.2 in Chapter 3) and the GDPR principles related to processing of personal data (see Table 3.3 in Chapter 3) are examples of FIPPs that the organization could adopt. You can find another useful FIPP list in the U.S. Office of Management and Budget report *Managing Federal Information as a Strategic Resource*[OMB16].

- **Structure of privacy program:** Provides a description of the structure of the privacy program and the resources dedicated to the privacy program.

- **Privacy roles:** Defines the privacy roles in the organization, such as privacy leader, data protection officer, and privacy champion. For each role, the document defines the range of responsibilities for the person or persons in that role. For example, the document *Best Practices: Elements of a Federal Privacy Program* [FCIO10] lists the following as representative responsibilities for a CPO:

  - Overall responsibility and accountability for ensuring the organization's implementation of information privacy protections, including the organization's full compliance with federal laws, regulations, and policies related to privacy protection.

  - Exercising a central role in overseeing, coordinating, and facilitating the organization's privacy compliance efforts. This role includes reviewing the organization's privacy procedures to ensure that they are comprehensive and current. Where additional or revised procedures are identified, the CPO consults and collaborates with the appropriate organization offices in developing, adopting, and implementing these procedures.

  - Ensuring that the organization's employees and contractors receive appropriate training and education regarding their privacy protection responsibilities. These programs inform employees about the underlying privacy laws, regulations, policies, and procedures governing the organization's handling of PII, documents, and records.

  - Playing a central policymaking role in the organization's development and evaluation of legislative, regulatory, and related policy proposals implicating privacy issues. Such issues include the organization's collection, use, sharing, retention, disclosure, and destruction of PII.

- **Coordination among organizational entities:** Describes coordination among organizational entities responsible for the different aspects of privacy. In addition, this section should indicate how privacy and security officers and groups coordinate so that protection of PII is incorporated in the security program.

The operational area of a privacy program plan provides a high-level view of the implementation and ongoing operation of privacy controls and policies to protect PII. It may encompass the following topics:

- **Managing PII:** This section should make explicit the requirements, or guidelines, that the organization uses to manage PII. For example, the U.S. Office of Management and Budget report *Managing Federal Information as a Strategic Resource* [OMB16] lists the following as responsibilities related to managing PII:

  - Maintain an inventory of agency information systems that involve PII and regularly review and reduce PII to the minimum necessary.

  - Eliminate unnecessary collection, maintenance, and use of Social Security numbers.

  - Follow approved records retention schedules for records with PII.

  - Limit the creation, collection, use, processing, storage, maintenance, dissemination, and disclosure of PII.

  - Require entities with which PII is shared to maintain the PII in an information system with a particular categorization level.

  - Impose conditions on the creation, collection, use, processing, storage, maintenance, dissemination, disclosure, and disposal of shared PII through agreements.

- **Privacy controls:** The privacy program plan is not the place to document specific privacy controls that are implemented. Rather, the program plan should indicate a commitment to using widely accepted privacy controls. In particular, the organization should commit to the use of privacy controls selected from NIST SP 800-53 and ISO 29151.

- **Budget and acquisition:** The privacy program needs to have the resources required to be effective. The program plan should indicate procedures and management responsibilities for the following:

  - Identifying resources needed

  - Including privacy requirements in new IT system acquisition plans

  - Upgrading, replacing, or retiring information systems that do not have adequate PII protection

- **Privacy impact assessments:** The privacy program does not document the privacy impact assessment details but should indicate procedures and management responsibilities for identifying and reducing the privacy impact of the organization's activities and notifying the public about any privacy impacts and steps taken to mitigate them.

- **Workforce management:** The privacy program plan should state that the privacy leader or other privacy official or group is responsible for assessing and addressing the hiring, training, and professional development needs of the organization with respect to privacy, including providing input into the performance of employees who have direct privacy responsibility.

- **Training and awareness:** Privacy training and awareness programs are key elements of building a culture of privacy throughout an organization. Training deals with assuring the implementation of privacy policy by responsible individuals. Awareness programs generally target all individuals with IT roles to assure that they are aware of the privacy requirements for handling PII. The program plan should define the training and awareness programs in the organization.

- **Incident response:** The program plan should indicate what policies are in place and what resources are devoted to dealing with incidents that compromise or could potentially compromise privacy. The program plan need not provide details but should indicate in overview fashion how the following responsibilities are met:

  - Documented incident management response policies and capabilities

  - Roles and responsibilities for oversight and coordination

  - Testing of incident response procedures

  - Process of after-action review and recommendations

  - Policies and procedure for reporting incidents

The oversight area of a privacy program plan provides a high-level view of the monitoring and accountability aspects of the privacy program. It may encompass the following topics.

- **Auditing:** The program plan indicates how and how often auditing is performed and by whom.

- **Accountability:** The program should commit the organization to implementing policies and procedures to ensure that all personnel are held accountable for complying with agency-wide privacy requirements and policies.

- **Notice and redress:** The program plan should document the contents and means of notification for a privacy notice to individuals whose PII is collected, stored, and processed by the organization. The program plan should also provide an overview of procedures by which individuals can amend or correct PII.

To summarize, the privacy program plan is the master plan documenting the organization's capability to protect PII. The more detailed and comprehensive the plan, the greater the assurance of stakeholders that the organization is effective in protecting privacy.

10.3 Information Privacy Management

Broadly speaking, the information privacy management function entails establishing, implementing, and monitoring an information privacy program under the direction of a senior responsible person, such as a privacy leader or CPO.

Privacy management involves multiple levels of management. Each level contributes to the overall privacy program with different types of expertise, authority, and resources. In general, executive managers (e.g., those at the headquarters level) better understand the organization as a whole and have more authority. On the other hand, frontline managers (at the IT facility and applications levels) are more familiar with the specific requirements, both technical and procedural, and problems of the systems and the users. The levels of privacy program management should be complementary; each can help the other be more effective.

Of course, the details of privacy management vary from one organization to the next, based on the size of the organization's IT operation, the amount of PII the organization handles, and various other factors, such as regulatory, contractual, and corporate image issues. This section provides a general overview, beginning with a discussion of key areas of privacy management. The section then discusses the key privacy management document: the information privacy policy. Finally, the section looks at a privacy management model.

Key Areas of Privacy Management

Figure 10.7 illustrates the main areas of concern for privacy management.

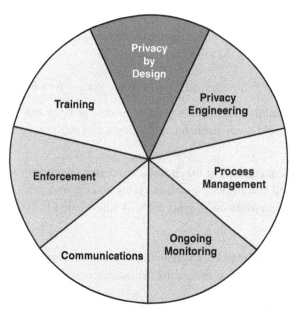

FIGURE 10.7   Key Areas of Privacy Management

The bulk of privacy management duties fall into one of these seven categories:

- **Privacy by design:** Privacy by design (PbD) is the keystone of information privacy management. PbD is concerned with ensuring that privacy features are designed into a system before implementation begins. PbD dictates how privacy is realized at every stage of the system development life cycle. Specifically, PbD involves privacy planning and policy, privacy risk, and impact assessment, as well as the selection of privacy controls. Chapter 2, "Information Privacy Concepts," discusses PbD principles.

- **Privacy engineering:** Privacy engineering involves taking account of privacy during the entire life cycle of ICT (information and communications technology) systems, such that privacy is and remains an integral part of their function. Privacy engineering involves implementing privacy in systems; ensuring that privacy is incorporated during system integration; privacy test and evaluation; and privacy auditing and incident response. Chapter 2 discusses privacy engineering principles.

- **Process management:** Process management is concerned with ensuring coordination of separate business functions within an organization. In this context, privacy managers coordinate with security managers, business unit managers, and others to ensure that privacy is incorporated in all management concerns.

- **Ongoing monitoring:** Monitoring is concerned with privacy audits and performance. An audit within an enterprise is an independent inspection of enterprise records to determine compliance with a standard or policy. More specifically, a privacy audit relates to the privacy policy and the mechanisms and procedures used to enforce that policy. Privacy performance monitoring deals with the measurable result of privacy controls applied to information systems.

- **Communications:** This area includes the development of privacy-related documents, employee handbooks and advisories, compliance procedures, and other privacy-related forms of communication within the organization and to external stakeholders and other interested parties.

- **Enforcement:** This area covers mechanisms for detecting and dealing with privacy breaches and policies and procedures for enforcing privacy policies.

- **Training:** This area covers the training required for all employees who handle or have access to PII.

Privacy Planning

Privacy planning involves the alignment of information privacy management and operation with enterprise and IT strategic planning. It also includes more detailed planning for the organization, coordination, and implementation of privacy. The manager or group responsible for privacy planning needs to consult and bring into the ongoing process of planning key actors within the organization, such as department heads and project managers.

A useful guide to privacy planning is NIST SP 800-18 (*Guide for Developing Security Plans for Federal Information Systems*). Although the focus of this document is security planning, it also incorporates privacy planning concepts. The following discussion is based on the concepts in this document.

The purpose of a system privacy plan is to provide an overview of the privacy requirements of the system and describe the controls in place or planned for meeting those requirements. The privacy plan also delineates responsibilities and expected behavior of all individuals who access the system. The privacy plan should be viewed as documentation of the structured process of planning adequate, cost-effective privacy protection for a system. The organization should take into account PbD and privacy engineering principles in developing privacy plans.

SP 800-18 recommends a separate plan document for each information system (IS), with an IS being defined as a discrete set of information resources organized for the collection, processing, maintenance, use, sharing, dissemination, or disposition of information. An IS consists of the hardware and software elements that collectively support a given application or set of related applications. The plan document for an IS should include the following elements:

- **IS name/identifier:** A name or other identifier uniquely assigned to each system. Assignment of a unique identifier supports the organization's ability to easily collect information and privacy metrics specific to the system as well as facilitate complete traceability to all requirements related to system implementation and performance. The identifier should remain the same throughout the life of the system and should be retained in audit logs related to system use.

- **IS owner:** The person responsible for managing this asset.

- **Authorizing individual:** The senior management official or executive with the authority to formally assume responsibility for operating an IS at an acceptable level of risk to agency operations, agency assets, or individuals.

- **Assignment of privacy responsibility:** The individual responsible for the privacy of the PII.

- **Privacy categorization:** Using the FIPS 199 categories, the acceptable level of risk (low, moderate, high) for confidentiality, integrity, and availability (for each distinct element of the system, if necessary).

- **IS operational status:** The status, such as operational, under development, or undergoing major modification.

- **IS type:** The type, such as major application or support system.

- **Description/purpose:** A brief description (one to three paragraphs) of the function and purpose of the system.

- **System environment:** A general description of the technical system, including the primary hardware, software, and communications equipment.

- **System interconnections/information sharing:** Other systems/information assets that interact with this IS.

- **Related laws/regulations/policies:** Any laws, regulations, or policies that establish specific requirements for confidentiality, integrity, or availability of the system and information retained by, transmitted by, or processed by the system.

- **Existing privacy controls:** Descriptions of the controls.

- **Planned privacy controls:** Descriptions of the controls and their implementation plans.

- **IS privacy plan completion date:** The target date.
- **IS privacy plan approval date:** The date the plan was approved.

This sort of documentation enables a privacy leader to oversee all privacy projects throughout the organization. The privacy leader should also coordinate a process for developing and approving these plans. One good description of such a process is provided in *Federal Enterprise Architecture Security and Privacy Profile* [OMB10]. The process involves three stages, each of which has goals, objectives, implementation activities, and output products for formal inclusion in agency enterprise architecture and capital planning processes:

1. **Identify:** A look at the research and documentation activities necessary to identify privacy requirements in support of the mission objectives so that they may be incorporated into the enterprise architecture.

2. **Analyze:** An analysis of organization privacy requirements and the existing or planned capabilities that support privacy.

3. **Select:** An enterprise evaluation of the solutions proposed in the preceding phase and the selection of major investments.

Step 1 refers to three types of requirements, defined as follows:

- **External requirements:** These are privacy requirements imposed external to the organization, such as laws, regulations, and contractual commitments.

- **Internal requirements:** These are privacy requirements developed as part of the privacy policy, such as the acceptable degree of risk and confidentiality, integrity, availability, and privacy guidelines.

- **Business requirements:** This refers to requirements other than privacy requirements that are related to the overall business mission. Examples include finance, accounting, and audit requirements. In general, these requirements refer to the organization's need to discharge business responsibilities.

Privacy Policy

An information privacy policy is an aggregate of directives, rules, and practices that prescribes how an organization manages, protects, and distributes information. It is helpful to distinguish five types of documents before proceeding:

- **Privacy program plan:** Relates to the long-term goals for maintaining security for assets and to privacy governance.

- **Privacy plan:** Relates to security controls in place and planned to meet strategic privacy objectives.

- **Privacy policy:** Relates to the rules and practices that enforce privacy. Also referred to as a *data protection policy*. It is concerned with specifying the policies and procedures that regulate how employees and non-employed personnel conduct themselves in relation to PII handled by the organization.

- **Privacy notice:** Relates to the information provided to outside users concerning privacy protection. This document is often referred to as a *privacy policy*, but to distinguish this document, this book uses the term *privacy notice*. Chapter 8, "Online Privacy," covers privacy notices.

- **Acceptable use policy:** Relates to how users are allowed to use assets. Chapter 12, "Privacy Awareness, Training, and Education," covers privacy notices.

Table 10.4 provides more detailed descriptions of these documents. All of these documents should be approved by a privacy leader or comparable executive. The privacy leader may task an individual or a team with document preparation. With these distinctions in mind, this section addresses privacy policy.

TABLE 10.4   Privacy-Related Documents

Document Type	Description	Primary Audience
Privacy program plan	A document used to communicate with the organization the organization's long-term goals with respect to information privacy, the actions needed to achieve those goals, and all the other critical elements developed during the planning exercise.	C-level executives
Privacy plan	A formal document that provides an overview of the security requirements for the information system and describes the privacy controls in place or planned for meeting those requirements.	C-level executives, security managers, and other managers
Privacy policy (data protection policy)	A set of laws, rules, and practices that regulate how an organization manages and protects PII and the rules for distribution of PII. It includes associated responsibilities and the information privacy principles to be followed by all relevant individuals.	All employees, especially those with some responsibility for an asset or assets
Privacy notice (external privacy policy)	A document that notifies external users of the measures in place to protect their PII and their rights with respect to their PII.	External users of organization data
Acceptable use policy	A document that defines, for all parties, the ranges of use that are approved for use of information, systems, and services within the organization with respect to PII.	All employees

The purpose of an information privacy policy is to ensure that all employees in an organization, especially those with responsibility of some sort for one or more assets, understand the privacy principles in use and their individual privacy-related responsibilities. Lack of clarity in information privacy policies can defeat the purpose of the privacy program and result in significant losses. An information privacy policy is the means by which the organization provides management direction and support for information privacy across the organization. The privacy policy document defines what is expected from employees and possibly others who have a role in the organization, such as contractors, outside partners or vendors, and visitors.

The privacy policy document should include the following major sections:

- **Overview:** Background information on the purpose of the document and what issues the policy addresses

- **People, risks, and responsibilities:** The scope of the policy, what risks it addresses, and the responsibilities of employees in various positions

- **Requirements for PII:** Details on the measures taken to protect PII

- **The external context:** Policies related to PII principals and other external parties

Table 10.5 suggests typical topics to be covered in each section.

TABLE 10.5 Elements of an Information Privacy Policy Document

Section	Description
Overview	
Introduction	Declares that the organization needs to collect and use certain PII and that this policy dictates how the PII is to be protected.
Rationale for Policy	Explains why the policy is needed–namely, to comply with regulations and laws; to protect rights of staff, customers, and business partners; and to protect against the risks of privacy violations.
Laws and Regulations	Lists and briefly describes the pertinent laws and regulations, such as the GDPR, U.S. Privacy Act, or any other law or regulation that applies.
FIPPs	Lists and defines the FIPPs that guide the policy and its implementation.
People, Risks, and Responsibilities	
Policy Scope	Describes the policy scope in terms of: ■ To whom it applies, such as the main office and all branches, all employees, and all contractors and suppliers ■ What data is protected—that is, what is considered PII, such as name, Social Security number, email address, and other PII
Data Protection Risks	Lists and briefly describes the kinds of privacy risks the organization faces, such as breaches of confidentiality, failure to offer choice to PII principals, and reputational damage.
Responsibilities	Briefly lists the responsibilities of each key officer, such as privacy leader, DPO, IT managers, and marketing managers.
General Staff Guidelines	Briefly describes the privacy-related responsibilities of all employees. Privacy awareness programs provide more detail.

Section	Description
Requirements for PII	
Data Storage	Describes the mandated measures to protect stored PII. This may include encryption, access control mechanisms, other information security measures, and approved physical locations and devices.
Data Use	Describes the mandated measures to protect PII while it is in use.
Data Accuracy	Describes employee responsibilities related to ensuring that PII is kept accurate and up to date.
The External Context	
PII Principal Requests	Describes the rights of PII principals to know what information the organization holds, how to gain access to it, how to keep it up to date, and how to correct errors. This document should describe in general terms the means by which PII principals can perform these tasks.
Disclosing Data	Indicates the circumstances that permit disclosure of PII to other parties, such as law enforcement agencies.
Providing Information	Commits the organization to maintaining a clear, easily accessible privacy notice.

10.4   OASIS Privacy Management Reference Model

The Organization for the Advancement of Structured Information Standards (OASIS) is a nonprofit consortium concerned with the development and adoption of open standards for the global information society. The consortium has more than 5000 participants representing more than 600 organizations and individual members in more than 65 countries. OASIS promotes industry consensus and produces worldwide standards, including in areas related to security and privacy. This section looks at two important OASIS contributions to privacy management practice.

Privacy Management Reference Model and Methodology (PMRM)

OASIS has developed the Privacy Management Reference Model and Methodology (PMRM) [OASI16], which is a methodology and analytic tool. The PMRM is, in effect, a detailed instruction manual for managing privacy by design. It is a step-by-step method of ensuring that the system design process incorporates and satisfies privacy requirements.

Figure 10.8 illustrates the overall PMRM process. The process begins with the selection of a use case. In essence, a use case is a business process, service, or function in which personal information (PI) and PII are used, generated, communicated, processed, stored, and erased.

> **Note**
>
> The PMRM recognizes a distinction between PI and PII, with PI referring to any attributes associated with a natural person and PII referring to data that are sufficient to uniquely identify a natural person. However, the document generally lumps these two concepts together in describing PRMR tasks.

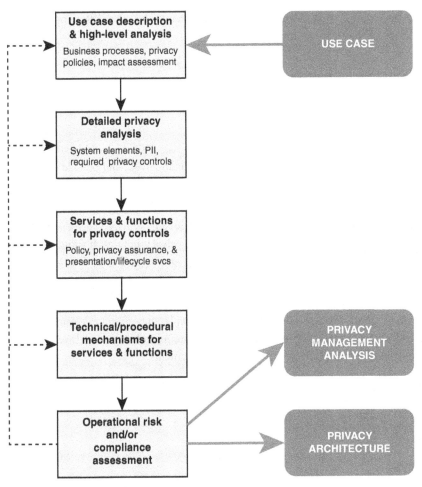

FIGURE 10.8   The PMRM Process

The PMRM defines a sequence of 19 tasks organized into 5 functional stages:

- Use case description and high-level analysis
- Detailed privacy analysis
- Services and functions for privacy controls
- Technical and procedural mechanisms for service and functions
- Operational risk and/or compliance assessment

A twentieth task is to iterate the analysis, as needed, to refine and add detail. The end result of the analysis consist of two documents: a privacy management analysis and a privacy architecture. For each task, the PMRM provides an example that enhances the utility of the model. The following sections describe the tasks within each of the stages of the PMRM.

Use Case Description and High-Level Analysis

The first set of tasks involve developing a detailed description of the use case and providing an initial high-level privacy analysis. The four tasks in this stage are:

- **Use case description:** This is a general description of the use case. This description should indicate the application, the individuals and organizational units involved, and outside entities involved.

- **Use case inventory:** This inventory should contain all the information needed for privacy analysis in subsequent steps. Examples include IT systems involved, applicable laws and regulations, PI collected, applicable privacy policy statements, and privacy notices. It should include any other factors that affect the collection, storage, processing, sharing, transmission, and disposal of PI.

- **Privacy policy conformance criteria:** This section spells out the specific conformance criteria for this use case to satisfy privacy requirements. For example, the criteria may include a requirement for two-factor authentication between specific systems and the use of IPsec for specific transmissions in order to satisfy specific policy requirements.

- **Assessment preparation:** This section should provide a preliminary and somewhat general description of potential risks and privacy impacts to guide detailed risk assessment and privacy impact assessment in subsequent steps.

Detailed Privacy Analysis

This stage, which is the heart of the PMRM, provides a structured approach that managers can use to ensure that privacy by design principles are incorporated into system development. It consists of 3 components and 12 tasks. The first component—the identification of all the key elements in the use case that have privacy implications—consists of the following tasks:

- **Identify participants:** Identify all the stakeholders responsible for any aspect of the life cycle of PI within the system, including the collection, storage, processing, sharing, transmission, and disposal of PI.

- **Identify systems and business processes:** Identify the systems and business processes involved in the collection, storage, processing, sharing, transmission, and disposal of PI. In this context, a *system* refers to an IT system, such as a workstation, server, data center, or cloud computing infrastructure. A *business process* is a set of structured, often chained, activities conducted by people and/or equipment to produce a specific product or service for a particular user or customer. The business process accomplishes a specific organizational goal within a use case.

- **Identify domains and owners:** A domain is a physical environment (e.g., an organization site, a third-party site) or a logical environment (e.g., a cloud service). An owner is an individual responsible for implementing and managing privacy controls within a domain.

- **Identify roles and responsibilities within a domain:** Within a use case, this tasks spells out the roles and responsibilities of individuals, business processes, and systems within a specific domain.

- **Identify touch points:** A touch point is an interface for a data flow between an individual and a system or between systems or between an individual or a system and a business process. This task identifies touch points related to the flow of PI.

- **Identify data flows:** This task identifies each data flow that carries PI or data related to a privacy control.

The second component of this stage deals with PI. The goal is to identify all the PI that is collected, stored, processed, shared, transmitted, and disposed. This component consists of the following tasks:

- **Identify incoming PI:** PI flowing into the domain.

- **Identify internally generated PI:** PI generated within a domain. Examples include physical location and timestamps that may be linked to an identity.

- **Identify outgoing PI:** PI flowing from one system or business process to another, either within the domain or to another domain.

The final component of this stage is the selection of privacy controls. These include management, technical, and physical controls. The controls account for all of the PI related to this domain and this use case. This component consists of the following tasks:

- **Specify inherited privacy controls:** These are privacy controls already in place for a domain, system, or business process and can be used to satisfy the privacy requirements of this use case.

- **Specify internal privacy controls:** These are privacy controls mandated by the privacy policies for this domain.

- **Specify exported privacy controls:** These are privacy controls that must be exported to other domains in order to satisfy the privacy requirements of this use case.

The end product of this stage is a set of privacy controls that implement the privacy policy and satisfy the privacy requirements for a use case. However, in the PMRM, privacy controls take the form of policy declarations or requirements that are not immediately actionable or implementable. Thus, the privacy controls in PMRM are not as detailed as those defined in NIST SP 800-53 and ISO 29151.

Service and Functions for Privacy Controls

The purpose of this stage is to define the services and functions that enable the implementation of the selected privacy controls. PMRM uses two key concepts in this regard:

- **Function:** Any hardware, software, or human activity that implements a privacy control.
- **Service:** A defined collection of related functions that operate for a specified purpose.

In effect, the PMRM recommends a classification of services designed to facilitate the management of the PbD process. The PMRM defines three categories of services:

- **Core policy services:** These services deal with defining what is allowable with respect to PI and how the PI is used in the use case.
- **Privacy assurance services:** These services related to ensuring that privacy controls are implemented as intended.
- **Presentation and life cycle services:** Relates to privacy controls that provide interfaces for PI principals and for employees with privacy responsibilities.

Table 10.6 defines the 10 services in the PMRM model [OASI16]. It is the responsibility of a privacy engineer, a system architect, or a technical manager to define the functions in each service and to implement technical mechanisms or describe procedural mechanisms for the functions.

TABLE 10.6 PMRM Services *(Copyright © OASIS Open 2016. All Rights Reserved.)*

PMRM Service	Service Functionality	Purpose
Core Policy Services		
Agreement	Defines and documents permissions and rules for the handling of PI, based on applicable policies, data subject preferences, and other relevant factors; provides relevant actors with a mechanism to negotiate, change, or establish new permissions and rules; expresses the agreements such that they can be used by other services.	Manage and negotiate permissions and rules
Usage	Ensures that the use of PI complies with the terms of permissions, policies, laws, and regulations, including PI subjected to information minimization, linking, integration, inference, transfer, derivation, aggregation, anonymization, and disposal over the life cycle of the PI.	Control IP use

PMRM Service	Service Functionality	Purpose
Privacy Assurance Services		
Validation	Evaluates and ensures the information quality of PI in terms of accuracy, completeness, relevance, timeliness, provenance, appropriateness for use, and other relevant qualitative factors.	Ensure PI quality
Certification	Ensures that the credentials of any actor, domain, system, or system component are compatible with their assigned roles in processing PI and verifies their capability to support required privacy controls in compliance with defined policies and assigned roles.	Ensure appropriate privacy management credentials
Enforcement	Initiates monitoring capabilities to ensure the effective operation of all services. Initiates response actions, policy execution, and recourse when audit controls and monitoring indicate operational faults and failures. Records and reports evidence of compliance to stakeholders and/or regulators. Provides evidence necessary for accountability.	Monitor proper operation, respond to exception conditions, and report on demand evidence of compliance where required for accountability
Security	Provides the procedural and technical mechanisms necessary to ensure the confidentiality, integrity, and availability of PI; makes possible the trustworthy processing, communication, storage, and disposition of PI; and safeguards privacy operations.	Safeguard privacy information and operations
Presentation and Life Cycle Services		
Interaction	Provides generalized interfaces necessary for presentation, communication, and interaction of PI and relevant information associated with PI, encompassing functionality such as user interfaces, system-to-system information exchanges, and agents.	Information presentation and communication
Access	Enables data subjects (as required and/or allowed by permission, policy, or regulation) to review their PI that is held within a domain and propose changes, corrections, or deletion for their PI.	View and propose changes to PI

The single task in this stage is:

- **Identify the services and functions necessary to support operation of identified privacy controls:** This task is performed for each data flow exchange between systems and domains.

Technical and Procedural Mechanisms Supporting Selected Services and Functions

This stage defines the specific mechanisms that implement the design produced by the preceding stages. The PMRM views a mechanism as the operational realization of a set of services and functions by human procedures or technical implementations. Mechanisms include specific procedures, applications, technical and vendor solutions, code, and other concrete tools that will actually make possible the delivery of required privacy controls. In essence, the preceding PMRM stages deal with *what* is needed to satisfy the use case's privacy requirements, and this stage deals with *how* to deliver the required functionality.

The single task in this stage is:

- **Identify mechanisms satisfying the services and functions necessary to support operation of identified privacy controls:** This task is performed for each data flow exchange between systems and domains.

Operational Risk and/or Compliance Assessment

The single task in this stage is:

- **Conduct risk assessment:** Perform a risk assessment from an operational point of view. This risk assessment is different from the initial risk assessment developed for this use case. This risk assessment looks at any risks that arise from the actual operation of the proposed design solution. If this assessment identifies risks that are not addressed by the privacy controls developed for this use case, then the analyst needs to iterate the design process by returning to one of the previous stages and going forward again.

PMRM Documentation

The PMRM methodology envisions two important documents as outputs of the process: a privacy management analysis (PMA) document and a privacy architecture document.

The PMA serves multiple stakeholders, including privacy officers, engineers and managers, general compliance managers, and system developers. The PMA is a high-level structured document that maps policy to privacy controls to services and functions, which in turn are implemented via mechanisms, both technical and procedural. The PMA documents the way in which this use case is handled and can serve as an input to shorten the analysis for other use cases. OASIS is currently working on a template for a PMA that can guide managers and analysts in the creation of this document.

A privacy architecture is the actual implementation of the privacy controls for this use case. It is an integrated set of policies, controls, services, and functions implemented in mechanisms. The privacy architecture document should be applicable to other use cases with similar requirements.

Privacy by Design Documentation for Software Engineers

OASIS has published a specification for software engineers that translates the seven privacy by design (PbD) principles to conformance requirements for documentation, either produced or referenced [OASI14]. Organizations may use the guidance in this document to produce documentation that demonstrates that privacy was considered at each stage of the software development life cycle (see Figure 10.9). This method has the advantage of demonstrating to stakeholders that PdB has been employed. Further, this method guides developers in the design and implementation stages to ensure that the Pbd principles are satisfied. (See Chapter 2 for a detailed discussion of PbD principles.)

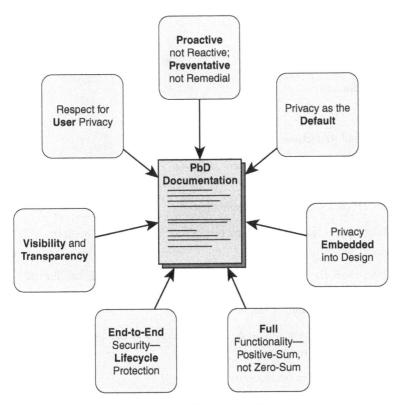

FIGURE 10.9   Privacy by Design Documentation

For each of the PbD principles, the OASIS document *Privacy by Design Documentation for Software Engineers Version 1.0* [OASI14] elaborates the principle into detailed sub-principles and indicates the required documentation. For example, for the Privacy as the Default principle, the document lists the following sub-principles:

- **2.1–Purpose Specificity:** Purposes must be specific and limited, and be amenable to engineering controls

- **2.2–Adherence to Purposes:** Methods must be in place to ensure that personal data is collected, used, and disclosed:

    - in conformity with specific, limited purposes

    - in agreement with data subject consent

    - in compliance with applicable laws and regulations

- **2.3–Engineering Controls:** Strict limits should be placed on each phase of data processing lifecycle engaged by the software under development, including:

  - Limiting Collection

  - Collecting by Fair and Lawful Means

  - Collecting from Third Parties

  - Limiting Uses and Disclosures

  - Limiting Retention

  - Disposal, Destruction; and Redaction

Privacy by Design Documentation for Software Engineers Version 1.0 then lists the following documentation requirements:

- **SHALL** list all [categories of] data subjects as a stakeholder

- **SHALL** clearly record the purposes for collection and processing, including retention of personal data

- **SHALL** document expressive models of detailed data flows, processes, and behaviors for use cases or user stories associated with internal software project and all data/process interaction with external platforms, systems, APIs, and/or imported code.

- **SHALL** describe selection of privacy controls and privacy services/APIs and where they apply to privacy functional requirements and risks.

- **SHALL** include software retirement plan from a privacy viewpoint

An annex to the OASIS document *Privacy by Design Documentation for Software Engineers Version 1.0* [OASI14] provides the following additional guidance to developers:

- A process to ensure that privacy requirements are considered throughout the entire software development life cycle from software conception to software retirement.

- A methodology for an organization and its software engineers to produce and reference privacy-embedded documentation to demonstrate conformance to this PbD-SE Version 1.0 specification.

- A Privacy Use Template that helps software engineers document privacy requirements and integrate them with core functional requirements.

- Privacy by Design Reference Architecture for software engineers to customize to their context, and Privacy Properties that software solutions should exhibit.

- Privacy by Design Patterns

- Privacy by Design for Maintenance and Retirement

Taken together, the main document and its annex are useful to privacy managers and system developers in ensuring that PbD is followed.

10.5 Key Terms and Review Questions

Key Terms

acceptable use policy	information security management system (ISMS)
C-level	information security strategic planning
chief counsel	
chief executive officer (CEO)	IT strategic planning
chief information officer (CIO)	personally identifiable information (PII)
chief information security officer (CISO)	privacy by design
chief operating officer (COO)	privacy champion
chief privacy officer (CPO)	privacy engineering
chief risk officer (CRO)	privacy management reference model (PMRM)
chief security officer (CSO)	privacy notice
data protection officer (DPO)	privacy policy
data protection policy	privacy program
enterprise strategic planning	privacy program plan
information privacy governance	process management
information privacy management	security program
information security governance	Senior Agency Official for Privacy (SAO)
information security management	

Review Questions

1. Briefly differentiate between information security governance and information security management.

2. List and describe the responsibilities of typical C-level executive positions.

3. List and describe the responsibilities of typical privacy positions.

4. What is a privacy program?

5. Briefly differentiate between privacy program plan, privacy plan, privacy policy, privacy notice, and acceptable use policy.

6. Briefly describe the OASIS privacy management reference model.

7. Briefly describe the OASIS privacy documentation for software engineers.

10.6   References

FCIO10: Federal CIO Council Privacy Committee. *Best Practices: Elements of a Federal Privacy Program.* https://www.cio.gov/resources/document-library/

IAPP18: International Association of Privacy Professionals. *IAPP-EY Annual Privacy Governance Report.* 2018. https://iapp.org/media/pdf/resource_center/IAPP-EY-Gov_Report_2018-FINAL.pdf

JUIZ15: Juiz, C., and Toomey, M. "To Govern IT, or Not to Govern IT?" *Communications of the ACM.* February 2015.

LEAC14: Leach, E. *Chief Privacy Officer: Sample Job Description.* IAPP blog, 2014. https://iapp.org/resources/article/chief-privacy-officer-sample-job-description/

OASI14: OASIS. *Privacy by Design Documentation for Software Engineers Version 1.0.* June 25, 2014. https://www.oasis-open.org/standards

OASI16: OASIS. *Privacy Management Reference Model and Methodology (PMRM) Version 1.0.* May 17, 2016. https://www.oasis-open.org/standards

OMB13: U.S. Office of Management and Budget and Federal Chief Information Officers Council. *Federal Enterprise Architecture Framework.* 2013.

OMB16: U.S. Office of Management and Budget. *Managing Federal Information as a Strategic Resource.* Circular A-130, 2016. https://obamawhitehouse.archives.gov/sites/default/files/omb/assets/OMB/circulars/a130/a130revised.pdf

SESS07: Sessions, R. A Comparison of the Top Four Enterprise-Architecture Methodologies. Microsoft Developer Network, May 2007.

SMG17: Strategic Management Group. *Strategic Planning Basics.* October 23, 2017. http://www.strategymanage.com/strategic-planning-basics/

STAL19: Stallings, W. *Effective Cybersecurity: A Guide to Using Best Practices and Standards.* Upper Saddle River, NJ: Pearson Addison Wesley, 2019.

ZIA15: Zia, T. " Organisations Capability and Aptitude towards IT Security Governance." *2015 5th International Conference on IT Convergence and Security (ICITCS),* August 2015.

Chapter | **11**

Risk Management and Privacy Impact Assessment

Learning Objectives

After studying this chapter, you should be able to:

- Explain the overall risk assessment process
- Provide a comparison of quantitative and qualitative risk assessment
- Present an overview of the NIST and ISO risk management frameworks
- Explain the major options for risk treatment
- Explain the purpose of a privacy threshold analysis
- Describe the major steps in a privacy impact analysis
- Explain the purpose of a privacy impact analysis report

The EU General Data Protection Regulation (GDPR) describes a *privacy impact assessment* (*PIA*), referred to in the regulation as a *data protection impact assessment*, in the following terms:

> Where a type of processing in particular using new technologies, and taking into account the nature, scope, context and purposes of the processing, is likely to result in a high risk to the rights and freedoms of natural persons, the controller shall, prior to the processing, carry out an assessment of the impact of the envisaged processing operations on the protection of personal data. A single assessment may address a set of similar processing operations that present similar high risks.

The GDPR mandates that a PIA include:

- A systematic description of the envisaged processing operations and the purposes of the processing, including, where applicable, the legitimate interest pursued by the controller

- An assessment of the necessity and proportionality of the processing operations in relation to the purposes

- An assessment of the risks to the rights and freedoms of data subjects

- The measures envisaged to address the risks, including safeguards, security measures, and mechanisms to ensure the protection of personal data and to demonstrate compliance with the GDPR, taking into account the rights and legitimate interests of data subjects and other persons concerned

A PIA is an essential element for effective privacy by design. It enables privacy leaders to be assured that the implementation of privacy controls satisfies regulations and organizational requirements and is key to determining what steps must be taken to manage privacy risk for the organization.

To aid in the understanding of the nature and role of PIAs, this chapter begins with a treatment of information security risk assessment and risk management in Sections 11.1 and 11.2. Sections 11.3 and 11.4 deal with privacy risk assessment and privacy impact assessment.

11.1 Risk Assessment

The ultimate objective of risk assessment is to enable organization executives to determine an appropriate budget for security and, within that budget, implement security controls to optimize the level of protection. This objective is met by providing an estimate of the potential cost to the organization of security breaches, coupled with an estimation of the likelihood of such breaches.

While the utility of risk assessment should be obvious—and indeed must be considered essential—it is important to recognize its limitations. If the scale of such an effort is too ambitious, projects may be large, complicated, and unreviewable, and there may be an incentive to leave out things that are not easily quantified. On the other hand, if effective ways of calculating risk are not employed, managers tend to underestimate the magnitude of the risk and may choose to invest in other areas that they understand better and that will lead to clear payoffs. Thus, responsible executives need to develop a plan for risk assessment that is balanced between too much and too little.

Risk Assessment Process

Figure 11.1 illustrates in general terms the universally accepted method for determining the level of risk.

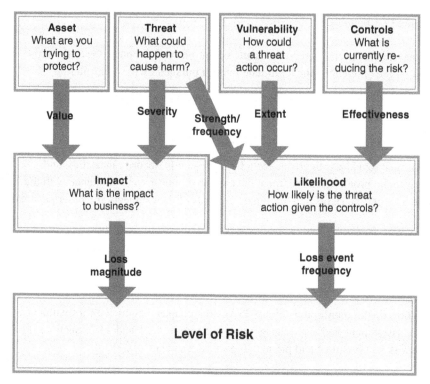

FIGURE 11.1   Determining Information Security Risk

The terms in Figure 11.1 can be defined as follows:

- **Asset:** An item of value to achievement of organizational mission/business objectives. An asset may be specifically related to information processing, including any data, device, or other component of the environment that supports information-related activities that can be illicitly accessed, used, disclosed, altered, destroyed, and/or stolen, resulting in loss. The asset category also includes organizational know-how, reputation, and image.

- **Threat:** Any circumstance or event with the potential to adversely impact organizational operations (including mission, functions, image, or reputation), organizational assets, or individuals through an information system via unauthorized access, destruction, disclosure, modification of information, and/or denial of service.

- **Threat severity:** The magnitude of the potential of a threat event to impose a cost on an organization. In other words, threat severity is a measure of how much damage a given threat can do.

- **Threat strength:** Also referred to as ***threat capability***, the probable level of force that a threat agent is capable of applying against an asset. As an example, consider an adversary attempting to obtain root privileges on a server. With root privileges, the adversary may be able to read, alter, or delete files and may be able to encrypt files for ransomware. Threat severity in this case is a measure of how many files can be attacked and the type of damage that can be done to the files. Threat capability in this case refers to the skill, resourcefulness, and determination of the adversary to gain root access.

- **Threat event frequency:** The probable frequency, within a given time frame, that a threat agent will act against an asset.

- **Vulnerability:** Weakness in an information system, system security procedures, internal controls, or implementation that could be exploited or triggered by a threat source. The *extent* of a vulnerability is some measure of how significant the weakness is.

- **Security control:** A safeguard or countermeasure prescribed for an information system or an organization that is designed to protect the confidentiality, integrity, and availability of its information and to meet a set of defined security requirements. The *effectiveness* of controls is a measure of how successful the controls are in blocking adversaries.

- **Impact:** The magnitude of harm that can be expected to result from the consequences of unauthorized disclosure of information, unauthorized modification of information, unauthorized destruction of information, or loss of information or information system availability. Note that threat severity is not the same as impact but only a factor in determining impact.

- **Likelihood:** Also called *loss event frequency*, the probable frequency, within a given time frame, that a threat agent will inflict harm upon an asset. Note the similarity to the definition of threat event frequency. The difference is that loss event frequency means that the threat event is successful. Thus, if a hacker unsuccessfully attacks a web server, this is a threat event but not a loss event.

- **Risk:** A measure of the extent to which an entity is threatened by a potential circumstance or event. Risk reflects the potential adverse impacts to organizational operations (including mission, functions, image, or reputation), organizational assets, individuals, and other organizations.

- **Level of risk:** The magnitude of a risk or a combination of risks, expressed in terms of the combination of consequences and their likelihood.

> **Note**
>
> The terms *risk* and *level* of *risk* are often used interchangeably.

Threats and vulnerabilities need to be considered together. A threat is the potential for a threat agent to intentionally or accidentally exploit a vulnerability, which is a weakness in a system's security procedures, design, implementation, or internal controls. A threat acting on a vulnerability produces a security violation, or breach. The level of risk is a measure that can be used by an organization in assessing the need for, and the expected cost of, taking remedial action in the form of risk treatment.

Figure 11.1 indicates two main threads, impact and likelihood, that should be pursued in parallel. The organization pursues the following tasks:

- **Impact:** Consider the two elements assets and threat in determining impact:
    - **Assets:** Develop an inventory of the organization's assets, which includes an itemization of the assets and an assigned value to each asset. Assets include intangible assets such as reputation and goodwill, as well as tangible assets, such as databases, equipment, business plans, and personnel.
    - **Threat:** For each asset, determine the possible threats that could reduce the value of that asset.

    Then, for each asset, determine the impact to the business, in terms of cost or lost value, if a threat action occurs.

- **Likelihood:** Consider the three elements threat, vulnerability, and controls in determining likelihood:
    - **Threat:** For each asset, determine which threats are relevant and need to be considered.
    - **Vulnerability:** For each threat to an asset, determine the level of vulnerability to the threat. That is, determine specifically for an asset how a threat action could be achieved.
    - **Controls:** Determine what security controls are currently in place to reduce the risk.

    Then, determine how likely it is that a threat action will cause harm, based on the likelihood of a threat action and the effectiveness of the corresponding controls that are in place.

Finally, the level of risk is determined as the combination of the cost if the threat occurs combined with the likelihood of the threat occurring. For example, a hacker (threat agent) may exploit known vulnerabilities (vulnerability) in the remote authentication protocol (vulnerability target) to disrupt (policy violated) remote authentication (asset exposed). The threat is unauthorized access. The assets are anything that can be compromised by an unauthorized access, such as files of PII. The vulnerability expresses how a threat action could occur (e.g., by access through a web interface). Existing security controls for this vulnerability can reduce the likelihood of a threat action.

Note that both impact and likelihood, are necessary in determining a budget allocation for security controls. If an organization focuses only on impact, the inclination will be to invest much of the security budget on high-impact threats, even if the likelihood of the impact is extremely small. Thus, the organization may give little attention to threats that produce a low or moderate impact and are realized frequently, with the net effect that the overall loss to the business is higher than it need be. Conversely, an organization errs in allocating security funds on the basis of likelihood alone. If a relatively rare security event that has very high impact costs is ignored, the organization is exposed to a very high security loss.

Risk Assessment Challenges

An organization faces enormous challenges in determining the level of risk. In general terms, these challenges fall into two categories: the difficulty of estimating and the difficulty of predicting. Consider first the problem of estimation of each of the four elements contributing to determining risk:

- **Asset:** An organization needs to put a value on individual assets and how that value may be reduced by a specific threat—in other words, the impact value. A single example indicates how difficult this is. If a company maintains a database of customer credit card numbers, what is the impact of the theft of that database? There are potential legal fees and civil penalties, loss of reputation, loss of customers, and lowering of employee morale. Assessing the magnitude of these costs is a formidable undertaking.

- **Threat:** In determining the threats facing an organization, there is past experience to go on and, as discussed subsequently, numerous publicly available reports that list current threats and their corresponding frequencies of attack. Even so, it should be clear that it is difficult to determine the entire range of threats that are faced as well as the likelihood that any threat is realized.

- **Vulnerability:** An organization may have security vulnerabilities that it is not aware of. For example, software vendors have been known to delay revealing a security vulnerability until a patch is available or even delaying releasing a patch to a portion of a vulnerability until a complete patch is available (e.g., [ASHO17], [KEIZ17]). Further, the patch may introduce new vulnerabilities. As another example, a company might have a fireproof barrier constructed around a data center enclosure; however, if the contractor does not install a barrier that meets the specification, there might not be any way for the company to know this.

- **Controls:** Controls are implemented to reduce vulnerability and therefore reduce the likelihood that particular threats are realized. However, it might be very difficult to assess the effectiveness of given controls, including software, hardware, and personnel training. For example, a particular threat action may be relatively unlikely, but controls may be introduced because of the high impact a successful threat action would have. But if the event rarely occurs, the organization has difficulty determining whether the control has the desired effect. The threat action may be artificially generated to test the system, but this artificial action may not be as realistic as is needed to get a true picture of how effective a control is.

Another challenge in risk assessment is the difficulty of predicting future conditions. Again, considering the four elements, the following problems emerge:

- **Asset:** Whether the planning period is one year, three years, or five years, changes in the value of an organization's assets complicate the effort to estimate the impact of a security threat. Company expansion, upgrade of software or hardware, relocation, and a host of other factors might come into play.

- **Threat:** It is difficult at best to assess the current threat capability and intentions of potential adversaries. Future projections are even more subject to uncertainty. Entire new types of attack may emerge in a very short period of time. And, of course, without complete knowledge of the threat, it is impossible to provide a precise assessment of impact.

- **Vulnerability:** Changes within the organization or its IT assets may create unexpected vulnerabilities. For example, if an organization migrates a substantial portion of its data assets to a cloud service provider, the organization may not know the degree of vulnerability of that provider with a high level of confidence.

- **Controls:** New technologies, software techniques, or networking protocols might provide opportunities for strengthening an organization's defenses. It is difficult, however, to predict the nature of these new opportunities, much less their cost, so resource allocation over the planning period might not be optimal.

Complicating matters is the many-to-many relationship between threats, vulnerabilities, and controls. A given threat may be able to exploit multiple vulnerabilities, and a given vulnerability may be subject to attack by multiple threats. Similarly, a single control may address multiple vulnerabilities, and a single vulnerability may require alleviation through the implementation of multiple controls. These facts complicate the planning of what controls to select and how much of the budget to allocate for various forms of mitigation.

With all these challenges, the responsible executives need to follow a systematic methodology of risk assessment based on well-established best practice.

Quantitative Risk Assessment

Organizations can treat two of the factors of risk assessment, impact and likelihood, either quantitatively or qualitatively. For impact, if it seems feasible to assign a specific monetary cost to each of the impact areas, then the overall impact can be expressed as a monetary cost. Otherwise, qualitative terms such as low, moderate, and high are used. Similarly, the likelihood of a security incident may be determined quantitatively or qualitatively. The quantitative version of likelihood is simply a probability value, and again the qualitative likelihood can be express in categories such as low, medium, and high.

If all factors can be expressed quantitatively, then a formula such as the following can be developed:

Level of risk = (Probability of adverse event) × (Impact value)

This is a measure of the cost of security breaches, expressed numerically. This can be expressed as a *residual risk* level, as follows:

In this equation, the mitigation factor reflects the reduction in the probability of an adverse event occurring, given the implementation of security controls. Thus, the residual risk level is equivalent to the expected cost of security breaches with the implementation of controls.

If the various factors can be quantified with a reasonable degree of confidence, these equations can be used to guide decisions concerning how much to invest in security controls. Figure 11.2 illustrates this point. As new security controls are implemented, the residual probability of an adverse event occurring declines and, correspondingly, the cost of security breaches declines. However, at the same time, the total cost of security controls increases as new controls are added. The upper curve represents the total security cost, calculated as follows:

Total cost = (Cost of security controls) + (Cost of security breaches)

The optimal cost point occurs at the lowest point of the total cost curve. This represents a level of risk that is tolerable and cannot be reduced further without the expenditure of costs that are disproportionate to the benefit gained.

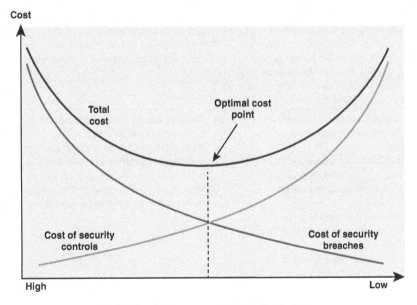

Cost

Total cost

Optimal cost point

Cost of security controls

Cost of security breaches

High

Low

(Probabilty of adverse event)/(mitigation factor)

FIGURE 11.2 Cost Analysis for Risk Assessment

Qualitative Risk Assessment

It is not reasonable to suppose that all impact costs and likelihoods can with confidence be expressed quantitatively. Organizations are often reluctant to reveal security breaches. Consequently, security incidence information is typically anecdotal or based on surveys and cannot be used to develop reliable or accurate probability or frequency values. At the same time, the total cost or potential loss due to a security breach is hard to quantify. The cost might depend on a variety of factors, such as length of downtime, amount and effect of adverse publicity, cost to recover, and other factors that are difficult to estimate.

However, it is possible, using reasonable judgment, to use qualitative risk assessment effectively. Qualitative assessment determines a relative risk rather than an absolute risk. Producing rough estimates of risk levels considerably simplifies the analysis. Qualitative risk assessment is usually sufficient for identifying the most significant risks and allowing management to set priorities for security expenditures with a reasonable degree of confidence that all the significant risks have been mitigated. Table 11.1 compares quantitative and qualitative risk assessment.

TABLE 11.1   Comparison of Quantitative and Qualitative Risk Assessment

Benefits and Drawbacks	Quantitative Risk Assessment	Qualitative Risk Assessment
Benefits	■ Risks are prioritized based on financial impact; assets are prioritized based on financial values. ■ Results facilitate management of risk by return on security investment. ■ Results can be expressed in management-specific terminology (e.g., monetary values and probability expressed as a specific percentage). ■ Accuracy tends to increase over time as the organization builds a historic record of data while gaining experience.	■ It enables visibility and understanding of risk ranking. ■ Reaching consensus is easier. ■ It is not necessary to quantify threat frequency. ■ It is not necessary to determine financial values of assets. ■ It is easier to involve people who are not experts on security or computers.
Drawbacks	■ Impact values assigned to risks are based on subjective opinions of participants. ■ The process to reach credible results and consensus is very time-consuming. ■ Calculations can be complex and time-consuming. ■ Specific numerical results for likelihood and other factors create a false sense of accuracy. ■ The process requires expertise, so participants cannot be easily coached through it.	■ There is insufficient differentiation between important risks. ■ It is difficult to justify investing in control implementation because there is no basis for a cost/benefit analysis. ■ Results are dependent on the quality of the risk management team that is created.

Note in Table 11.1 that "Impact values assigned to risks are based on subjective opinions of participants" is listed as a drawback of quantitative risk assessment. This is because it is not feasible to predict the cost of an impact within tight quantitative values. The official or group involved must make a subjective assessment of what the quantitative value will be for some future event. Disregarding this limitation may lead to a false impression of the accuracy of quantitative risk assessment. In addition, subjective opinions are used to make a qualitative estimate of impact, but in this latter case, it is clear that subjective estimates are inherent in the process.

Some clearly defined categories of impact, threat, likelihood, and vulnerability are required. For impact, FIPS 199 (*Standards for Security Categorization of Federal Information and Information Systems*) defines three security categories, based on the potential impact on an organization should certain events occur that jeopardize the IT assets needed by the organization to accomplish its assigned mission, protect its assets, fulfill its legal responsibilities, maintain its day-to-day functions, and protect individuals. The categories are:

- **Low:** Expected to have a limited adverse effect on organizational operations, organizational assets, or individuals. This might:
    - Cause a degradation in mission capability to an extent and duration that the organization is able to perform its primary functions, but the effectiveness of the functions is noticeably reduced
    - Result in minor damage to organizational assets
    - Result in minor financial loss
    - Result in minor harm to individuals

- **Moderate or medium:** Expected to have a serious adverse effect on organizational operations, organizational assets, or individuals. This might:
    - Cause a significant degradation in mission capability to an extent and duration that the organization is able to perform its primary functions, but the effectiveness of the functions is significantly reduced
    - Result in significant damage to organizational assets
    - Result in significant financial loss
    - Result in significant harm to individuals that does not involve loss of life or serious life-threatening injuries

- **High:** Expected to have a severe or catastrophic adverse effect on organizational operations, organizational assets, or individuals. This might:
    - Cause a severe degradation in or loss of mission capability to an extent and duration that the organization is not able to perform one or more of its primary functions

- Result in major damage to organizational assets

- Result in major financial loss

- Result in severe or catastrophic harm to individuals involving loss of life or serious life-threatening injuries

FIPS 199 provides a number of examples of qualitative impact assessment. For example, say that a law enforcement organization managing extremely sensitive investigative information determines that the potential impact from a loss of confidentiality is high, the potential impact from a loss of integrity is moderate, and the potential impact from a loss of availability is moderate. The resulting security category, SC, of this information type is expressed as:

SC investigative information = {(**confidentiality**, HIGH), (**integrity**, MODERATE), (**availability**, MODERATE)}.

Similarly, ranges of probability can be assigned to qualitative likelihood categories. SP 800-100 (*Information Security Handbook: A Guide for Managers*) suggests the following categories:

- **Low:** ≤ 0.1

- **Medium:** 0.1 to 0.5

- **High:** 0.5 to 1.0

Another possible categorization is based on an estimate of the number of times per year an event occurs:

- **Low:** < 1 time per year

- **Medium:** 1 to 11 times per year

- **High:** > 12 times per year

With these categories in mind, Figure 11.3 illustrates the use of matrices to determine risk. Part a of Figure 11.3 depicts the estimation of vulnerability. The vulnerability to a particular threat is a function of the capability, or strength, of the threat and the resistance strength of a system or an asset to that particular threat. Thus, for a given type of threat and a given ability of the system to resist that threat, the matrix indicates the estimated level of vulnerability. For this particular matrix, the risk analyst makes the determination that if the resistance strength is rated as higher than the threat capability, the vulnerability is low—and so on for the rest of the matrix entries.

Then, the likelihood of an adverse security event causing a particular threat is a function of the frequency, or likelihood, of the threat event occurring and the vulnerability to that threat, as illustrated in part b of Figure 11.3. In this example, for a particular type of threat, if the analyst estimates the threat event frequency to be low and the vulnerability to be high, then the analyst determines that the likelihood of threat event succeeding is low. Note that because the vulnerability can never be more than 100%, the likelihood will never be greater than the threat event frequency.

Part c of Figure 11.3 illustrates that impact is a function of asset class and the exposure to loss that a particular threat could cause.

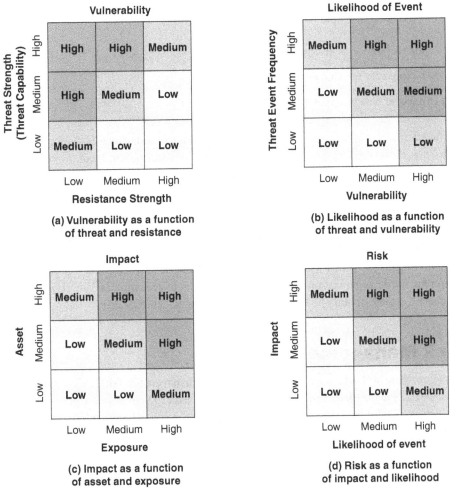

(a) Vulnerability as a function of threat and resistance

(b) Likelihood as a function of threat and vulnerability

(c) Impact as a function of asset and exposure

(d) Risk as a function of impact and likelihood

FIGURE 11.3 Qualitative Risk Determination

For example, an organization can classify assets in terms of the business impact of a loss, such as the following:

- **Low business impact:** Public information, high-level information

- **Medium business impact:** Network designs, employee lists, purchase order information

- **High business impact:** Financial data, personally identifiable information (PII), competitive product information

It can also classify assets in terms of the following exposure levels:

- **Low asset exposure:** Minor or no loss

- **Medium asset exposure:** Limited or moderate loss

- **High asset exposure:** Severe or complete loss

Finally, risk is a function of the impact and likelihood of an adverse event that causes the impact (part d of Figure 11.3). Thus, these matrices, coupled with an informed estimate of low, medium, or high for the various factors, provide a reasonable means of assessing risk.

It should be kept in mind, however, that results of such a coarse-grained analysis must be subject to judgment. For example, in part d of Figure 11.3, a low-likelihood, high-impact breach and a high-likelihood, low-impact breach are both rated as medium risk. Which should be given priority for scarce security resources? On average, each type of breach may be expected to yield the same amount of annual loss. Is it more important to deal with the former breach because although rare, if it does occur, it could be catastrophic for the organization? Or is it more important to deal with the latter type, which, unprotected, produces a steady stream of losses? That is for management to decide.

11.2 Risk Management

Risk assessment is one part of the broader security task of risk management. NIST SP 800-37 (*Risk Management Framework for Information Systems and Organizations A System Life Cycle Approach for Security and Privacy*) states that risk management includes a disciplined, structured, and flexible process for organizational asset valuation; security and privacy control selection, implementation, and assessment; system and control authorizations; and continuous monitoring. It also includes enterprise-level activities to help better prepare organizations to execute the RMF at the system level.

To place risk assessment into the context of risk management, this section summarizes risk management concepts defined by NIST and ISO.

NIST Risk Management Framework

NIST SP 800-37 defines a risk management framework that views the risk management process as consisting of six steps (see Figure 11.4):

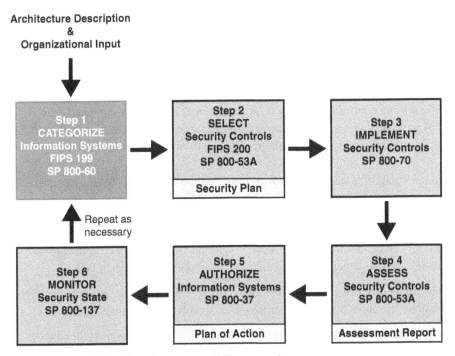

Architecture Description & Organizational Input

FIGURE 11.4 NIST Risk Management Framework

1. **Categorize:** Identify information that will be transmitted, processed, or stored by the system and define applicable levels of information categorization based on an impact analysis. The purpose of the categorization step is to guide and inform subsequent risk management processes and tasks by determining the adverse impact or consequences to the organization with respect to the compromise or loss of organizational assets—including the confidentiality, integrity, and availability of organizational systems and the information processed, stored, and transmitted by those systems. This is risk assessment.

2. **Select:** Select an initial set of baseline security controls for the system based on the security categorization as well as tailoring and supplementing the security control baseline as needed based on an organizational assessment of risk and local conditions.

3. **Implement:** Implement security controls and document how the controls are employed within the system and its environment of operation.

4. **Assess:** Assess the security controls using appropriate assessment procedures. Determine the extent to which the controls are implemented correctly, operating as intended, and producing the desired outcome with respect to meeting the security requirements for the system.

5. **Authorize:** Officially authorize a system to operate or continue to operate based on the results of the security control assessment. This management decision is based on a determination of the risk to organizational operations and assets resulting from the operation of the system and the determination that this risk is acceptable.

6. **Monitor:** Continuously monitor security controls to ensure that they are effective over time as changes occur in the system and in the environment in which the system operates. This includes assessing control effectiveness, documenting changes to the system or its environment of operation, conducting security impact analyses of the associated changes, and reporting the security state of the system to designated organizational officials.

One of the inputs to the Categorize step consists of architecture considerations. These considerations include:

- **Information security architecture:** This is a description of the structure and behavior for an enterprise's security processes, information security systems, personnel, and organizational sub-units, showing their alignment with the enterprise's mission and strategic plans.

- **Mission and business processes:** This refers to what the organization does, what the perceived mission or missions are, and what business processes are involved in fulfilling the mission.

- **Information system boundaries:** These boundaries, also referred to as *authorization boundaries*, establish the scope of protection for organizational information systems (i.e., what the organization agrees to protect under its direct management control or within the scope of its responsibilities) and include the people, processes, and information technologies that are part of the systems supporting the organization's missions and business processes.

The other major type of input to the Categorize step relates to organizational input and includes:

- Laws, directives, and policy guidance
- Strategic goals and objectives
- Priorities and resource availability
- Supply chain considerations

ISO 27005: *Information Security Risk Management*

A useful framework for developing a risk management process is the one defined in ISO 27005 (*Information Security Risk Management*), which describes a systematic approach to managing information security risk.

Figure 11.5 shows the overall risk management process defined in ISO 27005. This process consists of a number of separate activities:

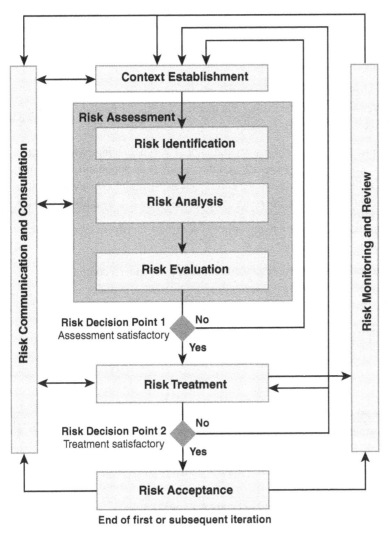

FIGURE 11.5   ISO 27005 Risk Management Process

- **Context establishment:** This management function involves setting the basic criteria necessary for information security risk management, defining the scope and boundaries, and establishing an appropriate organizational structure for information security risk management. Risk criteria are based on organizational objectives, and external and internal context. They can be derived from standards, laws, policies, and other requirements. Table 11.2, based on ISO 27005, lists guidelines for context establishment.

- **Risk assessment:** Figure 11.5 depicts risk assessment as consisting of three activities:

  - **Risk identification:** Involves the identification of risk sources, events, their causes, and their potential consequences. It can involve historical data, theoretical analysis, informed and expert opinions, and stakeholders' needs.

  - **Risk analysis:** Provides the basis for risk evaluation and decisions about risk treatment. Risk analysis includes risk estimation.

  - **Risk evaluation:** Assists in the decision about risk treatment by comparing the results of risk analysis with risk criteria to determine whether the risk and/or its magnitude are acceptable or tolerable.

- **Risk treatment:** This can involve avoiding risk by deciding not to start or continue with the activity that gives rise to the risk; taking or increasing risk in order to pursue an opportunity; removing the risk source; changing the likelihood; changing the consequences; sharing the risk with another party or parties (including contracts and risk financing); and retaining the risk by informed choice.

- **Risk acceptance:** One approach is to ensure that residual risks are explicitly accepted by the managers of the organization.

- **Risk communication and consultation:** An organization needs to conduct a continual and iterative processes to provide, share, or obtain information and to engage in dialogue with stakeholders regarding the management of risk.

- **Risk monitoring and review:** The organization needs to conduct ongoing monitoring and review of all risk information obtained from the risk management activities.

TABLE 11.2   Risk Management Context Establishment

Category	Consideration or Criteria
Purpose of risk management	■ Legal compliance and evidence of due diligence ■ Preparation of a business continuity plan ■ Preparation of an incident response plan ■ Description of the information security requirements for a product, a service, or a mechanism
Risk evaluation criteria	■ The strategic value of the business information process ■ The criticality of the information assets involved ■ Legal and regulatory requirements and contractual obligations ■ The operational and business importance of availability, confidentiality, and integrity ■ Stakeholders' expectations and perceptions, as well as negative consequences for goodwill and reputation
Impact criteria	■ Level of classification of the impacted information asset ■ Breaches of information security (e.g., loss of confidentiality, integrity, and availability) ■ Impaired operations (internal or third parties) ■ Loss of business and financial value ■ Disruption of plans and deadlines ■ Damage of reputation ■ Breaches of legal, regulatory, or contractual requirements

Category	Consideration or Criteria
Risk acceptance criteria	■ May include multiple thresholds, with a desired target level of risk but provision for senior managers to accept risks above this level under defined circumstances ■ May be expressed as the ratio of estimated profit (or other business benefit) to the estimated risk ■ Different criteria may apply to different classes of risk (e.g., risks that could result in noncompliance with regulations or laws may not be accepted, while acceptance of high risks may be allowed if this is specified as a contractual requirement) ■ May include requirements for future additional treatment (e.g., a risk may be accepted if there is approval and commitment to act to reduce it to an acceptable level within a defined time period)

As shown, the risk management process is a cyclic, repetitive process. As mentioned earlier, there are continual changes in business asset valuation, threat capability and frequency, vulnerability magnitude, and control technologies and techniques. In addition, implemented controls may not realize the anticipated benefits. Thus, the assessment and treatment of risk must be an ongoing activity.

Risk Evaluation

After a risk analysis is done, senior security management and executives can determine whether to accept a particular risk and, if not, determine the priority in assigning resources to mitigate the risk. This process, known as *risk evaluation*, involves comparing the results of risk analysis with risk evaluation criteria.

ISO 27005 makes a distinction between risk evaluation criteria and risk acceptance criteria. Evaluation criteria focus on the importance of various business assets and the impact that can be caused to the organization by various security events. The goal is to be able to specify priorities for risk treatment. Risk acceptance criteria relate to how much risk the organization can tolerate and can provide guidance on how much budget can be allocated for risk treatment.

SP 800-100 provides some general guidance for evaluating risk and prioritizing action based on a three-level model:

■ **High:** If an observation or a finding is evaluated as high risk, there is a strong need for corrective measures. An existing system may continue to operate, but a corrective action plan must be put in place as soon as possible.

■ **Moderate:** If an observation is rated as moderate risk, corrective actions are needed, and a plan must be developed to incorporate these actions within a reasonable period of time.

■ **Low:** If an observation is described as low risk, the system's authorizing official must determine whether corrective actions are still required or decide to accept the risk.

Risk Treatment

When the risk assessment process is complete, management should have available an identification of all the threats posed to all assets and an estimate of the magnitude of each risk. In addition, a risk evaluation provides input about the priority and urgency with which each threat should be addressed. The response to the set of identified risks is referred to as *risk treatment*, or *risk response*. ISO 27005 lists four options for treating risk (see Figure 11.6):

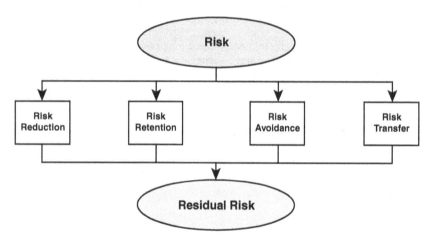

FIGURE 11.6   Risk Treatment

- **Risk reduction or mitigation:** Actions taken to lessen the probability and/or negative consequences associated with a risk. Typically, an organization achieves risk reduction by selecting additional security controls.

- **Risk retention:** Acceptance of the cost from a risk.

- **Risk avoidance:** Decision not to become involved in, or action to withdraw from, a risk situation.

- **Risk transfer or sharing:** Sharing with another party the burden of loss from a risk.

There is a many-to-many relationship between risks and treatments. A single treatment may affect multiple risks, and multiple treatments may be applied to a single risk. Further, the four options are not mutually exclusive. Multiple strategies may be adopted as part of a risk treatment plan.

Any risk treatment plan can reduce but not eliminate risk. What remains is referred to as *residual risk*. On the basis of the plan, the organization should update the risk assessment and determine whether the residual risk is acceptable or whether the plan needs to be updated.

Risk Reduction

Risk reduction is achieved by implementing security controls. Security controls might result in:

- Removing the threat source
- Changing the likelihood that the threat can exploit a vulnerability
- Changing the consequences of a security event

Risk Retention

Risk retention, also called *risk acceptance*, is a conscious management decision to pursue an activity despite the risk presented or to refrain from adding to the existing controls, if any, in place to protect an asset from a given threat. This form of treatment, which is in fact non-treatment, is acceptable if the defined risk magnitude is within the risk tolerance level of the organization. In particular cases, the organization may accept risk that is greater than the risk that is usually acceptable if a compelling business interest presents itself. In any case, the risk needs to be monitored, and response plans that are acceptable to the stakeholders need to be put in place.

Risk Avoidance

If the risk in a certain situation is considered too high and the costs of mitigating the risk down to an acceptable level exceed the benefits, the organization may choose to avoid the circumstance leading to the risk exposure. This could mean, for example, forgoing a business opportunity, relocating to avoid an environmental threat or a legal liability, or banning the use of certain hardware or software. Another type of avoidance that is of particular relevance in the context of privacy is that an organization may decide not to collect a certain category of data.

Risk Transfer

Sharing or transferring risk is accomplished by allocating all or some of the risk mitigation responsibility or risk consequence to some other organization. This can take the form of insurance or subcontracting or partnering with another entity.

11.3 Privacy Risk Assessment

This section deals with the subject of privacy risk assessment. Although Section 11.4 covers the broader area of privacy impact assessment, it is relevant to introduce some definitions at this point. NIST SP 800-53 (*Security and Privacy Controls for Information Systems and Organizations*) defines a *privacy impact assessment (PIA)*, also referred to as a *data protection impact assessment (DPIA)*, as an analysis of how information is handled to:

- Ensure that handling conforms to applicable legal, regulatory, and policy requirements regarding privacy

- Determine the risks and effects of creating, collecting, using, processing, storing, maintaining, disseminating, disclosing, and disposing of information in identifiable form in an electronic information system

- Examine and evaluate protections and alternate processes for handling information to mitigate potential privacy concerns

A privacy impact assessment is both an analysis and a formal document detailing the process and the outcome of the analysis. Thus, a PIA is a process for building and demonstrating compliance with an organization's privacy requirements.

PIA is part of the overall process of privacy risk management. The following definitions are useful for this discussion:

- **Privacy threat:** A potential for violation of privacy, which exists when there is a circumstance, a capability, an action, or an event that could violate privacy and cause harm. Chapter 4, "Information Privacy Threats and Vulnerabilities," includes a detailed discussion of privacy threats.

- **Privacy vulnerability:** A flaw or weakness in a system's design, implementation, or operation and management that could be exploited, intentionally or unintentionally, to violate the system's privacy policy and compromise PII. Chapter 4 includes a detailed discussion of privacy vulnerabilities.

- **Privacy breach:** A situation in which PII is processed in violation of one or more relevant privacy safeguarding requirements.

- **Privacy harm:** An adverse experience for an individual resulting from the processing of his or her PII.

- **Privacy impact:** The magnitude of cost or harm from a problematic data action.

- **Privacy control:** The administrative, technical, and physical safeguards employed within an organization to satisfy privacy requirements.

- **Privacy risk:** A combination of the likelihood that individuals will experience problems resulting from data processing and the impact should they occur.

- **Privacy risk assessment:** A process for identifying, evaluating, and prioritizing specific risks arising from data processing.

- **Privacy risk management:** A cross-organizational set of processes for identifying, assessing, and responding to privacy risks.

Figure 11.7, adapted from the NIST security risk management framework (see Figure 11.4), indicates the scope of PIA.

> **Note**
>
> This is the scope defined in ISO 29134 and the GDPR. Some documents restrict PIA to privacy risk assessment, and some expand PIA to include all of privacy risk management.

Note that the term *privacy impact assessment* is a misnomer on two counts. First, PIA does not simply assess impact but assesses privacy risk. Second, PIA is not limited to assessment but includes defining the controls for risk treatment.

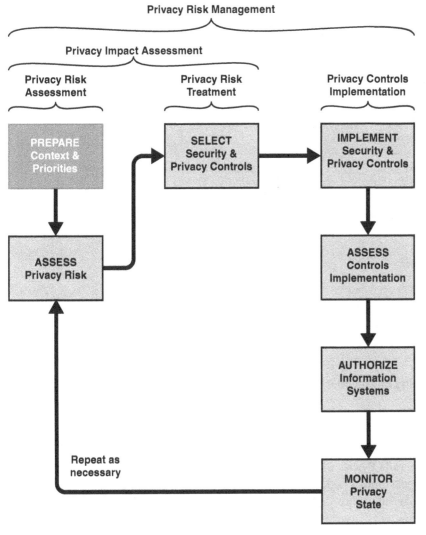

FIGURE 11.7 Privacy Risk Management Framework

The heart of the PIA process is privacy risk assessment, which this section examines. Section 11.4 discusses the overall PIA process.

Figure 11.8 illustrates the process of determining privacy risk, which is essentially the same as for determining information security risk (refer to Figure 11.1). The details presented in Figure 11.8 are based on concepts developed in a document from the French data protection office [CNIL12] and subsequently refined by an EU working group [SGTF18]. Another useful discussion of the PIA process is the document *Data Protection Impact Assessments* from the U.K. data protection office [ICO18].

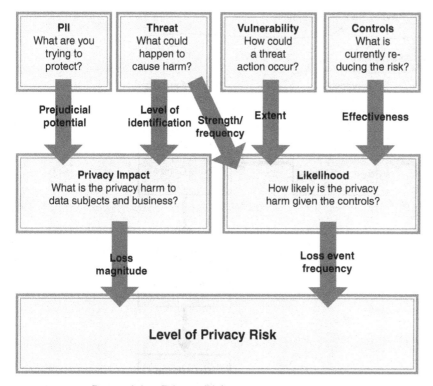

FIGURE 11.8   Determining Privacy Risk

Privacy Impact

The left-hand side of Figure 11.8 deals with determining privacy impacts. The analysis involves determining what PII is collected, processed, stored, and/or transmitted by the organization, as well as what data actions could constitute threats. The results of threats applied to PII are privacy impacts or, equivalently, privacy harms.

Threats

For a PIA, the primary focus is the impact of privacy violations on the individual. Chapter 4 discusses the potential threats to privacy. To summarize, threats to privacy can be classified as follows:

- **Appropriation:** The use of PII in ways that exceed an individual's expectation or authorization. Appropriation occurs when personal information is used in ways that an individual would object to or would have expected additional value for.

- **Distortion:** The use or dissemination of inaccurate or misleadingly incomplete personal information. Distortion can present users in an inaccurate, unflattering, or disparaging manner.

- **Induced disclosure:** Pressure to divulge personal information. Induced disclosure can occur when users feel compelled to provide information disproportionate to the purpose or outcome of the transaction. Induced disclosure can include leveraging access or privilege to an essential (or perceived essential) service.

- **Insecurity:** The improper protection and handling of PII. Identity theft is one potential consequence. Another possible consequence is the dissemination of false information about a person through alteration of that person's record.

- **Surveillance:** Tracking or monitoring of personal information that is disproportionate to the purpose or outcome of the service. The difference between the data action of monitoring and the problematic data action of surveillance can be very narrow. User behavior, transactions, or personal information may be tracked for operational purposes such as protection from cyber threats or to provide better services, but it becomes surveillance when it leads to privacy harms.

- **Unanticipated revelation:** Non-contextual use of data that reveals or exposes an individual or facets of an individual in unexpected ways. Unanticipated revelation can arise from aggregation and analysis of large and/or diverse datasets.

- **Unwarranted restriction:** Blocking tangible access to PII and limiting awareness of the existence of the information within the system or the uses of such information.

Privacy Harms

An organization determines potential privacy harm by developing a profile of PII that is stored and/or flows through the organization's information systems and cross-referencing that to potential threats. Again, Chapter 4 discusses the potential privacy harms. To summarize, the impacts can be classified as follows:

- **Loss of self-determination:** The loss of an individual's personal sovereignty or ability to freely make choices. This includes the following categories:

  - **Loss of autonomy:** Includes needless changes in behavior, including self-imposed restrictions on freedom of expression or assembly.

- **Exclusion:** Lack of knowledge about or access to PII. When individuals do not know what information an entity collects or can make use of, or when they do not have the opportunity to participate in such decision making, it diminishes accountability as to whether the information is appropriate for the entity to possess or the information will be used in a fair or equitable manner.

- **Loss of liberty:** Improper exposure to arrest or detainment. Even in democratic societies, incomplete or inaccurate information can lead to arrest, and improper exposure or use of information can contribute to instances of abuse of governmental power. More life-threatening situations can arise in non-democratic societies.

- **Physical harm:** Actual physical harm to a person. For example, if an individual's PII is used to locate and gain access to cyber-physical systems that interact with the individual, harms may include the generation of inaccurate medical device sensor readings, the auto-mated delivery of incorrect medication dosages via a compromised insulin pump, or the malfunctioning of critical smart car controls, such as braking and acceleration.

- **Discrimination:** The unfair or unequal treatment of individuals. This includes the following categories:

  - **Stigmatization:** A situation in which PII is linked to an actual identity in such a way as to create a stigma that can cause embarrassment, emotional distress, or discrimination. For example, sensitive information such as health data or criminal records, or merely accessing certain services such as food stamps or unemployment benefits, may attach to individuals, creating inferences about them.

  - **Power imbalance:** Acquisition of PII that creates an inappropriate power imbalance or takes unfair advantage of or abuses a power imbalance between the acquirer and the indi-vidual. For example, collection of attributes or analysis of behavior or transactions about individuals can lead to various forms of discrimination or disparate impact, including differential pricing or redlining.

- **Loss of trust:** The breach of implicit or explicit expectations or agreements about the han-dling of personal information. For example, the disclosure of personal or other sensitive data to an entity is accompanied by a number of expectations for how that data is used, secured, transmitted, shared, and so on. Breaches can leave individuals reluctant to engage in further transactions.

- **Economic loss:** Direct financial losses to data subjects as a result of identity theft as well as the failure to receive fair value in a transaction involving personal information.

As with information security risk assessment, for privacy risk assessment, an organization must assess the relative magnitude of each of the potential harms in terms of the amount of harm to the individual.

Assessing privacy impacts is challenging because individuals, not organizations, directly experi-ence privacy harms. Assigning a magnitude to a privacy impact is challenging because there may be significant variability in the harm perceived by individuals, especially for embarrassment or other psychologically based harms.

With respect to organizational losses, NISTIR 8062 (*An Introduction to Privacy Engineering and Risk Management in Federal Systems*) suggests that organizations may be able to use other costs as proxies to help account for individual impact, including:

- Legal compliance costs arising from the problems created for individuals

- Mission failure costs, such as reluctance to use the system or service

- Reputational costs leading to loss of trust

- Internal culture costs, which impact morale or mission productivity as employees assess their general mission to serve the public good against the problems individuals may experience

Assessment of Privacy Impact

A typical approach to estimating privacy impact is to look at the two factors that contribute to the impact (refer to Figure 11.8):

- **Prejudicial potential:** An estimation of how much damage would be caused by all the potential consequences of a threat

- **Level of identification:** An estimation of how easy it is to identify data subjects with the available data processed by the available software

A typical approach to characterizing potential impacts is to use five levels, such as very low, low, moderate, high, and very high. An analyst could take into consideration the type and amount of PII that is to be protected and the relevant threats that could violate the privacy of the PII principals (data subjects). Other factors include sensitivity of the PII breached, numbers of PII principals affected, and level of organizational impact. Table 11.3 provides examples of definitions, broken down into privacy harms to PII principals and costs to the organization.

TABLE 11.3 Definition of Privacy Impact Levels

Impact	Impact on PII Principals	Impact on the Organization
Very low	Virtually no noticeable impact	Virtually no noticeable impact
Low	Negligible economic loss; or small, temporary reduction of reputation; or no impact on other personal factors	No violation of law or regulation; or negligible economic loss; or small, temporary reduction of reputation
Moderate	Economic loss that can be restored; or small reduction of reputation or at most minor impact on other personal factors	Minor violation of law or regulation resulting in warning; or economic loss that can be restored; or some reduction of reputation

Impact	Impact on PII Principals	Impact on the Organization
High	Large economic loss that cannot be restored; or serious loss of reputation or other psychological damage by revealing sensitive information; or serious impact on other personal factors	Violation of law or regulation resulting in a fine or minor penalty; or large economic loss that cannot be restored; or serious and long-lasting loss of reputation
Very high	Considerable economic loss that cannot be restored; or serious loss of reputation or other psychological damage with long-lasting or permanent consequences; or serious impact on other personal factors	Serious violation of law or regulation resulting in a substantial fine or other penalty; or considerable economic loss that cannot be restored; or devastating and long-lasting loss of reputation

Table 11.4 provides a breakdown of five levels of identification, with an example of each one. For a given threat category, a PIA analyst can estimate how easy is it to identify an individual should the threat gain access to the PII residing on an organization asset.

TABLE 11.4   Levels of Identification

Level	Definition	Example (large population database)
Very low (1)	Identifying an individual using his or her personal data appears to be virtually impossible.	Searching using only an individual's first name
Low (2)	Identifying an individual using his or her personal data appears to be difficult but is possible in certain cases.	Searching using an individual's full name
Moderate (3)	Identifying an individual using his or her personal data appears to be of only moderate difficulty.	Searching using an individual's full name and year of birth
High (4)	Identifying an individual using his or her personal data appears to be relatively easy.	Searching using an individual's full name and date of birth
Very high (5)	Identifying an individual using his or her personal data appears to be extremely easy.	Searching using an individual's full name, date of birth, and mailing address

The following suggested methodology for combining prejudicial potential and level of identification is based on the document *Data Protection Impact Assessment Template for Smart Grid and Smart Metering Systems* from the E.U. Smart Grid Task Force [SGTF18]. The methodology includes the following steps:

1. Identify a list of privacy threat categories relevant to the organization's environment.

2. Identify the primary assets associated with each threat category. A primary asset is a set of one or more pieces of PII allocated on a specific IT system that requires protection.

3. For each primary asset, identify the relevant privacy harms that may occur.

4. For each potential harm resulting from a particular threat, associate the value of the level (1 = very low; up to 5 = very high) that best matches the prejudicial effect.

5. For each primary asset, determine the prejudicial effect as the maximum value of prejudicial effect for a potential harm.

6. For each primary asset of each threat category, take the sum of the level of identification and prejudicial effect and normalize to a scale of 1 to 5, using Table 11.5. The result is the privacy impact, or severity, for the primary asset.

7. The severity of a given threat category is the maximum value of severity for all associated primary assets.

TABLE 11.5 Privacy Impact Normalization Scale

Level of Identification + Prejudicial Effects	Impact or Severity
< 4	Very low (1)
4–5	Low (2)
6	Moderate (3)
7	High (4)
> 7	Very high (5)

Likelihood

NISTIR 8062 defines *likelihood* in privacy risk assessment as the estimated probability that a threat action will occur and be problematic for a representative or typical individual whose PII is processed by the system. This is a complex issue that involves assessing the following four factors (refer to Figure 11.8):

- The probability that a threat action will be attempted, either intentionally or unintentionally.
- The capability of the threat agent to perform the threat event.
- The vulnerabilities in the system that would enable the attempted threat action to occur.
- The reduction in probability due to the effectiveness of existing or planned security and privacy controls.

As with impact assessment, the risk analyst can use a five-level scale for each of these factors. The first two factors relate to the threat. Part a and b of Table 11.6 show typical definitions for threat capability and threat event frequency.

TABLE 11.6   Privacy Likelihood Factors

(a) Capability of Threat Source

Level	Capability
Very low	Source has no special capabilities to carry out a threat.
Low	Source has limited capabilities to carry out a threat.
Moderate	Source has malicious intent and moderate capability to carry out a threat.
High	Source has malicious intent and unlimited administrative privileges to carry out a threat.
Very high	Source has malicious intent and considerable expertise to carry out a threat.

(b) Threat Event Frequency

Level	Capability
Very low	< 0.1 times per year (less than once every 10 years)
Low	Between 0.1 and 1 times per year
Moderate	Between 1 and 10 times per year
High	Between 10 and 100 times per year
Very high	> 100 times per year

(c) Vulnerability

Level	Ease of privacy breach
Very low	Very difficult, requiring sustained effort and specialized expertise
Low	Cannot occur accidentally; or detailed knowledge of the system is needed; or requires help of authorized personnel
Moderate	Normal knowledge of the system is needed; or can be performed deliberately
High	Minor knowledge of the system is needed; or can be a result of wrong or careless usage
Very high	No technical knowledge of the system is needed; or can be a result of wrong or careless usage

(d) Control Effectiveness

Level	Capability
Very low	Only protects against the bottom 2% of an average threat population
Low	Only protects against the bottom 16% of an average threat population
Moderate	Protects against the average threat agent
High	Protects against all but the top 16% of an average threat population
Very high	Protects against all but the top 2% of an average threat population

With respect to vulnerabilities, Chapter 4 discusses potential privacy vulnerabilities. To summarize, the vulnerabilities can be:

- **Technical vulnerabilities:** Flaws in the design, implementation, and/or configuration of software and/or hardware components, including application software, system software, communications software, computing equipment, communications equipment, and embedded devices.

- **Human resource vulnerabilities:** Key person dependencies, gaps in awareness and training, gaps in discipline, and improper termination of access.

- **Physical and environmental vulnerabilities:** Insufficient physical access controls, poor siting of equipment, inadequate temperature/humidity controls, and inadequately conditioned electrical power.

- **Operational vulnerabilities:** Lack of change management; inadequate separation of duties; lack of control over software installation; lack of control over media handling and storage; lack of control over system communications; inadequate access control or weaknesses in access control procedures; inadequate recording and/or review of system activity records; inadequate control over encryption keys; inadequate reporting, handling, and/or resolution of security incidents; and inadequate monitoring and evaluation of the effectiveness of security controls.

- **Business continuity and compliance vulnerabilities:** Misplaced, missing, or inadequate processes for appropriate management of business risks; inadequate business continuity/contingency planning; and inadequate monitoring and evaluation for compliance with governing policies and regulations.

- **Policy and procedure vulnerabilities:** Privacy policies and procedures that are inadequate to fully protect PII, including conformance with fair information practice principles (FIPPs).

- **Data set vulnerabilities:** Weakness in de-identification measures; inadequate masking of PII in statistical data sets, and inadequate protection against discovery of PII by analysis of multiple datasets.

Part c of Table 11.6 provides sample definitions for a five-level estimation of the extent of vulnerability, expressed in terms of the ease of privacy breach. However, an analyst needs to modify these estimates by considering any controls already designed or planned for the system that provide protection to the primary assets (PII data). The result of this analysis is a residual ease of privacy breach. Then the analyst could use a 5×5 matrix similar to the 3×3 matrix in part a of Figure 11.3. Finally, the analyst could use a matrix similar to part b of Figure 11.3 to estimate likelihood as a function of threat event frequency and the extent of vulnerability. As an alternative, the analyst could use the numerical equivalent of each level (very low = 1 and so on), take the sum of two factors, and then normalize using the same normalization as shown in Table 11.5. Thus, vulnerability is calculated by taking the normalized sum of threat capability and resistance strength. Then likelihood is calculated by taking the normalized sum of vulnerability and threat event frequency.

As with impact assessment, with privacy assessment, an analyst needs to perform the likelihood analysis for each primary asset for each threat category.

Assessing Privacy Risk

Privacy risk assessment is based on an estimate of impact and of likelihood. An organization should carry out this assessment for each primary asset (PII stored on a system) and each threat category. The techniques used are essentially the same as those for information security risk assessment, described in Section 11.1.

Figure 11.9 gives two examples of a qualitative risk assessment matrix (compare with Figure 11.3). The matrix defines a risk level for each impact level and likelihood level. The structure of the matrix on the left in the figure is commonly used. For example, ISO 29134 (*Guidelines for Privacy Impact Assessment*) uses a 4×4 matrix with this structure. The structure on the right would be suitable for a more conservative or risk-averse organization.

For each primary asset and threat category, the organization should set a priority, based on where the risk is located in the matrix and on the risk criteria used by the organization. The following are typical guidelines for the five risk levels:

- **Very high:** These risks must be absolutely avoided or significantly reduced by implementing controls that reduce both their impact and their likelihood. Recommend practice suggests that the organization implement independent controls of prevention (actions taken prior to a damaging event), protection (actions taken during a damaging event), and recovery (actions taken after a damaging event) [SGTF18].

- **High:** These risks should be avoided or reduced by implementing controls that reduce the impact and/or likelihood, as appropriate. For example, the matrix on the left in Figure 11.9 has a high-risk entry for a very high impact and low likelihood; in this case, the emphasis is on reducing impact. The emphasis for these risks should be on prevention if the impact is relatively high and the likelihood is relatively low and on recovery if the impact is relatively low and the likelihood is relatively high.

- **Moderate:** The approach for moderate risk is essentially the same as for high risk. The difference is that moderate risks are of lesser priority, and the organization may choose to devote fewer resources to addressing them.

- **Low:** The organization may be willing to accept these risks without further control implementation, especially if the treatment of other security or privacy risks also reduce this risk.

- **Very low:** The organization may be willing to accept these risks because further attempts at reduction would not be cost-effective.

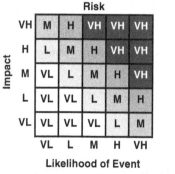
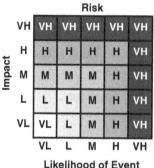

FIGURE 11.9   Two Examples of Privacy Risk Matrices

11.4 Privacy Impact Assessment

As shown in Figure 11.7, earlier in the chapter, a PIA involves both privacy risk assessment and a plan for privacy risk treatment. ISO 29134 provides useful guidance in performing a PIA. Figure 11.10 summarizes the PIA process defined in ISO 29134. The two boxes on the lower left of the figure are not in fact part of the PIA process but provide context for how PIA fits into the overall privacy risk management scheme. This section examines the steps defined in the other boxes.

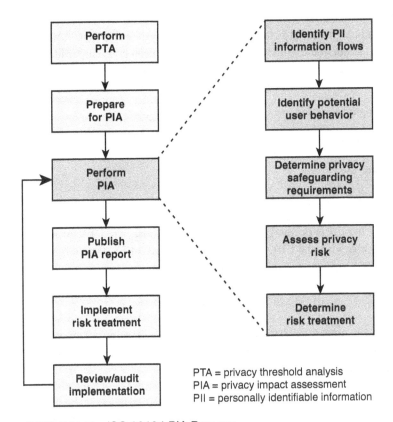

PTA = privacy threshold analysis
PIA = privacy impact assessment
PII = personally identifiable information

FIGURE 11.10 ISO 29134 PIA Process

Privacy Threshold Analysis

A privacy threshold analysis (PTA) is a brief assessment that requires system owners to answer basic questions on the nature of their systems and whether the systems contain PII, to identify systems that require PIA. This approach enables agencies to ensure that systems undergo the PIA process, if required, at the earliest stages of development.

SP 800-53 contains a useful description of conditions that would require a PIA:

> Conduct privacy impact assessments for systems, programs, or other activities that pose a privacy risk before:
>
> **a.** Developing or procuring information technology that collects, maintains, or disseminates information that is in an identifiable form; and
>
> **b.** Initiating a new collection of information that:
>
> **1.** Will be collected, maintained, or disseminated using information technology; and
>
> **2.** Includes information in an identifiable form permitting the physical or online contacting of a specific individual, if identical questions have been posed to, or identical reporting requirements imposed on, ten or more persons, other than agencies, instrumentalities, or employees of the organization.

A typical PTA includes the following information:

- Description of the system

- What PII, if any, is collected or used

- From whom the PII is collected

If no PII is collected or used, of if the PII is deemed to present no privacy risk, the PTA document would indicate no need for a PIA. Otherwise, the PTA document recommends a PIA. Typically, a privacy leader reviews the PTA to make a final decision about the need for a PIA.

Preparing for a PIA

Preparing for a PIA should be part of strategic security and privacy planning. The important components of PIA preparation are as follows:

- **Identify the PIA team and provide it with direction.** The privacy leader should have ultimate responsibility for the PIA. The privacy leader, together with other privacy personnel, should determine the scope of the PIA and the needed expertise. Depending on the size of the organization and the amount of PII involved, the team may need to include information security experts, a privacy counsel, operations managers, ethicists, business mission representatives, and others. The privacy leader or privacy team should define the risk criteria and ensure that senior management approve those criteria.

- **Prepare a PIA plan.** The person in charge of the PIA (the PIA assessor) should create a plan that specifies human resources, the business case, and a budget for conducting the PIA.

- **Describe the system or project that is the subject of this PIA.** This description should include an overview of the system or project, summarizing the system design, personnel involved, schedule, and budget. The description should focus on what PII is processed. The PII discussion should indicate what PII is collected/processed, the objectives, which PII principals are affected, what systems and processes are involved in the handling of PII, and what privacy policies govern the handling of the PII.

- **Identify stakeholders.** The assessor should indicate who is or might be interested in or affected by the project, technology, or service.

Identify PII Information Flows

Essential to understanding the privacy risks involved in the use of PII in a given system or project is a complete description of how PII flows into, through, and out of the system. A workflow diagram is a useful tool for ensuring that all aspects of PII handling are documented. Figure 11.11, from ISO 29134, is a typical example workflow of PII processing. An assessor should provide a commentary on and indicate the potential privacy impacts for each point in the workflow.

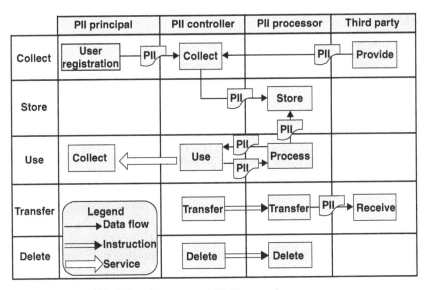

FIGURE 11.11 Workflow Diagram of PII Processing

Identify Potential User Behavior

An assessor needs to identify user behavior that could unintentionally have a privacy impact. Examples include incorrectly modifying operating system security settings on IT devices and susceptibility to social engineering attacks. This documentation can serve as a guide in user training and awareness programs.

Determine Relevant Privacy Safeguarding Requirements

An assessor needs to determine which privacy safeguarding requirements are relevant to this system or process. These requirements can be grouped in the following areas:

- **Legal and regulatory:** Determine what laws and regulations apply to this case.

- **Contractual:** Determine what privacy safeguards are required by applicable contracts.

- **Business:** Determine what privacy safeguards that are a normal part of business operations apply. These include industry guidelines, best practices documents, and standards typically used in information security and privacy system design by the organization, and organizational privacy policies that apply to this case.

- **Individual:** Determine which FIPPs are relevant to this case.

These safeguarding requirements serve as a guide to what privacy controls need to be implemented.

Assess Privacy Risk

Privacy risk assessment has three steps:

1. **Risk identification:** The assessor identifies the potential threats and the system vulnerabilities that are applicable to this case.

2. **Risk analysis:** The assessor calculates the level of risk for each potential impact, as described in Section 11.4.

3. **Risk evaluation:** The assessor determines the relative prioritization of privacy risk, based on the severity of privacy impact on PII principals as well as the overall impact to the organization.

Determine Risk Treatment

The final step of the PIA is to determine what risk treatments will be applied to the identified risks. This involves three tasks:

- Choose treatment options

- Determine controls

- Create risk treatment plans

Choose Treatment Options

Section 11.2 describes the risk treatment options risk reduction, risk retention, risk avoidance, and risk transfer. An assessor must recommend the most appropriate treatment option for each identified privacy risk. The treatment option decision for each risk involves balancing a number of factors, notably the cost of each option to the organization and the organization's obligation to protect the privacy of the PII.

Determine Controls

For each risk for which an assessor chooses risk reduction, the responsible privacy personnel need to select the appropriate combination of security and privacy controls to mitigate or eliminate the risk. The privacy leader may perform this task, or it may be assigned to one or more other privacy personnel, including the privacy assessor. The preference should be to use industry-standard controls, such as those defined in ISO 29151 (*Code of Practice for Personally Identifiable Information Protection*) and NIST SP 800-53.

Create Risk Treatment Plans

An assessor should develop a risk treatment plan for each identified risk that includes the following information:

- Rationale for the chosen treatment option
- Specific controls to be implemented
- Residual risk after treatment
- Result of a cost/benefit analysis
- Person responsible for implementation
- Schedule and resources
- How the implementation will be monitored and evaluated

The PIA Report

The PIA report documents the PIA process. However, the PIA process is an ongoing activity, as indicated by the return loop in Figure 11.10. New information may lead to a return to the PIA process, which in turn results in an updated PIA report. Objectives for the PIA report include:

- Demonstrate that the PIA process was performed in accordance with the organization's policy.
- Provide a basis for post-implementation review.
- Provide input to an information privacy audit.
- Provide a documented basis if iterations of the PIA process for this project are necessary.

Based on a review of numerous examples of PIA reports from Australia, Canada, New Zealand, the United Kingdom, and the United States, the PIAFProject [PIAF11] recommends that the PIA report should:

- Clarify whether the PIA was initiated early enough so that there was still time to influence the outcome

- Indicate who conducted the PIA

- Include a description of the project to be assessed, its purpose, and any relevant contextual information

- Map the information flows (i.e., how information is collected, used, stored, secured, and distributed and to whom and how long the data is retained)

- Check the project's compliance against relevant legislation

- Identify the risks to or impacts on privacy

- Identify solutions or options for avoiding or mitigating the risks

- Make recommendations

- Be published on the organization's website and be easily found there or, if the PIA report is not published (even in a redacted form), there should be an explanation as to why it has not been published

- Identify what consultation and with which stakeholders was undertaken

The PIAFProject report [PIAF11] contains a number of examples of PIA reports that can be useful guides for an organization designing its own report format.

Implement Risk Treatment

Once the PIA report has been approved by senior management, the individual or team responsible for privacy risk treatment can implement the controls that have been approved. Prior to implementation, the organization should provide the appropriate training for developers and users to ensure that privacy implications are fully considered.

Review/Audit Implementation

The organization should designate an individual or a group to assess the operational effectiveness of the privacy risk treatment implementation. Chapter 13, "Event Monitoring, Auditing, and Incident Response," addresses this topic. When it is determined that there are inadequacies or new requirements, the organization should mandate a new or updated PIA.

Examples

The reader may find it useful to examine real-world examples of PIAs. Two worthwhile documents are *Data Protection Impact Assessment Template for Smart Grid and Smart Metering Systems* from the E.U. Smart Grid Task Force [SGTF18], which deals with a smart grid application, and *Privacy Impact Assessment for the Integrated Data Infrastructure* from Statistics New Zealand [SNZ12], which covers the New Zealand Integrated Data Infrastructure. In addition, the U.S. Department of Homeland Security maintains an inventory of publicly available PIAs produced by various government agencies (https://www.dhs.gov/privacy-impact-assessments).

11.5 Key Terms and Review Questions

Key Terms

asset	privacy threshold analysis
data protection impact assessment	privacy vulnerability
impact	risk
level of risk	risk acceptance
likelihood	risk analysis
privacy breach	risk assessment
privacy control	risk avoidance
privacy harm	risk evaluation
privacy impact	risk identification
privacy impact assessment	risk management
privacy risk	risk reduction
privacy risk assessment	risk retention
privacy risk avoidance	risk transfer
privacy risk evaluation	risk treatment
privacy risk management	security control
privacy risk reduction	qualitative risk assessment
privacy risk retention	quantitative risk assessment
privacy risk transfer	threat
privacy risk treatment	vulnerability
privacy threat	

Review Questions

1. What are the four factors that determine risk, and how are they related to each other?

2. Differentiate between qualitative and quantitative risk assessment.

3. Explain the term *residual risk*.

4. Explain the steps in the NIST risk management framework.

5. Describe the various risk treatment options.

6. What is the difference between privacy risk assessment and privacy impact assessment?

7. How do privacy impacts differ from information security impacts?

8. What is privacy threshold analysis?

9. Describe recommended steps for preparing for a PIA.

10. What should go into a PIA report?

11.6   References

ASHO17: Ashok, I. "Hackers Spied and Stole from Millions by Exploiting Word Flaw as Microsoft Probed Bug for Months." *International Business Times*, April 27, 2017.

CNIL12: Commission Nationale de l'Informatique et des Libertés. *Methodology for Privacy Risk Management.* 2012 https://www.cnil.fr/sites/default/files/typo/document/ CNIL-ManagingPrivacyRisks-Methodology.pdf

ICO18: U.K. Information Commissioner's Office. *Data Protection Impact Assessments.* 2018. https://ico.org.uk/for-organisations/guide-to-data-protection/guide-to-the-general-data-protection-regulation-gdpr/data-protection-impact-assessments-dpias/

KEIZ17: Keizer, G. "Experts Contend Microsoft Canceled Feb. Updates to Patch NSA Exploits." *ComputerWorld*, April 18, 2017.

PIAF11: PIAFProject. *A Privacy Impact Assessment Framework for Data Protection and Privacy Rights.* Prepared for the European Commission Directorate General Justice. 21 September 2011. https://www.piafproject.eu/

SGTF18: E.U. Smart Grid Task Force. *Data Protection Impact Assessment Template for Smart Grid and Smart Metering Systems.* September 2018. https://ec.europa.eu/energy/en/topics/markets-and-consumers/smart-grids-and-meters/smart-grids-task-force/data-protection-impact-assessment-smart-grid-and-smart-metering-environment

SNZ12: Statistics New Zealand. *Privacy Impact Assessment for the Integrated Data Infrastructure.* 2012. http://archive.stats.govt.nz/browse_for_stats/snapshots-of-nz/integrated-data-infrastructure/keep-data-safe/privacy-impact-assessments/privacy-impact-assessment-for-the-idi.aspx

Chapter 12

Privacy Awareness, Training, and Education

Learning Objectives

After studying this chapter, you should be able to:

- Explain the four phases in the cybersecurity learning continuum
- Discuss the goals and desired content of a privacy awareness program
- Understand the elements of role-based training
- Discuss the role and typical content of an acceptable use policy

A critical element of an information privacy program is the privacy awareness, training, and education program. It is the means for disseminating privacy information to all employees, including IT staff, IT security staff, and management, as well as IT users and other employees. A workforce that has a high level of privacy awareness and appropriate privacy training for each individual's role is as important as, if not more important than, any other privacy countermeasure or control.

Two key NIST publications, SP 800-16 (*A Role-Based Model for Federal Information Technology/ Cybersecurity Training*) and SP 800-50 (*Building an Information Technology Security Awareness and Training Program*), are valuable resources in this area, and this chapter draws on both. NIST SP 800-50 works at a higher strategic level and discusses how to build and maintain an information security awareness and training program; NIST SP 800-16 addresses a more tactical level and discusses the awareness–training--education continuum, role-based training, and course content considerations. Both publications define and describe a cybersecurity learning continuum that depicts a progression of learning across the spectrum of roles across the organization, consisting of four levels (see Figure 12.1):

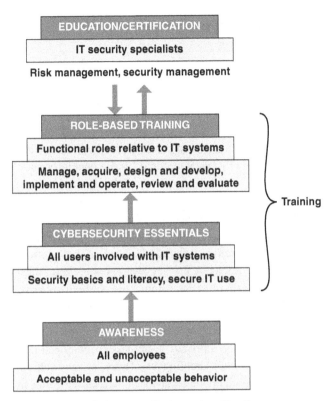

FIGURE 12.1   Cybersecurity Learning Continuum

- **Awareness:** A set of activities that explains and promotes security, establishes accountability, and informs the workforce of security news. Participation in security awareness programs is required for all employees.

- **Cybersecurity essentials:** Intended to develop secure practices in the use of IT resources. This level is needed for employees, including contractor employees, who are involved in any way with IT systems. It provides the foundation for subsequent specialized or role-based training by providing a universal baseline of key security terms and concepts.

- **Role-based training:** Intended to provide the knowledge and skill specific to an individual's roles and responsibilities relative to information systems. Training supports competency development and helps personnel understand and learn how to perform their security roles.

- **Education/certification:** Integrates all of the security skills and competencies of the various functional specialties into a common body of knowledge and adds a multidisciplinary study of concepts, issues, and principles (technological and social).

Although the concepts depicted in Figure 12.1 relate to security, they are equally applicable to privacy. Sections 12.1 and 12.2 cover privacy awareness, training, and education. Section 12.3 examines the related topic of acceptable use policies.

12.1   Information Privacy Awareness

Two key concepts are discussed in this section:

- **Privacy awareness:** The extent to which staff understand the importance of information privacy, the level of privacy required for personal information stored and processed by the organization, and their individual privacy responsibilities

- **Privacy culture:** The extent to which staff demonstrate expected privacy behavior in line with their individual privacy responsibilities and the level of privacy required for personal information stored and processed by the organization

Because all employees have some responsibilities related to the protection of personally identifiable information (PII), all employees must have suitable awareness training. This training seeks to focus an individual's attention on an issue or a set of issues. Awareness training is a program that continually pushes the privacy message to users in a variety of formats. A privacy awareness program must reach all employees, not just those with access to IT resources. Such topics as physical security, protocols for admitting visitors, social media rules, and social engineering threats are of concern with all employees.

The overall objective of the organization should be to develop a privacy awareness program that permeates to all levels of the organization and that is successful in promoting an effective privacy culture. To that end, the awareness program must be ongoing, focused on the behavior of various categories of people, monitored, and evaluated.

Specific goals for a privacy awareness program should include:

- Provide a focal point and a driving force for a range of awareness, training, and educational activities related to information privacy, some of which might already be in place but perhaps need to be better coordinated and more effective.

- Communicate important recommended guidelines or practices required to protect PII.

- Provide general and specific information about information privacy risks and controls to people who need to know.

- Make individuals aware of their responsibilities in relation to information privacy.

- Motivate individuals to adopt recommended guidelines or practices.

- Ensure that privacy awareness programs are driven by risk considerations. For example, risk levels can be assigned to different groups of individuals, based on their job function, level of access to assets, access privileges, and so on.

- Provide employees with an understanding of the different types of inappropriate behavior—namely malicious, negligent, and accidental—and how to avoid negligent or accidental unwanted behavior and recognize malicious behavior in others. Employees should understand the following concepts:

- **Malicious behavior:** Involves a combination of motive to cause harm and a conscious decision to act inappropriately (e.g., copying business files before taking employment with a competitor, leaking sensitive information, misusing information for personal gain)

- **Negligent behavior:** Does not involve a motive to cause harm but does involve a conscious decision to act inappropriately (e.g., using unauthorized services or devices to save time, increase productivity, or enable remote working)

- **Accidental behavior:** Does not involve a motive to harm or a conscious decision to act inappropriately (e.g., emailing sensitive information to unauthorized recipients, opening malicious email attachments, publishing personal information on publicly available servers)

- Create a stronger culture of privacy, with a broad understanding of and commitment to information privacy.

- Help enhance the consistency and effectiveness of existing information privacy controls and potentially stimulate the adoption of cost-effective controls.

- Help minimize the number and extent of information privacy breaches, thus reducing costs directly (e.g., data damaged by viruses) and indirectly (e.g. reduced need to investigate and resolve breaches).

Awareness Topics

ISO 29151 (*Code of Practice for Personally Identifiable Information Protection*) indicates three broad topics to be covered by an awareness program, in terms of the consequences of a privacy breach:

- For the organization (e.g., legal consequences, loss of business, brand or reputational damage)

- For PII principals (e.g., physical, material, and emotional consequences)

- For all staff members (e.g., disciplinary consequences)

A good example of an employee awareness component is a brief audiovisual presentation used by the U.S. Department of Homeland Security (https://www.dhs.gov/xlibrary/privacy_training/index.htm). The presentation covers the following topics:

- The fair information practice principles (FIPPs)

- Definition of PII

- Elements within the organization that collect/process PII

- Potential consequences of not protecting PII—for the organization, for the victim, and for the person causing the privacy incident

- When to report a privacy incident:

    - With lost, allowed, or witnessed unauthorized access to PII

    - With unintentional release of PII

    - With misuse of sensitive PII

    - When files or systems become compromised

    - When any of the above is suspected to have occurred

Awareness Program Communication Materials

The heart of an awareness training program consists of the communication materials and methods used to convey privacy awareness. There are two options for the awareness program design: in-house materials and externally obtained materials. A well-designed program will likely have materials from both sources.

NIST SP-100 (*Information Security Handbook: A Guide for Managers*) lists the following as necessary elements of an awareness program:

- **Tools:** Awareness tools promote information privacy and inform users of threats and vulnerabilities that impact their organization and personal work environment by explaining the *what* rather than the *how* of information privacy and by communicating what is and what is not allowed. Awareness training not only communicates information privacy policies and procedures that need to be followed but also provides the foundation for any sanctions and disciplinary actions imposed for noncompliance. Awareness training is used to explain the rules of behavior for using an organization's information systems and information and establishes a level of expectation related to the acceptable use of the information and information systems. Types of tools include:

    - Events, such as a privacy awareness day

    - Promotional materials

    - Briefings (program or system specific or issue specific)

    - Rules of behavior

- **Communication:** A large part of an awareness effort is communication with users, managers, executives, system owners, and others. A communications plan is needed to identify stakeholders, types of information to be disseminated, channels for disseminating information, and the frequency of information exchanges. The plan also needs to identify whether the communications are one way or two way. Activities that support communication include:

    - Assessment (as is/to be models)

    - Strategic plan

    - Program implementation

- **Outreach:** Outreach is critical for leveraging best practices within an organization. A web portal that provides a one-stop shop for privacy information can be an effective outreach tool. Policies, frequently asked questions (FAQs), privacy e-newsletters, links to resources, and other useful information should be easily accessible to all employees on a portal. This tool promotes a consistent and standard message.

The Privacy in a Suitcase resource (https://iapp.org/resources/article/privacy-in-a-suitcase/), provided by the International Association of Privacy Professionals (IAPP), is an excellent source of materials. It is composed of standalone modules that provide an overview of basic topics on privacy and security. Privacy in a Suitcase is meant to be used to educate nonprofit groups and small businesses about basic privacy principles and steps that they can take to protect their customers'/members' personal information.

Awareness Program Evaluation

Just as in other areas of information privacy, an organization needs an evaluation component to ensure that the awareness program is meeting objectives. ENISA has developed a set of metrics that are useful for awareness program evaluation [ENIS07], shown in Table 12.1.

TABLE 12.1 Metrics for Measuring the Success of Awareness Programs

Metric	Considerations
Number of security incidents due to human behavior	<ul><li>Can quickly show trends and deviations in behavior.</li><li>Can help understand root causes and estimate costs to the business.</li><li>May not be enough incidents to draw meaningful results.</li><li>May be other factors that affect the incidents.</li></ul>
Audit findings	<ul><li>Generally conducted by independent and knowledgeable people who can provide third-party assurance on behaviors.</li><li>Significant areas of awareness may not be reviewed.</li></ul>
Results of staff surveys	<ul><li>If used before and after specific training, can be used to gauge the effectiveness of campaigns.</li><li>If sufficiently large, can provide statistical conclusions on staff behaviors.</li><li>Need to be targeted at verifying key messages.</li><li>Have to be carefully designed since staff may respond with "expected" answers rather than true behaviors.</li></ul>
Tests of whether staff follow correct procedures	<ul><li>Very good way of actually measuring behaviors and highlighting changes after training.</li><li>Have to be carefully planned and carried out since could be breaches of employment and data protection laws.</li><li>Need a big enough sample if results are to be meaningful.</li></ul>
Number of staff completing training	<ul><li>Need to decide what combination of classroom and computer-based training to use.</li><li>Have to consider what training to make mandatory.</li><li>May need to be tailored for different areas or regions.</li><li>May need regular and potentially costly updates.</li></ul>

12.2 Privacy Training and Education

Privacy training is targeted at IT and other personnel who have access and/or are responsible for collecting, storing, processing, and disposing of PII. The goal of training is to provide these individuals with the knowledge and skills that enable them to protect PII. The organization's privacy training policy should cover the following areas:

- Roles and responsibilities for training

- Training prerequisites for receiving access to PII

- Frequency of training and refresher training requirements

SP 800-122 (*Guide to Protecting the Confidentiality of Personally Identifiable Information*) lists the following topics that an organization should communicate to all employees with PII access or responsibilities:

- The definition of PII

- Applicable privacy laws, regulations, and policies

- Restrictions on data collection, storage, and use of PII

- Roles and responsibilities for using and protecting PII

- Appropriate disposal of PII

- Sanctions for misuse of PII

- Recognition of a security or privacy incident involving PII

- Retention schedules for PII

- Roles and responsibilities in responding to PII-related incidents and reporting

As part of the training program, an organization should have all relevant personnel take a cybersecurity essential training course. Beyond that, the organization's training program should be tailored to the specific roles of individuals.

Cybersecurity Essentials

A cybersecurity essentials program serves two purposes. Its principal function is to target users of IT systems and applications, including company-supplied mobile devices and BYOD, and to develop sound security practices for these employees. Secondarily, it provides the foundation for subsequent specialized or role-based training by providing a universal baseline of key security terms and concepts.

SP 800-16 defines a cybersecurity essentials program as a program that improves an individual's familiarity with and ability to apply a core knowledge set that is needed to protect electronic information and systems. All individuals who use computer technology or its output products, regardless of their specific job responsibilities, must know these essentials and be able to apply them. The training at this level should be tailored to a specific organization's IT environment, security policies, and risks.

Key topics that should be covered include:

- Technical underpinnings of cybersecurity and its taxonomy, terminology, and challenges

- Common information and computer system security vulnerabilities

- Common cyber-attack mechanisms, their consequences, and motivation for their use

- Different types of cryptographic algorithms

- Intrusion, types of intruders, techniques, and motivation

- Firewalls and other means of intrusion prevention

- Vulnerabilities unique to virtual computing environments

- Social engineering and its implications to cybersecurity

- Fundamental security design principles and their role in limiting points of vulnerability

Role-Based Training

Role-based training is intended for all users, privileged and non-privileged, who have some role with respect to IT systems and applications. In this context, the term *role* refers to the responsibilities and functions that a person is performing within the organization. Role-based privacy training allows employees in different roles, such as human resources and IT, to receive education tailored to their specialties.

The most significant difference between training and awareness is that training seeks to teach skills that allow a person to perform a specific function, while awareness seeks to focus an individual's attention on an issue or a set of issues.

The nature of role-based training depends on the role of the individual in the organization. SP 800-16 develops training recommendations based on a differentiation of four major roles:

- **Manage:** The individual's job functions encompass overseeing a program or technical aspect of a security program; overseeing the life cycle of a computer system, network, or application; or have responsibilities for the training of staff.

- **Design:** The individual's job functions encompass scoping a program or developing procedures, processes, and architectures; or design of a computer system, network, or application.

- **Implement:** The individual's functions encompass putting programs, processes, and policies into place; or operation/maintenance of a computer system, network, or application.

- **Evaluate:** The individual's functions encompass assessing the effectiveness of any of the above actions.

SP 800-50 gives as an example of training an IT security course for system administrators, which should address in detail the management controls, operational controls, and technical controls that should be implemented. Management controls include policy, IT security program management, risk management, and life cycle security. Operational controls include personnel and user issues; contingency planning; incident handling, awareness, and training; computer support and operations; and physical and environmental security issues. Technical controls include identification and authentication, logical access controls, audit trails, and cryptography.

The U.S. Office of Personnel Management [OPM04] offers another useful breakdown of roles. OPM lists the following training objectives based on roles:

- **All users** of organization information systems must be exposed to security awareness materials at least annually. Users include employees, contractors, students, guest researchers, visitors, and others who may need access to organization information systems and applications.

- **Executives** must receive training in information security basics and policy level training in security planning and management.

- **Program and functional managers** must receive training in information security basics; management and implementation level training in security planning and system/application security management; and management and implementation level training in system/application life cycle management, risk management, and contingency planning.

- **Chief Information Officers (CIOs), IT security program managers, auditors, and other security-oriented personnel** (e.g., system and network administrators, and system/application security officers) must receive training in information security basics and broad training in security planning, system and application security management, system/application life cycle management, risk management, and contingency planning.

- **IT function management and operations personnel** must receive training in information security basics; management and implementation level training in security planning and system/application security management; and management and implementation level training in system/application life cycle management, risk management, and contingency planning.

An extremely useful resource is SP 800-181 (*National Initiative for Cybersecurity Education (NICE) Cybersecurity Workforce Framework*). This document structures training and education objectives for those with cybersecurity responsibilities into four areas:

- **Knowledge:** A body of information applied directly to the performance of a function. The document lists 630 separate knowledge areas related to cybersecurity.

- **Skill:** An observable competence to apply tools, frameworks, processes, and controls that have an impact on the cybersecurity posture of an organization or individual. The document lists 374 separate skill areas related to cybersecurity.

- **Ability:** Competence to perform an observable behavior or a behavior that results in an observable product. The document lists 176 separate ability areas related to cybersecurity.

- **Task:** A specific defined piece of work that, combined with other tasks, composes the work in a specific work role. The document lists 1007 separate task areas related to cybersecurity.

SP 800-181 characterizes the cybersecurity workforce into seven categories. Each category is broken down into a number of specialty areas, and each specialty area is further broken down into a number of specific work roles. SP 800-181 provides a mapping between work roles and the required knowledge, skills, abilities, and tasks. This extraordinarily detailed framework is suitable as a guide for large organizations.

Education and Certification

An education and certification program is targeted at those who have specific information privacy responsibilities, as opposed to IT workers who have some other IT responsibility but must incorporate privacy concerns.

Information privacy education is normally outside the scope of most organization awareness and training programs. It more properly fits into the category of employee career development programs. Often, this type of education is provided by outside sources, such as college or university courses or specialized training programs. The following are examples of such programs:

- **International Association of Privacy Professionals:** IAPP is the principal organization offering privacy-related certifications, with three offerings: Certified Information Privacy Professional (CIPP), Certified Information Privacy Manager (CIPM), and Certified Information Privacy Technologies (CIPT).

- **International Information System Security Certification Consortium (ISC)² Certified HealthCare Information Security and Privacy Practitioner (HCISSP):** Designed for information security professionals charged with guarding protected health information (PHI).

In addition, those with information privacy responsibilities will find the following information security programs useful:

- **SANS Computer Security Training & Certification:** SANS provides intensive immersion training designed to help participants master the practical steps necessary for defending systems and networks against the most dangerous threats—the ones being actively exploited.

- **Global Information Assurance Certification (GIAC) Security Essentials (GSEC):** This program is designed for IT pros who want to demonstrate skills in IT systems hands-on roles with respect to security tasks. Ideal candidates for this certification possess an understanding of information security beyond simple terminology and concepts.

- **ISACA Certified Information Security Manager (CISM):** This program is for candidates who are inclined toward organizational security and want to demonstrate the ability to create a relationship between an information security program and broader business goals and objectives. This certification ensures knowledge of information security and development and management of an information security program.

- **European Institute of Public Administration (EIPA):** EIPA offers a number of courses related to information privacy (called *data protection* in most EU policy and regulation documents) that lead to a Data Protection Certificate.

12.3 Acceptable Use Policies

An acceptable use policy (AUP) is a type of security or privacy policy targeted at all employees who have access to one or more organization assets. It defines what behaviors are acceptable and what behaviors are not acceptable. An AUP should be clear and concise, and it should be a condition of employment that each employee sign a form indicating that he or she has read and understood the policy and agrees to abide by its conditions.

Information Security Acceptable Use Policy

The MessageLabs whitepaper *Acceptable Use Policies—Why, What, and* How [NAYL09] suggests the following process for developing an AUP:

1. **Conduct a risk assessment to identify areas of concern.** That is, as part of the risk assessment process, those elements that need to go into an AUP should be identified.

2. **Create a policy.** The policy should be tailored to the specific risks identified and should include liability costs. For example, the organization is exposed to liability if customer data is exposed. If the failure to protect the data is due to an employee's action or inaction, and if this behavior violates the AUP, and if this policy is clear and enforced, then this may mitigate the liability of the organization.

3. **Distribute the AUP.** This includes educating employees on why an AUP is necessary.

4. **Monitor compliance.** A procedure is needed to monitor and report on AUP compliance.

5. **Enforce the policy.** An AUP must be enforced consistently and fairly when it is breached.

An example of a template for an AUP is provided by the SANS Institute (https://www.sans.org/security-resources/policies/general/pdf/acceptable-use-policy). The heart of the document is the Policy section, which covers the following areas:

- **General use and ownership:** Key points in this section include:
  - Employees must ensure that proprietary information is protected.
  - Access to sensitive information is only to the extent authorized and necessary to fulfill duties.
  - Employees must exercise good judgment regarding the reasonableness of personal use.
- **Security and proprietary information:** Key points in this section include:
  - Mobile devices must comply with the company's BYOD policies.
  - System- and user-level passwords must comply with the company's password policy.
  - Employees must use extreme caution when opening email attachments.
- **Unacceptable use—system and network activities:** Key points in this section include prohibition of the following:
  - Unauthorized copying of copyrighted material
  - Accessing data, a server, or an account for any purpose other than conducting company business, even if you have authorized access
  - Revealing your account password to others or allowing use of your account by others
  - Making statements about warranty unless it is a part of normal job duties
  - Circumventing user authentication or security of any host, network, or account
  - Providing information about, or lists of, company employees to outside parties
- **Unacceptable use—email and communication activities:** Key points in this section include prohibition of the following:
  - Any form of harassment
  - Any form of spamming
  - Unauthorized use, or forging, of email header information
- **Unacceptable use—blogging and social media:** Key points in this section include:
  - Blogging is acceptable, provided that it is done in a professional and responsible manner, does not otherwise violate company policy, is not detrimental to the company's best interests, and does not interfere with an employee's regular work duties.
  - Any blogging that may harm or tarnish the image, reputation, and/or goodwill of the company and/or any of its employees is forbidden.
  - Employees may not attribute personal statements, opinions, or beliefs to company.

PII Acceptable Use Policy

With respect to information privacy, an AUP should cover the employee responsibilities with respect to PII. The AUP should apply to any user of an information system that processes, stores, and/or transmits PII, and should cover the following areas:

- **PII impact level:** The user should ensure that any set of PII that is used has been assessed for impact level and that the user accepts responsibility for the protection of the PII accordingly.

- **Mobile computing devices:** Specific approval is required for storing or processing PII on mobile devices. The policy should specify other measures, such as logging and tracking procedures, the use of encryption, approval for removing devices from the workplace, screen locks, and other measures.

- **Remote access:** The policy should indicate that remote access is discouraged and permitted only for compelling operational needs—and only using authorized devices. The policy should specify required measures, such as certificate-based authentication, a limited period of inactivity while connected, and restriction on remote storage of PII.

- **Reporting privacy breach:** The policy should specify user responsibilities in the event of loss or suspected loss of PII or other privacy breach.

- **PII training:** The policy should indicate that the user must have completed PII training, including refresher training.

12.4   Key Terms and Review Questions

Key Terms

accidental behavior	privacy certification
acceptable use policy	privacy culture
cybersecurity essentials	privacy education
malicious behavior	privacy training
negligent behavior	role-based training
privacy awareness	

Review Questions

1. What are the four levels of the cybersecurity learning continuum?

2. Briefly explain the difference between privacy awareness and privacy culture.

3. Differentiate between malicious behavior, negligent behavior, and accidental behavior.

4. What topics should be covered by a privacy awareness program?

5. What are some tools used to impact awareness training?

6. What topics should be covered by a cybersecurity essentials program?

7. What is role-based training?

8. Explain the concept of an acceptable use policy.

12.5 References

ENIS07: European Union Agency for Network and Information Security. *Information Security Awareness Initiatives: Current Practice and the Measurement of Success.* July 2008. https://www.enisa.europa.eu

NAYL09: Naylor, J. *Acceptable Use Policies—Why, What, and How.* MessageLabs whitepaper, 2009. http://esafety.ccceducation.org/upload/file/Policy/AUP%20Legal%20advice.pdf

OPM04: Office of Personnel Management. *Information Security Responsibilities for Employees Who Manage or Use Federal Information Systems.* 5 CFR Part 930. 2004.

Chapter | 13

Event Monitoring, Auditing, and Incident Response

Learning Objectives

After studying this chapter, you should be able to:

- Understand the difference between a security event and a security incident
- List useful information to collect in security audit trails
- Summarize the SP 800-53 security audit controls
- Present a typical privacy audit checklist
- Present an overview of the privacy incident management process

This chapter deals with activities an organization pursues after privacy controls and policies have been implemented. The key objectives are to assess the effectiveness of the privacy program and to respond to privacy breaches. Sections 13.1 through 13.3 deal with collecting and assessing information related to the effectiveness of security and privacy controls. Section 13.4 discusses the process of responding to a privacy breach.

13.1 Event Monitoring

This section begins with a discussion of the methods used for logging, monitoring, and managing information security events and then discusses the application of these methods to information privacy.

Security Event Logging

In the information security field, a distinction is commonly made between events and incidents:

- **Security event:** An occurrence considered by an organization to have potential security implications to a system or its environment. Security events identify suspicious or anomalous activity. Events sometimes provide indication that an incident is occurring.

- **Security incident:** An occurrence that actually or potentially jeopardizes the confidentiality, integrity, or availability of an information system; or the information the system processes, stores, or transmits; or that constitutes a violation or imminent threat of violation of security policies, security procedures, or acceptable use policies. Also called a *security breach*.

A related concept, which is a type of security incident, is an indicator of compromise (IOC). IOCs are specific techniques used in the course of an attack that may appear as anomalous behavior. NIST SP 800-53 (*Security and Privacy Controls for Information Systems and Organizations*) defines IOCs as forensic artifacts from intrusions that are identified on organizational information systems (at the host or network level). IOCs provide organizations with valuable information on objects or information systems that have been compromised. IOCs for the discovery of compromised hosts can include, for example, the creation of registry key values. IOCs for network traffic include, for example, uniform resource locator (URL) or protocol elements that indicate malware command and control servers. The rapid distribution and adoption of IOCs can improve information security by reducing the time that information systems and organizations are vulnerable to the same exploit or attack.

The term *security event* covers both events that are security incidents and those that are not. In a certification authority workstation, for example, a list of security events might include the following:

- Logging an operator into or out of the system
- Performing a cryptographic operation (e.g., signing a digital certificate or certificate revocation list)
- Performing a cryptographic card operation (e.g., creation, insertion, removal, backup)
- Performing a digital certificate life cycle operation (e.g., rekey, renewal, revocation, or update)
- Posting a digital certificate to an X.500 directory
- Receiving a key compromise notification
- Receiving an improper certification request
- Detecting an alarm condition reported by a cryptographic module
- Failing a built-in hardware self-test or a software system integrity check

Only the final four events in this list are security incidents.

Security Event Logging Objective

A log is a record of the events occurring within an organization's systems and networks. The objectives of security event logging are to help identify threats that may lead to an information security incident, maintain the integrity of important security-related information, and support forensic investigations. Effective logging enables an enterprise to review events, interactions, and changes that may be relevant to security. With a record of events such as anomalies, unauthorized access attempts, and excessive resource usage, the enterprise is able to perform an analysis to determine the cause.

Potential Security Log Sources

There is a wide variety of sources of security events that can be logged, including:

- Server and workstation operating system logs

- Application logs (e.g., web server, database server)

- Security tool logs (e.g., antivirus, change detection, intrusion detection/prevention system)

- Outbound proxy logs and end user application logs

- Firewalls and other perimeter security devices for traffic between the local user and remote database or server (referred to as north–south traffic)

- Security devices between data center storage elements that communicate across a network (referred to as east–west traffic); such traffic may involve virtual machines and software-based virtual security capabilities

The abundance of log sources presents a considerable challenge to enterprise security management. An organization should create a central repository to store logs in a standardized format. This may require conversion software and consolidation software to keep the amount of log information manageable.

What to Log

In determining what types of events to log, an organization must take into consideration a number of factors, including relevant compliance obligations, institutional privacy policies, data storage costs, access control needs, and the ability to monitor and search large data sets in an appropriate time frame. The following are examples of events that are potentially security related that could be logged:

- **Operating system logs:** Successful user logon/logoff, failed user logon, user account change or deletion, service failure, password changes, service started or stopped, object access denied, and object access changed

- **Network device logs:** Traffic allowed through a firewall, traffic blocked by a firewall, bytes transferred, protocol usage, detected attack activity, user account changes, and administrator access

- **Web servers:** Excessive access attempts to nonexistent files, code (SQL, HTML) seen as part of the URL, attempted access to extensions not implemented on the server, web service stopped/started/failed messages, failed user authentication, invalid requests, and internal server errors

Security Event Management

Security event management (SEM) is the process of identifying, gathering, monitoring, analyzing, and reporting security-related events. The objective of SEM is to extract from a large volume of security events those events that qualify as incidents. SEM takes data input from all devices/nodes and other similar applications, such as log management software. The collected events data are analyzed with security algorithms and statistical computations to trace out any vulnerability, threat, or risk (see Figure 13.1).

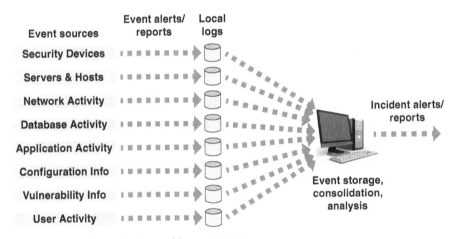

FIGURE 13.1 Security Event Management

The first phase of event management is the collection of event data in the form of logs, as discussed in the preceding section. As event data are generated, they are generally stored in logs local to the devices that generate them. A number of steps need to be taken at this point:

- **Normalization:** For effective management, the log data needs to be in a common format to enable further processing.

- **Filtering:** This step includes assigning priorities to various types of events. On the basis of priority, large numbers of events may be set aside and not subject to further analysis but may be archived in case there is a need to review them later.

- **Aggregation:** The IT facility of a large enterprise can generate millions of events per day. It should be possible to aggregate these events by categories into a more manageable amount of data. For example, if a particular type of traffic is blocked a number of times, it may be sufficient to record as a single aggregate event the type of traffic and the number of times it was blocked over a particular time frame.

These preliminary steps will reduce the volume of data. The objective of the next steps is to analyze the data and generate alerts of security incidents. Aspects of analysis include:

- **Pattern matching:** This involves looking for data patterns within the fields of stored event records. A collection of events with a given pattern may signal a security incident.

- **Scan detection:** An attack is likely to begin with scans of IT resources by the attacker, such as port scans, vulnerability scans, or other types of pings. A substantial number of scans from a single source or a small number of sources may signal a security incident.

- **Threshold detection:** A straightforward form of analysis is the detection of a threshold crossing. For example, if the number of occurrences of a type of event exceeds a given threshold in a certain time period, that can constitute an incident.

- **Event correlation:** Correlation consists of using multiple events from a number of sources to infer that an attack or suspicious activity has occurred. For example, if a particular type of attack proceeds in multiple stages, the separate events that record those multiple activities need to be correlated in order to see the attack. Another aspect of correlation involves correlating particular events with known system vulnerabilities, which might result in a high-priority incident.

Event Logging Related to PII

Organizations generally limit the definition of *security event* to occurrences that have potential security implications. Such events may or may not be suspicious or anomalous. From a privacy perspective, any occurrence that involves access to personally identifiable information (PII) is an event.

Thus, a privacy event log should record the following for each access to PII:

- Which PII was accessed

- Which PII principals' PII was accessed

- What action was performed (e.g., read, print, add, modify, transmit, delete) as a result of the event

- When the action occurred

- Who is the individual responsible for the action

- What level of privileged access, if any, was used (e.g., by system administrators or operators)

The log itself may contain PII related to the incident. Therefore, an organization should use security measures such as access control and encryption to ensure that logged information is used only for its intended purpose and to maintain log file integrity.

NIST SP 800-53 provides the following guidance for privacy protection related to logs:

> Automated monitoring techniques can create unintended privacy risks because automated controls may connect to external or otherwise unrelated systems. The matching of records between these systems may create linkages with unintended consequences. Organizations assess and document these risks in their privacy impact assessment and make determinations that are in alignment with their privacy program plan.

An actual privacy breach or violation of privacy policy constitutes a privacy incident. Organizations should define what they consider anomalous activity as a means of detecting suspected privacy incidents.

13.2 Information Security Auditing

In general terms, an audit within an enterprise is an independent inspection of enterprise records to determine compliance with a standard or policy. More specifically, a security audit relates to security policies and the mechanisms and procedures used to enforce those policies.

Two definitions are relevant for this section:

- **Security audit:** An independent review and examination of a system's records and activities to determine the adequacy of system controls, ensure compliance with established security policy and procedures, detect breaches in security services, and recommend any changes that are indicated for countermeasures.

- **Security audit trail:** A chronological record of system activities that is sufficient to enable the reconstruction and examination of the sequence of environments and activities surrounding or leading to an operation, a procedure, or an event in a security-relevant transaction from inception to final results.

Security audit mechanisms are not involved directly in the prevention of security violations. Rather, they are concerned with the detection, recording, and analysis of events. The basic audit objective is to establish accountability for system entities that initiate or participate in security-relevant events and actions. Thus, means are needed to generate and record a security audit trail and to review and analyze the audit trail to discover and investigate security violations.

Data to Collect for Auditing

The choice of data to collect is determined by a number of requirements. One issue is the amount of data to collect, which is based on the range of areas of interest and the granularity of data collection. There is a trade-off here between quantity and efficiency. The more data are collected, the greater is the performance penalty on the system. Larger amounts of data may also unnecessarily burden the various algorithms used to examine and analyze the data. Further, the presence of large amounts of data creates a temptation to generate excessive numbers of security reports or reports that are especially long.

With these cautions in mind, the first order of business in security audit trail design is the selection of data items to capture. These may include:

- Events related to the use of the auditing software

- Events related to the security mechanisms on the system

- Any events that are collected for use by the various security detection and prevention mechanisms, including items relevant to intrusion detection and firewall operation

- Events related to system management and operation

- Operating system access (e.g., via system calls)

- Application access for selected applications

- Remote access

The auditing function should capture both normal and abnormal events. For example, each connection request, such as a TCP connection request, may be a subject for a security audit trail record, whether or not the request was abnormal and whether or not the request was accepted. This is an important point. Data collection for auditing goes beyond the need to generate security alarms or to provide input to a firewall module. Data representing behavior that does not trigger an alarm can be used to identify normal versus abnormal usage patterns and thus serve as input to intrusion detection analysis. Also, in the event of an attack, an analysis of all the activity on a system may be needed to diagnose the attack and arrive at suitable countermeasures for the future.

As a security administrator designs an audit data collection policy, it is useful to organize the audit trail into categories for purposes of choosing data items to collect. The following are typical categories used for this purpose:

- **System-level audit trails:** These are generally used to monitor and optimize system performance but can serve a security audit function as well. The system enforces certain aspects of security policy, such as access to the system itself. A system-level audit trail should capture data such as both successful and unsuccessful login attempts, devices used, and OS functions performed. Other system-level functions may be of interest for auditing, such as system operation and network performance indicators.

- **Application-level audit trails:** These can detect security violations within an application or detect flaws in the application's interaction with the system. For critical applications or those that deal with sensitive data, an application-level audit trail can provide the desired level of detail to assess security threats and impacts. For example, for an email application, an audit trail can record sender and receiver, message size, and types of attachments. An audit trail for a database interaction using SQL (Structured Query Language) queries can record the user, type of transaction, and even individual tables, rows, columns, or data items accessed.

- **User-level audit trails:** These trace the activity of individual users over time. They can be used to hold users accountable for their actions. Such audit trails are also useful as input to an analysis program that attempts to define normal versus anomalous behavior. A user-level audit trail can record user interactions with the system, such as commands issued, identification and authentication attempts, and files and resources accessed. An audit trail can also capture the user's use of applications.

- **Network-level audit trails:** These capture a wide variety of network activity. Enterprises use such audit trails to evaluate system performance and perform load balancing. These audit trails can also include security-related data, such as data generated by firewalls, virtual private network managers, and IPsec traffic.

- **Physical access audit trails:** These are generated by equipment that controls physical access and are then transmitted to a central host for subsequent storage and analysis. Examples of such equipment are card-key systems and alarm systems.

Internal and External Audits

A sound auditing policy should include both internal and external security audits. Internal audits are carried out by the organization itself, typically on a quarterly basis or after a significant security event. External audits are carried out by someone from outside, typically on an annual basis.

The objectives of an internal security audit should be to:

- Identify security weaknesses

- Provide an opportunity to improve the information security management system

- Provide management with information about the status of security

- Review compliance of security systems with the information security policy of the organization

- Find and resolve noncompliance

The objectives of an external security audit should be to:

- Assess the process of internal auditing
- Determine the commonality and frequency of recurrence of various types of security violations
- Identify the common causes
- Provide advisory and training inputs to tackle the neglect of procedures
- Review and update the policy

Security Audit Controls

A useful guide to developing a security audit program is the family of audit controls defined in NIST SP 800-53. The controls are designed to be flexible and customizable and to be implemented as part of an organization-wide process to manage risk.

The audit and accountability family consist of 16 controls. Some of the controls include one or more control enhancements, which add functionality or specificity to a base control or increase the strength of a base control. The 16 control categories are as follows:

- **Audit and Accountability Policy and Procedures:** This category defines the governance strategy for a security audit policy.

- **Audit Events:** This category focuses on the type of events to be audited. Additional guidance for this category includes the following: Specify the event types to be audited; verify that the system can audit the selected event types; provide a rationale for why the auditable event types are deemed to be adequate to support after-the-fact investigations of security and privacy incidents; and coordinate the security audit function with other organizational entities requiring audit-related information.

- **Content of Audit Records:** This category deals with the content of audit records, including the following issues:

  - Specify the content of an audit record, such as what type of event occurred, when the event occurred, where the event occurred, the source of the event, the outcome of the event, and the identity of any individuals or subjects associated with the event.

  - Provide centralized management and configuration of the content to be captured.

  - Limit personally identifiable information contained in audit records.

- **Audit Storage Capacity:** This category allocates sufficient storage capacity to accommodate record retention requirements.

- **Response to Audit Processing Failures:** This category provides guidance on alerting specific personnel of an audit processing failure and what additional actions to take.

- **Audit Review, Analysis, and Reporting:** This category deals with reviewing and analyzing security audit records at a specified frequency, with reports to specified individuals.

- **Audit Reduction and Report Generation:** This category provides summary information from audit records that is more meaningful to analysts.

- **Timestamps:** This category deals with recording timestamps from internal system clocks and with synchronizing all clocks to a single reference time source.

- **Protection of Audit Information:** This category provides technical or automated protection of audit information.

- **Non-repudiation:** This category protects against an individual falsely denying having performed selected audit-related activities.

- **Audit Record Retention:** This category provides guidance for developing a records retention policy.

- **Audit Generation:** This category provides guidance for defining an audit record generation capability for the auditable event types.

- **Monitoring for Information Disclosure:** This category discusses monitoring of open source information (e.g., from social networking sites) for evidence of unauthorized disclosure of organizational information.

- **Session Audit:** This category provides and implements the capability for authorized users to select a user session to capture/record or view/hear.

- **Alternate Audit Capability:** This category provides an alternate audit capability in the event of a failure in primary audit capability that implements organization-defined alternate audit functionality.

- **Cross-Organizational Audit:** When organizations use systems and/or services of external organizations, the auditing capability necessitates a coordinated approach across organizations. This category provides for such a capability.

This set of controls provides comprehensive guidance for planning and implementing an effective security auditing function. In addition, some of the control categories address privacy requirements, as indicated in the final column of Table 13.1 (S = security control, P = privacy control).

TABLE 13.1 Audit and Accountability Control Categories

Code	Name	Security (S)/Privacy (P)
AU-1	Audit and Accountability Policy and Procedures	S
AU-2	Audit Events	S
AU-3	Content of Audit Records	S, P
AU-4	Audit Storage Capacity	S
AU-5	Response to Audit Processing Failures	S

Code	Name	Security (S)/Privacy (P)
AU-6	Audit Review, Analysis, and Reporting	S
AU-7	Audit Reduction and Report Generation	S
AU-8	Timestamps	S
AU-9	Protection of Audit Information	S
AU-10	Non-repudiation	S
AU-11	Audit Record Retention	S, P
AU-12	Audit Generation	S, P
AU-13	Monitoring for Information Disclosure	S
AU-14	Session Audit	S
AU-15	Alternate Audit Capability	S
AU-16	Cross-Organizational Audit	S, P

13.3   Information Privacy Auditing

Privacy auditing encompasses both a detailed review of policies and procedures and an assessment of the effectiveness of the privacy controls in place at the time of the audit. Objectives of a privacy audit include:

- Determining the degree of compliance with applicable privacy laws and regulations

- Determining the degree of compliance with contractual commitments

- Revealing gaps, if any, between required and actual privacy management, operational, and technical controls

- Providing a basis for a privacy remediation and improvement plan

- Enhancing effectiveness and completeness of security auditing and assessment process by addressing privacy-specific criteria

Privacy Audit Checklist

A privacy audit should encompass both a review of event logs and an assessment of policies, procedures, and operations. A checklist serves as a useful guide to ensure that all issues are considered. The following discussion is based on a checklist presented in the document *Privacy Audit Checklist* [ENRI01].

Preliminary Work

Before beginning the actual audit, some preliminary work is required to guide the auditing process. First, the auditor should establish the context for the organization, including covering the following topics:

- Assess the statutory/regulatory climate(s) affecting the organization

- Account for industry/trade organization affiliations (Are there any self-regulatory initiatives with which your policies and practices must comport?)

- Consider the media climate (Are there certain practices on which you should focus during your assessment? [i.e., cookie use, web bug use, or other media hot-button issues])

Next, the auditor should conduct, or have access to, a privacy impact assessment (PIA). The PIA will include a catalog of all PII within the organization and especially sensitive PII (e.g., medical, financial, children under the age of 13). The PIA will also document data flows, which helps to determine the level of privacy-related exposure.

Information Collected from Users

The auditor should determine what information is collected with a user's knowledge and/or consent, including:

- **Log files:** Examples include IP addresses, browser type, and date/time of access. The auditor should determine the purpose for collecting each class.

- **Cookies:** Why are cookies used? Are other companies allowed to deliver cookies to the user via your website?

- **Partners, third parties:** What PII flows to/from other organizations, such as business partners or third-party vendors?

The audit should address the issue of information sharing, including the following considerations:

- Does your website/organization share, transfer, or release any information to third parties?

- Does your website contain links to other websites? What are the privacy implications?

- Does your organization supplement the information received directly from a user with additional information received from third parties or information received by mechanisms other than those to which the user has explicitly consented?

The audit should document what opt-in/opt-out mechanisms are available to the user regarding control of collection, use, and distribution of personal information.

Security Issues

The auditor should document and assess the effectiveness of the security mechanisms in place with regard to PII. This should encompass the following areas:

- **Access control:** Who has access to PII, and why? What measures have been taken to prevent access by unauthorized individuals and to prevent unauthorized actions by those who have access?

- **Authentication:** Assess the authentication controls to verify the identity of individuals accessing PII.

■ **Data integrity:** This encompasses the following concerns:

   ■ What restrictions are in place to control merging of sensitive data with unprotected data?

   ■ Is there a mechanism in place to allow users access to their information in order to verify that the data are accurate and have not been modified or corrupted?

   ■ What information does your organization allow users to access, modify, and correct?

   ■ What verification mechanisms are in place to verify the identity of users wishing to access/correct their personal information?

   ■ How will a user be informed if there is a change in the use of his or her PII?

Privacy Policy Assessment

The auditor should verify that the internal privacy policy statement addresses all the regulatory and organizational privacy policies and supports fair information practice principles (FIPPs). The auditor should ensure that the privacy policy is complete and easy to understand, as well as that the appropriate training and awareness programs are in place regarding this policy.

The auditor should conduct a similar assessment of the organization's external privacy policy or privacy notice statement. Chapter 8, "Online Privacy," discusses privacy notices, and Chapter 10, "Information Privacy Governance and Management," discusses privacy policies.

Privacy Controls

As indicated in Table 13.1, four of the audit and accountability control categories in SP 800-53 include privacy elements:

■ **AU-3 Content of Audit Records:** The control enhancement AU-3(3) deals with limiting PII elements in the content of audit records. The organization should specifically list what elements may be recorded in an audit record. The AU-3(3) guidance in this regard is that limiting PII in audit records when such information is not needed for operational purposes helps reduce the level of privacy risk created by a system.

■ **AU-11 Audit Record Retention:** The organization should specify a time period for retaining audit records to provide support for after-the-fact investigations of security and privacy incidents and to meet regulatory and organizational information retention requirements.

■ **AU-12 Audit Generation:** The control enhancement AU-12(4) deals with query parameter audits of PII, expressed as "Provide and implement the capability for auditing the parameters of user query events for data sets containing PII." Query parameters are explicit criteria that a user or an automated system submits to a system to retrieve data. Auditing of query parameters within systems for data sets that contain PII augments an organization's ability to track and understand the access, usage, or sharing of PII by authorized personnel.

- **AU-16 Cross-Organizational Audit:** The organization should use organization-defined methods for coordinating organization-defined audit information among external organizations when audit information is transmitted across organizational boundaries. Maintaining the identity of individuals who requested specific services across organizational boundaries may often be very difficult, and doing so may have significant performance and privacy ramifications.

13.4 Privacy Incident Management and Response

ISO 27000 (*Information Security Management Systems—Overview and Vocabulary*) defines *information security incident management* as consisting of processes for detecting, reporting, assessing, responding to, dealing with, and learning from information security incidents. Similarly, information privacy incident management deals with these issues with respect to information privacy incidents, also referred to as *privacy breaches*.

An organization should use a broad definition of *breach* to maximize the chance of detecting any privacy violation. The following definition of *privacy breach*, from a U.S. Office of Management and Budget memorandum [OMB17], is useful:

> The loss of control, compromise, unauthorized disclosure, unauthorized acquisition, or any similar occurrence where (1) a person other than an authorized user accesses or potentially accesses PII or (2) an authorized user accesses or potentially accesses PII for an other than authorized purpose.

Objectives of Privacy Incident Management

The following objectives are relevant for information privacy incident management. An organization should:

- Detect privacy-related events and deal with them efficiently, in particular deciding when they should be classified as privacy breaches.

- Assess and respond to identified privacy breaches in the most appropriate and efficient manner.

- Minimize the adverse effects of privacy breaches on the organization and its operations through appropriate controls as part of incident response.

- Coordinate with relevant elements from crisis management and business continuity management through an established escalation process.

- Assess and mitigate information privacy vulnerabilities to prevent or reduce incidents.

- Quickly learn from information privacy incidents, vulnerabilities, and their management. This feedback mechanism is intended to increase the chances of preventing future information privacy incidents from occurring, improve the implementation and use of information privacy controls, and improve the overall information privacy incident management plan.

The following documents can provide useful guidance for developing a privacy incident management plan:

- **NIST SP 800-122:** *Guide to Protecting the Confidentiality of Personally Identifiable Information*
- **ISO 29151:** *Code of Practice for Personally Identifiable Information Protection*
- **EU Data Protection Working Party WP250:** *Guidelines on Personal Data Breach Notification Under the GDPR*
- **OMB Memorandum M-17-12:** *Preparing for and Responding to a Breach of Personally Identifiable Information*

Many organizations react in an ad hoc manner when a privacy incident occurs. Because of the potential cost of privacy incidents, it is cost-beneficial to develop a standing capability for quick discovery and response to such incidents. This capability can also serve to support the analysis of past privacy incidents with a view to improving the ability to prevent and respond to incidents.

SP 800-61 (*Computer Security Incident Handling Guide*) defines a four-phase incident management process (see Figure 13.2). SP 800-122 recommends that privacy incident management be added to each of these phases, taking advantage of management structures and procedures already developed for information security incident management.

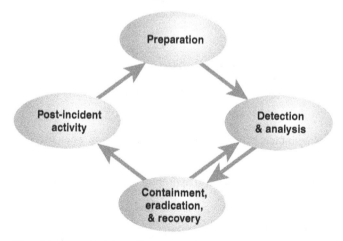

FIGURE 13.2   Incident Response Life Cycle

Privacy Incident Response Team

Most organizations will want to create a formal *privacy incident response team (PIRT)*. A PIRT is a team of appropriately skilled and trusted members of the organization that handles security incidents during their life cycle. At times, external experts may supplement this team. Individuals with the following backgrounds/skill sets should be selected as members of the PIRT:

- Understanding of known threats, attack signatures, and vulnerabilities

- Understanding of the enterprise network, security infrastructure, and platforms

- Experience in privacy breach response and/or troubleshooting techniques

- Experience in forensic techniques and best practices

- Understanding of regulations and laws that pertain to privacy and disclosure and evidentiary requirements

- Understanding of systems, threats and vulnerabilities, and remediation methods in a particular area of business responsibility

Part-time or liaison members of the PIRT should include representation from the following key areas:

- Information technology

- Information security

- Corporate communications

- Human resources

- Legal

- Business unit management and technology specialists

- Corporate security (including physical security)

The PIRT's primary responsibility is to respond to incidents throughout the incident response life cycle. The PIRT may also be involved in making recommendations for improving privacy practices and implementing new privacy controls.

Preparing for Privacy Incident Response

An effective incident response capability requires the participation of a number of people within the organization. Making the right planning and implementation decisions is key to establishing a successful incident response program. Tasks involved in preparing for incident response include:

- Develop an organization-specific definition of the term *privacy incident* so that the scope of the term is clear.

- Create a privacy incident response plan.

- Establish a cross-functional PIRT that develops, implements, tests, executes, and reviews the privacy incident response plan.

- Staff and train the PIRT.

- Develop incident response and reporting procedures.

- Establish guidelines for communicating with external parties.

- Define the services that will be provided by the PIRT.

- Establish and maintain accurate notification mechanisms.

- Develop written guidelines for prioritizing incidents.

- Have a plan for the collection, formatting, organization, storage, and retention of incident data.

The Office of Management and Budget [OMB17] recommends that the privacy incident response plan should, at a minimum, include the following elements:

- **Privacy incident response team:** Including the specific officials and job titles comprising the PIRT, as well as their respective roles and responsibilities when responding to a breach

- **Identifying applicable privacy compliance documentation:** Including the responsibility to identify any individual with responsibility for PII, privacy impact assessments (PIAs), and privacy notices that may apply to the potentially compromised information

- **Information sharing to respond to a breach:** Including the potential information sharing within the organization or with other organizations or government agencies that may arise following a breach to reconcile or eliminate duplicate records, to identify potentially affected individuals, or to obtain contact information to notify potentially affected individuals

- **Reporting requirements:** Including the specific officials responsible for reporting a breach to law enforcement and oversight entities

- **Assessing the risk of harm to individuals potentially affected by a breach:** Including the factors the organization shall consider when assessing the risk of harm to potentially affected individuals

- **Mitigating the risk of harm to individuals potentially affected by a breach:** Including whether the organization should provide guidance to potentially affected individuals, purchase identity theft services for potentially affected individuals, and offer methods for acquiring such services

- **Notifying individuals potentially affected by a breach:** Including if, when, and how to provide notification to potentially affected individuals and other relevant entities (Under some legal frameworks, it might be necessary to also inform some categories of individuals that were not affected.)

The organization should provide employees with a clear definition of what constitutes a breach involving PII and what information needs to be reported. SP 800-122 recommends that the following information be obtained from employees who are reporting a known or suspected breach involving PII:

- Person reporting the incident

- Person who discovered the incident

- Date and time the incident was discovered

- Nature of the incident

- Name of the system and possible interconnectivity with other systems

- Description of the information lost or compromised

- Storage medium from which information was lost or compromised

- Controls in place to prevent unauthorized use of the lost or compromised information

- Number of individuals potentially affected

- Whether law enforcement was contacted

Detection and Analysis

Perhaps the most challenging phase of the incident response life cycle is detection and analysis, which consists of determining whether an incident has occurred and, if so, the type, extent, and magnitude of the problem.

Incident Detection

The preceding sections of this chapter discuss event logging and management in some detail. The task of privacy incident detection is to detect privacy incidents from among the numerous security and privacy events that have been logged and recorded.

Key aspects of incident detection include the following. The organization should:

- Train all IT personnel and users regarding procedures for reporting failures, weaknesses, and suspected incidents; methods to recognize and detect problems with security and privacy protections; and how to escalate reporting appropriately.

- Implement technical controls for the automated detection of security and privacy incidents from event logs, coupled with reporting that is as near real time as possible. Key technical tools include intrusion detection systems (IDSs) and continuously monitoring antivirus software.

- Collect situational awareness information from internal and external data sources, including local system and network traffic and activity logs; news feeds concerning ongoing political, social, or economic activities that might impact incident activity; and external feeds on incident trends, new attack vectors, current attack indicators, and new mitigation strategies and technologies.

■ Ensure that digital evidence is gathered and stored securely and that its secure preservation is continually monitored, in case the evidence is required for legal prosecution or internal disciplinary action.

Analysis

When an incident is detected, an organization should do a preliminary analysis of the potential impact of the breach. The organization should consider the following factors:

■ **Nature and sensitivity of the PII potentially compromised by the breach:** Including the potential harms that an individual could experience due to the compromise of that type of PII

■ **Likelihood of access and use of PII:** Including whether the PII was properly encrypted or rendered partially or completely inaccessible by other means

■ **Type of breach:** Including the circumstances of the breach, as well as the actors involved and their intent

■ **Impact on the organization:** Including legal liability, financial liability, and reputational harm

The analysis may also determine whether immediate action is needed to remove the vulnerability or to block the action that enabled the incident to occur. Such analysis may also be part of the post-incident activity phase.

Containment, Eradication, and Recovery

The containment, eradication, and recovery phase are the central tasks of incident management. If prevention measures have failed and an incident occurs, the enterprise needs to stop the attack if it is ongoing and recover from the attack. Actions taken during this phase may uncover another incident, which feeds back to the detection and analysis phase, as shown previously in Figure 13.2.

Containment

Most incidents require some sort of containment. The objective is to prevent the spread of the effects of the incident before they overwhelm resources or in some other way increase damage.

Strategies for dealing with various types of incidents should have been planned well in advance. The strategy will vary depending on the type of incident. Thus, email-borne virus, denial of service, and intrusion coupled with escalation of privilege all require different strategies. In some cases, a system may need to be removed from the network until it is cleaned. User- or system-level accounts may need to be disabled or changed. Active sessions may need to be terminated.

The nature of the strategy and the magnitude of resources devoted to containment should depend on criteria that have been developed ahead of time. Examples of criteria include potential damage to and theft of resources, the need to preserve evidence, the effectiveness of the strategy, the time and resources needed to implement the strategy, and the duration of the solution.

Eradication

Once the ongoing damage has been stopped, it may be necessary to perform some sort of eradication to eliminate any residual elements of the incident, such as malware and compromised user accounts.

Recovery

During recovery, IT personnel restore systems to normal operation to the extent possible and, if applicable, harden systems to prevent similar incidents. Possible actions include:

- Restoring systems with the clean version from the latest backup

- Rebuilding systems from scratch

- Replacing compromised files with clean versions

- Installing patches

- Changing passwords

- Tightening network perimeter security (e.g., firewall rule sets)

SP 800-122 indicates the following actions at this stage that are specific to privacy breaches:

- Perform additional media sanitization steps when PII needs to be deleted from media during recovery.

- Determine whether the PII must be preserved as evidence before sanitizing the PII.

- Use proper forensics techniques to ensure preservation of evidence.

- Determine whether PII was accessed and how many records or individuals were affected.

Notification to Affected Individuals

One of the first orders of business for an organization after or even during a privacy incident is notification. There may be legal, regulatory, or contractual requirements for notifying government agencies, business partners, stakeholders, and affected PII principals. The notification should include details of the incident and the organization's response. Organizations should provide affected PII principals access to appropriate and effective remedies, such as correction or deletion of incorrect information.

When providing notice to individuals, organizations should make affected individuals aware of their options.

The EU GDPR provides useful guidance in this regard. The GDPR states that when a personal data breach is likely to result in a high risk to the rights and freedoms of natural persons, the controller shall communicate the personal data breach to the data subjects without undue delay. The communication should provide the following in clear and plain language:

- A description of the nature of the breach

- The name and contact details of the data protection officer or other contact point

- A description of the likely consequences of the breach

- A description of the measures taken or proposed to be taken by the controller to address the breach, including, where appropriate, measures to mitigate its possible adverse effects

The EU document WP250 provides a number of examples of data breaches and the types of notification that are appropriate.

Post-Incident Activity

There should be an incident logging capability for recording incidents and notes about the incident. After an incident has been dealt with in the containment, eradication, and recovery phase, the organization should conduct an evaluation process. This process should include lessons-learned meetings and after-action reports. Depending on the type of incident and the security policy, a comprehensive forensic investigation may be warranted, or a loss comprehensive analysis may be undertaken.

Once the PIRT has reviewed and analyzed the effects of the incident and the magnitude of the effort required for recovery, the PIRT may recommend further action, such as:

- Review of the incident handling process to determine whether the process needs to be modified and/or more resources should be committed. Such changes depend on the novelty of the incident and its severity.

- Determine whether policy and process changes may be warranted. Questions to consider include the following: Were any procedures missing, were any communications unclear, or were any stakeholders not appropriately considered? Did the technical staff have appropriate resources (information as well as equipment) to perform the analysis and/or the recovery?

- Consider other improvements outside the incident management process that may be needed, including new or revised technical security controls, updates to awareness and acceptable use policies, and improvements in the areas of threat intelligence and vulnerability assessment.

Table 13.2, from SP 800-61, is a useful checklist for ensuring that the organization completes all phases of the incident response life cycle.

TABLE 13.2 Incident Handling Checklist

	Detection and Analysis
1.	Determine whether an incident has occurred
1.1	Analyze the precursors and indicators
1.2	Look for correlating information
1.3	Perform research (e.g., search engines, knowledge base)
1.4	As soon as the handler believes an incident has occurred, begin documenting the investigation and gathering evidence
2.	Prioritize handling the incident based on the relevant factors (functional impact, information impact, recoverability effort, etc.)
3.	Report the incident to the appropriate internal personnel and external organizations
	Containment, Eradication, and Recovery
4.	Acquire, preserve, secure, and document evidence
5.	Contain the incident
6.	Eradicate the incident
6.1	Identify and mitigate all vulnerabilities that were exploited
6.2	Remove malware, inappropriate materials, and other components
6.3	If more affected hosts are discovered (e.g., new malware infections), repeat the detection and analysis steps (1.1, 1.2) to identify all other affected hosts and then contain (5) and eradicate (6) the incident for them
7.	Recover from the incident
7.1	Return affected systems to an operationally ready state
7.2	Confirm that the affected systems are functioning normally
7.3	If necessary, implement additional monitoring to look for future related activity
	Post-Incident Activity
8.	Create a follow-up report
9.	Hold a lessons-learned meeting (mandatory for major incidents and otherwise optional)

13.5 Key Terms and Review Questions

Key Terms

event monitoring	log files
external audit	privacy audit
information privacy auditing	privacy breach
information security auditing	privacy control
internal audit	privacy incident management

privacy incident response	security event logging
privacy incident response team (PIRT)	security event management
security audit	security incident
security audit trail	security log
security event	

Review Questions

1. Differentiate between a security event and security incident.

2. For security event logging, what events should be captured in operating system logs, network device logs, and web server logs?

3. What information should a privacy event log record?

4. What are key objectives for a security audit?

5. Define the terms *security audit* and *security audit trail*.

6. What is meant by *external security audit*? What should be the key objectives of such an audit?

7. What topics should be covered by a privacy audit checklist?

8. List and describe the privacy-specific controls that are part of the SP 800-53 audit and accountability control set.

9. What should be the objectives for information privacy incident management?

10. Describe the four phases of the incident management process.

11. What skills and training are important for selecting members of a PIRT?

12. What topics should be covered by a privacy incident response plan?

13. What factors should be considered in assessing the severity of a privacy breach?

13.6 References

ENRI01: Enright, K. *Privacy Audit Checklist.* 2001. https://cyber.harvard.edu/ecommerce/privacyaudit.html

OMB17: Office of Management and Budget. *Preparing for and Responding to a Breach of Personally Identifiable Information.* OMB Memorandum M-17-12. January 3, 2017.

PART VI

Legal and Regulatory Requirements

Chapter | **14**

The EU General Data Protection Regulation

Learning Objectives

After studying this chapter, you should be able to:

- Understand the organization of the GDPR and its supporting guideline documents
- Explain the principles of the GDPR
- Explain the rights of data subjects defined in the GDPR
- Summarize the roles of the controller and processor
- Present an overview of the data protection impact assessment process

The General Data Protection Regulation (GDPR) is a European Commission regulation for the protection of data in the European Union (EU). The European Commission published the GDPR on April 27, 2016, and it entered into force on May 25, 2018. The GDPR builds on the foundations of and repeals its predecessor, Directive 95/46/EC, which had provided the basis for EU member states' data protection laws. As a regulation instead of a directive, the GDPR enters directly into force without the need for implementation in law by the member states. This regulation makes data protection stronger and more specific in some areas while expanding the rights of consumers over their data. Thus, while many of the provisions look familiar, taken together, they radically change the impact of data protection within the EU.

The GDPR is enforceable in all the nations in the European Economic Area (EEA), which consists of the 28 member states of the EU, plus Iceland, Liechtenstein, and Norway. The GDPR also regulates the flow of personal data outside the EU. Its main objective is to protect the privacy of citizens of the EU and unify the data regulation rules of the EU's member nations. Its rules apply to private organizations and government agencies, including the police and military. Mandates in the GDPR apply to all personal data of EU citizens, whether or not the organization collecting the data in question is located within the EU, as well as all people whose data is stored within the EU, whether or not they are actually EU citizens.

This chapter focuses on areas of the GDPR that are of particular interest to information privacy designers and implementers. The first three sections provide an overview, discussing key roles and terms in the GDPR, the structure of the GDPR document, and the objectives and scope of the GDPR. Sections 14.4 through 14.6 focus on the rights of data subjects, including a description of the principles used to define these rights, restrictions on collecting and processing certain types of personal data, and the specific rights of data subjects that are protected by the GDPR. The remaining sections detail the operational and management requirements imposed by the GDPR. Section 14.7 looks at the roles and responsibilities of the controller, the processor, and the data protection officer. Section 14.8 deals with the GDPR requirements for a data protection impact assessment.

14.1   Key Roles and Terms in the GDPR

A number of actors or roles are defined in the GDPR, including the following:

- **Natural person:** A human being.

- **Legal person:** A non-human entity, such as a corporation, partnership, or sole proprietorship, that is recognized as having privileges and obligations, such as having the ability to enter into contracts, to sue, and to be sued. Sometimes the term *legal person* encompasses natural persons and well as non-human entities, but the GDPR limits the term *legal person* to non-human entities.

- **Data subject:** An identified or identifiable natural person, which is one who can be identified, directly or indirectly, in particular by reference to an identifier such as a name, an identification number, location data, an online identifier, or one or more factors specific to the physical, physiological, genetic, mental, economic, cultural, or social identity of that natural person.

- **Controller:** The natural or legal person, public authority, agency, or other body that determines the purposes and means of processing personal data, regardless of whether such data are collected, stored, processed, or disseminated by that party or by an agent on its behalf.

- **Processor:** The natural or legal person, public authority, agency, or other body responsible for processing personal data on behalf of and in accordance with the instructions of a controller. The controller and the processor may be the same entity.

- **Third party:** A natural or legal person, public authority, agency, or body other than the data subject, controller, processor, and persons who, under the direct authority of the controller or processor, are authorized to process personal data.

- **Data protection officer (DPO):** An independent member of the privacy team who reports directly to senior management. The responsibilities of the DPO include:

  - Assisting the controller or the processor in monitoring internal compliance with the GDPR

  - Providing advice where requested regarding to the data protection impact assessment and monitoring its performance

  - Cooperating with the supervisory authority and acting as a contact point. A supervisory authority is a government entity with the authority to enforce the GDPR

  - Prioritizing activities and focusing efforts on issues that present increased data protection risks

  - Creating inventories and holding a register of processing operations based on information provided by the various departments in the organization responsible for the processing of personal data

- **Supervisory authority:** An independent public authority established by a EU member state that is responsible for monitoring the application of the GDPR. Some, but not all, EU member states refer to this body as a ***data protection authority (DPA)***, although this term does not appear in the GDPR.

The GDPR uses some terms that differ from those that were heretofore common in the information privacy literature and regulations. Table 14.1 shows GDRP terms and equivalent terms in common use.

TABLE 14.1 Key GDPR Terms

GDPR Term	Equivalent Term
Data controller	PII controller
Data processor	PII processor
Data protection	Information privacy
Data protection by default	Privacy by default
Data protection by design	Privacy by design
Data protection impact assessment	Privacy impact assessment
Data protection officer	Chief privacy officer, privacy leader
Data subject	PII principal
Personal data	PII
Personal data breach	Privacy breach, privacy violation

14.2   Structure of the GDPR

The GDPR consists of a set of 99 articles, organized into 11 chapters. These 99 articles are the specific rules put forth in the regulation. In addition, the GDPR document includes 173 recitals, which provide commentary and additional explanation of the GDPR. Each recital, with the exception of recital 172, is associated with one or more specific articles.

> **Note**
>
> In the English-language version of the regulation, the articles occupy 57 pages, and the recitals occupy 31 pages.

Table 14.2 summarizes the topics covered by each chapter and indicates the corresponding articles and recitals.

TABLE 14.2   Structure of the GDPR

Chapter	Description	Articles	Recitals
1: General Provisions	Defines the regulation objectives, scope with respect to personal data, territorial scope, and terminology.	1–4	1–37
2: Principles	Discusses how an organization should treat personal data and how the person who is processing the data has to demonstrate compliance. This chapter also brings in consent, categories for personal data, and when processing does not require identification.	5–11	38–57
3: Rights of the Data Subject	Explains the rights of the person whose data are handled by the processor, controller, or someone who receives the data.	12–23	58–73
4: Controller and Processor	Deals with a number of procedural issues. Covers the roles of controller, processor, and data protection officer. Mandates use of data protection by design and data protection impact assessment. Also outlines requirements for notification of a personal data breach.	24–43	13, 39, 74–100
5: Transfer or Personal Data to Third Countries or International Organizations	Deals with transfer of personal data to a third country (a country outside the EU or EAA) or to an international organization.	44–50	101–116

Chapter	Description	Articles	Recitals
6: Independent Supervisory Authorities	Focuses on requirements and mandates for EU member states.	51–59	117–132
7: Cooperation and Consistency	Discusses how supervisory authorities can remain consistent and cooperate with one another. This chapter also defines the purpose of the European Data Protection Board and discusses its purpose.	60–76	124–128, 130–131, 133–140
8: Remedies, Liability and Penalties	Reviews the rights of data subjects and how they proceed with complaints. This chapter also covers penalties for processors and controllers.	77–84	141–152
9: Provisions Relating to Specific Processing Situations	Discusses how member states can provide exemptions, conditions, or rules in relation to specific processing activities.	85–91	153–165
10: Delegated Acts and Implementing Acts	Discusses the EU Commission's power to adopt delegated acts and the process in which that occurs. This refers to acts that are not specifically part of EU legislation.	92–93	166–170
11: Final Provisions	Discusses how the EU Commission must report on the regulation every four years. This chapter also discusses the differences between previous directives and the GDPR.	94–99	102, 171, 173

To provide more detailed guidance, the Article 29 Data Protection Working Party issued a number of documents. This advisory body was made up of a representative from the data protection authority of each EU member state, the European Data Protection Supervisor, and the European Commission. In 2018, it was replaced by the European Data Protection Board (EDPB) under the GDPR. The EDPB has issued additional guidance documents. With respect to the focus of this book, the most relevant documents are the following:

- *Guidelines 2/2019 on the Processing of Personal Data Under Article 6(1)(b) of the GDPR in the Context of the Provision of Online Services to Data Subjects*

- *Guidelines 3/2018 on the Territorial Scope of the GDPR* (Article 3)

- *Guidelines on Transparency Under Regulation 2016/679 (wp260rev.01)*

- *Guidelines on Automated Individual Decision-Making and Profiling for the Purposes of Regulation 2016/679 (wp251rev.01)*

■ *Guidelines on Personal Data Breach Notification Under Regulation 2016/679 (wp250rev.01)*

■ *Guidelines on Consent under Regulation 2016/679 (wp259rev.01)*

■ *Guidelines on the Lead Supervisory Authority (wp244rev.01)*

■ *Guidelines on Data Protection Officers ("DPOs") (wp243rev.01)*

■ *Guidelines on the Right to "Data Portability" (wp242rev.01)*

■ *Guidelines on Data Protection Impact Assessment (DPIA) (wp248rev.01)*

14.3 GDPR Objectives and Scope

Chapter 1 of the GDPR lays out the objectives for this regulation and the scope of its applicability.

Objectives

The GDPR has the following key objectives:

■ Provide the fundamental right to the protection of personal data for every individual

■ Harmonize the protection of fundamental rights and freedoms of natural persons in respect of processing activities and to ensure the free flow of personal data between member states

■ Balance privacy rights against other fundamental rights, in accordance with the principle of proportionality

■ Define a strong and more coherent data protection framework in the EU, backed by strong enforcement, given the importance of creating the trust that will allow the digital economy to develop across the internal market

■ Enable, to the extent possible, natural persons to have control of their own personal data

■ Ensure consistent and homogenous application of the rules for the protection of the fundamental rights and freedoms of natural persons with regard to the processing of personal data throughout the European Union

■ Strengthening and setting out in detail the rights of data subjects and the obligations of those who process and determine the processing of personal data, as well as equivalent powers for monitoring and ensuring compliance with the rules for the protection of personal data and equivalent sanctions for infringements in the member states

■ Take account of the specific needs of micro, small, and medium-sized enterprises in the application of the GDPR

Scope of the GDPR

The GDPR defines both a material scope and a territorial scope for its application. These terms can be defined as follows:

- **Material scope:** The actions covered by a particular law or regulation. In the context of this chapter, material scope refers to the types of processing of personal data that are covered by the GDPR.

- **Territorial scope:** The jurisdictional reach of a law or regulation. In the context of this chapter, territorial scope refers to what physical locations of enterprises and data subjects are covered by the GDPR.

Material Scope

The GDPR applies to the processing of personal data wholly or partly by automated means and to the processing other than by automated means of personal data that form part of a filing system or are intended to form part of a filing system. Recital 15 clarifies this as follows:

> In order to prevent creating a serious risk of circumvention, the protection of natural persons should be technologically neutral and should not depend on the techniques used. The protection of natural persons should apply to the processing of personal data by automated means, as well as to manual processing.

The GDPR defines *personal data* as:

> Any information relating to an identified or identifiable natural person (data subject); an identifiable natural person is one who can be identified, directly or indirectly, in particular by reference to an identifier such as a name, an identification number, location data, an online identifier or to one or more factors specific to the physical, physiological, genetic, mental, economic, cultural or social identity of that natural person.

The regulation defines a filing system as "any structured set of personal data which are accessible according to specific criteria, whether centralized, decentralized or dispersed on a functional or geographical basis." One example is chronologically ordered sets of manual records containing personal data; in this case, records are accessible by date.

There are four key elements to the GDPR definition of personal data:

- **Any information:** In essence, the GDPR considers any data that can be used to identify an individual as personal data. It includes, for the first time, things such as genetic, mental, cultural, economic, and social information. There may be a wide variety in terms of the nature and content of the information, as well as its technical format.

- **Relating to:** This phrase implies that the regulation applies to information that relates to an individual on the basis of its content, purpose, or result. This phrase also covers information that may have an impact on the way in which an individual is treated or evaluated.

- **Identified or identifiable:** Recital 26 states that to determine whether a person is identifiable, account should be taken of all the means reasonably likely to be used to identify the person. To ascertain whether means are reasonably likely to be used to identify the natural person, account should be taken of all objective factors, such as the costs of and the amount of time required for identification, taking into consideration the available technology at the time of the processing and technological developments. Thus, personal data include not only data that by itself identifies a person but also data that, together with other available information and means, can be used to identify the person. The principles of protection do not apply to data rendered anonymous in such a way that the data subject is no longer identifiable.

- **Natural person:** Personal data apply to natural persons, not to non-human legal persons.

In the United States and many other countries, a somewhat restrictive view is taken of PII, which frequently focuses on whether the data is actually linked to an *identified* person. However, EU privacy laws and regulations, culminating in the GDPR, are more expansive and broadly define PII to encompass all data that can be used to make a person *identifiable*. As pointed out in "Reconciling Personal Information in the United States and European Union," from the *California Law Review* [SCHW14], in the EU interpretation, "even if the data alone cannot be linked to a specific individual, if it is reasonably possible to use the data in combination with other information to identify a person, then the information is PII."

The regulation does not apply in certain cases, such as in some cases related to national security, foreign policy, or certain law enforcement activities of member states. In addition, the regulation does not apply to a natural person in the course of a purely personal or household activity.

Territorial Scope

The processing of EU residents' data anywhere in the world is subject to the GDPR. The GDPR applies to organizations that are established solely outside EU territory if they "(i) offer goods or services to EU residents; or (ii) monitor the behavior of EU residents." Table 14.3 illustrates the territorial scope requirement. Note that a business unit within an organization needs to consider whether any other entity—whether in the same organization or another organization—with which it collaborates in the processing of data is covered by the GDPR.

TABLE 14.3   Territorial Scope of the GDPR

Who	Doing What	Whose Personal Data	Processed Where	For What
Data controller or processor established in the EU	Processing personal data	Belonging to natural persons	Within or outside the EU	In the context of the activities of the establishment
Data controller or processor established outside the EU	Processing personal data	Belonging to natural persons who are in the EU	Within or outside the EU	Related to offering goods/services (paid or free) OR Relating to monitoring the behavior of natural persons taking place within the EU
Data controller established outside the EU	Processing personal data	Belonging to natural persons	Outside the EU, but member state law applies because of public international law	Diplomatic mission or consular position

The subject of territorial scope is a complex one. Two useful sources are the EDPB document *Guidelines 3/2018 on the Territorial Scope of the GDPR (Article 3)* and "What Does Territorial Scope Mean Under the GDPR?" from *The Privacy Advisor* [KISH18].

14.4 GDPR Principles

The GDPR is built on a foundation of principles and rights (see Figure 14.1). The principles drive the development of an organization's privacy policies and controls, and the rights of data subjects define the constraints on the collection, processing, and storage of personal data. This section examines GDPR principles, and Section 14.5 discusses rights of data subjects.

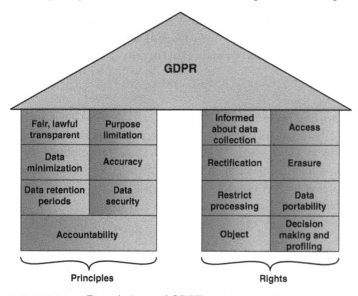

FIGURE 14.1 Foundations of GDPR

Chapter 2 of the GDPR defines a set of principles that govern the processing of personal data. These principles are similar to the fair information practice principles (FIPPs) set forth by the OECD (see Table 3.2 in Chapter 3, "Information Privacy Requirements and Guidelines") and consist of the following:

- **Fair, lawful, and transparent processing:** The requirement to process personal data fairly and lawfully is extensive. It includes, for example, an obligation to tell data subjects what their personal data will be used for.

- **Purpose limitation:** Personal data collected for one purpose should not be used for a new, incompatible, purpose. Further processing of personal data for archiving, scientific, historical, or statistical purposes is permitted, subject to appropriate laws and regulations.

- **Data minimization:** Subject to limited exceptions, an organization should process only personal data that it actually needs to process in order to achieve its processing purposes.

- **Accuracy:** Personal data must be accurate and, where necessary, kept up to date. Every reasonable step must be taken to ensure that personal data that are inaccurate are either erased or rectified without delay.

- **Storage limitation:** Personal data must be kept in a form that permits identification of data subjects for no longer than is necessary for the purposes for which the data were collected or for which they are further processed. Data subjects have the right to erasure of personal data, in some cases sooner than the end of the maximum retention period.

- **Integrity and confidentiality:** Technical and organizational measures must be taken to protect personal data against accidental or unlawful destruction or accidental loss, alteration, unauthorized disclosure, or access

- **Accountability:** The controller is obliged to demonstrate that its processing activities are compliant with the data protection principles.

This section elaborates on some key aspects of these principles.

Fairness

Organization should collect and process data in the spirit of fairness to the data subjects. The GDPR does not explicitly indicate what is meant by the term *fair*. The EDPB document *Guidelines on Automated Individual Decision-Making and Profiling for the Purposes of Regulation 2016/679 (wp251rev.01)* discusses the potential for profiling to be unfair and create discrimination, such as by denying people access to employment opportunities, credit, or insurance or by targeting them with excessively risky or costly financial products. Under the GDPR, **profiling** is any automated evaluation of a natural person, especially when the goal of the processing is predictive or used for targeting purposes. Profiling works by creating derived or inferred data about individuals that has not been provided directly by the data subjects themselves. Individuals have different levels of comprehension and may find it challenging to understand the complex techniques involved in profiling and automated decision-making processes.

The document gives the example of a data broker that sells consumer profiles to financial companies without consumer permission or knowledge of the underlying data. The data broker puts individuals into categories based on their personal data and may put them at an unwarranted financial disadvantage.

In general, processing that may cause injury to an individual or a group of individuals may be unfair. For example, a resume-aggregating service may collect and use an individual's gender as a factor in matching applicants to employers, but the algorithm used may be inadvertently biased against women.

Another aspect of the principle of fairness relates to the reasonable expectations of the data subject. This includes the data subjects understanding the possible adverse consequences of personal data that are processed for a given purpose (Recital 47). It also includes that the controller should have due regard to the relationship and potential effects of imbalance between the data subject and the controller with respect to processing personal data for purposes other than the original one (Recital 50).

Lawful

The GDPR requires an organization to identify a legal basis for processing at the time of collection, before processing occurs, and must furnish the data subject with both the purpose of the processing and its legal basis at the time data are collected. Article 6 lays out six different legal bases that satisfy the lawfulness requirement. At least one of the following must apply:

- The data subject has given informed consent to the processing of his or her personal data for one or more specific purposes. Note that consent is only one alternative for lawfulness. WP259 (*Guidelines on Consent Under Regulation 2016/679*) provides a detailed discussion of this topic.

- Processing is necessary for the performance of a contract to which the data subject is party or in order to take steps at the request of the data subject prior to entering into a contract.

- Processing is necessary for compliance with a legal obligation to which the controller is subject.

- Processing is necessary in order to protect the vital interests of the data subject or of another natural person.

- Processing is necessary for the performance of a task carried out in the public interest or in the exercise of official authority vested in the controller.

- Processing is necessary for the purposes of the legitimate interests pursued by the controller or by a third party, except where such interests are overridden by the interests or fundamental rights and freedoms of the data subject, which require protection of personal data, in particular where the data subject is a child.

Transparency

Transparency implies that the organization provide data subjects with information about the processing of their personal data that complies with the following rules:

- It must be concise, intelligible, and easily accessible.

- Clear and plain language must be used.

- The requirement for clear and plain language is of particular importance when providing information to children.

- It must be in writing or by other means, including, where appropriate, by electronic means.

- Where requested by the data subject, it may be provided orally.

- It must be provided free of charge.

The EDPB document *Guidelines on Transparency Under Regulation 2016/679 (wp260rev.01)* gives a number of examples that satisfy the transparency requirement, including discussing privacy notices on websites. A link to this privacy statement/notice should be clearly visible on each page of a website under a commonly used term (such as *Privacy*, *Privacy Policy*, or *Data Protection Notice*). Positioning or color schemes that make a text or link less noticeable or hard to find on a web page are not considered easily accessible.

14.5 Restrictions on Certain Types of Personal Data

The GDPR imposes two special restrictions on the types of personal data that may be collected and processed: children's personal data and special categories of personal data.

Children's Personal Data

The GDPR provides enhanced protection for children under the age of 16 because, compared to adults, they may be less aware of the risks, consequences, and safeguards concerned and of their rights in relation to the processing of personal data. Article 8 of the GDPR applies when both of the following conditions are met:

- The processing is based on consent (i.e., the processing is based on the first of the alternative conditions for lawfulness described in Section 14.4).

■ The processing is related to the offer of information society services directly to a child under the age of 16. The term *information society services* covers contracts and other services that are concluded or transmitted online.

If these two conditions are met, then collection and/or processing of a child's PII is lawful only if and to the extent that consent is given or authorized by the holder of parental responsibility over the child. Figure 14.2 illustrates the Article 8 conditions.

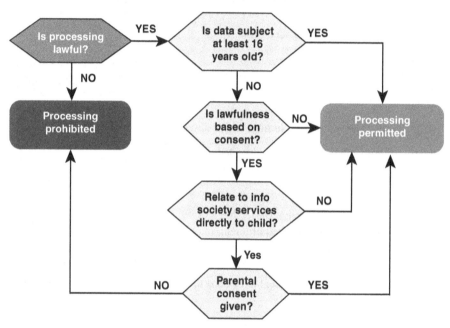

FIGURE 14.2   Conditions Applicable to a Child's Consent

Special Categories of Personal Data

The term *special categories of data* refers to data that are particularly sensitive in relation to fundamental rights and freedoms and merit specific protection as the context of their processing could create significant risks to the fundamental rights and freedoms. Article 9 lists the following:

> Personal data revealing racial or ethnic origin, political opinions, religious or philosophical beliefs, or trade-union membership, and the processing of genetic data, biometric data for the purpose of uniquely identifying a natural person, data concerning health or data concerning a natural person's sex life or sexual orientation.

Two separate conditions must be satisfied in order to process special category data (see Figure 14.3).

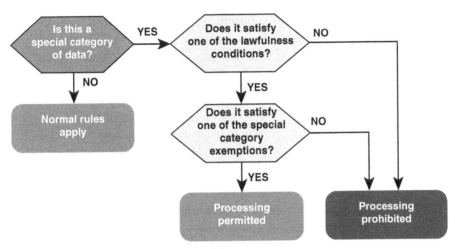

FIGURE 14.3 Conditions for Processing Special Category Personal Data

First, there must be a lawful basis using one of the six conditions defined in Article 6 (listed in Section 14.4). Second, one of the following 10 conditions must be met:

(a) The data subject has given explicit consent to the processing of those personal data for one or more specified purposes, except where Union or Member State law provide that the prohibition referred to in paragraph 1 may not be lifted by the data subject;

(b) Processing is necessary for the purposes of carrying out the obligations and exercising specific rights of the controller or of the data subject in the field of employment and social security and social protection law in so far as it is authorized by Union or Member State law or a collective agreement pursuant to Member State law providing for appropriate safeguards for the fundamental rights and the interests of the data subject;

(c) Processing is necessary to protect the vital interests of the data subject or of another natural person where the data subject is physically or legally incapable of giving consent;

(d) Processing is carried out in the course of its legitimate activities with appropriate safeguards by a foundation, association, or any other not-for-profit body with a political, philosophical, religious, or trade union aim and on condition that the processing relates solely to the members or to former members of the body or to persons who have regular contact with it in connection with its purposes and that the personal data are not disclosed outside that body without the consent of the data subjects;

(e) Processing relates to personal data that are manifestly made public by the data subject;

(f) Processing is necessary for the establishment, exercise, or defense of legal claims or whenever courts are acting in their judicial capacity;

(g) Processing is necessary for reasons of substantial public interest, on the basis of Union or Member State law, which shall be proportionate to the aim pursued, respect the essence of the right to data protection, and provide for suitable and specific measures to safeguard the fundamental rights and the interests of the data subject;

(h) Processing is necessary for the purposes of preventive or occupational medicine, for the assessment of the working capacity of the employee, medical diagnosis, the provision of health or social care or treatment or the management of health or social care systems and services on the basis of Union or Member State law or pursuant to contract with a health professional and subject to the conditions and safeguards detailed in Article 9;

(i) Processing is necessary for reasons of public interest in the area of public health, such as protecting against serious cross-border threats to health or ensuring high standards of quality and safety of health care and of medicinal products or medical devices, on the basis of Union or Member State law, which provides for suitable and specific measures to safeguard the rights and freedoms of the data subject, in particular professional secrecy;

(j) Processing is necessary for archiving purposes in the public interest, scientific or historical research purposes, or statistical purposes in accordance with Article 89(1) based on Union or Member State law, which shall be proportionate to the aim pursued, respect the essence of the right to data protection, and provide for suitable and specific measures to safeguard the fundamental rights and the interests of the data subject.

Note that the choice of lawful basis under Article 6 does not dictate which special category condition an organization must apply and vice versa. The *Data Protection Impact Assessments* from the U.K. Information Commissioner's Office [ICO18] gives several examples: If you use consent as your lawful basis, you are not restricted to using explicit consent for special category processing under Article 9. You should choose whichever special category condition is the most appropriate in the circumstances—although in many cases there may well be an obvious link between the two. For example, if your lawful basis is vital interests, it is highly likely that the Article 9 condition for vital interests will also be appropriate.

14.6   Rights of the Data Subject

Chapter 3 of the GDPR enumerates the following rights of data subjects:

- **The right to be informed where personal data are collected from the data subject:** The controller should, at the time when personal data are obtained, provide the data subject with information about the collection and use of the subject's personal data, including identity and the contact details of the controller, contact details of the data protection officer, purposes of the processing for which the personal data are intended as well as the legal basis for the processing; recipients or categories of recipients of the personal data, if any; and, where applicable, the fact that the controller intends to transfer personal data to a third country or international organization, reference to the appropriate or suitable safeguards, and the means by which to obtain a copy of them or where they have been made available.

- **The right to be informed where personal data have not been collected from the data subject:** The controller must provide the same information as listed in the preceding bullet within a reasonable time period of obtaining the personal data from another source.

- **The right of access by the data subject:** The controller must allow a data subject access to personal data held by the controller. The GDPR requires that responses be within a month, generally without charge, and with additional information, such as data retention periods.

- **The right to rectification:** Individuals have the right to have inaccurate personal data corrected or completed if they are incomplete.

- **The right to erasure (right to be forgotten):** Individuals have the right to have their personal data erased, subject to certain restrictions.

- **The right to restrict processing:** Individuals have the right to request the restriction or suppression of their personal data. Methods by which to restrict the processing of personal data could include temporarily moving the selected data to another processing system, making the selected personal data unavailable to users, or temporarily removing published data from a website.

- **The right to data portability:** The right to data portability allows individuals to obtain and reuse their personal data for their own purposes across different services. It allows them to move, copy, or transfer personal data easily from one IT environment to another in a safe and secure way, without affecting its usability. Doing this enables individuals to take advantage of applications and services that can use this data to find them a better deal or help them understand their spending habits.

- **The right to object:** The data subject has the right to object, on grounds relating to his or her situation, at any time to processing of personal data concerning him or her. The controller cannot process unless demonstrating legitimate grounds for the processing that override the interests, rights, and freedoms of the data subject.

- **Rights in relation to automated decision making and profiling:** Profiling involves (1) automated processing of personal data and (2) using that personal data to evaluate certain personal aspects relating to a natural person. Specific examples include analyzing or predicting aspects concerning that natural person's performance at work, economic situation, health, personal preferences, interests, reliability, behavior, location, or movements. An organization can only carry out this type of decision-making where the decision is any of the following:

  - Necessary for the entry into or performance of a contract

  - Authorized by union or member state law applicable to the controller

  - Based on the individual's explicit consent

14.7   Controller, Processor, and Data Protection Officer

Chapter 4 of the GDPR covers a number of topics related to the responsibilities of the controller, the processor, and the data protection officer. This section focuses on topics that are particularly relevant to this book.

Data Protection by Design and Default

Article 25 mandates the following responsibilities of the controller:

- **Data protection by design:** The controller should implement appropriate technical and organizational measures, both at the design phase of the processing and at its operation, that satisfy the requirements articulated in the data protection principles. De-identification is an example of a technical measure; privacy awareness is an example of an organizational measure.

- **Data protection by default:** The technical and organizational measures should ensure that, by default, only personal data that are necessary for each specific purpose of the processing are processed.

An advisory opinion issued by the European Data Protection Supervisor [EDPS18] distinguishes between these concepts and the concept of privacy by design, which is discussed in Chapter 2. In essence, the EDPS uses the term *privacy by design* to designate the broad range of measures for ensuring privacy. *Data protection by design* and *data protection by default* designate specific legal obligations under the GDPR and may not encompass the wider visionary and ethical considerations of privacy by design.

Data Protection by Design

The European Data Protection Supervisor [EDPS18] lists the following dimensions of obligation for data protection by design:

- **Outcome of a design project:** The design process should encompass the whole system development life cycle and focus on the protection of individuals and their personal data consistent with project requirements and the GDPR.

- **Risk management approach:** The organization should implement a privacy risk management approach, including a data protection impact assessment.

- **Appropriate and effective measures:** The effectiveness is to be benchmarked against the purpose of those measures: to ensure and be able to demonstrate compliance with the GDPR; to implement the data protection principles; and to protect the rights of individuals whose data are processed.

- **Safeguards integrated into the processing:** The organizational and technical measures should not be after-the-fact add-ons but should be effectively integrated into the system.

Useful sources of guidance by which an organization can ensure that it has adequately met the data protection by design requirement are ISO 28151 (*Code of Practice for Personally Identifiable Information*) and NIST SP 800-122 (*Guide to Protecting the Confidentiality of Personally Identifiable Information*).

Data Protection by Default

Data protection by default requires an organization to ensure that it processes only the data that are necessary to achieve its specific purpose. It links to the fundamental data protection principles of data minimization and purpose limitation.

The European Data Protection Supervisor [EDPS18] gives the example of an app for car sharing. The user expects that his or her location is used for the individual to know where the closest car is parked and that the user's contact details will be used to get in touch with the user in the context of the service. But, by default, the user's location and contact details should not be sent over to local bike sellers so they can send the user advertising and offers.

Records of Processing Activities

The GDPR contains explicit provisions concerning the documenting of an organization's personal data processing activities. Each controller must maintain a record that includes:

- The name and contact details of the controller and, where applicable, the joint controller, the controller's representative, and the data protection officer

- The purposes of the processing

- A description of the categories of data subjects and of the categories of personal data

- The categories of recipients to whom the personal data have been or will be disclosed, including recipients in third countries or international organizations

- Where applicable, transfers of personal data to a third country or an international organization, including the identification of that third country or international organization and the documentation of appropriate safeguards

- Where possible, the envisaged time limits for erasure of the different categories of data

- Where possible, a general description of the technical and organizational security measures implemented

Processors must maintain a similar record. This documentation must be provided to the supervisory authority. Although there is some burden imposed by this requirement, it can help an organization comply with other aspects of the GDPR and improve data governance.

Article 30 does provide the potential for exemption for small businesses and other organizations. Specifically, the record-keeping requirement does not apply to an enterprise or an organization employing fewer than 250 persons unless one of the following conditions exist:

- The processing it carries out is likely to result in a risk to the rights and freedoms of data subjects.

- The processing is not occasional. The term occasional is not defined in the GDPR or any of the guidance documents. Occasional processing can be considered as processing which is coincidental, unforeseen, or not usual (e.g. processing activities relating to customer management, human resources, or supplier management). Accordingly, the term not occasional corresponds roughly to the term regular, which is defined in WP243 as meaning one or more of the following:

  - ongoing or occurring at particular intervals for a particular period

  - recurring or repeated at fixed times

  - constantly or periodically taking place

- The processing includes special categories of data, as referred to in Article 9 (discussed in Section 14.5), or personal data related to criminal convictions and offences.

Figure 14.4 illustrates the conditions of Article 30.

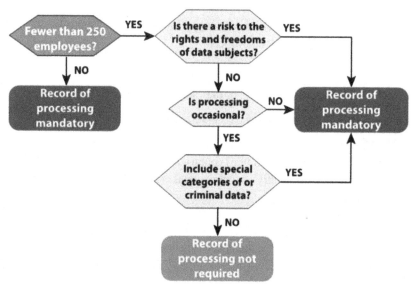

FIGURE 14.4   Conditions for Maintaining a Record of Processing Activities

Security of Processing

Security of processing is a foundational principle of the GDPR. Article 5 mandates that personal data shall be processed in a manner that ensures appropriate security of the personal data, including protection against unauthorized or unlawful processing and against accidental loss, destruction, or damage. This principle is further incorporated in Article 32, which mandates the implementation of appropriate technical and organizational measures to ensure a level of security appropriate to the risk. Article 32 lists the following specific measures:

- The pseudonymization and encryption of personal data

- The ability to ensure the ongoing confidentiality, integrity, availability, and resilience of processing systems and services

- The ability to restore the availability and access to personal data in a timely manner in the event of a physical or technical incident

- A process for regularly testing, assessing, and evaluating the effectiveness of technical and organizational measures for ensuring the security of the processing

Useful sources of guidance by which an organization can ensure that it has adequately met the security requirement are ISO 27001 (*Information Security Management Systems—Requirements*) and ISO 27002 (*Code of Practice for Information Security Controls*).

Data Protection Officer

The GDPR mandates that many organizations subject to the regulation must appoint a data protection officer (DPO). An organization should designate a DPO on the basis of professional qualities and, in particular, expert knowledge of data protection law and practices.

When Organizations Need a DPO

Article 37 mandates that the controller and/or processor must designate a DPO if one of these conditions is met:

- The processing is carried out by a public authority or body, except for courts acting in their judicial capacity.

- The organization's core activities consist of processing that requires regular and systematic monitoring of data subjects on a large scale.

- The organization's core activities consist of processing on a large scale special categories of data, as defined in Article 9, or personal data related to criminal convictions and offenses.

Three terms need to be clarified here: regular and systematic monitoring, large scale, and special categories of data.

The term *regular and systematic monitoring* includes the following concepts:

- **Monitoring:** This includes all forms of tracking and profiling on the Internet, including for the purposes of behavioral advertising. Monitoring also encompasses offline tracking and profiling using personal data collected by an organization.

- **Regular:** As discussed above, this term refers to an activity that is ongoing or that occurs at periodic intervals.

- **Systematic:** The term refers to an activity that is in some sense an integral part of a data collection and processing activity.

Neither Article 37 nor the relevant Recital 97 provides specific guidance on what constitutes *large scale*. The EDPB guidance document *Guidelines on Data Protection Officers (wp243rev.01)* indicates that an organization should consider the following factors in determining whether processing is on a large scale:

- The number of data subjects concerned, either as a specific number or as a proportion of the relevant population

- The volume of data and/or the range of different data items being processed

- The duration, or permanence, of the data processing activity

- The geographical extent of the processing activity

The document provides the following as examples of large-scale processing:

- Processing of patient data in the regular course of business by a hospital

- Processing of travel data of individuals using a city's public transport system (e.g., tracking via travel cards)

- Processing of real-time geolocation data of customers of an international fast food chain for statistical purposes by a processor specialized in providing these services

- Processing of customer data in the regular course of business by an insurance company or a bank

- Processing of personal data for behavioral advertising by a search engine

- Processing of data (content, traffic, location) by telephone providers or Internet service providers

Thus, a hospital, social media site, or mobile fitness app probably needs a DPO with several years of experience in privacy law and compliance, while a hair salon probably does not. Large multinational organizations are likely to need to appoint a DPO with advanced professional credentials—perhaps even a law degree—while smaller organizations may be able to appoint someone who can use on-the-job training time to gain the knowledge required to fulfill the DPO duties.

The term *special categories of data* is discussed in Section 14.5

Tasks of the DPO

Guidelines on Data Protection Officers ("DPOs") [WP243] lists the following as tasks for which the DPO is responsible:

- **Monitor compliance with the GDPR:** Inform, advise, and issue recommendations to the employer regarding GDPR compliance.

- **Support the data protection impact assessment (DPIA) process:** Advise the controller and/or processor on the following aspects of the DPIA:

  - Whether or not to carry out a DPIA

  - What methodology to follow when carrying out a DPIA

  - Whether to carry out a DPIA in-house or outsource it

  - What safeguards (including technical and organizational measures) to apply to mitigate any risks to the rights and interests of the data subjects

  - Whether or not the DPIA has been correctly carried out and whether its conclusions (whether or not to go ahead with the processing and what safeguards to apply) comply with the GDPR

- **Cooperate with the supervisory authority:** Act as a contact point to facilitate access by the supervisory authority to the documents and information it needs.

- **Follow a risk-based approach:** Prioritize activities and focus efforts on issues that present higher data protection risks.

- **Support record keeping:** Maintain the record of processing operations under the responsibility of the controller as one of the tools enabling compliance monitoring, informing, and advising the controller or the processor.

14.8   Data Protection Impact Assessment

Article 35 mandates the use of a data protection impact assessment (DPIA) under certain conditions and describes the content of such an assessment. A DPIA is equivalent to a privacy impact assessment (PIA), which Chapter 11, "Risk Management and Privacy Impact Assessment." of this book covers in detail.

Risk and High Risk

The GDPR frequently uses the term *risk*, which is not defined in the regulation. Recital 75 indicates that the types of risk to be considered are risks "to the rights and freedoms of natural persons, of varying likelihood and severity, which may result from personal data processing and could lead to physical, material, or non-material damage." The recital includes the following examples:

- Discrimination

- Identity theft or fraud

- Financial loss

- Damage to the reputation

- Loss of confidentiality of personal data protected by professional secrecy

- Unauthorized reversal of pseudonymization

- Any other significant economic or social disadvantage by which data subjects might be deprived of their rights and freedoms or prevented from exercising control over their personal data

- Where personal data processed reveal racial or ethnic origin, political opinions, religion or philosophical beliefs, or trade union membership

- The processing of genetic data, data concerning health or sex life, or data concerning criminal convictions and offenses or related security measures

- Where personal aspects are evaluated, in particular analyzing or predicting aspects concerning performance at work, economic situation, health, personal preferences or interests, reliability or behavior, location, or movements, in order to create or use personal profiles

- Where personal data of vulnerable natural persons—in particular of children—are processed

- Where processing involves a large amount of personal data and affects a large number of data subjects

Each of the risks listed here can become high risk, depending on the likelihood and severity of the risks as determined in a risk assessment process by reference to the nature, scope, context, and purpose of processing.

Determining Whether a DPIA Is Needed

The process of determining whether a DPIA is needed is equivalent to the privacy threshold analysis discussed in Chapter 11. Under the GDPR, a DPIA is mandatory for a processing operation in which processing is likely to result in a high risk to the rights and freedoms of natural persons.

The following are categories where a DPIA may be required:

- When the personal data being processed could pose a high risk to the data subjects if an incident were to occur (Recital 84)

- Prior to the first time any new business process involving personal data is completed (Recital 90)

- Where a business process involving personal data has not undergone a DPIA in the past (Recital 90)

- When processing old data sets or personal data (Recital 90)

- When personal data, including IP addresses, are being used to make decisions regarding a data subject (Profiling) (Recital 91)

- When public areas are being monitored on a large scale (Recital 91)

- When sensitive categories of data, criminal data, or national security data are being processed on a large scale (Recital 91)

- When a business process incorporates a new technology (Article 35)

- When a business process involves automated decision making (Article 35)

- When the processing of personal data involves the systematized processing of personal data. (Article 35)

- When there is a change of the risk represented by processing operations (Article 35)

Figure 14.5, from the *Guidelines on Data Protection Impact Assessment (wp248rev.01)*, illustrates the principles related to the decision to use a DPIA.

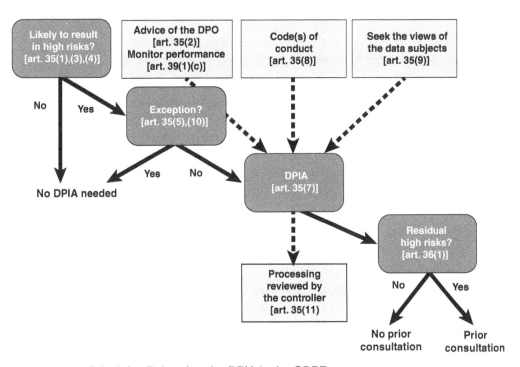

FIGURE 14.5 Principles Related to the DPIA in the GDPR

If the processor or controller determines that this process involves a high risk, a DPIA has to be carried out unless one of two exception categories apply:

- The supervisory authority may define a set of processing operations that do not require a DPIA.

- If the organization has already carried out a DPIA as part of a general impact assessment mandated by some EU or member state law, it need not carry out the DPIA.

As discussed in Chapter 11, a DPIA involves an assessment of data protection risk and a determination of risk treatment. One of the risk treatment options (refer to Figure 11.6) is risk retention, in which the controller accepts the cost from a risk. Another option is partial mitigation of the risk identified for the processing operation. In either case, if the resulting risk treatment plan leaves a residual high risk, the data controller must seek prior consultation for the processing from the supervisory authority. As part of this, the DPIA must be fully provided to the supervisory authority, which may provide its advice. This amounts to a prior authorization requirement.

The lighter-shaded boxes in Figure 14.5 indicate background or supporting tasks, including the following:

- The DPO should provide advice to the controller regarding the DPIA and should monitor the DPIA process to ensure that it satisfies the GDPR.

- The controller should perform the DPIA in conformance with a code of conduct that has been defined by the organization. GDPR codes are voluntary accountability tools that set out specific data protection rules for categories of controllers and processors. They can be useful and effective accountability tools, providing a detailed description of the most appropriate, legal, and ethical set of behaviors of a sector. From a data protection viewpoint, codes can therefore operate as a rule book for controllers and processors who design and implement GDPR-compliant data processing activities, which give operational meaning to the principles of data protection set out in European and national law.

- Where appropriate, the controller should seek the views of data subjects or their representatives on the intended processing, without prejudice to the protection of commercial or public interests or the security of processing operations.

- Where necessary, the controller should carry out a review to assess whether processing is performed in accordance with the DPIA, at least when there is a change in the risk represented by processing operations.

DPIA Process

Figure 14.6, from the *Guidelines on Data Protection Impact Assessment* [WP248], illustrates the recommended process for carrying out a DPIA, which includes the following steps:

FIGURE 14.6   Iterative Process for Carrying Out a DPIA

1. **Description of the envisaged processing:** This is a systematic description of the processing operation and its purposes. It should include the following:

   - A description of how the organization will collect, use, store, and delete personal data and whether personal data will be shared with third parties. A useful way to describe the processing is by using a flow diagram, as described in Chapter 11.

   - A definition of the scope of the processing, including the nature of the personal data, how much will be collected and processed, how long the data will be stored, and how many individuals will be affected.

2. **Assessment of the necessity and proportionality:** This is a justification of the details of the processing operation in relation to the purposes.

3. **Measures already envisaged:** This documents the security and privacy controls already planned for this processing.

4. **Assessment of the risks to the rights and freedoms:** This is a risk assessment that considers impact and likelihood. Chapter 11 addresses this process in detail.

5. **Measures envisaged to address the risk:** This risk treatment plan documents the security and privacy controls used to mitigate the risks. The treatment plan should document how the controls ensure the protection of personal data and comply with the GDPR.

6. **Documentation:** The summary should include a complete description of the risk treatment plan, a description of residual risks, and a summary of DPO advice, if any.

7. **Monitoring and review:** The DPO should monitor the DPIA process, and the controller should carry out a review to assess whether processing is performed in accordance with the DPIA.

GDPR Requirements

A document from the Smart Grid Task Force of the European Commission [SGTF18] provides a checklist to be used in the DPIA process to verify that the process or application complies with the relevant GDPR rules and to document how such compliance is achieved. Although this document addresses the smart grid environment, the checklist applies generally to any DPIA.

The checklist includes the following items:

- Purpose limitation (Article 5)

- Data minimization (Article 5)

- Storage limitation (Article 5)

- Integrity and confidentiality (Article 5)

- Accurate and up-to-date data (Article 5)

- Processing based on lawfulness conditions provided by the GDPR (Article 6)

- Where the processing is based on consent, consent of the data subject to processing of his or her personal data (Article 7)

- Processing of special categories of personal data according to the measures provided by the GDPR (Article 9)

- Information provided to the data subject by the data controller (Articles 13 and 14)

- The guaranteed right of access by the data subject (Article 15)

- The guaranteed right to rectification (Article 16)

- The guaranteed right to erasure (Article 17)

- The guaranteed right to restriction of processing (Article 18)

- Whether recipients of the personal data are sent notification when the data subject requested a rectification, erasure, or restriction of processing and whether a procedure is available (Article 19)

- The guaranteed right of data portability (Article 20)

- The guaranteed right to object to a processing (Article 21)

- The right to object to a decision based solely on automated processing, including profiling (if applicable) (Article 22)

- Principles of data protection by design and data protection by default (Article 25)

- An agreement with eventual joint controllers (Article 26)

- An appointed processor that provides guarantees to implement appropriate technical and organizational measures and ensure the protection of the rights of the data subjects (Article 28)

- Those in charge of the processing acting under instructions of the controller (Article 29)

- Records of processing activities (Article 30)

- Security measures (Article 32)

- Procedures for dealing with data breaches and notification of breaches to the supervisory authority or to the affected individuals (if applicable) (Articles 33 and 34)

- A preexisting DPIA (Article 35)

- A prior consultation (Article 36)

- An appointed DPO (Article 37)

- A code of conduct for the data controller or data processor (Article 40)

- Data controller or data processor certification (Article 42)

- Transfer of personal data outside the EU according to the GDPR provisions (Articles 44–49)

In the DPIA, the controller should indicate whether the system is in compliance with each item and provide a rationale or description.

Criteria for an Acceptable DPIA

Guidelines on Data Protection Impact Assessment [WP248] proposes that data controllers can use the following criteria to assess whether a DPIA, or a methodology to carry out a DPIA, is sufficiently comprehensive to comply with the GDPR:

- Provides a systematic description of the processing:

  - Takes into account the nature, scope, context, and purposes of the processing

  - Records the personal data, recipients, and the period for which the personal data will be stored

  - Provides a functional description of the processing operation

  - Identifies the assets on which personal data rely (e.g., hardware, software, networks, people, paper, paper transmission channels)

  - Complies with approved codes of conduct

- Describes and assesses the necessity and proportionality of measures contributing to the processing on the basis of:
  - Specified, explicit, and legitimate purpose(s)
  - Lawfulness of processing
  - Adequate, relevant, and limited to what is necessary data
  - Limited storage duration
- Describes and assesses the necessity and proportionality measures contributing to the rights of the data subjects:
  - Information provided to the data subject
  - Right of access and to data portability
  - Right to rectification and to erasure
  - Right to object to restriction of processing
  - Relationships with processors
  - Safeguards surrounding international transfer(s)
  - Prior consultation
- Appreciates the origin, nature, particularity, and severity of data protection risks. More specifically, the DPIA addresses each risk (illegitimate access, undesired modification, and disappearance of data) from the perspective of the data subjects:
  - Takes into account risks sources
  - Identifies potential impacts to the rights and freedoms of data subjects, in case of events including illegitimate access, undesired modification, and disappearance of data
  - Identifies threats that could lead to illegitimate access, undesired modification, and disappearance of data
  - Estimates likelihood and severity (Recital 90)
- Determines measures envisaged to treat the risks in the preceding list.
- Involves interested parties:
  - Seeks the advice of the DPO
  - Seeks the views of data subjects or their representatives, where appropriate

14.9 Key Terms and Review Questions

Key Terms

article	legal person
controller	material scope
data protection by default	natural person
data protection by design	processor profiling
data protection impact assessment (DPIA)	recital
data protection officer (DPO)	risk
data subject	supervisory authority
fairness	territorial scope
General Data Protection Regulation (GDPR)	third party
high risk	transparent
lawful	

Review Questions

1. What is the difference between a natural person and a legal person?

2. What is the difference between a controller and a processor?

3. List some of the key responsibilities of a DPO.

4. What is the difference between an article and a recital in the GDPR?

5. List and briefly describe the main objectives of the GDPR.

6. Explain the concepts of material scope and territorial scope.

7. List and briefly describe the GDPR principles.

8. Explain the concept of fairness in the GDPR.

9. List and briefly describe rights of data subjects enumerated in the GDPR.

10. What is the difference between data protection by design and data protection by default?

11. What is meant in the GDPR by the term *processing on a large scale*?

12. Distinguish between the concepts of risk and high risk.

13. List and briefly describe the key steps in carrying out a DPIA.

14.10 References

EDPS18: European Data Protection Supervisor. *Preliminary Opinion on Privacy by Design.* Opinion 5/2018, May 31, 2018. https://iapp.org/media/pdf/resource_center/Preliminary_Opinion_on_Privacy_by_Design.pdf

ICO18: U.K. Information Commissioner's Office. *Data Protection Impact Assessments.* 2018. https://ico.org.uk/for-organisations/guide-to-data-protection/guide-to-the-general-data-protection-regulation-gdpr/data-protection-impact-assessments-dpias/

KISH18: Kish, K. "What Does Territorial Scope Mean Under the GDPR?" *The Privacy Advisor*, January 23, 2018. https://iapp.org/news/a/what-does-territorial-scope-mean-under-the-gdpr/

SCHW14: Schwartz, P, and Solove, D. "Reconciling Personal Information in the United States and European Union." *California Law Review*, Vol. 102, No. 4, August 2014.

SGTF18: Smart Grids Task Force of the European Commission. *Data Protection Impact Assessment Template for Smart Grid and Smart Metering Systems.* September 13, 2018. https://ec.europa.eu/energy/en/topics/markets-and-consumers/smart-grids-and-meters/smart-grids-task-force/data-protection-impact-assessment-smart-grid-and-smart-metering-environment

Chapter | **15**

U.S. Privacy Laws

Learning Objectives

After studying this chapter, you should be able to:

- Discuss the main differences between the information privacy environment in the United States and in the European Union
- Describe the key federal laws related to privacy
- Give a presentation on HIPPA
- Give a presentation on HITECH
- Give a presentation on COPPA
- Compare the GDPR and the California Consumer Privacy Act

The characteristics of privacy law in the United States contrast sharply with the situation within the European Union. The EU depends on a single regulation, the General Data Protection Regulation (GDPR), which is common across all member states, each of which has a supervisory authority or data protection authority to monitor and enforce the regulation. The GDPR came into effect in 2018, and particularly in the area of information privacy, it embraces modern concepts of privacy by design and privacy engineering. For example, the GDPR mandates the use of data protection impact assessments (DPIAs) and provides requirements and guidance on the DPIA process and the content of a DPIA report.

The U.S. privacy landscape consists of a variety of federal and state privacy laws and regulations, some dating back to the 1970s, as well as common law created by judicial precedent. Typically, each privacy law regulates privacy matters in a segment of the economy or deals with the responsibilities of government agencies. Many of these laws mandate that various federal agencies issue regulations to flesh out the requirements of the law. These regulations are thus subject to changes in different presidential administrations. Further, a significant range of state privacy laws mimic GDPR's consent compliance burdens, including the recently enacted California Consumer Privacy Act that will be enforced beginning in 2020, as well as even stricter proposed laws in other states that have yet to be enacted.

Section 15.1 provides a brief survey of key U.S. federal privacy laws. Sections 15.2 through 15.4 look at the three federal privacy laws that are perhaps the most significant from the point of view of this book. Finally, Section 15.5 examines the most important and far-reaching state privacy law, the California Consumer Privacy Act.

15.1   A Survey of Federal U.S. Privacy Laws

Table 15.1 lists important federal laws that deal, in whole or in part, with privacy.

TABLE 15.1   U.S. Federal Laws Related to Privacy

Category	Federal Law	Date
Health care	Health Insurance Portability and Accountability Act (HIPAA)	1996
	Health Information Technology for Economic and Clinical Health (HITECH) Act	2009
Genetics research	DNA Identification Act	1994
	Genetic Information Nondiscrimination Act (GINA)	2008
Business/workplace	Children's Online Privacy Protection Act (COPPA)	1998
	Controlling the Assault of Non-Solicited Pornography and Marketing (CAN-SPAM) Act	2003
Financial Sector	Gramm–Leach–Bliley Act (GLBA)	1999
	Fair Credit Reporting Act (FCRA)	1970
	Fair and Accurate Credit Transactions Act	2003
	Right to Financial Privacy Act	1978
Education/students	Family Educational Rights and Privacy Act (FERPA)	1974
Law enforcement	Omnibus Crime Control and Safe Streets Act	1968
	Electronic Communications Privacy Act (EPCA)	1986
National security	The Uniting and Strengthening America by Providing Appropriate Tools Required to Intercept and Obstruct Terrorism Act (USA PATRIOT Act)	2001
	REAL ID Act	2005
Government	Freedom of Information Act (FOIA)	1966
	The Drivers Privacy Protection Act (DPPA)	1994
	Privacy Act of 1974	1974
	Computer Matching and Privacy Protection Act	1988
	E-Government Act	2002
	Federal Information Security Management Act (FISMA)	2002

The following list provides details on the laws listed in Table 15.1:

- **Health Insurance Portability and Accountability Act (HIPAA):** Requires covered entities (such as medical and health insurance providers and their associates) to protect the security and privacy of health records.

- **Health Information Technology for Economic and Clinical Health (HITECH) Act:** Broadens the scope of privacy and security protections under HIPAA and also expands on the penalties for noncompliance.

- **DNA Identification Act:** Specifies the requirements for participation in the National DNA Index System (NDIS) and the DNA data that may be maintained at NDIS, including data on convicted offenders, arrestees, legal detainees, forensic casework, unidentified human remains, missing persons, and relatives of missing persons.

- **Genetic Information Nondiscrimination Act (GINA):** Prohibits discrimination during employer hiring and prohibits insurance companies from denying coverage or charging higher premiums based on the results of genetic tests. It also prevents the disclosure of genetic information, with some exceptions.

- **Children's Online Privacy Protection Act (COPPA):** Gives parents a way to control the online information that is collected from their children under the age of 13. COPPA defines general requirements for website operators to follow and authorizes the Federal Trade Commission (FTC) to promulgate regulations to clarify and implement its requirements.

- **Controlling the Assault of Non-Solicited Pornography and Marketing (CAN-SPAM) Act:** Applies to anyone who advertises products or services via electronic mail. The act prohibits false or misleading headers, deceptive subject lines, and the sending of message to individuals who requested not to receive future emails. It also requires an opt-out function for future emails and that emails warn when they contain sexually oriented materials. The act mandates that opt-out lists, also known as *suppression lists*, be used only for compliance purposes.

- **Gramm–Leach–Bliley Act (GLBA):** Applies to financial institutions and contains privacy and information security provisions that are designed to protect consumer financial data. This law applies to how institutions collect, store, and use financial records containing personally identifiable information (PII) and places restrictions on the disclosure of individuals' nonpublic personal information.

- **Fair Credit Reporting Act (FCRA):** Ensures that consumer reporting agencies exercise their responsibility to adopt reasonable procedures to meet commercial needs in a manner that is fair and equitable to consumers in regard to confidentiality, accuracy, and privacy. FCRA details the information that consumer credit reports may contain and how and by whom a consumer's credit information can be used.

- **Fair and Accurate Credit Transactions Act:** Requires entities engaged in certain kinds of consumer financial transactions to be aware of the warning signs of identity theft and to take steps to respond to suspected incidents of identity theft.

- **Right to Financial Privacy Act:** Entitles bank customers to a limited expectation of privacy in their financial records by requiring that law enforcement officials follow certain procedures before information can be disclosed. Unless a customer consents in writing to the disclosure of his or her financial records, a bank may not produce such records for government inspection unless ordered to do so by an administrative or judicial subpoena or a lawfully executed search warrant.

- **Family Educational Rights and Privacy Act (FERPA):** Protects students and their families by ensuring the privacy of student educational records and ensuring a parent's rights to access his or her child's education records, correct mistakes in those records, and know who has requested or obtained the records. Educational records are agency- or institution-maintained records containing personally identifiable student and educational data. FERPA applies to primary and secondary schools, colleges and universities, vocational colleges, and state and local educational agencies that receive funding under any program administered by the U.S. Department of Education.

- **Omnibus Crime Control and Safe Streets Act:** Governs the use of electronic surveillance in both the public and the private sectors. In the public sector, the act outlines detailed procedures the federal government must follow before conducting any form of electronic surveillance. In the private sector, the act prohibits any person from intentionally using or disclosing information that has been knowingly intercepted by electronic or mechanical means without the consent of the interested person.

- **Electronic Communications Privacy Act (EPCA):** Amends the federal wiretap statute to extend protection against unauthorized interception of specific types of electronic communications, such as email, radio-paging devices, cell phones, private communications carriers, and computer transmissions. It also extends the prohibition on interception to the communications of wire or electronic communication services.

- **The Uniting and Strengthening America by Providing Appropriate Tools Required to Intercept and Obstruct Terrorism Act (USA PATRIOT Act):** Introduces a number of legislative changes that have significantly increased the surveillance and investigative powers of law enforcement agencies in the United States. The law allows financial institutions to share information with one another in order to identify and report activities involving money laundering and terrorist activities. The act does not, however, provide for the system of checks and balances that traditionally safeguards civil liberties in the face of such legislation.

- **REAL ID Act:** Creates a de facto national identification card for the United States. The act establishes new national standards regarding both technological and verification procedures for state-issued driver's licenses and non-driver identification cards to be accepted by the federal government for official purposes, such as boarding commercially operated airline flights and entering federal buildings and nuclear power plants.

■ **Freedom of Information Act (FOIA):** In most instances other than those related to national security, foreign policy, or other classified areas, FOIA guarantees the right of Americans to request a copy of any reasonably identifiable record kept by a federal agency. However, it contains limitations on the disclosure of agency information when such disclosure would constitute a "clearly unwarranted invasion of personal privacy."

■ **The Drivers Privacy Protection Act (DPPA):** Restricts disclosure of personal information obtained by state departments of motor vehicles (DMVs) in connection with a motor vehicle record. A motor vehicle record is defined as "any record that pertains to a motor vehicle operator's permit, motor vehicle title, motor vehicle registration, or identification card issued by a department of motor vehicles." The DPPA specifies when and how state DMVs may disclose such information.

■ **Privacy Act of 1974:** Designed to protect the privacy of records created and used by the federal government. The law states the rules that a federal agency must follow to collect, use, transfer, and disclose an individual's PII. The act also requires agencies to collect and store only the minimum information that they need to conduct their business. In addition, the law requires agencies to give the public notice about any records that it keeps that can be retrieved using a personal identifier (e.g., name or Social Security number).

■ **Computer Matching and Privacy Protection Act:** Amended the Privacy Act of 1974 to specify the requirements for federal agencies matching information on individuals with information held by other federal, state, or local agencies.

■ **E-Government Act:** Requires federal agencies to review and assess the privacy risks to their IT systems and publicly post privacy notices about their data collection practices. This law complements the Privacy Act of 1974 and was intended to promote access to electronic government resources. Under this law, an agency that collects PII must conduct a privacy impact assessment before it collects that information. The privacy impact assessment must specify the data the agency will collect, how it is collecting those data, how it will use and/or share the data, whether individuals have the opportunity to consent to specific uses of the data (e.g., any use not otherwise permitted by law), how the agency will secure the data, and whether the data collected will reside in a system of records as defined by the Privacy Act.

■ **Federal Information Security Management Act (FISMA):** Protects the security of federal information technology systems and the data contained within those systems. This law and its provisions apply to federal agencies and to contractors and affiliates of those agencies. FISMA requires federal agencies to implement risk-based information security programs that conform to certain national standards. It also requires those programs to be independently reviewed each year.

15.2 Health Insurance Portability and Accountability Act

The Health Insurance Portability and Accountability Act of 1996 (HIPAA) is intended to standardize the electronic exchange of health information and to improve the privacy and security of health information. HIPAA applies to health plans, health care clearinghouses, and health care providers that transmit health information electronically (covered entities). HIPAA authorizes the secretary of Health and Human Services (HHS) to issue rules to accomplish the purpose of HIPAA. HIPAA is perhaps the most important federal privacy law because it affects virtually every U.S. resident.

This section provides a brief overview of HIPAA and then focuses on its privacy aspects.

HIPAA Overview

HIPAA has two main goals:

- Mandate continuous health insurance coverage for workers who lose or change their job

- Reduce the administrative burdens and cost of health care by standardizing the electronic transmission and protection of health care–related administrative and financial transactions

The law consists of five titles:

- **Title I: HIPAA Health Insurance Reform:** Protects health insurance coverage for individuals who lose or change jobs. It also prohibits group health plans from denying coverage to individuals with specific diseases and preexisting conditions and from setting lifetime coverage limits.

- **Title II: HIPAA Administrative Simplification:** Directs the U.S. HHS to establish national standards for processing electronic health care transactions. It also requires health care organizations to implement secure electronic access to health data and to remain in compliance with privacy regulations set by HHS.

- **Title III: HIPAA Tax-Related Health Provisions:** Includes tax-related provisions and guidelines for medical care.

- **Title IV: Application and Enforcement of Group Health Plan Requirements:** Further defines health insurance reform, including provisions for individuals with preexisting conditions and those seeking continued coverage.

- **Title V: Revenue Offsets:** Includes provisions on company-owned life insurance and the treatment of those who lose their U.S. citizenship for income tax purposes.

The part of HIPAA that is most visible to the public is Title II. Title II includes the following compliance elements:

- **National Provider Identifier Standard:** Each covered entity must have a unique 10-digit national provider identifier (NPI) number. The covered entities are health plans, health care providers, health care clearinghouses, and business associates. A business associate is a person or an organization, other than a member of a covered entity's workforce, that performs certain functions or activities on behalf of, or provides certain services to, a covered entity that involve the use or disclosure of individually identifiable health information.

- **Transactions and Code Sets Standard:** Health care organizations must follow a standardized mechanism for electronic data interchange (EDI) in order to submit and process insurance claims.

- **HIPAA Privacy Rule:** Officially known as the Standards for Privacy of Individually Identifiable Health Information, this rule requires safeguards to protect the privacy of patient data by setting limits and conditions on what information can be used and disclosed without patient authorization.

- **HIPAA Security Rule:** The Security Standards for the Protection of Electronic Protected Health Information establishes national standards to protect the confidentiality, integrity, and availability of individuals' electronic health information through appropriate administrative, physical, and technical safeguards.

- **HIPAA Enforcement Rule:** This rule establishes guidelines for investigations into HIPAA compliance violations.

HIPAA Privacy Rule

HIPAA required HHS to issue regulations that provide details on the requirements of the Privacy Rule. The Privacy Rule is intended to:

- Give patients greater control over their health information

- Place limitations on the use and release of medical records

- Establish standards for safeguarding personal health information

- Provide for the disclosure of health information when a covered entity has a public responsibility to do so (e.g., under emergency circumstances)

The HIPAA Privacy Rule protects most individually identifiable health information held or transmitted by a covered entity or its business associate, in any form or medium, whether electronic, on paper, or oral. *Individually identifiable health information*, also referred to as *protected health information (PHI)*, is information that is a subset of health information, including demographic information collected from an individual, and:

(1) Is created or received by a health care provider, health plan employer, or health care clearinghouse

(2) Relates to the past, present, or future physical or mental health or condition of an individual; the provision of health care to an individual; or the past, present, or future payment for the provision of health care to an individual; and

(i) That identifies the individual; or

(ii) With respect to which there is a reasonable basis to believe the information can be used to identify the individual

PHI includes many common identifiers (e.g., name, address, birth date, Social Security number) when they can be associated with the health information from the preceding list.

A guidance document from the U.S. Department of Health and Human Services [HHS12] gives the following examples: A medical record, laboratory report, or hospital bill would be PHI because each document would contain a patient's name and/or other identifying information associated with the health data content. By contrast, a health plan report that only noted the average age of health plan members as 45 years would not be PHI because that information, although developed by aggregating information from individual plan member records, does not identify any individual plan members, and there is no reasonable basis to believe that it could be used to identify an individual.

PHI involves both personal information and related health information. Identifying information alone, such as personal names, residential addresses, or phone numbers, would not necessarily be designated as PHI. For instance, if such information were reported as part of a publicly accessible data source, such as a phone book, then this information would not be PHI because it is not related to health data. If such information were listed with health condition, health care provision, or payment data, such as an indication that the individual was treated at a certain clinic, then this information would be PHI.

Disclosures

A covered entity is required to disclose PHI without an individual's authorization under one of the following conditions:

- The individual who is the subject of the information (or the individual's personal representative) authorizes disclosure in writing.

- HHS is undertaking a compliance investigation or review or enforcement action.

A covered entity is permitted to use or disclose PHI for the following purposes or situations:

- To the individual

- For treatment, payment, and health care operations

- As an opportunity to agree or object

- Incident to an otherwise permitted use and disclosure

- For public interest, law enforcement, and benefit activities

- For the purposes of research, public health, or health care operations, where direct identifiers relating to individuals, their families, and employers are removed from the limited dataset

Otherwise, a covered entity must obtain an individual's written permission for any use or disclosure of PHI.

Administrative Requirements

The Privacy Rule mandates the following administrative requirements. A covered entity must:

- **Privacy policies and procedures:** Develop and implement both an internal privacy policy and an external (privacy notice) policy.

- **Privacy personnel:** Designate a privacy official responsible for the privacy policies and a contact person or office.

- **Workforce training and management:** Train all workforce members on its privacy policies and procedures, as necessary and appropriate for them to carry out their functions. A covered entity must have and apply appropriate sanctions against workforce members who violate its privacy policies and procedures or the Privacy Rule.

- **Mitigation:** Mitigate, to the extent practicable, any harmful effect caused by use or disclosure of PHI in violation of its privacy policies and procedures or the Privacy Rule.

- **Data safeguards:** Implement appropriate security and privacy controls to prevent intentional or unintentional use or disclosure of PHI in violation of the Privacy Rule.

- **Complaints:** Provide a process for individuals to make complaints concerning the covered entity's policies and procedures required by the Privacy Rule; or its compliance with such policies and procedures; or its compliance with the requirements the Privacy Rule.

- **Retaliation and waver:** A covered entity must not retaliate against a person for exercising rights provided by the Privacy Rule, for assisting in an investigation by HHS or another appropriate authority, or for opposing an act or a practice that the person believes in good faith violates the Privacy Rule.

- **Documentation and record retention:** A covered entity must maintain, until six years after the later of the date of their creation or last effective date, its privacy policies and procedures, its privacy practices notices, disposition of complaints, and other actions, activities, and designations that the Privacy Rule requires to be documented.

De-Identification

The Privacy Rule imposes no restrictions on the use or disclosure of de-identified health information. Chapter 7, "Privacy in Databases," defines *de-identification* of PII as having the following characteristics for each individual in the group:

- The resulting data do not suffice to identify the PII principal to whom they relate.

- A re-identification parameter is associated with the de-identified data such that the combination of that parameter and the de-identified data enable identification of the associated PII principal.

- An adversary not in possession of the re-identification parameter cannot identify the PII from the de-identified data by reasonable efforts.

Thus, de-identification retains *linkability*. Different data associated with the same re-identification parameter can be linked. Chapter 7 also defines *anonymization* of PII as having the following characteristics for each individual in the group:

- The resulting data do not suffice to identify the PII principal to whom they relate.

- An adversary not in possession cannot identify the PII from the de-identified data by reasonable efforts.

The Privacy Rule specifically addresses de-identified PHI but, by implication, also exempts anonymized PHI. De-identified health information neither identifies nor provides a reasonable basis to identify an individual. The Privacy Rule indicates two ways to de-identify information (see Figure 15.1, from [HHS12]).

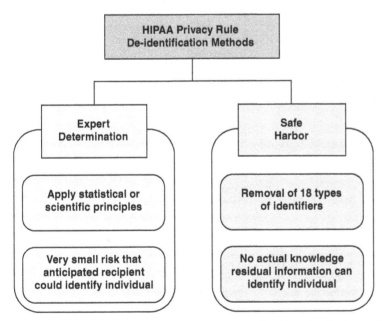

FIGURE 15.1 Two Methods to Achieve De-identification in Accordance with the HIPAA Privacy Rule

For the *expert determination method*, a person who is technically qualified applies de-identification or anonymization techniques and determines that the risk is very small that the information could be used, alone or in combination with other reasonably available information, by an anticipated recipient to identify an individual who is a subject of the information. Any of the methods discussed in Chapter 7—such as suppression, generalization, perturbation, swapping, and *k*-anonymity—can serve as techniques for de-identification.

Table 15.2 suggests a set of principles to be used in assessing the risk of any de-identification method [HHS12].

TABLE 15.2   Principles Used by Experts in the Determination of the Identifiability of Health Information

Principle	Description	Examples
Replicability	Prioritize health information features into levels of risk according to the chance it will consistently occur in relation to the individual.	**Low:** Results of a patient's blood glucose level test will vary.
		High: Demographics of a patient (e.g., birth date) are relatively stable.
Data source availability	Determine which external data sources contain the patients' identifiers and the replicable features in the health information, as well as who is permitted access to the data sources.	**Low:** The results of laboratory reports are not often disclosed with identity beyond health care environments.
		High: Patient name and demographics are often in public data sources, such as vital records—birth, death, and marriage registries.
Distinguishability	Determine the extent to which the subject's data can be distinguished in the health information.	**Low:** It has been estimated that the combination of year of birth, gender, and five-digit zip code is unique for approximately 0.04% of residents in the United States. This means that very few residents could be identified through this combination of data alone.
		High: It has been estimated that the combination of a patient's date of birth, gender, and five-digit zip code is unique for over 50% of residents in the United States. This means that over half of U.S. residents could be uniquely described just with these three data elements.
Assess risk	The greater the replicability, availability, and distinguishability of the health information, the greater the risk for identification.	**Low:** Laboratory values may be very distinguishing, but they are rarely independently replicable and are rarely disclosed in multiple data sources to which many people have access.
		High: Demographics are highly distinguishing, highly replicable, and available in public data sources.

The *safe harbor method* involves the removal of specified identifiers of the individual and of the individual's relatives, household members, and employers; this removal is adequate only if the covered entity has no actual knowledge that the remaining information could be used to identify the individual. This method requires the removal of potentially identifying information, including:

- Names
- All geographic subdivisions smaller than a state, including street address, city, county, precinct, and zip code
- All elements of dates (except year) for dates that are directly related to an individual, including birth date, admission date, discharge date, death date, and all ages over 89 and all elements of dates (including year) indicative of such age
- Telephone numbers
- Fax numbers
- Email addresses
- Social Security numbers
- Medical record numbers
- Health plan beneficiary numbers
- Account numbers
- Certificate/license numbers
- Vehicle identifiers and serial numbers, including license plate numbers
- Device identifiers and serial numbers
- URLs
- IP addresses
- Biometric identifiers, including fingerprints and voice prints
- Full-face photographs and any comparable images

For de-identified PHI, the Privacy Rule includes an implementation specification for re-identification as follows: A covered entity may assign a code or other means of record identification to allow de-identified information to be re-identified, provided that:

- The code or other means of record identification is not derived from or related to information about the individual and is not otherwise capable of being translated so as to identify the individual.
- The covered entity does not use or disclose the code or other means of record identification for any other purpose and does not disclose the mechanism for re-identification.

Researchers in many fields use de-identified or anonymized health data. For some purposes, the safe harbor method is adequate, but for many types of health-related research, the greater detail available from the expert determination method is needed. The topic of re-identification risks for PHI is beyond the scope of this book. A good starting point is the article "Evaluating Re-identification Risks with Respect to the HIPAA Privacy Rule," from the *Journal of the American Medical Informatics Association* [BENI10].

15.3   Health Information Technology for Economic and Clinical Health Act

The Health Information Technology for Economic and Clinical Health (HITECH) Act is part of the American Recovery and Reinvestment Act of 2009 (ARRA). A primary goal of the HITECH Act is to promote and expand the adoption of health information technology.

The HITECH Act enhances the privacy and security protections defined under HIPAA. Two noteworthy aspects of the act are the breach notification rules and the description of technologies for the protection of health information, including encryption and data destruction.

The HITECH Act also increases legal liability for noncompliance and allows for more enforcement actions by the secretary of the HHS as well as state attorneys general.

Breach Notification

The HITECH Act defines a *breach* as an impermissible use or disclosure under the HIPAA Privacy Rule that compromises the security or privacy of the PHI. An impermissible use or disclosure of protected health information is presumed to be a breach unless the covered entity or business associate, as applicable, demonstrates that there is a low probability that the PHI has been compromised based on a risk assessment of at least the following factors:

- The nature and extent of the PHI involved, including the types of identifiers and the likelihood of re-identification

- The unauthorized person who used the PHI or to whom the disclosure was made

- Whether the PHI was actually acquired or viewed

- The extent to which the risk to the PHI has been mitigated

If a breach occurs, the covered entity must provide notice to the following:

- **Affected individuals:** The covered entity must notify affected individuals by mail or email within 60 days of the discovery of the breach.

- **HHS:** The covered entity must notify HHS via the HHS web-based breach report form within 60 days of the discovery of the breach if 500 or more individuals are involved or on an annual basis for smaller breaches.

- **Media:** Covered entities that experience a breach affecting more than 500 residents of a state or jurisdiction must provide notice to prominent media outlets serving the state or jurisdiction.

Covered entities must only provide the required notifications if the breach involved unsecured PHI. Unsecured PHI is PHI that has not been rendered unusable, unreadable, or indecipherable to unauthorized persons through the use of a technology or methodology specified by HHS guidance. The HITECH Act specifies two types of technologies: encryption and media sanitization.

The HITECH Act refers to the four commonly recognized data states (the first three of which are discussed further in Chapter 9, "Other PET Topics"):

- **Data at rest:** Data that reside in databases, file systems, and other structured storage methods

- **Data in motion:** Data that are moving through a network, including wireless transmission

- **Data in use:** Data in the process of being created, retrieved, updated, or deleted

- **Data disposed:** Data such as discarded paper records or recycled electronic media

The HITECH Act identifies two methods that may be used to secure PHI: encryption of data at rest and in motion and destruction of data disposed. The HITECH Act does not address data in use. HHS issued detailed guidance on these areas in the *Federal Register* of August 24, 2009. The guidance makes use of specifications issued by NIST. The remainder of this section summarizes the guidance.

Encryption of PHI

In essence, HHS mandates the use of a secure encryption algorithm in which measures are taken to ensure the protection of the key or keys so as to prevent decryption by unauthorized persons.

However, HHS doesn't require encryption and instead lists it as *addressable* as opposed to *required*, meaning that it should basically be used when reasonable and appropriate. There aren't too many times when encryption wouldn't be reasonable and appropriate, but encryption is not a firm requirement.

Data at Rest

For data at rest, the encryption scheme must be consistent with NIST SP 800-111 (*Guide to Storage Encryption Technologies for End User Devices*). SP 800-111 lists four approaches that can be used:

- **Full disk encryption:** Encrypts the entire disk, except for software needed to boot the disk. This scheme uses an authentication method to enable booting. Once the device is booted, there is no protection of the data.

- **Virtual disk encryption:** Encrypts the contents of a container, which are protected until the user is authenticated for the container.

- **Volume encryption:** Provides the same protection as virtual disk encryption but for a volume instead of a container.

- **File/folder encryption:** Protects the contents of encrypted files (including files in encrypted folders) until the user is authenticated for the files or folders.

SP 800-111 describes the strengths and weaknesses of each approach. It also designates approved encryption and authentication algorithms. As discussed in Chapter 1, "Security and Cryptography Concepts," recent publications, such as SP 800-131A (*Transitioning the Use of Cryptographic Algorithms and Key Lengths*), provide guidance on specific key lengths.

Data in Motion

Protection of data in motion involves protection of PHI as it is communicated across a network. This involves encrypting the PHI and employing an appropriate secure protocol. HHS indicates three approved approaches:

- **Transport Layer Security (TLS):** TLS is designed to make use of Transmission Control Protocol (TCP) to provide a reliable end-to-end secure service. TLS is a complex protocol that allows users to authenticate each other and to employ encryption and message integrity techniques across a transport connection. SP 800-52 (*Guidelines for the Selection and Use of Transport Layer Security Implementations*) is the NIST specification.

- **Virtual private networks (VPNs) using IPsec:** A VPN is a private network that is configured within a public network (a carrier's network or the Internet) in order to take advantage of the economies of scale and management facilities of large networks. VPNs are widely used by enterprises to create wide area networks that span large geographic areas, to provide site-to-site connections to branch offices, and to allow mobile users to dial up their company LANs. From the point of view of the provider, the pubic network facility is shared by many customers, with the traffic of each customer segregated from other traffic. Traffic designated as VPN traffic can only go from a VPN source to a destination in the same VPN. It is often the case that encryption and authentication facilities are provided for the VPN. IPsec is a set of Internet standards that augment Internet Protocol (IP) and enable the development of VPNs at the IP level. SP 800-77 (*Guide to IPsec VPNs*) is the NIST specification. (Note that Secure Sockets Layer (SSL) is an earlier version of TLS and has been replaced by TLS.

- **VPNs using TLS:** A TLS VPN consists of one or more VPN devices that users connect to using their web browsers. The traffic between a web browser and a TLS VPN device is encrypted with the TLS protocol. TLS VPNs provide remote users access to web applications and client/server applications, as well as with connectivity to internal networks. They offer versatility and ease of use because they use the SSL protocol that is included with all standard web browsers, so the client usually does not require configuration by the user. SP 800-113 (*Guide to SSL VPNs*) is the NIST specification.

Data Destruction

For the destruction of data, the HHS specifies that the media on which the PHI is stored or recorded must be destroyed in one of the following ways:

- Paper, film, or other hard copy media must be shredded or destroyed such that the PHI cannot be read or otherwise cannot be reconstructed. Redaction is specifically excluded as a means of data destruction.

- Electronic media must be cleared, purged, or destroyed consistent with SP 800-88 (*Guidelines for Media Sanitization*) such that the PHI cannot be retrieved.

SP 800-88 defines *media sanitization* as a process to render access to target data (i.e., the data subject to the sanitization technique) on the media infeasible for a given level of recovery effort. Three increasingly secure actions for sanitization are defined:

- **Clear:** Applies logical techniques to sanitize data in all user-addressable storage locations for protection against simple non-invasive data recovery techniques; typically applied through the standard Read and Write commands to the storage device, such as by rewriting with a new value or using a menu option to reset the device to the factory state (where rewriting is not supported).

- **Purge:** Applies physical or logical techniques that render target data recovery infeasible using state-of-the-art laboratory techniques. This can be achieved by performing multiple overwrites. For a self-encrypting drive, cryptographic erasure can be used. If the drive automatically encrypts all user-addressable locations, then all that is required is to destroy the encryption key, which can be done using multiple overwrites.

- **Destroy:** Renders target data recovery infeasible using state-of-the-art laboratory techniques and results in the subsequent inability to use the media for storage of data. Typically the medium is pulverized or incinerated at an outsourced metal destruction or licensed incineration facility.

Based on the risk assessment for the office device, the organization can assign a security category to the data on the device and then use the flowchart of Figure 15.2 to determine how to dispose of the memory associated with the device.

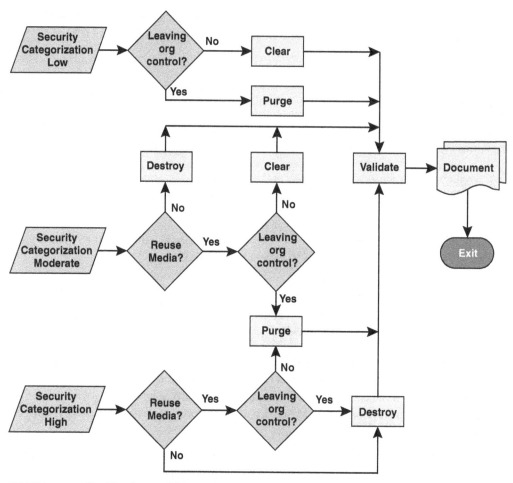

FIGURE 15.2 Sanitization and Disposition Decision Flow

15.4   Children's Online Privacy Protection Act

The Children's Online Privacy Protection Act (COPPA) is a federal law that prohibits a website operator from knowingly collecting information from children under the age of 13 unless the operator obtains parental consent and allows parents to review their children's information and restrict its further use. The primary goal of COPPA is to place parents in control of what information is collected, used, and disclosed from their young children online.

General Provisions

COPPA defines *personal information* as information that is individually identifying, including:

- First and last name
- Home or physical address

- Email address

- Phone number

- Social Security number

- Any other identifier determined by the Federal Trade Commission (FTC) to permit the physical or online contacting of a specific individual:

  - A persistent identifier that can be used to recognize a user over time and across different websites or online services. Such persistent identifiers include, but are not limited to, a customer number held in a cookie, an Internet Protocol (IP) address, a processor or device serial number, or a unique device identifier

  - A photograph, video, or audio file where such file contains a child's image or voice

  - Geolocation information sufficient to identify the street name and name of a city or town

- Other information about the child or parent that the website collects online from the child and is combined with any of the above-described identifiers

To achieve the objective of controlling website collection of children's personal information, COPPA includes the following:

- Requires notice of the collection, use, and disclosure of children's personal information

- Requires verifiable parental consent for the collection, use, and disclosure of children's personal information

- Provides a reasonable means for a parent to review the personal information collected from a child and to refuse to permit its further use or maintenance

- Prohibits the collection of more personal information than is reasonably necessary from a child in order for the child to participate in an online activity, such as a game

- Requires that operators establish reasonable procedures to protect the security, integrity, and confidentiality of children's personal information

The COPPA Final Rule

FTC issued a Final Rule that adds more detail to COPPA's general requirements. Of special note, the Final Rule mandates that website operators must provide a link on their site to a privacy notice that contains the following information:

- The name, address, phone number, and email address of the website operator

- The types of personal information collected from children

- Whether children's personal information is collected directly or passively (e.g., cookies)

- How the operator uses such information

- Whether children's personal information is disclosed to third parties (and, if so, other information about such third parties, including the type of business in which the third party is engaged and whether the third party has agreed to maintain the confidentiality, security, and integrity of the personal information)

- A statement that the operator cannot condition a child's participation in an activity on the disclosure of more personal information than is reasonably necessary to participate in the activity

- A parent's right to agree to the collection of his or her child's information without agreeing to the disclosure of the information to third parties

- A parent's right to review and delete previously collected information

- A parent's right to refuse the further collection of his or her child's collected personal information

15.5   California Consumer Privacy Act

The California Consumer Privacy Act (CCPA) is perhaps the most significant state-level data privacy law in the United States. It is likely to become a model for other state privacy laws. The CCPA creates substantial new privacy rights for consumers, comparable to the access, restriction, and erasure rights that European citizens enjoy under the EU General Data Protection Regulation (GDPR). The extensiveness of covered personal information and industry applicability under the CCPA goes beyond what is typically covered by U.S. privacy laws. The CCPA will significantly impact data-driven businesses' data practices, with new and demanding compliance obligations regarding consumer data collection and use. Businesses that fail to comply with the CCPA may be subject to monetary penalties, regulatory enforcement actions, and private rights of action.

The CCPA was passed in 2018 and goes into effect January 1, 2020.

Basic Concepts

Three key concepts in CCPA are consumers, personal information, and businesses.

Consumers

The CCPA applies to individuals designated as consumers. A consumer is a natural resident of California, however identified, including by any unique identifier. Thus, anyone who is a resident of California and can be identified in any way is a consumer. The term *resident* includes (1) every individual who is in the state for other than a temporary or transitory purpose and (2) every individual who is domiciled in the state who is outside the state for a temporary or transitory purpose. All other individuals are nonresidents.

Personal Information

The CCPA defines *personal information* as any information that identifies, relates to, describes, is capable of being associated with, or could reasonably be linked, directly or indirectly, with a particular consumer or household. Personal information includes, but is not limited to, the following:

- Identifiers such as a real name, alias, postal address, unique personal identifier, online identifier, Internet Protocol address, email address, account name, Social Security number, driver's license number, passport number, or other similar identifiers.

- Any categories of personal information described in subdivision (e) of Section 1798.80. This includes signature, physical characteristics or description, address, telephone number, state identification card number, insurance policy number, education, employment, employment history, bank account number, credit card number, debit card number, or any other financial information, medical information, or health insurance information.

- Characteristics of protected classifications under California or federal law. These include race, religious creed, color, national origin, ancestry, physical disability, mental disability, medical condition, and marital status.

- Commercial information, including records of personal property; products or services purchased, obtained, or considered; or other purchasing or consuming histories or tendencies.

- Biometric information.

- Internet or other electronic network activity information, including, but not limited to, browsing history, search history, and information regarding a consumer's interaction with an Internet website, application, or advertisement.

- Geolocation data.

- Audio, electronic, visual, thermal, olfactory, or similar information.

- Professional or employment-related information.

- Education information, defined as information that is not publicly available personally identifiable information, as defined in the Family Educational Rights and Privacy Act (20 U.S.C. section 1232g, 34 C.F.R. Part 99).

- Inferences drawn from any of the information identified in this subdivision to create a profile about a consumer reflecting the consumer's preferences, characteristics, psychological trends, preferences, predispositions, behavior, attitudes, intelligence, abilities, and aptitudes.

Personal information does not include publicly available information that is lawfully made available to the general public from federal, state, or local government records. It also does not include protected or health information that is collected by a covered entity governed by the California Confidentiality of Medical Information Act or governed by the privacy, security, and breach notification rules issued by HHS pursuant to the Health Insurance Portability and Accountability Act of 1996. This is an extraordinarily broad definition of personal information. Table 15.3 compares this definition with comparable definitions from ISO 29100 (*Privacy Framework*) and the GDPR.

TABLE 15.3   Definitions of Personal Information

Standard/Regulation	Term	Definition
ISO 29100	Personally identifiable information (PII)	Any information that (a) can be used to identify the PII principal to whom such information relates or (b) is or might be directly or indirectly linked to a PII principal.
GDPR	Personal data	Any information relating to an identified or identifiable natural person; an identifiable natural person is one who can be identified, directly or indirectly, in particular by reference to an identifier such as a name, an identification number, location data, an online identifier, or to one or more factors specific to the physical, physiological, genetic, mental, economic, cultural, or social identity of that natural person.
CCPA	Personal information (PI)	Information that identifies, relates to, describes, is capable of being associated with, or could reasonably be linked, directly or indirectly, with a particular consumer or household.

This definition creates the potential for extremely broad legal interpretation around what constitutes personal information, holding that personal information is any data that could be linked with a California individual or household. The key phrase in the definition is "capable of being associated with, or could reasonably be linked, directly or indirectly, with a particular consumer or household." This goes well beyond information that is easily associated with an identity, such as name, birth date, or Social Security number. It is much more difficult for an organization to avoid collecting or even identifying that it has collected this "indirect" information, such as product preference or geolocation data. For small organizations, the personal information definition can impose a significant resource burden to ensure that any personal information that is collected satisfies the CCPA consent requirement. Large organizations potentially have a great number of applications and data stores for collecting up to petabytes of information, ranging from highly identifiable to indirect. This massive volume of data may reside across a combination of structured and unstructured data stores in the data center and the cloud, making it difficult for organizations to have an accurate picture of whose data they really have, where it resides, and how it is being used.

Businesses

The CCPA is a law that regulates the activities of businesses. The law defines a business as meeting the following conditions:

■ Is a sole proprietorship, partnership, limited liability company, corporation, association, or other legal entity that is organized or operated for the profit or financial benefit of its shareholders or other owners

- Collects consumers' personal information, or on the behalf of which such information is collected

- Alone, or jointly with others, determines the purposes and means of the processing of consumers' personal information

- Does business in the State of California

- Satisfies one or more of the following thresholds:

  - Has annual gross revenues in excess of $25 million

  - Annually buys, receives for the business' commercial purposes, sells, or shares for commercial purposes, alone or in combination, the personal information of 50,000 or more consumers, households, or devices

  - Derives 50% or more of its annual revenues from selling consumers' personal information

Figure 15.3 illustrates this definition.

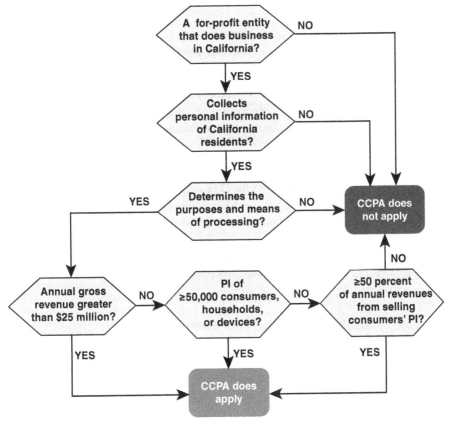

FIGURE 15.3   Applicability of CCPA

Rights of Consumers

The CCPA lists the following as the enforceable rights with respect to consumers' personal information:

- The right of Californians to know what personal information is being collected about them

- The right of Californians to know whether their personal information is sold or disclosed and to whom

- The right of Californians to say no to the sale of personal information

- The right of Californians to access their personal information

- The right of Californians to equal service and price, even if they exercise their privacy rights

The sections that follow examine each of these rights in more detail.

Right to Know

The right to know covers both generic and specific collection of personal information, including the following:

- **Disclosure of generic collection practices upon request:** Upon a consumer's request, a business shall disclose the categories and specific pieces of personal information the business has collected.

- **Disclosure of generic collection practices upon collection:** At or before collection of a consumer's personal information, a business shall inform consumers as to the categories of personal information to be collected and the purposes for which the categories of personal information shall be used. The business shall not collect undisclosed categories, or make undisclosed uses, of personal information.

- **Disclosures about collected personal information to the consumer:** Upon a consumer's request, a business shall disclose to the consumer the (1) categories of personal information it has collected about that consumer, (2) categories of sources from which the personal information is collected, (3) business or commercial purpose for collecting or selling personal information, (4) categories of third parties with whom the business shares personal information, and (5) specific pieces of personal information it has collected about that consumer. The last element should be provided in a format to facilitate data portability.

Rights Concerning Sold or Disclosed Personal Information

If a business sells consumer information, upon a consumer's request, a business shall disclose to the consumer the categories of personal information that the business (1) collected about the consumer, (2) sold about the consumer and the categories of third parties to whom the personal information was sold, by category or categories of personal information for each third party to whom the personal information was sold, and (3) disclosed about the consumer for a business purpose.

Right to Refuse the Sale of Personal Information

This right covers two separate situations:

- A business collects personal information about a consumer and then sells that information to a third party. For example, an online retail establishment may sell purchase information to an advertiser, which then sends ads to the consumer.

- A business collects personal information about a consumer, sells that information to a third party, and then the third party sells that information to another organization.

With respect to the first category, consumers can opt out of sales of their personal information, and the business can't ask them to change that for at least 12 months. In addition, a business that knows (or willfully disregards the consumer's age) personal information related to consumers under age 16 may not sell the personal information unless the consumer (ages 13[nd]16) or parent/guardian (under 13) opts in.

With respect to this second category, a third party shall not sell personal information about a consumer that has been sold to the third party by a business unless the consumer has received explicit notice and is provided an opportunity to exercise the right to opt out. If a business sells personal information, then it must provide a clear and conspicuous link on the business's Internet home page, titled *Do Not Sell My Personal Information*, to an Internet web page that enables a consumer, or a person authorized by the consumer, to opt out of the sale of the consumer's personal information.

Right to Access and Delete Personal Information

A consumer has the right to request that a business that collects a consumer's personal information disclose to that consumer the categories and specific pieces of personal information the business has collected.

The business must provide the information in a readily usable format that enables porting the data to another entity without hindrance. Consumers may make this request to a business no more than twice in a calendar year. A business is not required to include data that are obtained in a one-time transaction or to re-identify or link information that is not in identifiable form.

The right to access also includes the right to deletion. Upon a consumer's request, a business shall delete any personal information about the consumer that the business collected from the consumer. Businesses can refuse deletion requests when it is necessary for the business or service provider to maintain the consumer's personal information for one of the following reasons:

- To complete the transaction or a reasonably anticipated transaction

- To find, prevent, or prosecute security breaches or illegal activity

- To debug, identify, and repair errors that impair existing intended functionality

- To exercise free speech (of the business or a third party) or exercise another right provided for by law

- To comply with the California Electronic Communications Privacy Act

- To engage in certain types of research in limited cases

- To enable solely internal uses that are reasonably aligned with the expectations of the consumer based on the consumer's relationship with the business

- To comply with a legal obligation

- To otherwise use the consumer's personal information, internally, in a lawful manner that is compatible with the context in which the consumer provided the information

It is noteworthy that the law does not include a right to amend inaccurate personal information, unlike the GDPR, which provides the right of rectification.

Right to Equal Service and Price

The CCPA prohibits companies from:

- Denying goods or services to the consumer

- Charging different prices or rates for goods or services

- Providing a different level or quality of goods or services to the consumer

- Suggesting that the consumer will receive a different price or rate for goods or services or a different level or quality of goods or services

A business shall not discriminate against a consumer because the consumer exercised any of the consumer's rights under this title, although a business may charge a consumer a different price or rate or provide a different level or quality of goods or services to the consumer if that difference is reasonably related to the value provided to the consumer by the consumer's data. Businesses may offer financial incentives to compensate for the collection, sale, or deletion of data but not if the financial incentives are unjust, unreasonable, coercive, or usurious in nature.

Comparison with the GDPR

The GDPR and the CCPA are the two most significant developments in information privacy regulation in recent years. Both take into account the current technological ecosystem and threats to privacy. The GDPR is considerably more complex (88 pages for the English-language version of the GDPR versus 24 pages for the CCPA). The GDPR mandates specific operational and management requirements, such as a data protection officer (DPO) and a data protection impact assessment (DPIA). The CCPA is instead focused primarily on outcomes, enumerating rights and mandating obligations to protect those rights. The GDPR applies to all types of organizations, including for-profit, nonprofit, and government agencies, whereas the CCPA applies only to for-profit businesses.

Another noteworthy difference between the two is that the CCPA's definition of *personal information* is considerably broader than that the GDPR definition of *personal data*.

Table 15.4 summarizes key differences between the CCPA and the GDPR.

TABLE 15.4   Comparison of the GDPR and the CCPA

Concept	GDPR	CCPA
PII	Any information relating to an identified or identifiable natural person	Anything that identifies, relates to, describes, is capable of being associated with, or could be reasonably linked to a particular person or household
Covered entity	Any entity that controls or processes personal data	Any for-profit business that collects personal data
Disclosure/ transparency obligations	An entity is required to provide the identity and the context details of the data controller, the recipients of that data, the legal basis and purposes for processing, the retention period, the right of access, and more	Businesses need to inform consumers at or before the point of collection what information is being collected and why it is necessary
Right of access	Right to access all personal data processed	Right to access personal data collected in the past two months
Scope	EU residents plus persons whose PII is processed by organizations established in the EU	California residents
Right to portability	Must export and import certain EU personal data in a user-friendly format	All access requests must be exported in user-friendly format; no import requirement
Right to correct	Right to correct errors in personal data processed	Not included in the CCPA
Right to stop processing	Right to withdraw consent or otherwise stop processing of personal data	Right to opt out of selling personal data only.
Right to stop automated decision making	Right to require a human to make decisions that have legal effect	Not included in the CCPA
Right to stop third-party transfer	Right to withdraw consent for data transfers involving second purposes of special categories of data	Right to opt out of selling personal data to third parties
Right to erasure	Right to erase personal data, under certain conditions	Right to erase personal data collected, under certain conditions
Right to equal services and price	Not included in GDPR	Required
Private right of action damages	No floor or ceiling	Floor of $100 and ceiling of $750 per incident
Regulator enforcement penalties	Ceiling of 4% of global annual revenue	No ceiling; $7500 per violation

15.6   Key Terms and Review Questions

Key Terms

anonymization	Health Information Technology for Economic and Clinical Health (HITECH) Act
Children's Online Privacy Protection Act (COPPA)	Health Insurance Portability and Accountability Act (HIPAA)
clear	
de-identification	HIPAA Privacy Rule
destroy	HIPAA Security Rule
expert determination method	linkability
file/folder encryption	media sanitization
full disk encryption	purge
data at rest	safe harbor method
data disposed	virtual disk encryption
data in motion	virtual private network (VPN)
data in use	volume encryption

Review Questions

1. What are some of the key differences between the information privacy environment in the United States and that in the European Union?

2. Briefly describe the privacy aspects of the Fair Credit Reporting Act.

3. Briefly describe the privacy aspects of the Fair and Accurate Credit Transactions Act.

4. Briefly describe the privacy aspects of the Right to Financial Privacy Act.

5. Briefly describe the privacy aspects of the Family Educational Rights and Privacy Act.

6. What are the main goals of HIPAA?

7. What is the HIPAA Privacy Rule?

8. To what categories of personal health information does HIPAA apply?

9. Under what circumstance may a HIPAA covered entity use or disclose PHI?

10. Describe the two methods of de-identification permitted under HIPAA.

11. Under the HITECH Act, what risk assessment factors must a covered entity take into account in determining whether a breach notification is needed?

12. Describe the technical measures mandated by the HITECH Act for the protection of data at rest.

13. Describe the technical measures mandated by the HITECH Act for the protection of data in motion.

14. Describe the three technical measures authorized by the HITECH Act for media sanitization.

15. How is PII defined for the purposes of COPPA?

16. What are the main requirements imposed by COPPA?

15.7 References

BENI10: Benitez, K., and Malin, B. "Evaluating Re-Identification Risks with Respect to the HIPAA Privacy Rule." *Journal of the American Medical Informatics Association*, March 2010. https://academic.oup.com/jamia/article/17/2/169/809345

HHS12: U.S. Department of Health & Human Services. *Guidance Regarding Methods for De-identification of Protected Health Information in Accordance with the Health Insurance Portability and Accountability Act (HIPAA) Privacy Rule.* November 26, 2102. https://www.hhs.gov/hipaa/for-professionals/privacy/special-topics/de-identification/index.html

Index

kit (virus generator), 148
knowledge factors, 125

L

lawfulness in GDPR, 422–423
L-diversity, 198–199
legal person, 413
level of risk, 337
life cycle, 36
lightweight cryptographic algorithms, 24–25
likelihood
  defined, 337
  privacy risk assessment, 361–363
linkability, 453
local hardware WAF, 221
local software WAF, 221
location services, 227
logging security events, 389–391
logic bombs, 148
loss event frequency, 337
loss of autonomy, 103, 357
loss of governance, 284
loss of liberty, 103, 358
loss of self-determination, 103, 357
loss of trust, 104, 284, 358
low-level EA artifacts, 304

M

MaaS (malware as a service), 148
MAC (mandatory access control), 131
macrodata tables, 180
magnitude tables
  defined, 180
  protection, 203–204
malicious behavior, 377
malware (malicious software)
  defined, 146
  nature of threat, 149

practical protection measures, 150–153
  types of, 147–149
malware as a service (MaaS), 148
malware protection software, 153–154
  capabilities, 153–154
  managing, 154
manageability
  defined, 83
  in IoT, 276
mandatory access control (MAC), 131
masquerades, 8
material scope, 418–419
measured service, 281
media protection, 80
media sanitization, 459
messaging, 264
metadata for attribute-based access control (ABAC), 137–139
microcontrollers, 267
microdata tables
  defined, 180
  de-identification of quasi-identifiers, 190–196
mid-level artifacts, 304
minimization, 122
misuse detection, 167
mobile app security, 224–231
  BYOD policies, 227–229
  device vulnerabilities, 225–227
  mobile ecosystem, 224–225
  privacy notices, 246–248
  privacy threats, 232–234
  resources, 230–231
  vetting, 229–230
mobile code, 148
mobile device protection, 265
mobile devices, 165
  BYOD policies, 227–229
  defined, 224

pseudorandom number generators, 14

public application stores, 225

public cloud, 282

public keys, 18

public-key certificates, 25–26

public-key infrastructure (PKI), 25–28

architecture, 27–28

certificates, 25–26

PUP (potentially unwanted program), 148

purge (sanitization), 459

purpose limitation in GDPR, 421

purpose specification

defined, 64, 65, 122

privacy authorization, 124

Q

qualitative risk assessment, 342–346

quantitative risk assessment, 340–341

quarantine, 153–154

quasi-identifiers (QI)

defined, 179

de-identification, 190–196

query language usage, 122

query restriction, 206, 207–209

queryable databases, 204–211

categories of, 204

defined, 180–181

privacy threats, 205–206

protection, 206–211

R

RA (registration authority), 28

radio-frequency identification (RFID), 267

random rounding, 202

ransomware, 148

rapid elasticity, 281

RAT (remote access Trojan), 148

RBAC (role-based access control), 131, 133–134

read access, 130

read privileges, 119

REAL ID Act, 447–448

records of processing activities, 429–430

recovery, 407

registration authority (RA), 28

regular (monitoring), 432

regulations (privacy), 66–68

re-identification

attacks, 183–187

disclosure risks, 186–187

examples, 183–184

motivation of attackers, 186

privacy controls, 187

types of, 184–186

defined, 61

release of message contents, 8

relying party, 28

relying party (RP), 128

remediation level, 114

remote access, 264

remote access Trojan (RAT), 148

replay attacks, 8

report confidence, 114

repository, 28

repurposing data, 96

residual risk, 341

resource pooling, 281

resources, 135

respect for context, 235

response perturbation, 206, 209–211

responsibility ambiguity, 284

RFID (radio-frequency identification), 267

RFID tags in IoT, 276

Right to Financial Privacy Act, 447

rights of consumers, 466–468

rights of data subjects, 426–427